Developmentalism and Beyond

Society and Politics in Egypt and Turkey

Edited by Ayşe Öncü
Çağlar Keyder
Saad Eddin Ibrahim

The American University in Cairo Press

113 Sharia Kasr el Aini
Cairo, Egypt

Dar el Kutub No. 8548/93
ISBN 977 424 329 3

Printed in Egypt at the Printshop of the American University in Cairo

Developmentalism and Beyond

Contributors

Abdel Monem Said Aly
Galal A. Amin
Korkut Boratav
Ayşe Buğra
Ali E. Hillal Dessouki
Atila Eralp
Nadia Ramsis Farah
Saad Eddin Ibrahim
Amani Kandil
Çağlar Keyder
Ayşe Öncü
İlkay Sunar

Contents

Interest Articulation and the Management of Discontent

Tables

Acknowledgments

This volume grew out of a project which the editors designed and proposed to the Middle East Research Competition (MERC) of the Ford Foundation for funding. Contributors to the volume met at two conferences, the first in Istanbul in 1990 and the second in Cairo in 1991, where they presented and discussed the papers which eventually evolved into the versions found in this collection. Many colleagues and friends in Cairo and Istanbul made the meetings enjoyable and fruitful; we must especially mention Dr. Necla Tschirgi of the Ford Foundation in Cairo, whose enthusiasm for the project contributed greatly to its continuation. Finally we would like to acknowledge gratefully the financial support of MERC, without which this volume would not have been possible.

Acknowledgments

[illegible]

Introduction
Comparing Egypt and Turkey

Çağlar Keyder, Ayşe Oncü

The essays in this volume explore a particular analytical terrain: the interaction between politics and economics in Turkey and Egypt.

The cases of these two Middle Eastern countries invite comparison because they display a broad range of common features, yet remain a study of contrasts. The similarities in size, historical and religious heritage, status in the world economy, and geopolitical position require little elaboration. In their history, the two countries share the cultural legacy of a multiethnic empire and the state-centered high culture of Islam. As nation-states, both were consolidated in the early decades of the twentieth century, when the ethnic and political map of the region was being redrawn through superpower rivalries. Today, they are the two most populous, oil-poor, labor-surplus economies of the region, with roughly comparable levels of development. As part of the same 'crisis-prone' region, to use the trendy terminology of the post–Gulf War era, they share a series of constraints which arise from their similar location within the world economic and political order.

At the same time, Egypt and Turkey represent, within the region, two markedly different trajectories of political-cum-economic transformation. Egypt in 1922 and the Turkish Republic in 1923 emerged from radically different political backgrounds. Each embodied a distinctive configuration of social forces in terms of the role of the state and the political power of various classes, paving the way for what is frequently referred to as the 'liberal age' of the interwar decades in Egypt in contrast to the consolidation of 'etatism' in Turkey. The years 1950 and 1952, respectively in Egypt and Turkey, signaled important transformations in the context of the post-1945 world system under American hegemony. Both countries embarked upon grand developmentalist projects, but of different varieties. The contrast between Egypt's "populist-socialism" and Turkey's "populist-capitalism" as experiments in national development are interesting, not because one can be gauged to be more successful than the other along any single scale of achievements, but because they elucidate the various ways in which Egypt and Turkey encountered and dealt with universal problems such as capital accumulation, agrarian transformation, social protest, and political legitimation. Similarly, the years 1973 in Egypt and 1980 in Turkey represent important breaks in the trajectories of the two countries, coinciding with the official inauguration of a set of radical economic policy changes known as *Infitah.* But the strategies of Infitah have unfolded, each in its own discursive fashion, to yield different matrices of political and economic developments in the two countries.

This unique set of common and dissimilar parameters point toward and underline the significance of an analytical terrain that stands somewhere between putatively general macro social processes, to be found, variously, in modernization, dependency, world-system, etc. theories, and the unfolding of unique historical events in the individual countries. They suggest that the most interesting analytical issues reside at the level between the most general and the particular; a realm of second-order possibilities wherein the distinctive ways 'politics' is interwoven with 'economics' in the two countries provides fertile ground for new historical and empirical research.[1]

As a collective effort, the contributions to this volume set out to explore this particular analytical terrain of second-order possibilities. Our aim is neither to underline the richly textured, unique historicity of each case, nor to highlight the generalizing processes of development and/or peripheralization due to the shared regional and global positions of the two countries. These we simply take for granted. The set of contributions we offer are an attempt to move beyond the historical uniqueness and toward exploring the distinctive unfolding of social forces which have shaped the divergent political-cum-economic trajectories of Egypt and Turkey.[2]

At the point of departure are two fairly simple analytical premises which allow us to proceed with focused and delimited comparisons between the two cases. The studies in this volume stand together because they all focus on what we designate below as major historical turning points in the twentieth-century trajectories of the two countries. Each seeks to understand, from a variety of disciplinary perspectives and theoretical inclinations, the ways in which the nature, projects, and activities of social groups and classes have shaped the different outcomes.

Historical Turning Points

We use the notion of historical turning points to refer to periods of major restructuring in the international political economy that contain the potential for a number of competing outcomes. They are critical junctures of conflict and of realignments in the global context, corresponding to shifts in hegemonic power and cycles of growth and depression. They are also moments of fluidity in the national arena, when historical opportunities are presented and strategic options are available—at least for the duration and unfolding of the conjuncture until the system acquires a new definition. The question is whether there are domestic social forces willing to exploit the opportunities, whether they can override opposing interests, and whether they enjoy the necessary organizational capacities. If the answer to these questions is in the affirmative, then we would expect a change in the prevailing class alliances, in principal economic policy (such as a shift from import substitution to export orientations), in the role of the state in the economy (and in state administrative capacities) and in the ideologies of legitimation. If the answer is negative, then the reasons for failure must once again lie in the nature, capabilities, and prevailing balance of social forces in the domestic arena.[3] How the 'external' opportunity space is 'internalized', i.e. perceived, defined, and translated into an agenda for change, can only be understood with reference to the projects and activities of groups and classes in each society.

Three such historical turning points, each of which corresponds to major transitions in both Egypt and Turkey, are relevant in our comparative analysis. The first of these may be designated as the global commercial crisis and uncertainty culminating in World War I, which paved the way for the dismemberment of the Ottoman Empire in the Middle East and led to Egyptian independence in 1922 and the declaration of the Turkish Republic in 1923. The second major turning point, corresponding to the crystallization of the post-1945 bipolar world order and the ascendance of American hegemony in Europe, complete with its international institutions, marks major shifts in 1950 and 1952, respectively, in Turkey and Egypt. The last major turning point, beginning in the 1970s and crystallizing in the 1980s, coincides with a qualitative shift in the degree of internationalization of the world economy and the collapse of 'national development' models in a variety of underdeveloped and socialist countries. The years 1973 and 1980 mark this watershed in Egypt and Turkey respectively. The periods bracketed by these turning points—Egypt's interwar 'liberal age' in contrast to Turkey's 'Etatism'; Egypt's post–World War II experiment in state directed 'socialism' in juxtaposition to Turkey's state sponsored 'capitalism'; as well as the variable course of the two Infitah projects—remain a study in contrasts.

By anchoring our comparative analysis on such turning points, we aim to develop explanations for different outcomes in the two cases, based on the specific configuration of choices and constraints available to different social groups and classes contending for power in each national context. Our preference thus is for a formulation that privileges the existing power constellations in the 'domestic' context in order to understand the particular direction of the impact of 'external' conditions, both regional and global.

Bringing 'Society' Back In

Both Egypt and Turkey have been stereotyped as highly centralized societies. In the Turkish case, the legacy of the 'Ottoman state tradition' has most frequently been invoked; in the Egyptian case, 'hydraulic society', 'oriental despotism', and 'Asiatic Mode of Production' have often been used interchangeably to account for such 'centralization'. From this perspective, the key to understanding the genesis of social classes and all institutions is the state, which retains the prerogative of allowing, denying, or transforming dynamics arising outside of itself. Political life is also understood in the context of state primacy, whereby resistance to the encroachment of the state (despotic, modernizing, or liberalizing, depending on the period) constitutes the principal stuff of political analysis.[4]

We would not dispute the centrality of the state as an autonomous actor. We would argue however, that the apparent continuities in the state tradition in the Middle East are illusory, and that the character, mission, and capacities of the state have undergone significant transformations which may only be understood with reference to the projects and activities of diverse groups and classes in the society. This is not to suggest that the state simply mirrors the balance of forces in society. As institutional structures, states have histories and traditions. As organizations, they affect societies through their interventions—or inertia—and through their relationships with groups. Bureaucrats, as officialdom, tend to defend their power and privileges. Hence there is little doubt that states have an independent impact on the course of social change. But state autonomy or primacy cannot be explained by the continuity of a strong state tradition; this autonomy is subject to erosion and reconstruction, and its perpetuation depends on interaction with society.

We have thus chosen, in the present volume, to highlight 'society' as opposed to the state and to move from cultural essentialism to context-specific analysis. Our interest is in how various societal actors—including the state—have shaped the outcomes, and in turn been shaped by them, during the critical historical moments.

Comparative Themes

Within the general axes of comparison we have charted above, the contributing authors have defined and interpreted their own mandates differently. Some have attempted direct comparisons, others have remained grounded in one case, using the other as the implicit contrast. Some have focused on specific historical periods, others have pursued a single substantive theme over different periods. All of the contributors had to struggle with the problems of comparative method and chose their own strategies. Below, we will briefly touch on some of the salient comparative themes in various contributions and outline our own understanding of their significance from the perspective of major turning points in the historical trajectories of the two countries.

1. Variable Paths Toward National Independence

While Egypt and present-day Turkey share a common historical legacy as territories of the Ottoman Empire, the broader rhythms of European economic and political penetration in the region affected them very differently. The impact of the world system on changes in the region from about 1800 to 1914 constitutes the point of departure in the two complementary essays by Keyder and Ibrahim in the first part of this volume. They focus on landlords and the bourgeoisie as the two dominant social forces which have singly and together shaped the modern history of the two countries. The analysis they provide on the different origins, nature, and alliances of landlords and the bourgeoisie in the two cases, although couched within a much wider time frame, allows us to juxtapose the divergent sociopolitical equations that paved the way for the 1922 granting of independence in Egypt and the 1923 declaration of the Turkish Republic.

The origins of Egypt's powerful landed interests date back to the collapse of Muhammed Ali's project to create an economically independent Egypt in the early part of the nineteenth century. During Muhammed Ali's rule, Egypt became an independent actor in the interstate system while still nominally a province of the Ottoman Empire, and remained so until the British occupation in 1882. Muhammed Ali's project was to turn Egypt into a centrally managed agrarian estate. State monopolies would earn a revenue and finance the modernization efforts in the building of an army, bureaucracy, and educational institutions. The paradoxical outcome of this scheme was that while Egypt underwent substantial economic growth (a point emphasized by Galal Amin in his essay), the agrarian-based interests which grew out of it eventually undermined the effort to manage Egypt as a single state. What sealed the fate of the project was the unsustainability of economic independence during a period of world history when Britain was establishing its systemic hegemony based on free trade. In fact, Muhammed Ali's industrialization scheme was dismantled following the 1838 free trade treaty, and an agrarian structure based on large landownership was set in place.

Egypt's big landlords became a pivotal social force during increasing foreign penetration of the economy and society in the second half of the nineteenth century, their interests rapidly coalescing with the newly forming commercial bourgeoisie and foreign capital. The volume of trade rose steadily together with an inflow of foreign capital, in the form of investment in land, canals, banks, mortgage institutions, and commerce, as well as public debt advanced to government. Foreigners arrived in Egypt to own, manage, and provide personnel for all stages of Egypt's incorporation into the imperialist system. The establishment of a colonial administration opened the way for a smooth interpenetration of foreign and local interests and for Egypt's transformation into an export economy.

By the time World War I signaled the end of British rule in Egypt, a native commercial bourgeoisie had evolved out of the class of large landholders, gaining strength through its intricate and integral relationship with foreign capital, but now sufficiently powerful to demand access to the political center. The massive popular upheaval of 1919 against British presence enhanced the bargaining power of Egypt's 'landed bourgeoisie', leading to the granting of formal independence to Egypt in 1922.

Patterns of European penetration into present-day Turkey were markedly different. Anatolia, the heartland of the Ottoman Empire, was dominated by the classical equation of an agrarian empire, with a small land-owning peasantry maintained by the laws and practices of a central authority whose principal source of revenue was the tax collected from these producers. Ottoman sultans were able to maintain this structure, and the 1838 treaty (which sealed the fate of Muhammed Ali's imperial adventure in Egypt) allowed the European penetration of Anatolia to proceed on the basis of an agrarian structure characterized by small peasant ownership.

There were several consequences. First, compared to Egypt, the level of capitalist penetration remained much lower and the rate of growth of trade was smaller; the average peasant was less commercialized. Second, direct foreign investment in agriculture was nonexistent and it remained much more limited in infrastructure to promote trade. Consequently, a considerably smaller foreign presence was confined to the port cities, where foreigners mostly engaged in international commerce. Third, the intermediary positions in trade that required dealing with a large number of petty producers in agriculture were necessarily occupied by locals, and the Greek and Armenian minorities emerged as the natural candidates for these positions.

This balance sheet meant that Turkey would enter World War I with an inventory substantially different from that of Egypt: an agrarian structure wherein small peasant land-holding prevailed; a bureaucracy that retained its monopoly over the state and could therefore engage in reformism and modernization from above, and a native Christian bourgeoisie which was unwittingly drawn into conflicts that eventually led to the nationalist dismemberment of the empire.

2. Divergent Sociopolitical Equations in the Interwar Decades

The 1923 declaration of the Turkish Republic and the 1922 granting of independence for Egypt came under very different circumstances and embodied different equations both in terms of leadership and the social composition of the population.

In the Turkish case, republican leadership represented a continuation of the Ottoman intelligentsia in its cultural and political prerogatives. In the absence of an entrenched landed oligarchy or a sufficiently powerful would-be bourgeoisie, their nation-building project remained unchallenged. The new population of republican Turkey contained, in its overwhelming majority, a fairly homogeneous peasantry, provincial merchants, and a small urban petite bourgeoisie. Most of the metropolitan bourgeoisie and modern working class had been Christians, and having suffered deportation, emigration, and expulsion, they were no longer a significant presence.

In the case of Egypt, the promise of independence provided scope for the 'nationalist' aims of an aspiring native bourgeoisie of agrarian origin, allowing it access to an administrative apparatus hitherto monopolized by the

British, without, however, severing its organic links to landownership or foreign capital. The broader parameters of Egypt's ancien regime remained intact; the 'landed bourgeoisie', confident of its class position and the prerogatives of this position, could afford to experiment with economic liberalism, which further served to consolidate the bourgeoisie's ascendance during the interwar decades.

The impact of the world depression towards the end of the 1920s crystallized the divergence of social forces in the two cases, foreclosing some choices and paving the way for others. In the Turkish case, the economic crisis implied that Muslim merchants, who in the 1920s had been successful in filling the lucrative opportunity space left after the departure of the Christian bourgeoisie, remained politically emasculated. Instead, the proto–Third-Worldist ideology and anti-market sentiments of the military–civilian bureaucratic cadres prevailed. Etatist—i.e. state capitalistic—economic policies were coupled with corporatist legislation and institutions, reminiscent of other models then current around the Mediterranean.

In terms of rapid growth and progress along capitalist lines, interwar Egypt boasted a much wealthier, more sophisticated economy than republican Turkey. And, again by contrast, Egypt's rich urban culture and liberal ideological climate were striking. Whether this was Egypt's golden 'liberal age' or the dark ages of 'quasi-colonialism' remains a controversy—one that underlies the different interpretations of the Nasser decades and its accomplishments offered by various authors in this volume. When juxtaposed with interwar Turkey, the social forces unleashed by Egypt's uneven economic growth present complex matrices, the world crisis serving to exacerbate existing cleavages and paving the way for new ones.

For 'native' Egyptian capital, the depression years, which stimulated local manufacturing, provided the opportunity to undertake 'import substituting' investments. Foreign capital continued to play a major role and maintained control over some of the major monopolies or semimonopolies in key sectors of the economy, but the numbers of Egyptian-owned and -operated firms steadily increased. Hence, comprador or not, Egypt's local bourgeoisie matured during the interwar period and began to dominate the exclusive elite circles of Cairo and Alexandria. This indigenous bourgeoisie seemed to be an organic extension of the traditional landholding class, making the transition from agrarian landownership to commercial and manufacturing investment.

The depression and falling cotton prices also unleashed from the land a vast dispossessed peasantry, flooding the large cities to depress the wages of unskilled workers in manufacturing establishments and contributing to notorious density of the industrial slums that grew around the port and railway terminals of Cairo and Alexandria. Within this broader panorama of growing polarization in interwar Egypt, the growing cadres of what has been termed a 'new middle class', occupying the middle echelons of the newly created banks and industrial enterprises, employed as technocrats and bureaucrats in various state organs and as officers in the army, found the gateways to economic and political power closed. Their misgivings vis-à-vis the Egyptian landed bourgeoisie were just as grave as those about the British and the royal family. The growing restlessness of this stratum led it into an alliance with the gathering momentum of anti-imperialist social forces, and, given the inability of Egypt's bourgeoisie to overcome the inertia of its own vested interests, ultimately provided the necessary ingredient for the success of Egypt's nationist revolution.

3. Contrasting the Grand Developmentalist Projects of the Post-1950 Era

The years 1950 and 1952 were obvious turning points in the trajectories of the two countries—but not necessarily in directions to be anticipated on the basis of prevailing equations we have depicted above. Interwar Egypt, with its mono-crop export economy, its landed oligarchy, its growing 'new middle class', and its impoverished but increasingly politicized and mobilized 'popular classes', resembles Latin American equations of the period. Such equations do not 'naturally' give birth to socialist experiments. Turkey, with its statist regime astride a small–middle peasant population, is reminiscent of interwar Spain, a case where the regime did not 'naturally' yield to popular discontent or international pressure to hold popular elections.

In both cases, the ascendance of American hegemony in Europe in the post-1945 period and the crystallization of a bipolar global order provided new opportunities but also limited the choices. The new era of growth and expansion in the world economy was accompanied by a restructuring of the linkages between the core and peripheral countries and a shift from trade-based domination towards one permitting a certain kind of industrial development. In the Middle East, this shift was accompanied by a decline in British–French domination and growing Soviet–American rivalry. Two complementary essays in this volume, by Ali and Eralp, underline the significance of superpower rivalries in the region as both parameters and variables in the emergent political configurations in the two countries. They point out that in both Egypt and Turkey, the industrialization drive of the post–World War II decades was contingent upon massive infusions of foreign aid and credit, albeit from different sources. While Turkey played its strategic card on the American option, the regional conflicts restricted Egypt's maneuvering capacity; the appeal to the Soviet Union during the Suez crisis made the American option increasingly difficult to pursue. Within a world context characterized by bipolarity, these choices proved to be mutually exclusive.

The underpinnings of these choices in the preexisting lines of contestation and conflict in the two contexts is discussed by Sunar in his comparative article. He emphasizes that the coalitional basis of "popular-democratic capitalism" in Turkey was defined in contradistinction to an etatist, bureaucratic power bloc of the interwar decades. The ideological discourse of Turkish populists was consistently antibureaucratic, antistatist, liberal, and capitalist. The Democratic Party appealed to and mobilized groups who sought to curb state interventionism and enhance marketization—i.e. urban and rural producers as well as the commercial bourgeoisie—*against* the bureaucratic power bloc. Populism in Egypt confronted the preestablished 'liberal' order of oligarchic landowning and commercial groups, foreign and domestic. The discourse of Egyptian populism appealed to the 'national' classes, its ideological content was initially antioligarchic and antiliberal. Its strategy was premised on forging a coalition for an interventionist state that would promote nationalization. What underlined the anticapitalist dimension of Egyptian populism and shaped its eventual socialist path, at the expense of the nationalist bourgeoisie who were among its original supporters, was, we believe, the external template. The regional conflicts in the transition from British to American hegemony, and Egypt's role in this conflict, progressively restricted the maneuvering capacity of Egypt's revolutionary officers, undermining alternative political and social solutions as populism congealed into socialism.

Populist mobilization in Turkey was based on the promise of economic and political liberalism. The Democratic Party's landslide electoral victory of May 1950 hinged upon its pledge of liberating the economic potential of the country by allowing the market free reign. In fact, when the export boom of the first euphoric years subsided, economic policy shifted towards protectionism. The aspiring Turkish bourgeoisie, eager to capitalize on the promise of foreign aid, was now ready to embrace import substitution with its protectionist, developmentalist edifice. The 1960 military coup brought the bureaucratic cadres back into the ruling coalition, replacing the liberal, pro-market discourse of the earlier period with planning-oriented rhetoric. In the subsequent two decades of inflationary expansion, heavily reliant upon foreign aid and credit, the Turkish bourgeoisie consolidated itself around what became the hallmark of private enterprise—the giant family-owned holding companies. As described by Buğra in her essay, these private conglomerates, with their vast networks of affiliated companies, have diversified into an extensive range of industrial, commercial, and financial activities to become the oligopolistic giants of the Turkish economy. Their growth throughout the 1960s and 1970s depended on state protectionism, which combined tariff barriers with investment incentives in the form of state-subsidized credit. The heavy reliance of private conglomerates on domestic public credit, as well as on state-controlled foreign credit, resulted in a high degree of interpenetration and interlocking between the public and private sectors through the banking system. The capital concentration in private enterprise flourished next to, and interdependent with, a vast state sector that continued to expand in the post-1950 decades. Three decades of near continuous inflationary expansion of the economy made massive state investments in infrastructure, in health, and in education affordable. Stagnant agrarian structures were transformed; commercialization in agriculture and rural emigration was accompanied by expanding opportunities for urban employment in both private industry and the state sector. Populist developmentalism in Turkey entailed private accumulation through state intervention, its trials and tribulations contingent upon sustainability of inflationary growth which would allow for both.

In Egypt, populist mobilization was based upon the promise of justice and equity, through state intervention against the economic power of the upper classes. After the Suez crisis and the mass departure of foreign and minority businessmen and the transfer of largest companies to the public sector, aspirations for justice through redistribution were supplemented by an emphasis on industrial growth and economic development through socialist planning. The accomplishments of the Nasser regime in terms of extending major benefits to hitherto excluded groups, through extensive land reform, rent-control measures, expansion of public sector employment, and a variety of other subsidies, are outlined by Galal Amin in his contribution to this volume. Egypt's agenda for 'planned industrialization' and 'populist redistribution' presents remarkable parallels with that of Turkey in the post-1960 period. But populist developmentalism in Egypt was premised upon a state which assumed the functions of both capital accumulation and equitable distribution. Bureaucratic supremacy, in both the economy and polity, enhanced the role of state functionaries, who gradually began to merge ranks with the old bourgeoisie (disenfranchised, but still continuing to enjoy wealth and social status) as the momentum of Egypt's socialism began to subside after 1967.

4. The Trajectories of 'Liberalization' in the Two Countries

The official inauguration of Infitah, in 1973 in Egypt and 1980 in Turkey, entailed a repudiation of more than three decades of inward-oriented developmentalism in both countries. The political discourse and espoused aims of the two cases of Infitah have been remarkably similar. And in neither case does the promise of an open-door economy, paving the path towards a new era of export-oriented growth, appear to have fully materialized. But the ethos of liberal internationalism and its economic strategies have generated new opportunities in both cases, and, given the preexisting balance of contending social forces, have entailed different potential beneficiaries.

In Turkey, Infitah followed on the heels of a major balance-of-payments crisis, brewing since the mid-1970s, but held at bay through workers' remittances from Europe and a succession of governments which spent all their energy to secure loans from abroad to delay the day of reckoning. The political equation of populist-capitalism had been based on the comfortable ascendance of a bourgeoisie, whose accumulation through import substitution depended upon an expanding domestic consumer market—ensured by state-protected barriers and state-mediated redistributive policies. The Turkish bourgeoisie was content to remain out of the political limelight so long as electoral politics could contain distributive conflicts. But the escalating demands of an increasingly politicized labor movement, together with the growing radicalism of the urban petite bourgeoisie (including state employees)—progressively divided among the competing claims of Islamic fundamentalism and neo-fascistic nationalism—strained the limits of this political equation. The familiar signals of an import-substitution crisis—spiraling inflation and foreign exchange shortages—meant that distributive conflicts could not be held at bay through state subsidies and patronage mechanisms.

When the military stepped in, ostensibly to put an end to civil strife in 1980, it was apparent that a new cycle of credit and aid from international sources depended on major restructuring toward closer integration into worldwide capital and commodity flows. Hence it was under direct military rule between 1980 and 1983 that economic transformation policies that had been on the drawing board for almost two years could actually be implemented. After 1983, the political management of Turkey's Infitah was overtaken by a narrowly based center–right coalition, which faced little challenge in the dramatically restricted political arena. The coalition, however, could and did elicit the support of the international financial community, multinational agencies, etc. to forge ahead with 'liberalization' in pursuit of export markets and foreign capital.

The new era of internationalization paved the way for the Turkish bourgeoisie, given its organizational base in giant oligopolistic holdings, to link directly with international financial markets, providing access to fresh capital both through borrowing and joint ventures with foreign capital. Hitherto entirely dependent on subsidized state credit, chafing under the political uncertainties such dependency entailed, and yet reluctant to relinquish family control to pursue alternative strategies such as issuing shares (as discussed by Buğra), Turkish family holdings have seized the opportunity to integrate with global capital markets. The attendant outcomes of this 'successful' integration, i.e. declining social expenditures, reductions in state subsidies, and worsening income distribution, have been dramatic. Korkut Boratav points out, in his discussion of the post-1980 economic transformation in Turkey, that the overall framework and components of the stabilization/adjustment recipes have been similar to those implemented in a number of other countries. But the decline in the relative and absolute positions of workers, peasants, and state employees has been unprecedented in magnitude and duration. Ayşe Öncü underlines the weakness of resistance and opposition at the level of street politics and argues that it has contributed to the effectiveness of "incomes policy" as a key component of the Turkish Infitah. Thus Infitah in Turkey has engendered a radical restructuring of state–society relations, enhancing the role of Turkey's (now) internationalized bourgeoisie as an autonomous political and economic actor, enabling it to stamp its vision and demands upon the polity and the economy.

The pattern of Egypt's integration into regional and global capital and commodity flows during the Infitah decades represents, in contrast to Turkey, the reorientation of an etatist economy and polity. Etatist, because the redistributive promise and capacity of populist-socialism has already reached its limits by June of 1967. The war with Israel sealed its demise, disillusionment eroding revolutionary sensibility, leaving behind an omnipresent state apparatus which controlled resources and mediated access, with state franchises and monopolistic favors flowing through party channels. Party officials and military–civilian bureaucrats who intermingled in the executive committees of national banks, state enterprises, and cooperatives, once the vanguards of a compelling mission, now became the mediators between particularistic demands and state resources. Enhanced possibilities of accumulation through state favors—import–export licenses, contracts awarded for major construction projects, etc.—provided room for Egypt's traditional landed bourgeoisie to revive and recuperate much of its wealth, without allowing it to consolidate an organizational and institutional base within the state-dominated economy.

Thus the official inauguration of Infitah, announcing a series of sweeping policy measures in 1974, ushered Egypt's bourgeoisie into the new era of liberalization, but without the institutional underpinnings upon which the Turkish bourgeoisie had built its economic ascendance, i.e. oligopolistic family holdings. Hence foreign capital and aid which flowed into Egypt was mediated through state-controlled agencies, thereby strengthening the state bureaucracy and subordinating the domestic bourgeoisie to bureaucratic channels of decision-making and authority. At the risk of overstating the difference, we would argue that integration of the Egyptian economy into regional and global financial markets has reinforced the powers of the state bureaucracy in Egypt, whereas in Turkey Infitah has led to the political marginalization of the bureaucratic cadres and has enabled the Turkish bourgeoisie to translate its social and economic dominance into political power for the first time in the republican era. Nadia Farah provides an extensive discussion on the continued political power of Egypt's bureaucratic elite over entrepreneurial groups, despite (or in conjunction with) immense accumulation of both old and new wealth. In contrast to the puritan 'free market' discourse of Turkey's liberalizers, the engineers of Egypt's Infitah have been in search of what Ali Dessouki calls "a hybrid formula," the typical lexicon of bureaucratic politics.

The macroeconomic policies of Infitah in Egypt and Turkey, as well as their common distributive outcomes—social polarization and political exclusion—remind us of a variety of other experiments around the world, daring experiments with liberalization which contain few, if any, victories. To say that Infitah has fallen dramatically short of its professed aims in either of the cases would be to restate the obvious. But the politico-economic equations within which the broader processes of Infitah have unfolded in the two cases remain unique and distinct, allowing us to conclude, somewhat optimistically, that history does offer choices and opportunities to be seized.

Organization of the Volume

The studies in this volume have been organized around five broad themes which provide a basis for developing the broader, comparative framework we have outlined above. Each of these broad themes chart out a set of core questions which complementary texts on Egypt and Turkey jointly address. These broad themes and the ways individual authors have chosen to approach them are, briefly, as follows:

Landlords and the Bourgeoisie

Landlords and the bourgeoisie have been dominant social actors in the modern history of both Egypt and Turkey. We are interested in how their different roles and alliances during periods of social, economic, and political transformation (nationally, regionally, and internationally) have influenced the trajectories of both society and the state. Saad Eddin Ibrahim and Çağlar Keyder focus on differences in the origins, paths of evolution, and variable alliances of landlords and bourgeoisies in Egypt and Turkey, respectively.

State Formation, Transformation, and Legitimizing Ideologies

In both Turkey and Egypt, institutions of the state have been the source as well as the vital object of political struggles between contending social forces in their pursuit of different social visions and alternative social projects. Our major interest in this context is in how and why different ideologies gained momentum to challenge preestablished forms of the state power and its legitimization in the two contexts, and the factors which shaped the success of alternative strategies of mobilization within particular historical junctures. İlkay Sunar and Ali Hillal Dessouki approach this question by outlining the various ideologies which have competed in Egypt and Turkey (e.g. nationalist, liberal, socialist, and religious) and the ways they have articulated the demands of different social forces in the two contexts.

State Economic Policies and Regime Performance

'Social equity' and 'economic growth' have been embedded in the discourse of successive political regimes in both Egypt and Turkey. Our interest here is in understanding how they have been addressed and reconciled in practice. Specifically, we wanted to know how major shifts in state economic policies have had variable implications in terms of growth and distribution. Three essays in this volume provide complementary assessments of overall and sectoral growth rates as well as leading indicators of distribution in the two countries. Galal Amin focuses on the Nasser experiment in Egypt, comparing its social and economic performance with previous as well as subsequent periods. Nadia Ramsis Farah discusses the constellation of politico-economic forces that gave birth to Infitah policies in Egypt and shaped its subsequent course. Korkut Boratav discusses Turkey's pursuit of Infitah over the past decade and provides a balance sheet in terms of groups that have gained and lost in the process.

The International Context and State Policies

The twentieth-century trajectories of Egypt and Turkey are bound up with cycles of growth and depression of the world economy, as well as superpower rivalries at the global and regional level. Our central concern was to go beyond very broad generalizations in order to address the question of varying impact. Atila Eralp and Abdel Monem Said Aly focus on issues of foreign aid, trade, and debt as both parameters and variables in major state policies in the two contexts.

Interest Articulation and Management of Discontent

The institutional bases and organizational capacities of various social groups in propagating and/or defending their interests are crucial in understanding the relative autonomy of the state vis-à-vis societal pressures and constraints. We are here mainly interested in differences between Egypt and Turkey in the capabilities of various groups to promote their interests or articulate discontent, and how states in turn deal with them through co-optation, accommodation, and coercion. There are three contributions on this theme. Buğra discusses the organizational bases of Turkey's powerful business interests, the family holdings, and outlines their origins and growth. Kandil emphasizes the role of professional associations in Egypt and discusses their potential power and limits. Öncü focuses on differences in modes of articulating discontent and repertories of political action among workers in Egypt and Turkey.

In choosing to organize our comparative effort around these five themes, with complementary pieces on Egypt and Turkey on each theme, we have sought to highlight the unique features of each case and to draw out the contrasts between them. Such an analytical strategy helps reinforce the overall aim of the project concerning the need to go beyond broad commonalities and generalizing processes, and allows us to proceed with more controlled comparisons. It also poses a methodological problem in that real societies and sociohistorical processes cannot be broken at will into neat thematic compartments. Individual authors (including the project convenors themselves) had to confront this problem; they had to grapple with the dilemma of how to remain within the confines of an analytical theme while not losing sight of the unified whole. Some rigorously delimited themselves in time and place to maintain thematic focus, while others adopted a holistic approach to emphasize interlinkages between different spheres of society and preserved the historical reality of the individual case, but at the expense of lengthy chronological narratives. Many attempted to do both at once, and with varying degrees of success, as the reader will discover.

There have been remarkably few efforts to juxtapose and compare trajectories of change systematically among Middle Eastern countries. We hope that our collective enterprise, aiming to adapt some of the categories and analytical concerns of the vast literature on social and economic transformation and political outcomes to two important examples, will serve as a contribution in this direction. Also, we hope that the discussion of these two specific and significant cases, in terms that are easily translatable to the historical and analytical traditions of comparative social inquiry, will help introduce the Middle East into a literature which has for so long ignored its potentially rich contribution.

Notes

1 Evans and Stephens point out that the most fruitful lines of investigation over the past two decades have been in this direction. See Peter Evans and John D. Stephens, "*Studying Development Since the Sixties: The Emergence of a New Comparative Political Economy,*" in Theory and Society vol. 17, 1988, pp. 713–45.

2 What we set out to accomplish comes close to what Skocpol and Somers have called "comparative history as the contrast of contexts." See Theda Skocpol and Margaret Somers, "*The Uses of Comparative History in Macrosocial Inquiry,*" in Comparative Studies in Society and History vol. 25, no. 2, 1980, pp. 174–97.

3 The classic reference would be Fernando Cardoso and Enzo Faletto, *Dependency and Development in Latin America* (Berkeley: University of California Press, 1979).

4 We would dispute, at least in the case of Egypt and Turkey, Lisa Anderson's generalization that the literature on the Middle East has been "society centered." See Lisa Anderson, "*The State in the Middle East and North Africa,*" in Comparative Politics vol. 20, no. 1, 1987, pp. 1–18. In fact, both the orientalist and the Marxist literature on Egypt and Turkey have privileged the state.

Landlords and the Bourgeoisie

1

Egypt's Landed Bourgeoisie

Saad Eddin Ibrahim

Introduction

This essay deals with a crucial socioeconomic formation in the evolution of modern Egypt: the big landowning bourgeois class. The main propositions expounded in this essay are the following:

1. Fertile land has been a scarce commodity, hence the most valuable asset, in the otherwise arid country of Egypt. Control and management of this asset have constituted much of the sociopolitical discourse in modern Egypt.

2. The concept of landowning was initiated by the Egyptian state in the mid-nineteenth century, and the country's modern class structure has been woven around it, as has its main social conflict.

3. Once under way, the processes involved in obtaining and owning land sorted and sifted out an 'upper class' which continued a century-long striving to maximize its share of Egypt's land. In the process, the upper class has engaged in a complex interplay with the state, the rest of society, and the outside world.

4. In the interwar period (1918–39), big landowners engaged in bourgeois-like economic activities. Hence, the same landowners also became a major integral part of the grande bourgeoisie. During the same period this social formation has become a 'class in itself' as well as a 'class for itself'.

5. In its quest for total domination of state, economy, and society, this Egyptian upper class changed its domestic and internal alliances more than once, and grew more oblivious of and insensitive to the classes below, especially the lower-middle class. Growing in number but not as much in wealth or power, the latter was steadily alienated. Ultimately in 1952, through its own young army officers, it revolted against the Egyptian upper class and its domestic and foreign allies.

6. The period 1952–72 witnessed a dramatic rise of the middle class to power, and a steady decline in the power and wealth of Egypt's upper-class landed bourgeoisie. This is the 'populist–nationalist' period in modern Egyptian history, and the worst one for the old upper class. Control of state power by a

middle-class military–technocratic elite was employed domestically for sociopolitical mobilization, redistribution of wealth, and rapid economic development. It was a period that also witnessed the rise of pan-Arabism and the projection of Egyptian regional power within a context of nonalignment vis-à-vis the two superpowers of the United States and the Soviet Union.

7. The populist–nationalist phase, symbolized by Nasser, began to draw to an end after Egypt's defeat by Israel in 1967. In the subsequent seven years (1967–74), the old upper-class landed bourgeoisie resurfaced and allied itself with the new 'embourgeoised' elements of the Nasser era at home and its Arab and Western counterparts abroad. This alliance inched its way up to state power under Sadat. By the early 1980s the old upper-class landed bourgeoisie had been completely rehabilitated and renewed, and had succeeded in amalgamating itself with aspiring like-minded elements from below and relinking with the world capitalist system. The Open-Door Economic Policy (*Infitah*) was the result of its lobbying, and has been the context of its socioeconomic comeback. This comeback has been accompanied by a gradual political pluralism, in the form of a restoration of a limited multiparty system.

8. Elements of the current enlarged bourgeoisie are now members of Egypt's top political elite and sub-elites. Through the ruling National Democratic Party (NDP) and some opposition parties (such as the Wafd), this class has been engaged in a renewed quest for total political domination of the state, the economy, and society. Its success in this quest is contingent not only on its own internal cohesion and skillful use of its resource base, but also on its ability to manage and expand the Egyptian economy in general, to accommodate the minimum interests of other classes from below, and incorporate in its own ranks the ambitious members of these classes.

9. Early indications, fifteen years after the start of its comeback, suggest that Egypt's landed bourgeoisie has not as yet succeeded in evolving the kind of credible vision of socioeconomic performance which would make the progress of its ascent to total power proceed without serious challenge from below. Some of the symptoms which had caused its earlier decline (1942–52) and fall (1952–72) have reappeared, and are generating the same discontent, alienation, resentment, and frustration among other classes.

10. The same lower-middle class which led the fight against Egypt's landed bourgeoisie in the 1940s and 1950s, under populist–nationalist slogans, is now engaged in a similar fight under populist–Islamic banners. The question in the 1990s will be only whether such a fight will be with ballots or with bullets. The 1980s witnessed previews of both possibilities, e.g., the killing of a president (1981), and the participation of Islamic activists in parliamentary elections (1984 and 1987).

This essay will only concentrate on the century-long rise, decline, fall, and comeback of the landed bourgeoisie. While this long march of one class is our focus, it goes without saying that the analysis would be incomplete, indeed meaningless, without understanding both the rest of the domestic scene (i.e. the state and other social classes) and the international setting in which it evolved, impacted, and by which it was affected. Other essays in this volume attempt to do that.

The Formation of Egypt's Landed Bourgeoisie

Social classes do not form overnight. While the moment of their inception might be roughly fixed within a relatively short period (of a few years) in time, their unfolding as full-fledged 'classes' is a protracted social process which may take several generations or even centuries. Egypt's landed bourgeoisie is no exception. When the 1952 Revolution fought and defeated it, this class was already one century old. During that century, Egypt's big landowners had struggled to institutionalize the legal ownership of land, which until 1862 was all state-owned and merely leased for use. They eventually succeeded also in consolidating and expanding their own land holdings. Only in its third generation did the descendants of this class venture with their surplus capital into commercial, banking, and industrial activities, thus becoming a 'landed bourgeoisie'. In the process, a class consciousness, a value system, and a lifestyle crystallized. Its political involvement, alliances, and coalitions at home and abroad varied and shifted over time, sometimes guided by 'enlightened self-interest', and often misguided by narrow 'selfish interest'.

The Genesis of the Landed Bourgeoisie

Initially made up of big landowners, this class owes its genesis to Muhammad Ali's land distribution scheme that was implemented between 1847 and 1889. He granted sizable plots of land to members of his own family (at an average of 5,000–10,000 feddans each), to top aides and army commanders (at an average of 1,000 feddans each), to high state officials and Bedouin tribal chiefs (at an average of 500 feddans each), and to middle state functionaries and local notables (at an average of 50–100 feddans each).[1] All in all, this land amounted to half of all of Egypt's cultivable area at the time, and involved some two thousand individual grantees. Except for members of his own family, Muhammad Ali did not at the beginning make these grants outright legal properties. He allowed the recipients and their descendants the right to hold, utilize, and rent the land, but not to sell it. He seemed to have intended to create a stable class of big landowners over several generations to come. He was also attempting to circumvent the possible fallout from the implementation of the London Treaty of 1840, which called for opening the Egyptian economy to foreign activities—including investment in agricultural land and urban real estate.[2]

1. Consolidation and Egyptianization

Complete property rights were obtained, however, during the rule of Muhammad Ali's successors—namely under Said, Ismail, and Tawfiq (under British occupation).[3] This in turn allowed for the sale and exchange of land among members of this privileged class and their descendants, and between them and other Egyptians and foreigners alike. Thus, while in the mid-nineteenth century the original two thousand big landholders were mostly of Turkish–Circasssian–Albanian background, by the end of the century they had become more diverse, with a majority of native or mixed Egyptians, Syrians, and an assortment of Europeans. Interestingly enough, big urban merchants and successful professionals joined this category by buying land as an investment or for prestige. Likewise, during and after World War I, several of the original big landowners invested some of their surplus in commercial and industrial activities. As we shall see later, all of the original founders of Bank Misr, the first major Egyptian bank, were from this landed aristocracy. So intensive was this interchangeability during the interwar period, which coincided with Egyptian independence (1922), that the entire upper class consisted of both landowners and shareholders in urban businesses and industrial enterprises. This fact was overlooked by several Marxist and leftist analysts who assumed an inherent conflict between big landowners and industrial–commercial capitalists.

2. Concentration of Landownership

By 1950, this upper class (owners of more than fifty feddans) had consolidated its hold on nearly 50 percent of Egypt's total cultivable land (of about six million feddans). Land property also became more concentrated in fewer owners and bigger holdings. At the turn of the century owners of more than fifty feddans numbered about 14,000, holding about two million feddans (at an average of 143 feddans each). By 1950 their number had declined to 12,000, owning 2.6 million feddans (at an average of 217 feddans each). A counter trend took place among poor peasants during the same period, i.e., the number of owners of smaller holdings increased. Thus, at the turn of the century the number of owners of less than one feddan was 780,000, owning a total of 364,000 feddans (at an average of half a feddan each). By 1950 their number had grown to about two million owning a total land area of 724,000 feddans (at an average of less than one third of a feddan each).[4]

Factors of Expansion

The ability of the Egyptian upper class to expand and tighten its hold on this very valuable means of production—fertile land in an otherwise vast arid country—was aided by several factors. Among these were certain historical moments, e.g., the American Civil War in the 1860s, the two world wars, and the Korean War, in which demand on agricultural products, especially cotton, rose very sharply. The windfall profits were reinvested in buying or reclaiming more land. Meanwhile the concentration of large landholdings continued. When small landowners could not pay their taxes or make ends meet, as happened frequently, big owners bought them out. Even Khedive

Ismail, under pressure to pay public and personal debts, was forced to sell some of his vast holdings to owners of large and middle-sized holdings. The British occupation, too, assisted in this process of land concentration. It courted the upper landed class early on (1882 to 1922) in the hope of creating for itself a friendly social base in Egypt, or at least of neutralizing the attitude of its members. In fact, both sides shared a common interest, since Britain was the major buyer of cotton. Thus, banks operating in Egypt, which until 1922 were merely extensions of London banks, advanced credit facilities to big landowners to finance and capitalize on their agriculture or to reclaim more land.

However, it was with the coming of independence in 1922 that big landowners reaped the greatest benefits. Dominating the parliament, under different party banners, its members passed several laws advancing their own interests. Land taxes were held to a minimum, and a government-sponsored agricultural credit bank, supposedly established to help small farmers through low-interest credit, ended up aiding the big landowners more.[5] The native Egyptian elements of this class, the only ones who could run for and serve in parliament, passed successive laws (between 1922 and 1951) restricting then prohibiting foreigners from ownership of cultivable land.[6] These laws (especially Law 37 of 1951) had the effect of transferring some 12 percent of the country's total agricultural land (about 600,000 feddans), previously held by foreigners, to native Egyptian ownership, mostly big landowners.

Another means by which big landowners expanded their economic base was through pressure on the government to sell them its own holdings. In 1893, the year which marks the complete institutionalization of private ownership of land, the Egyptian government was in possession of more than half a million feddans, about 10 percent of the country's cultivable land. Shortly after independence, a heated debate (similar to the current one on privatization) broke out over whether the government should own or could manage agricultural land. Critics of the government invoked considerations of 'optimum management' and 'rational utilization' of the country's resources which, it was claimed, could only be ensured by 'private ownership'.[7] In the end, the government yielded to pressure, and sold 507,000 feddans—about 132,000 in small plots (of less than 10 feddans) and about 344,000 feddans in bigger plots (20–100 feddans) which went mostly to landowners of middle and big land holdings.[8]

The demand on land, as a scarce resource, reached an all-time high in the late 1940s and early 1950s, when the average price of a feddan rose to LE1,000 (at the time LE1 equaled US$2.6). In other words, the total landholdings of this Egyptian upper class (2.6 million feddans) was valued at LE2.6 billion (more than $6 billion). The steep rise in cotton prices at the time (because of the Korean War) also sent the annual rent up to an unprecedented high of LE100 per feddan.[9]

Embourgeoisation of the Landed Aristocracy

Having reaped windfall profits from the sale of agricultural products during World War I, Egypt's upper class was bound to search for new investment opportunities, besides buying more land and/or indulging in intensive capitalization of agriculture. Individual bank deposits rose more than five-fold between 1914 and 1919.[10] Some of these accumulated savings went into import-substitution industries to meet inelastic domestic demands, and benefited greatly from governmental tariff protection. This trend was to expand after independence, during Egypt's Liberal Age (1922–52).

Bank Misr, established in 1920 by eight Egyptians, all of whom were also big landowners,[11] rapidly grew to become a conduit and a blender of native landed and business bourgeoisie. By the early 1930s the number of its shareholders rose from the original eight founders to about 10,000. The bank's deposits rose rapidly from LE200,000 in 1920, to LE5.5 million in 1927, to LE45 million in 1947, to about LE80 million in 1952. In the three decades (1920–50), Bank Misr took the initiative in establishing more than twenty industrial and commercial enterprises, ranging from textiles, to airlines, to motion pictures. It also helped establish the Egyptian Federation of Industries (EFI) as early as 1922, which acted as an effective lobby with both parliament and the government for the entire period of the Liberal Age (1922–52). Several prominent members of the EFI became cabinet members and prime ministers,12 and many were members in both houses of parliament. In fact, the upper house (the Senate or the Council of Sheikhs) was almost exclusively confined to this class, since eligibility for membership, according to the law, required that members own at least a certain specified minimum amount of wealth.[13]

Other native Egyptian industrial groups, besides Bank Misr, appeared and flourished between 1922 and 1952. Prominent among them were the Ahmed Abboud Group, the Amin Yehia Group, and the M. Farghaly Group. They competed with each other, and all of them competed with foreign-held companies. In the same way they had dealt with landownership, the Egyptian upper bourgeoisie also lobbied to squeeze foreign interests out of the commercial and industrial fields. First, they managed to overhaul the entire customs and tariff system in 1930, making it much more protective of their interests.[14] Second, they managed to pass a law (Law 138 of 1947) making it mandatory that native Egyptians possess at least 51 percent of all shares in any new joint-stock company registered in the country. This, along with earlier measures, mainly the 1937 Montreux Treaty terminating the Capitulations, increased the share of Egyptians in new joint-stock companies from less than 5 percent in 1920, to 9 percent in 1933, a jump of 47 percent in 1939, to 84 percent in 1948. However, there were older joint-stock companies in which the majority shares were still held by foreigners, and these remained so until 1956, when following the Suez War all such foreign holdings were nationalized.

The industrialization of Egypt grew steadily between 1914 and 1945, and was especially aided by the two world wars. In 1914 the share of industry in the GNP was less than 2 percent. By 1947 it had increased more than fourfold to 8 percent. With the sprouting of an Egyptian bourgeoisie, a modern 'working class' was bound to grow. The number of industrial workers grew from less than 100,000 in 1917 to 274,000 in 1937 to over 400,000 in 1947.[15] The total capital invested in industry by 1950 was estimated at about LE550 million, at least 40 percent of which (LE220 million) belonged to some 11,000 major shareholders, i.e., averaging LE20,000 each. Many of these were members of the same families.[16]

Thus, it is safe to conclude that the same 12,000 families of big landowners who held some 50 percent of all of Egypt's cultivable land also included the 11,000 major shareholders who held some 40 percent of Egypt's joint-stock companies. At the time of the 1952 Revolution these owners and their families represented less than half of 1 percent of Egypt's population. Such figures attest to the glaring concentration of wealth that existed at the time.

State and Politics of the Landed Bourgeoisie in the Liberal Age (1922–52)

During its consolidation and embourgeoisation, Egypt's landed aristocracy had two other major political factors to contend with in its quest for control of the state: British occupation and the monarchy. The relationship between these three major actors on the Egyptian socioeconomic political scene was complicated by shared interests, rivalry, and antagonism. Hence, each side of the triangular relationship zigzagged along a cooperation–conflict continuum but was never subjected to a total rupture. The British streamlined the government's previously troubled fiscal affairs, improved Egypt's irrigation and transportation systems, and provided stable markets for the country's agricultural products, especially cotton—measures which mutually enhanced the interests of both sides. However, the terms of economic exchange and relative share of power had remained a matter of contention between Egypt's landed bourgeoisie and the British, with the former steadily feeling short-changed. As for the monarchy, it had larger common economic–political interests with the landed bourgeoisie. For one thing, Egypt's royal family was the biggest landowner at the turn of the century, and despite previous sales (between 1870 and 1890), the family still owned some 250,000 feddans of the best agricultural land, thus having a definite common interest with other big landowners.[17] As other landowners of large holdings initiated commercial–industrial activities in the interwar period, members of the royal family followed suit, becoming shareholders and presidents of many of the newly created joint-stock companies.[18] While the royal family and the landed bourgeoisie shared the common objective of reducing British power or ridding Egypt of it altogether, there remained the question of how much of that power would go to each side.

Between 1918 and 1952, the political behavior of the upper class (bourgeoisie) went through two distinct phases, roughly separated by the years 1936–37. In the years immediately following World War I, this class allied itself with the middle and lower classes in leading the national struggle for independence (from the British) and constitutionalism (vis-à-vis the monarchy). The struggle, culminating in the 1919 Revolution, resulted in a series of remarkable national gains: a declaration of partial independence in 1922, a national constitution in 1923, elections and the beginning of parliamentary life in 1924, a consolidation of political independence through the 1936 Treaty with Britain, and the 1937 International Montreux Treaty ending the Capitulations. However, every one of these gains seemed to have fallen somewhat short of the expectations of the classes below. Growing numbers from the lower classes were disgruntled and began to desert the implicit 'grand coalition' of the 1919 Revolution (as symbolized at the time by the Wafd Party), and to form their own political parties.

The second phase stretched from 1939 to 1952, and it was during this time that social issues were added to the agenda of Egypt's political discourse. Barring some notable exceptions, the majority of the upper bourgeoisie maintained its hold on the machinery of the state and the practice of politics as usual. Most of the bills addressing social issues that were submitted to parliament were variously ignored, harshly trimmed, or rejected out of hand. For example, several land reform bills, quite moderate compared with what came after the July 1952 Revolution, were rejected. Warnings by authors of such bills about a 'coming crisis' fell on deaf ears.[19] World War II, as noted earlier, had a positive economic impact on the fortunes of the upper bourgeoisie, but an extremely negative one on the lot of other classes. Hence it compounded the effect of the already existing income disparities.

Despite tension and occasional conflict among various wings of the upper-class landed bourgeoisie, or between them and either the palace or the British, the three actors remained in broad agreement on maintaining the socioeconomic status quo. If the state was to interfere at all in an otherwise free-market economy, it was to enhance the interests of the landed bourgeoisie. In the seven years between the end of World War II and the 1952 Revolution, some elements of this bourgeoisie increasingly entered into partnership with foreign counterparts, thereby partly reversing the interwar trend of Egyptianizing the national economy. Some bills that became law relaxed earlier stringent conditions for such partnerships. In other words, when it had suited their interests to squeeze out foreign economic involvement, the Egyptian bourgeoisie had invoked 'national independence' to pass necessary laws to this effect. Later, when it served their interests to link up with foreign capital, this same bourgeoisie invoked 'economic rationality' and 'national interest' to pass laws to this effect. Meanwhile, by the late 1940s neither the free-market system nor this new partnership with foreign capital was developing the economy fast enough to create the necessary jobs for an ever-increasing number of the young and the poor, or trickling down enough benefits to pacify the middle class.

The nationalist zeal of the upper bourgeoisie had long since eroded with the 1936 treaty, and that fact, coupled with the use by the British of an ultimatum to force the king to install a government of their choice in 1942, and the defeat in Palestine in 1948, meant that by 1950 it was no longer possible to trade off the neglect of the social issue with a political cause. Widespread and frequent flare-ups in both rural and urban areas were clear indications not just that the rule of the upper-class landed bourgeoisie was opposed by the lower classes, but that the entire system had lost its legitimacy. When the 1952 revolutionaries struck against both the system and the landed bourgeoisie, few if any voices were raised in defense of the latter. Indeed no social force with any real weight was willing to stand up on behalf of the old regime.

The Fall of the Landed Bourgeoisie

The long march of Egypt's landed bourgeoisie was suddenly and harshly brought to an abrupt halt in 1952. In fact, by 1956, it looked as if this class was completely destroyed economically and politically, though not socio-demographically. However, three decades later it turned out that its resilience and co-optation skills should not have been underestimated. In this part of the essay we look at the years of defeat and retreat of Egypt's landed bourgeoisie (1952–72), and in the next part we will look at its recovery and comeback.

The army officers' coup d'état of 23 July 1952 was soon to emerge as a full-fledged social revolution, transforming the role of the state and the structure of society in mid-century Egypt. The July Revolution promptly forged a sociopolitical coalition of three social classes: the middle petite bourgeoisie, the urban working class, and the rural poor. The target enemy of this coalition was Egypt's upper-class landed bourgeoisie. As the conflict unfolded, whether by design or due to the swift march and logic of events, the Egyptian state grew bigger in size and strength, and its links with the region and the world altered qualitatively from what it had been before 1952.

The New Middle Class and the Expansion of the State

A review of the eighteen years between 1952 and 1972 reveals clearly that all three parties of the July Revolution's coalition had benefited markedly both at the expense of the upper, landed bourgeoisie and as a direct result of the state's expansionist–interventionist role.

To start with, the officers who staged the 1952 coup d'état were all from the middle petit-bourgeois class. Their entry into the Egyptian Military

Academy, as cadets, had followed the signing of the Anglo–Egyptian Treaty of 1936, which allowed the Egyptian government a greater measure of freedom to build a bigger national army. The need for more officers opened the door wide, for the first time in this century, for youngsters of the middle class to join the officer corps. As young officers, they were part of that class generation which had experienced the waning power and increasing failure of the ruling elite and the politically dominant landed bourgeoisie.

The initial declarations of the young officers who led the 1952 revolt indicated clearly that their movement was a populist one, i.e., encompassing general objectives which addressed the aspirations of the vast majority of Egyptians. What was not immediately clear were the ways and means of achieving these objectives. Thus there was a phase (1952–56) in which the young revolutionaries essentially just tried to do the same things that had been done by the old regime that they had just ousted, but in better ways, mainly by streamlining the governmental machinery to make it more efficient and less corrupt. With the exception of the Agrarian Reform Laws, the general socioeconomic orientation of the Liberal Age continued, but with more zeal, and without favoritism or corruption. The first series of economic laws, passed during 1952–54, all aimed at expediting development and industrialization. These laws were intended to encourage domestic and foreign investment through tax exemption on profits for five to seven years. They were as generous and as liberal as in the heyday of the bourgeois-dominated Liberal Age of an earlier time, and as generous and liberal as those of twenty years later under Sadat's Infitah policies.

At first the new ruling elite held the simplistic belief that political power and economic power could operate separately or independently from one another. An equally mistaken view that also prevailed then, possibly under the influence of Marxist thought at the time, was that big landowners represent a separate 'feudalist class' whose interest is in direct conflict with a 'capitalist class', as was the case in seventeenth-century Europe. On both counts, the expected outcomes based on these assumptions did not materialize. The big landowners and industrial capitalists being one and the same, the Egyptian landed bourgeoisie—badly hurt by agrarian reform—was not about to risk whatever capital it had in more industrial investments under a government in which it had little or no say. The appeal to their patriotism and the incentives built into the new economic laws of 1953–54 fell on deaf ears. With the reluctance of indigenous capitalists in evidence, potential foreign investors showed even greater hesitance. As a result, little in the way of development came from the private sector in this initial phase after the 1952 Revolution. Whatever was done in this regard came from the government itself or through bilateral agreements with other governments.[20] Nor was it much of an inducement for the private sector to invest when the young revolutionaries Egyptianized what remained of foreign interests in Egypt following the 1956 Suez Crisis. Six major laws were then passed in 1957–58 transferring the majority share of all joint-stock companies, as well as their management and top personnel, to mostly private Egyptian hands[21]—a result that the nationalist movement in general, and the Egyptian landed bourgeoisie in particular, had fought for with only partial success since the 1920s. The Egyptian bourgeoisie welcomed these measures, and did take advantage of them, but it was not sufficiently attracted to inject enough new capital investment of its own, as the young officers had hoped. Upper-class skepticism, misgivings, or fears vis-à-vis the officers' total monopoly of political power persisted, and thus discouraged private capital investments.

It was only in the late 1950s, some seven years after seizing power, that the leaders of the July Revolution fully recognized that politics and economics are inseparable, on both the internal and external fronts. Attaining their vision of a strong, independent, and just society in Egypt would take more than conducting 'business as usual', albeit in cleaner and more efficient ways. Therefore, the young revolutionaries concluded that the state itself had to undertake all the major socioeconomic tasks. Starting in 1959, they embarked on the task of overhauling the entire economy and society as well. Central planning, the establishment of a public sector, massive nationalization, major income-redistribution policies, and other social policies were undertaken. Together, these policy measures and practices came to be known as 'Arab Socialism'.

By the mid-1960s the public sector had assumed control of over 80 percent of all such related activities. This phenomenal expansion came about as a result of a series of nationalizations of major privately owned Egyptian joint-stock companies. Starting in February 1960, with control of the two largest banks in the country, the National Bank of Egypt and Bank Misr, the government was able to use the necessary resources and tools to launch its first five-year plan (1960–65).[22] In June and July of the following year (1961), six laws and about ten presidential decrees were issued, aimed at transferring total ownership of the country's forty-two largest companies from private to public hands, and the transfer of majority shares (more than 50 percent) of the next largest eighty-two companies to ownership of public-sector organizations. Moreover, concessions to major public utility companies were terminated (e.g., Lebon Gas, the Electricity Company of Alexandria, and the Cairo Tramway), and their assets transferred to state hands. All in all, the largest two hundred enterprises in the country had come under state control. These included all banks, insurance companies, industrial transportation, and a variety of commercial, financial, import–export, and land-reclamation companies. Clearly the state intended not only to control the 'heights' of the economy, but also wished to prevent the creation of strong private enterprises of any sort. Additional presidential decrees stipulated that all state construction and public works whose contract value exceeded LE30,000 be carried out by companies owned totally or mostly by the state.[23]

Though no direct measure was proclaimed specifically to have been designed to benefit the Egyptian middle class (petite bourgeoisie), the overall policies of the July Revolution gave that class the biggest gains. In fact, the new rulers of Egypt came right from the midst of this class and consequently symbolized its values, aspirations, and also its limitations. To begin with, the removal of every member of the older upper class from every position of political and economic power automatically meant an opening and an opportunity for a middle-class member to move up and fill the vacancy. Secondly, the exit of every foreigner previously residing and working in Egypt meant a handsome house or flat and a well-paid job for some middle-class Egyptian.

Likewise, the expansion of the machinery of the state (the civil bureaucracy, the armed forces, and the public sector) was primarily an act by the middle class for the middle class. In 1952, Egypt had 350,000 public employees (2.2 percent of the population). By 1970 the figure increased nearly fourfold to 1.2 million state employees (3.8 percent of the population).[24] In similar fashion the social services (education, health, and the like) were considerably expanded.[25]

War of Attrition Against the Landed Bourgeoisie

The above measures were officially proclaimed as necessary to expedite economic development, ensure social justice, and consolidate national independence. Many of the same measures were also applied to Syria, which had been united with Egypt in 1958 as the United Arab Republic (UAR). When Syria seceded from the union after a coup d'état in September 1961, it was blamed on "reactionary forces." Hence, one added justification for the above measures and new nationalizations and sequestrations in Egypt was deemed as "protection of the people from counter-revolutionary forces," which generally meant the landed bourgeoisie.

Another proclaimed reason for the massive nationalizations was "social justice." While this objective had been stated earlier as one of the six basic principles of the 1952 Revolution, it had remained hitherto (until 1961) largely confined to the first Agrarian Reform Law, of September 1952. Another, but far smaller, measure was urban rent control in 1958.[26] But it was in 1961 that several more drastic measures were implemented with far-reaching redistributive effects. They were all clearly in favor of the three social classes that made up the sociopolitical coalition of the 1952 Revolution, and in effect amounted to a 'war of attrition' against the landed bourgeoisie. Of these measures, the following four were the most far-reaching:

1. Agrarian Reform

We have already alluded to the first Land Reform Law of 1952, which limited maximum ownership to two hundred feddans per family (excluding adult offspring). Then this ceiling was successively reduced, in two stages, down to fifty feddans. Equally far-reaching, but less discussed in the literature, was the rent regulation of agricultural land, which put an end both to speculation and to the arbitrary dismissal of tenant farmers by landowners. Indeed, this latter measure made about one million small tenants de facto owners of the land they tilled. All in all some 900,000 feddans (about 14.5 percent of Egypt's agricultural land at the time) were taken from big landowners (about two thousand families) and redistributed to small farmers and destitute peasants. About 1.3 million of the poorest Egyptian men (comprising with their families some 7.5 million people) benefited immensely from these specific redistributive measures. There were other socioeconomic spillover ramifications which we need not go into here, but which had the added effect of improving the overall income distribution in the Egyptian countryside.[27] The net losers in the whole process were the members of the landed bourgeoisie.

2. Progressive Taxation

In 1950, a progressive income tax was already in effect, reaching 70 percent of individual incomes above LE50,000. Following the July Revolution, the tax rate was rapidly increased and eventually reached, in 1961, a rate of 90 percent on annual incomes above LE10,000. In the same way, the taxes on real estate were steeply raised. The annual transfers resulting from these laws did not go directly to other classes (as in the Agrarian Reform), but rather to the state, thus enabling it to pursue more of its expansionist–interventionist socioeconomic policies. Again, the net loser was the landed bourgeoisie.

3. Labor-Related Measures

The second major constituency of the 1952 Revolution was the urban-based working class. It benefited both from the direct measures which addressed its previous grievances, and indirectly from measures which promoted overall social equity and economic development issues. A series of labor laws addressed outstanding labor issues: the working day was reduced to seven hours; a social insurance system was created to cover all workers; a standard 25 percent of annual company profits was mandatorily set aside for provision of social services to companies' workforces; workers were represented on the companies' boards of directors. These measures along with others that prohibited arbitrary firing, and the establishment of a new ministry of labor and a special labor court, had the effect of empowering Egypt's working class as never before.

Indirectly, the overall state-sponsored economic expansion, especially through industrialization, nearly tripled the job opportunities for the working class, thereby greatly increasing its size in the eighteen years between 1952 and 1970.[28] This class (together with many in the middle class too) also benefited indirectly from two rent reductions of urban housing (in 1958 and 1961), totaling some 40 percent of the previous rents.[29] Their children (along with the children of all classes) also now enjoyed free and expanding education at all levels, as well as free medical care.[30]

The organized working class considered the new expanding public sector to be its own, and in later years (the 1970s and 1980s) it would defend it relentlessly against all liquidation or privatization attempts. On the other hand, Egypt's landed bourgeoisie perceived these same measures as one more blow to its economic power.

4. Stripping the Landed Bourgeoisie of Sociopolitical Power

More direct measures were enacted to reduce the sociopolitical power of Egypt's landed bourgeoisie. One of the earliest measures (September 1952) was the abolition of 'civilian titles'. Symbolic as they may seem, such titles as *pasha, bey, effendi*, etc., carried immense social prestige. More drastically, many of the landed bourgeoisie and other prerevolutionary public figures were deprived of all political rights.[31]

All in all, in a series of steps over a ten-year period (1952–62), the July Revolution managed to remove the landed bourgeoisie from its previously privileged position at the top of society—both socially and politically. To many observers at the time, it looked as if a class, which took one long century to form and become established, was irreversibly destroyed in one short decade. For nearly twenty years the leading names and faces of that class were blacked out in the public media, with the possible exception of the obituary page in some newspapers.

The Resurrection of the Egyptian Bourgeoisie (1974–90)

Though politically marginalized and with their wealth drastically reduced, the old upper class (grande bourgeoisie) still owned the legally allowed maximum of agricultural land (fifty feddans per person by 1968), real estate, and shares in non-nationalized companies. Hence, despite demoralization and a low profile, the prerevolutionary upper class continued to enjoy considerable wealth and social status. Consequently, often the upwardly mobile middle-class elements, who distinguished themselves with more power or wealth than the average ranks of their own class, frequently displayed a marked eagerness to intermarry with the old upper class. A case in point was President Sadat's children, who married into that class.[32]

With the debacle of the Nasser regime in 1967, the old upper class felt increasingly emboldened to make a comeback. Its spokesmen attributed Egypt's mounting difficulties in the late Nasser years to socialism, the absence of liberal democracy, and anti-Western policies. This argument was gradually endorsed by some elements of the middle-class intelligentsia. The following decade (1967–77) was to witness a gradual resurrection of Egypt's landed bourgeoisie. Those ten years brought about several major turning points in Egypt's recent socioeconomic–political development: Nasser left the scene (1970), a successful war was waged by his successor, President Anwar Sadat (1973), a new Open-Door Economic Policy (Infitah) was adopted, and Egypt's regional and global alignment shifted Westward. Thus, the comeback of Egypt's landed bourgeoisie coincided with and was encouraged by a host of domestic, regional, and international factors.

The reemergence of the landed bourgeoisie was not an exact replay of their old years of privilege. Nor did it entail for them the same degree of their old political dominance of state, economy, and society. For one thing, those who did 'come back' were mostly a new generation, the descendants of the prerevolutionary era. Second, they were more 'bourgeois' than 'landed'. Third, they returned to an arena which had become far more complex during their eclipse (1952–72)—one in which the population had doubled, new classes, ideas and values had become established, and the state had become vastly expanded and unwieldy. In this section we look at some of these conditions.

The Landed Bourgeoisie and The New Social Coalition Under Sadat

The formal declaration of the Open-Door Economic Policy (ODEP) or Infitah, in February 1974, marked a qualitative shift in Egypt's economic course from what it had been since 1960. The debacle of the 1967 war brought into question the regime's socialist orientation. It was considered by one side of the debate not just a military but a total defeat of the sociopolitical–economic orientation of the Nasser years. Secure in power, and with a victory of sorts in the October 1973 war, Sadat, who sided with this point of view, forged and presided over a new sociopolitical coalition made up of the old landed-bourgeois class and the upwardly mobile middle class. Regional and international factors at the time (early 1970s) reinforced this new coalition and the new ODEP.

The Changing Middle Class

As indicated earlier, the biggest gains from the expanding state and the socialist orientation of the Nasser years were made by the middle (petit bourgeois) class. By the late 1960s the upper slice of that class had nearly exhausted what it could get from the state's socialist orientation. This slice was typically made up of top state bureaucrats, technocrats, and managers of the public sector. To this group two other groups from the same class may be added. The first was that of medium-sized private contractors, suppliers, and distributors to whom the expanding public sector had farmed out numerous subcontracts. The second was that of high-level manpower working abroad, especially in the oil-rich Arab countries. The two groups had accumulated substantial private savings, with no real opportunities to invest either in Egypt's state-controlled economy or in the oil-rich host countries (which only allowed their own citizens such opportunities).[33]

By no means did the three aforementioned groups constitute a numerical majority of their own middle class. However, they were so articulate and strategically situated as to be of tremendous influence. Several of their members had already occupied cabinet posts in the 1960s (under Nasser) and early 1970s (under Sadat).

Their advocacy of deregulating socioeconomic affairs was couched in nationalistic political terms—a call for 'a stronger more prosperous Egypt.'[34] Such advocacy entailed promises for more opportunities and better incomes for the rest of the middle class and for the working class, both inside Egypt and in the Arab world generally.[35] The fact that the real growth rates of GNP had been falling since 1967 strengthened their argument.

A New Enlarged Bourgeoisie

Thus, the upper slice of Egypt's middle class, including top professionals (e.g., doctors, lawyers, professors, engineers, and accountants), was ready and eager to engage in free-enterprise activities. They would join the surviving ranks of Egypt's old landed bourgeoisie to constitute a formidable socioeconomic–political coalition. As it turned out, the various wings of the coalition complemented one another. The old landed bourgeoisie had the name, prestige, and Western (especially European) connections. The former managers and technocrats of the public sector had the recognized entry into and the organizational skills useful to the state bureaucracy, while the middle-sized entrepreneurs, sub-contractors of the public sector, and high-level manpower working in rich Arab countries had the capital and the regional connections.

Though different in background, values, experience, and lifestyles, these groups had common economic interests that were quickly to amalgamate them into a new enlarged bourgeois class around a core of the surviving members of the old landed bourgeoisie. The 'embourgeoisation' of the upper slice of the middle class was promoted by a marked incidence of intermarriage among the offspring of old and new money on one hand and the ruling elite on the other.[36] The process was equally encouraged by regional and international factors.

Regional and International Factors

The 1967 defeat discredited Nasser and other like-minded progressive regimes in the Arab world. The fact that they had to turn to conservative Arab regimes for financial aid at the Arab Summit in Khartoum in 1967 added humiliation to injury. The magnanimous and compassionate response of the conservative regimes to the hard-pressed Arab progressives gave the former a new lease of life and enhanced their pan-Arab standing. In a sense, the conservatives benefited indirectly from the progressives' debacle in 1967. They were also to benefit even more from the progressives' victory in 1973. Under the pretext of helping the latter, the conservative Arab regimes, led by

Saudi Arabia, imposed a partial embargo on the production and export of their oil to pro-Israeli Western countries.37 With a contrived shortage of oil supplies, oil prices more than tripled between October and December 1973, resulting in a spectacular rise of revenues for the oil-rich countries. Thus, the Arab defeat of 1967 strengthened the conservative Arab regimes politically, and the Arab victory of 1973 benefited them financially.

Despite their launching of ambitious development plans, the conservative regimes could not absorb the surplus money they were fast accumulating.[38] In other words, they had more to dispense in aid, loans, and direct investments elsewhere. Capital-short Egypt was in dire need of some of that surplus. The obstacle to getting it, as was said at the time, were the tight state controls, fear of nationalization, and lack of investment incentives. It was argued that if these apprehensions were addressed, Arab capital would flow into Egypt. The aforementioned new social coalition, which was in the process of forming in Egypt at that juncture, wasted no time in endorsing this message. It was an added argument in its advocacy of changing Egypt's socioeconomic course.[39]

On the international front, Egypt's ruling elite and the new sociopolitical coalition became convinced that inasmuch as the Soviets helped in wartime it was only the capitalist West that could help the country in its postwar reconstruction. The West, especially the United States, also gave signals to this effect, again indicating that the only obstacle to the flow of Western capital, technology, and managerial know-how was apprehension about state controls, nationalization, and lack of investment incentives. If these considerations were seriously addressed, it was argued, there would be a Marshall Plan for Egypt.[40] Thus, the Egyptian stage was set for a new socioeconomic reorientation, and a new set of policies to put it into operation. The Sadat regime provided those policies which came to be known as the Open-Door Policy.

The Open-Door Economic Policy (Infitah)

Although some liberalization of the economy had already begun as early as 1968,[41] it was the sweepingly liberal nature of Law 43 of 1974, which provided considerable incentives to attract foreign investment, that in reality ushered Sadat's Open-Door Economic Policy (ODEP). Passed only four months after the 1973 October War, it strongly indicates a close link between external and domestic turning points in Egypt's modern evolution. This suggestion is reminiscent of similar links in the past: in 1840 (the Muhammad Ali developmental campaign and the British–Turkish intervention), 1882 (the Urabi revolt and British occupation), 1919–22 (revolt, independence, the Liberal Age, and the flourishing of a newly sprouting bourgeoisie), and 1956 (Suez Crisis, Egyptianization, and nationalization).

1. Pillars of the New Policy

Law 43 provided very generous incentives and iron-clad guarantees to Arab and foreign investors. It released them from many of the import–export restrictions and labor-law requirements, and provided a tax exemption for the first five years of operation. Coinciding with greatly improved relations with the United States and other Western countries, and with the oil boom in neighboring Arab countries, Law 43 was hailed in these quarters as a political–economic breakthrough. Several other measures were taken to supplement Law 43, including the lifting of earlier restrictions on labor-migration and importing through private-sector companies, as well as the termination of the public-sector monopoly on trade representation of foreign corporations.

Other laws supportive of the new policy were issued in the subsequent three years. Complaints from the private sector, about the tremendous economic edge that public-sector holding companies still had, led to the issuing of new laws intended to 'reorganize the public sector.' Public-sector firms were allowed to operate autonomously and were given the freedom to invest or enter into joint ventures with private capital, and to transact with all parties with no preferential treatment given to public-sector units, as had been the case before. Moreover, all privileges granted to foreign investors were also extended to Egyptian capital, including the right of private entrepreneurs to possess and transact business in foreign currency with external firms. Presidential decrees, which lifted the earlier restrictions on the employment of former top public-sector officials in the private sector at home or abroad, were also issued. Another measure was enacted returning previously sequestered properties and assets to their original owners. These laws were considered a great triumph for Egypt's enlarged bourgeoisie, the old core, and the new wings alike.

2. Immediate Impacts

The above liberalizing measures set in motion several new socioeconomic dynamics, the evaluation of which has been polemical among Egyptian writers.[42] Firstly, there was massive labor migration, of all levels of Egyptian manpower to oil-rich Arab countries, which reached an estimated peak of three million by the early 1980s. Secondly, there was an exodus of top managers from the public sector to the newly flourishing private sector. Thirdly, there was the return of hundreds of members of the former Egyptian upper class and businessmen who had been living or working abroad since the early 1960s. Fourthly, many elements of the old bourgeoisie resurfaced and took an active role in economic life. Many of the last two groups quickly established or revived connections with their Western, especially European, counterparts.[43]

3. Sequence of Infitah Enterprises

Some of the earliest investments were in new banks or branches of foreign banks,[44] many of which were established with joint private and public Egyptian capital. Next to come were trading, tourist, and consumer-goods companies. Many of these were joint ventures between foreign capital and elements of the old Egyptian bourgeoisie. At a later stage (late 1970s) more names of former leaders of the public-sector and ex-government officials began to appear among major shareholders of Infitah companies, and also by that time enterprising Egyptians working in the oil-rich Arab countries began to figure prominently among major shareholders.[45] In the early 1980s two new sub-formations joined the previously mentioned Infitah business elite. One group, which had no previous record in public or private economic life, had capital from unknown sources, though it is believed to have accumulated such capital from illegal and parasitic activities.[46] The second came into the picture under the popular banner of 'Islamic investments'.[47] By the mid-1980s, there was a marked mixing among the five sub-groupings.

Conclusion: The Politics of the Infitah Bourgeoisie

Revived and enlarged, the current generation of the Egyptian bourgeoisie has been treading shrewdly in economic and political affairs. It has gradually and persistently worked towards liberalizing the economy and politics, and in the process has so far successfully shielded itself behind international and regional covers. With every gain achieved, this bourgeoisie lobbied for more liberalization.

Thus, the early Infitah laws (1974–77) were advocated by the bourgeoisie under the pretext of attracting Arab and foreign capital, modern technology, and better management. In that phase the Egyptian bourgeoisie confined itself to brokerage, representation, and minor partnerships with Arab and foreign capital. Once these were established, it pushed and pressured for similar (Law 32 of 1977) or better treatment (Law 230 of 1989) for purely indigenous investors. By 1990 the Egyptian bourgeoisie was pushing and pressuring for the 'privatization' of public-sector companies, floating the Egyptian pound, and for doing away with, or at least reducing, public subsidies on most basic goods and services. In this respect, the Egyptian bourgeoisie has the International Monetary Fund (IMF), the Paris Club, and other aid donors as formidable allies. The ruling elite of the Mubarak regime is divided and generally inept at responding to such demands. But on the whole it ends up by yielding piecemeal.

One of the most successful tactics used by the Egyptian bourgeoisie in putting pressure on the state to push it in the direction desired consists of withholding or slowing down investments, a move which invariably acts as a brake on Arab and foreign capital. The phenomenon of 'internationalization of capital' makes such a tactic quite effective. Some sources estimate private Egyptian capital abroad at about $50 billion, that is, equal to Egypt's foreign debt in 1990. President Mubarak and other Egyptian officials keep pleading with "fellow citizens" to bring this money home.[48] The representatives of the bourgeoisie argue that such capital would return to the country if the state acted favorably to their "reasonable demands." The recent events in the former Soviet Union and Eastern Europe have added tremendous weight to those arguments which call for the dismantling of the public sector, deregulation, and privatization[49] The counter-arguments are becoming increasingly feeble.

Politically, Egypt's bourgeoisie has organized itself in what seems on the surface to be an apolitical manner, e.g., business associations, chambers of commerce, unions of industries, and the like. But since these organizations have former and current senior office-holders—such as prime ministers and prominent ruling National Democratic Party (NDP) figures—as leading members, they have become very effective pressure groups.[50] Two of these pressure groups illustrate the point. The first is the American Chamber of Commerce in Egypt (ACCE), which was initiated in 1981 with the blessing of President Sadat and subsequently authorized by his successor, President Mubarak, the following year.[51] Its membership list in 1985 included the names of ten cabinet members, including those for defense, foreign affairs, economy, finance, energy, petroleum, tourism, and agriculture.[52] The same list included the names of eleven former ministers, and five others who became ministers after 1985. Along with these political figures, the membership included most of the leading Egyptian bankers and businessmen,[53] and 312 institutional members. The last category comprises "American companies with branches, agents, or representative offices in Egypt, Egyptian companies with American equity, and Egyptians who have significant business relationships with the United States."[54] The ACCE has been an active lobby in promoting Egyptian–American economic and political links as well as in advocating privatization in Egypt. It has persuaded US authorities to earmark a growing percentage of the annual aid to Egypt as credit facilities for the Egyptian private sector, and more recently another portion for facilitating the transfer of publicly owned companies to private hands.[55]

The other case in point is the Egyptian Society of Businessmen (ESB), which was established in the late 1970s, again with the blessing of the late President Sadat. Unlike the ACCE, the ESB's membership is confined to Egyptian citizens, and has had a much higher profile in public debates on socioeconomic–political issues. Its annual meetings have become the functional equivalent of parliamentary hearings. Hardly any top decision-maker, including all prime ministers since 1979, has declined an invitation to speak to members of the ESB, as each eagerly hopes to obtain an endorsement of his policy.[56] Like the ACCE, the ESB has been outspokenly pro-privatization, and also favors more liberal laws of investment and taxation. There is a considerable overlap in the membership of ACCE and ESB, which together read like a who's who of the old landed-aristocracy and the new bourgeois families.

In the more overtly political arena, growing numbers of Egypt's enlarged bourgeoisie have joined political parties, been elected to parliament (the

People's Assembly), and have been appointed to the cabinet as ministers. It has been observed that members of the new wings of the present bourgeoisie, especially former ministers and managers of the public sector, tend to join the ruling NDP, while members of the older landed bourgeoisie tend to join the major opposition Wafd Party. But both generally advocate the same socio-economic policies in their respective parties. Should any of them change party affiliation, it is generally to the other party (i.e., from the Wafd to the NDP, and vice versa) but rarely to any of the other minor opposition parties that are right or left of center. In other words, the NDP and the Wafd have evolved into favorite centrist parties of the various wings of Egypt's bourgeoisie. The Wafd has been more consistent in its advocacy of a liberal market economy since its prerevolutionary beginnings in the 1920s. The NDP still oscillates between a historical commitment to Nasser's populist orientation and Sadat's Open-Door policies, with a growing tilt towards the latter. It is through membership of these two major parties that a growing number of the bourgeoisie (old and new) has been elected to the People's Assembly since 1976. Some eighty members of them (from a total of 450) were elected as deputies in the 1987 Assembly, compared with fewer than twenty in 1976.[57]

In cabinet appointments, the percentage of businessmen and professionals rose steadily in the 1970s and 1980s; from 2.4 percent in 1970, to 9.8 percent in 1971–72, to 14.7 percent between 1974 and 1981 (post-Infitah years).[58] Their percentage in the successive cabinets under President Mubarak (1981–90) has risen further to about 20 percent. In this respect much of the gain by businessmen and professionals has been at the expense of the military, whose percentage of representation in cabinet posts has steadily declined from 38 percent in 1970 (Nasser's death), to 27 percent in 1972–74, to 12 percent since 1974 (post-Infitah).[59] Equally interesting is the fact that many former cabinet members who have no previous business experience are quickly picked up by the private sector as board chairmen, presidents, general managers, or advisers of major Infitah companies.[60] Thus, there is a growing interchange between the political and business elites.

In conclusion, the enlarged Egyptian bourgeoisie has made a spectacular comeback after twenty years (1952–72) of total eclipse. It has done so on the coattails of Arab and foreign investments and still shields itself behind them, though in reality it is the major economic actor of the Open-Door policy. Its share in total private investments since 1974 has risen to more than 64 percent, compared with about 20 percent Arab and 16 percent foreign capital. After inching its way into the economy, this bourgeois class has started doing the same in politics.

Nevertheless, in its present round, the Egyptian bourgeoisie is still far from attaining the level of political–economic domination it enjoyed in the Liberal Age (1922–52), and probably will never be able to do so. The reason, as previously mentioned, is that the socioeconomic scene it 'came back' to (in

1974) had grown far more complex than when it had been removed from it (in 1952). Now, there is a population which has more than doubled, a working class which has more than quadrupled, lower-middle and middle classes which have more than tripled, a public sector which still controls some 60 percent of the nonagricultural formal economic activities, and a state bureaucracy which has grown fourfold. To deal with, much less accommodate, all these actors has not been—and probably will never be—an easy task. Making the task more difficult is the modest performance, so far, of the bourgeoisie in helping Egypt out of its numerous socioeconomic problems. Though the enlarged bourgeoisie has done extremely well for itself since 1974, the country as a whole is suffering from a growing heavy external debt (from $1.6 billion in 1973 to $55 billion in 1990) and widespread unemployment (from less than 10 percent in 1973 to over 15 percent in 1973 to over 25 percent in 1990).

The Egyptian bourgeoisie may not be solely responsible for the negative indicators above, especially as its representatives do not fully control the decision-making process. However, the fact that its comeback has been associated with the Infitah policies (1974) makes the bourgeoisie look partly, or even totally, responsible for Egypt's problems in the eyes of the disadvantaged and the more deprived, i.e., all the classes below. On some occasions this perception was translated into mob-rioting and looting against the state and, more significantly, against the properties and institutions associated with the bourgeoisie, such as the food riots of 1977 and the Central Security riots of 1986.

If rioting and looting are the response of the 'absolutely deprived' urban lumpen proletariat, Islamic militancy has been the response of the 'relatively deprived' youngsters of the lower-middle class. Both kinds of response represent an equal threat to the Egyptian state and the Egyptian bourgeoisie in the 1990s.

Notes

1 See more details in A. Ramadan, *Class Conflict in Egypt: 1937-1952* (in Arabic) (Cairo: al-Mu'assasa al-'Arabiya li-l-Dirasat wa-l-Nashr, 1978), pp. 33–187, and Ali Dessouki, *Big Landowners and Their Role in Egyptian Society* (in Arabic) (Cairo: Dar al-Thaqafa al-Gadida, 1975), pp. 13–51.

2 Ramadan, pp. 54–57.

3 Dessouki, p. 10.

4 Ramadan, pp. 74–84.

5 Ibid., pp. 130–42.

6 Dessouki, pp. 210–80.

7 The newspaper debate over this issue reported in *al-Siyasa*, 8 August 1924, *al-Ahram* 29 April 1925, *al-Siyasa*, 20 July 1926, all cited in Dessouki, pp. 40–45.

8 Ibid., p. 42.
9 Charles Issawi, *Egypt in Revolution: An Economic Analysis* (London: Oxford University Press, 1963), pp. 34–37.
10 Ramadan, p. 95.
11 Ibid., p. 98.
12 Ibid., pp. 199–200.
13 Dessouki, pp. 210–14. The requirement for candidacy to the Upper House (Council of Sheikhs) was the ownership of a minimum of 150 feddans of land, according to Article 50 of the 1923 constitution.
14 Until 1930 there was a uniform tax of 8 percent on all imports. The new system (1930) had a different tax structure on imports, e.g., reducing such taxes to as low as 5 percent on essentials and raising it to as high as 50 percent on luxury items and those products that have an equivalent which is produced domestically. See Afify Hafez, *On The Periphery of Egyptian Politics* (in Arabic) (Cairo: Dar al-Kutub al-Misriya, 1938), pp. 101–92.
15 The figures for industrial workers vary widely in successive Egyptian statistical annual records, and sometimes even for the same year, depending on the definition adopted in each, which may or may not include workers in extractive industries, gas, and electricity. The above figure of 400,000 for 1947 does include them.
16 For documentation of names and families see Ramadan, pp. 106–40, and M. Mourad, *Who Ruled Egypt?* (in Arabic) (Cairo: Madbuli, 1975).
17 Dessouki, pp. 32–33.
18 Ibid., p. 94. For example, King Farouk had twenty thousand shares in the Pepsi-Cola Company. His uncle Sherif Sabry was the president of a chemical company of the Ahmed Abboud Group.
19 The best-known of these land-reform proposals was submitted as a bill to the parliament by the Deputy Muhammad Khattab in 1945. It took two years of protracted deliberations in subcommittees of both houses, then was finally rejected on 24 March 1947.
20 These governmental efforts, nevertheless, resulted in an average rate of economic growth of about 7 percent annually during the period 1952–60. For figures and details, see A. Mohyeddin and S. E. Ibrahim, "State Socialism and Economic Development" in S. E. Ibrahim, ed., *Egypt in a Quarter of a Century* (Beirut: Arab Institute of Development Studies, 1980), pp. 301–35.
21 Ibid., pp. 331–32.
22 Ibid., p. 332.
23 Issawi, pp. 58–59.
24 For an elaborate treatment of the state machinery, both civil and military, see Nazih Ayubi, *Bureaucracy and Politics in Contemporary Egypt* (London: Ithaca Press, 1980).
25 S. E. Ibrahim, "The Social Project," in Ibrahim, *Egypt in a Quarter of a Century*, pp. 139–43, and S. E. Ibrahim, "Income Distribution and Social

Mobility in Egypt," in G. Abdel Khalek and R. Tignor, eds., *The Political Economy of Income Distribution in Egypt* (New York: Holmes and Meier, 1981).

26 Reducing urban rents by 25 percent, and making it virtually impossible for landlords to raise the rents or evict tenants or their descendants.

27 M. Adel Fadil, *Development, Income Distribution and Social Change in Rural Egypt: 1952–1970* (Cambridge: Cambridge University Press, 1975), pp. 17–102.

28 The reduction of the number of working hours, and the real expansion of the industrial base contributed to an absolute increase of nearly 900,000 workers between 1952 and 1970. See Qassem, *Evolution of Egyptian Industry*, p. 349, and CAPMAS, *Statistical Indicators 1952–1973* (Cairo, 1974), table p. 206.

29 For details see S. E. Ibrahim, "The Social Project of the July Revolution," in S. E. Ibrahim, ed., *Egypt, Arabism, and the July Revolution* (in Arabic) (Beirut: Center for Arab Unity Studies, 1982), pp. 133–36.

30 Ibid., p. 138.

31 Ibid., pp. 121–46.

32 S. E. Ibrahim, *The New Arab Social Order* (Boulder: Westview Press, 1982), pp. 65–68.

33 S. E. Ibrahim, "The Social Project" pp. 138–43. For a more elaborate treatment see Abdel Khalek and Tignor, *The Political Economy of Income Distribution.*

34 For an account of the debate, see Ibrahim Issawi, "The Internal Factors Leading to the Infitah (Open-Door)," in Abdel Khalek, ed., *The Open-Door Policy (Infitah), op. cit.*, pp. 71–90.

35 Ibrahim, *The New Arab Social Order, op. cit.*, pp. 67–69.

36 See an elaborate documentation of this amalgamation in Mata Zaalouk, "Commercial Agents in Egypt: A Case Study in Development," Ph.D. thesis submitted to the University of Hull, 1982: e.g., all three daughters of Sadat's second wife, Mrs. Gihan Sadat, married into the old upper class, one to a big landowner, another to the son of a former pasha, and the third to a grand-bourgeois capitalist.

37 Ibrahim, *The New Arab Social Order, op. cit.*, pp. 130–32.

38 Galal Amin, "The External Factors Leading to the Infitah (Open-Door)," in Abdel Khalek, ed., *The Open Door Policy, op. cit.*, pp. 91–124.

39 Adel Hussein, *Egyptian Economy From Independence to Dependency: 1974–1979*, 2 vols., (in Arabic) (Cairo: Dar al-Mustaqbal al-'Arabiya, 1982), pp. 200–34.

40 Enid Hill, "Legislating Development in Egypt: 1971–1986," paper presented to the Conference on Dynamics of States and Societies in the Middle East, Center for Political Research and Studies, Cairo, 17–19 June 1989, p. 3.

41 Ibid., pp. 7–12.

42 The Infitah (Open-Door Policy) has come under sharp criticism, especially from leftist writers. See for example Hussein, *Egyptian Economy*; and F. Morsy, *This Open-Door Economic Policy* (Beirut: Dar al-Wihda, 1981).

43 Samia Imam, *Who Owns Egypt? An Analytical Study of the Social Origins of the Infitah Elite: 1974–1980* (in Arabic) (Cairo: Dar al-Mustaqbal al-'Arabiya, 1986), pp. 22–122.

44 Ibrahim Mokhtar, *Egypt's Banks* (in Arabic) (Cairo: Kitab al-Ahram al-Iqtisadi, 1988), pp. 37–54.

45 Imam, pp. 83–122.

46 Ibid., pp. 123–36.

47 On these companies see, *Islamic Investment Companies: The Rise, The Collapse, and the Future* (Cairo: Kitab al-Ahram al-Iqtisadi, June 1988).

48 See for example, President Mubarak's speech on the 38th Anniversary of the July Revolution, published in *al-Ahram*, 23 July 1990.

49 See a typical argument of the bourgeoisie as in *al-Wafd* newspaper, 8 July 1990, reporting on a seminar of Egyptian investors in London, held 29 June–2 July 1990.

50 For a detailed documentation and analysis of their effective lobbying see Amani Kandil, "Public Policy-Making in Egypt: A Case Study of Economic Policy: 1974–1981," Ph.D. dissertation in Political Science, submitted to Cairo University, 1985, and also by the same author "Interest Groups and Foreign Policy," paper presented to the Second Annual Conference of Political Research, Cairo University, 3–5 December 1988.

51 See the Introduction to *The American Chamber of Commerce Membership Directory, 1984/1985*, p. 5.

52 Ibid., p. 15.

53 Ibid., pp. 15–22.

54 Ibid., p. 23.

55 Kandil, "Interest Groups and Foreign Policy," pp. 6–7, 10–11 (for details of the ACCE meeting with President Mubarak, 8 March 1988).

56 See the detailed list of top Egyptian officials who have addressed the Egyptian Society of Businessmen (ESB) in the Society's *Annual Report 1987*, published in April 1988.

57 The figures are for those who identified themselves or were identified by the newspapers as known businessmen. There may be more who choose to be identified by some other affiliation. Other than 'farmers' and 'workers', the Egyptian constitution lumps 'professionals' and 'national capitalists' under the label 'categories'.

58 Raymond Hinnebusch, "Egypt under Sadat: Elites, Power Structure, and Political Change in a Post-Populist State," in *Social Problems*, vol. 28, no. 4, April 1981, pp. 442–63. The figures are extracted from Table 2, p. 448.

59 Ibid., p. 448.

60 For more documentation and analysis of this phenomenon, see Imam, *Who Owns Egypt?*, especially appendices 1–8, pp. 241–347.

2

The Agrarian Background and the Origins of the Turkish Bourgeoisie

Çağlar Keyder

The Turkish bourgeoisie is a creation of the Turkish state—the product of a slow and ambivalent process. Yet the creation of a bourgeoisie never became a declared or acknowledged goal of the regime, mostly because republican bureaucrats nursed a lingering self-conception as inheritors of the mantle from the autonomous ruling class of the precapitalist empire. Instead, the project gradually gained shape within the world-system context as both the bureaucrats and the bourgeois actors responded to economic constraints and to political designs radiating from hegemonic centers. In the absence of a credible and popular ideology which would sustain their historical autonomy, the bureaucracy eventually capitulated to the ascendancy of the capitalist class. Had they been successful in formulating a developmentalist project to legitimate the economic undertaking, their relationship with the bourgeoisie might have been one of mutuality and coordination—as in the East Asian examples. As it was, the evolving bourgeoisie never trusted the bureaucracy; it resented the arbitrary power the state elite continued to brandish. It was not until the 1980s, when world balances changed drastically, that the bourgeoisie could finally attain a clear domination in both the political and ideological realms.

The birth of the Turkish bourgeoisie is contemporaneous with the foundation of the Turkish state. In other words, the peripheral Ottoman bourgeoisie did not historically evolve into the Turkish bourgeoisie. The majority of the business groups in the Ottoman economy had been Greeks and Armenians. Their expulsion during and after World War I implied that a class of entrepreneurs had to be constituted anew within the new Turkish state.

During the initial period of the Turkish state it was very much the nation-building project of the Kemalist republicans that guided the creation of the entrepreneurial class. The subsequent 1930s Great Depression and the war greatly facilitated the implementation of national economic policies and guaranteed the dependence of the bourgeoisie on the state. This equation was to change radically after the war: while urging the dismantlement of etatist policy-making, American hegemony also created a new set of opportunities which were seized by a new group of businessmen. During the late 1950s and 1960s an import-substitution policy emerged, partly at the instigation of the hegemonic power but also conforming to the aspirations of the new industrial entrepreneurs. Significantly, this new policy assigned to the bureaucracy a not-negligible role in planning and regulating the accumulation process. Import substitution was a success from the point of view of the maturation of the bourgeois class. By the 1970s the internal structure of the bourgeoisie came to be characterized by interlocking enterprises organized in 'holding companies' whose control was effected by families with a privileged access to the state (see Buğra in this volume). Thus, the crisis of import substitution, the debt squeeze, and the unavoidable restructuring of the economy during the 1980s all served to consolidate capitalist ascendancy. The bourgeoisie's organizational strength and newly found confidence vis-à-vis the state permitted Turkish capitalism to negotiate successfully the transformation in world economic conditions and state policies of the late 1970s.

The Character of the 'Precapitalist' Environment

1. Increases in foreign trade during the nineteenth century led to a new orientation in Middle Eastern economies. Differences in landownership patterns and in the relation of the cultivator to the political authority made for qualitatively divergent trajectories of social differentiation and class formation. The experiences of the two countries illustrate the range of such divergence: as the volume of foreign trade increased, large landholdings dominated in Egypt while the actual peasant producers were able to protect their possession rights in Turkey.

There are various ways in which this divergence may be explained.[1] We may look at the differences in the historical formation of landholding patterns, with reference to customary law, tradition of social conflict, and to the force of past practice and inertia. A second tack would be to privilege the degree of autonomy of the state from the landholders, arguing that a strong centralized state opts for an independent peasantry from which it can draw taxes and conscripts. Big landlords not only tend to hoard land and leave the peasantry landless, but they also take over the political authority in order to perpetuate their domination of the main productive resource. A third possibility is to argue for the decisiveness of turning points where alternative trajectories are potentially feasible. Turning points contain the potential of alternative outcomes when conflicting class projects are at balance; at these junctures history may go either way. Hence any additional input into the historical conjuncture has a disproportionate impact. During the nineteenth century this additional input took the form of active intervention by outside powers.

It seems to me that the story of the divergence of the Egyptian and Turkish trajectories of class formation may be told by underscoring any single one of these explanatory tacks, but the various accounts are, in fact, complementary.

2. In Egypt the agrarian structure resorted to its earlier form upon the demise of Muhammad Ali's project.[2] The *multazims*, the dynastic family, and the new cotton merchants who wanted to establish themselves in land, became large landlords at the expense of the peasants, who, in turn, sank to the status of sharecroppers, tenants, or landless workers. This process was further reinforced during the cotton boom of the 1860s, and yet again under British occupation. Hence, the peasantry was more or less, but always, dependent, and a class controlling the land always prevailed (see Ibrahim in this volume). On the other hand, the identity of the political authority with a landlord class, whose revenue derived precisely from the extraction of surplus from the peasantry, meant that there were no significant obstacles against the tendency to reduce the rural population to dependent peons. Since the landed class dominated the state structure, the bureaucracy did not develop as an autonomous body controlling administrative resources and did not look for an ally in the independent peasantry. Egypt during the nineteenth century remained a society in which the ruling class, comprising the large landholders, had overwhelming control over the political apparatus, leaving the peasantry both economically and politically powerless.

The Turkish story is very different.[3] First, the Anatolian agrarian structure had always been dominated by small and independent family farms. At the level of physical and economic geography, the model of dispersed, nucleated villages, where the surplus produced by each unit was never very great, seemed to be a feature of the *longue durée*. The administrative logic of both the Byzantine and the Ottoman empires was based on the collection of small surpluses from a large number of peasant families. This collection was usually carried out by a large number of appointed functionaries or tax-farmers who were supposed to relay to the center whatever surplus they could legally collect.

The prevalence of the small peasantry depended crucially on the strength of the central state. Land codes considered the peasant family the essential unit of production, and stipulated that it should have access to sufficient land in order to be able to pay taxes to the central authority. Accordingly, the state attempted to prevent local usurpers from expropriating peasant lands and often resorted to legal and military means in order to defend the small producers' access to land. The final episode of this nature, when the central government suppressed a potential class of large landholders, took place in the eighteenth and the beginning of the nineteenth centuries.[4] A weak central authority had initially permitted the rise of a quasi-official notability called the *ayan;* during the early part of the nineteenth century, however, a strengthened central authority turned against these local powers and put an end to centrifugal development.

During the time of their ascendance, the *ayan* of Anatolia monopolized local official positions—they captured tax-farming contracts and acted as merchants—but they were unable to establish large managed estates. Thus, although they transgressed the limits imposed by the state in squeezing the peasantry more than the ideal model allowed, their inability to establish new relations on land led to the easy reversal of their fortunes. By the mid-nineteenth century the *ayan* were history and the role they had played in local economies was set to be taken over by a very different group of intermediaries oriented to the growing world economy.

Despite the long-term stability of agrarian relations, it is possible to identify turning points in the nineteenth century when alternative outcomes in the evolution of class balances were possible. Muhammad Ali's experiment in Egypt supplies one such moment.[5] Had it been successful, the peasantry would arguably have emerged more independent and autonomous, with a state bureaucracy ruling over a society in which economic power was more evenly distributed. Although there were other, internal, reasons why the experiment failed, the active intervention of the hegemonic power delivered the decisive blow. The 1838 Treaty, which was imposed on Egypt through the collusion of Britain and the Porte, constituted a turning point. It guaranteed that the experiment could not be revived.

Similarly in 1882, when the British intervened again on occasion of the Urabi 'revolt', the imperialist prerogative was utilized in favor of safeguarding and accelerating a development based on the commercialization of large landed properties. If the Urabi revolt had been successful, it might have checked the development of large estates and their total integration through commerce and credit into the networks of European capitalism.[6] Both in 1838 and 1882, the clash of class interests was overlaid by conflict at the interstate level. The outcome was determined to a large extent by the intervention of the hegemonic power. Without such intervention class balances characterizing the agrarian structure in Egypt might have evolved differently.

By contrast, the impact of the interstate system on the core areas of the Ottoman empire tended to strengthen the hold of the central authority. This meant that state centrism was upheld at crucial turning points; alternative outcomes which would favor local grandees were discouraged. The first instance of such intervention is again provided by the 1838 Treaty, whose impact on Anatolia was the mirror image of its impact on Egypt. With this treaty, which capped the centralization attempts of Selim III and Mahmud II, Britain implicitly guaranteed that the hegemonic power would be on the side of the Porte against attempts at local autonomy by the *ayan* or other potential challengers.[7]

The policy adopted by the creditor powers, following Ottoman and Egyptian declarations of insolvency later in the century, was even more revealing. While Caisse de la Dette in Cairo became a crucial mediator in encouraging foreign investment, especially in land, the Public Debt Administration in Istanbul accepted the Ottoman agrarian structure as given, and attempted to duplicate the Ottoman administration in collecting taxes from the small peasantry.[8] In other words, at a time when the fiscal crisis was at its most severe, and when they could easily extract legislative concession, the 'great powers' instead reinforced the small-peasant-dominated agrarian structure in Anatolia. Hence, the history of the two countries differed on all counts: the genesis of landholding patterns, the relation between the state and the peasantry, and the character of external intervention in shaping the agrarian structure. The result was large landholding in Egypt and small peasantry in Anatolia. We shall now discuss the implications of this difference on the formation of the bourgeoisies.

The Origins of the Bourgeoisies

1. The concentration of landownership in Egypt during the 1850s and 1860s accelerated under the impact of the cotton boom and led to the creation of an entire structure of commerce, insurance, transportation, land reclamation, and finance.[9] Foreign capital and new settlers were attracted to the booming country. Soon, under the auspices of the Egyptian state, a merged class of foreign financiers and local landlords evolved, with shared interests in the cotton economy. The original source of accumulation continued to be agriculture: the usual urban businesses of trade and finance and manufacturing developed around it. Foreign loans went directly to improving agricultural productivity, and when foreigners could, as private persons, purchase land, there evolved a smooth merger between agrarian exploitation and foreign capital. Landholding and exploitation of the peasantry remained at the foundation of the entire edifice.[10] (See Ibrahim in this volume.)

The formation of the Egyptian bourgeoisie was thus a process in which two distinct elements gradually merged: the foreign finance- and trade-oriented businessmen with close connections to European banks and merchant houses, and the large landholding families whose accumulation in land was channeled to trade and, later, industry. Throughout the latter part of the nineteenth century it had become apparent that what was squeezed out of the peasantry financed both these factions; the two groups shared the same interest in maintaining the agrarian structure. Subsequently the merged groups made the transition to manufacturing investment catering to urban needs. It was certainly true that the Egyptian-born component of the bourgeoisie gained ground against the foreigners during the interwar years, but the nationalist conflict was essentially one of rival business groups and did not in any way inhibit the momentum of capitalist development.[11]

2. The Egyptian case was more conventional: precapitalist, agrarian accumulation led to the formation of a bourgeoisie, which then continued to

accumulate in the capitalist manner.[12] Against this backdrop the Turkish case appears anomalous. As already argued, small peasant property was the rule in Ottoman Anatolia. With one important regional exception that we will discuss below, large landlords did not emerge, and accumulation on the basis of landownership remained improbable. For all the reasons mentioned above, it was impossible to consolidate large landed properties through expropriation of the peasantry, and at the same time it was difficult to find dependent peasants who would submit to the kind of exploitation that was common in Egypt.[13] Historical tradition and social relations established in rural society, the manner in which the village community defended its access to land, the ideology which served to legitimate the imperial order, the legislative and law-keeping practice of the state, and the absence of outside intervention in the direction of privatization and concentration of land, were factors which militated against the transformation of the agrarian structure.[14]

Consequently, Anatolia was integrated into the nineteenth-century world economy at a considerably lower level than Egypt. In 1914 per capita trade in Egypt was 2.5 times greater than in the Ottoman empire. This was both the reason for and a consequence of the differences in levels of foreign investment: the empire received about one third of the foreign capital that Egypt did; hence structuring by foreign investment was a limited process as well.[15] This difference in performance was partly due to a much lower fertility of land in Anatolia; the real problem, however, was the unchanging pattern of landownership.

One consequence of the agrarian structure was that Anatolia did not develop as the supplier of one significant export crop. Instead, exports originated in diverse peasant surpluses, no single crop ever exceeding 15 percent of the total revenues.[16] There were many export products, including various grains, raw materials for dyes, ores, figs, raisins, hazelnuts, cotton, and in the latter part of the century, tobacco. None took a preponderant position in export revenues, basically because it would have been difficult to induce a large number of producers, by means of price incentives, to assume the risks associated with switching to a single crop.

Hence, neither the preincorporation order itself, nor the changes imposed upon this order by integration into the world market, led to a concentration of the agrarian surplus in a few hands. Yet there was money to be made from the new trading activity. There were positions of intermediation in trade and finance, in collecting the agrarian surplus, channeling it towards ports of export, and in supplying the advance funds necessary to induce the peasantry to switch to world-market crops. In an agrarian structure where surplus is concentrated, large landlords are often themselves merchants; they may establish more equal relationships with merchants or dominate them economically and (as in most of Eastern Europe) subordinate them politically. In a situation characterized by thousands of small suppliers, however, both the economic and political balances favor the merchants. In other words, the merchants or financiers dealing in Egypt's cotton were not in a position to dominate the large landlords. The conditions were there for the emergence of a dominant landlord class extracting and circulating the agrarian surplus. In Anatolia, by contrast, the intermediary class was formed outside the agrarian economy itself and, since it dealt with a dispersed peasantry (by definition powerless), achieved a superordinate position.17

This intermediary class, at first subsidiary to foreign merchants who were privileged by the 1838 Treaty, gradually acquired an independent status and was successful in isolating the local economy from the direct control of the foreigners.[18] In other words, unlike in Egypt, foreigners remained outsiders. There were a few 'Levantine' families, mostly of older than nineteenth-century origin, who continued to be active in finance and trade, but the core of the new class nurtured in the new orientation of the economy were natives. At first, foreign merchant houses and banks had needed them and used them; but by the 1890s, there was no doubt that this group had become an independent bourgeoisie, bound neither to a landlord class nor, any longer, to foreign capital.[19]

The vast majority of this intermediary class was non-Muslim. Before the nineteenth century, the economic difference between Muslims and non-Muslims was not overwhelming; the social and political differences were. As foreign trade became important, foreign merchants required intermediaries to deal with the large number of dispersed producers, and they chose the Greeks and the Armenians, who were culturally and linguistically closer to themselves.[20] In addition to this real or invented affinity, the Capitulations allowed legal extra-territoriality to be extended by foreign consulates to protected individuals.[21] As a result, thousands of non-Muslims acquired passports of European powers, which effectively placed them beyond the reach of Ottoman law and Ottoman tax authorities.[22] The ethnic division of labor which had prevailed in the multiethnic empire thus evolved into a class differentiation.

The new class was relatively large, precisely because the requisite intermediation was extensive, reaching a large number of producers—each responsible for a small amount of surplus. In all the large cities of trade, as well as in smaller towns on the road network, Greeks and Armenians began to live in refracted bourgeois styles, adopting consumption patterns, cultural emoluments, and manners as befitted the nineteenth-century European ideal.[23] This transformation in lifestyle often separated them from the Muslim population more radically than did their economic activities.

3. Towards the end of the century, the forms of enterprise that the intermediary class engaged in had also changed: in addition to finance and commerce they began to undertake properly capitalist production. As new lifestyles and consumption patterns spread, so grew the need for a rudimentary import substitution, consisting of manufacturing the perceived necessities of urban life which were difficult or costly to import.[24] Here is yet another dif-

ference from Egypt: the new bourgeoisie's manufacturing concerns were found in import substitution rather than in investments linked with the export product. The Anatolian bourgeoisie did not control agricultural production and was not in any position to guarantee a sustained supply of raw materials for the requirements of industrial processing. In addition, very wealthy families were exceedingly rare in Anatolia. Hence, the manufacturing undertakings of the bourgeoisie were small, and oriented to the consumption demand of the bourgeoisie itself.

Nonetheless, these manufacturing undertakings were important because, in the entire economic landscape of pre–World War I Anatolia, they were the only ones which carried the potential of transforming the social structure.[25] The old guild system was practically moribund; it had no potential of evolving into a form that could create a bourgeoisie and a working class. State manufactures that were undertaken by the palace, mostly with the intention of provisioning the army, remained artificial implants which did not serve to catalyze other investment. Other forms of production in manufactures used cheap domestic labor in putting-out type relationships; hence they articulated with existing conditions without disturbing the social structure—in this case household-based peasant production.

Import-substituting urban manufacturing, however, was couched in a package of transforming lifestyles. As such it promised to constitute a more lasting element of the social structure. The entrepreneurs had actually made the transition from being intermediaries to producers and had accepted the change in logic, attitude, and political behavior this change entailed. Most importantly, they now had to employ a genuine working class: urban, dispossessed, and politically conscious.[26] Most of these workers were also non-Muslims, but as became evident during the war years, the urban Muslim population, probably dispossessed artisans, were also gradually drawn to wage employment. In short, the bourgeoisie we have identified as the agent of capitalist accumulation introduced into the social fabric a transformatory dynamic which possessed the requisite potential of creating a new, capitalist, class structure.

4. The nationalist reaction against the non-Muslim bourgeoisie also evolved differently in the two countries. In Egypt nationalism became an important force during the interwar period, when the domestic bourgeoisie of agrarian origin felt strong enough to demand a greater share of the economic pie from the foreigners. In Turkey, however, there was no rival group within the bourgeoisie to press a demand for Turkification. Rather, it was the state elite which felt that the non-Muslim bourgeoisie in ascendance threatened the traditional social structure of the empire, as well as endangering the status of the bureaucracy itself. Furthermore, the bureaucrats thought that the integrity of the empire was threatened and suspected the Greek and Armenian populations of engaging in nationalist, irredentist, and separatist politics. This suspicion, in turn, contributed to the further estrangement of the

Greek and Armenian elites from the Ottoman state. The structural reasons for a conflict between the Muslim bureaucracy, representing a traditional order based on an unchanging economic structure, and a non-Muslim bourgeoisie, embracing the market and capitalist accumulation, were certainly there. To these were added the attitudinal reasons which gradually spread to the population at large.

By the advent of the constitutional regime in 1908, despite the temporary euphoria and dreams of coexistence under the mantle of a reformed empire, local conflicts between the Muslim and non-Muslim population had become frequent, and a popular hostility against the Christian bourgeoisie, accompanied by a demand for Muslimization—if not yet Turkification—was emerging. The Committee of Union and Progress (CUP) was initially dominated by an ideology of Ottomanism which had allowed for the formation of a multiethnic alliance against Hamidian absolutism. Very soon after its accession to power in 1909, however, the CUP began to exploit ethnic conflict to guarantee the support of the Muslim population. In settling Muslim immigrants from the Balkans, arranging boycotts of foreign goods and non-Muslim businesses, and orchestrating strikes, they sent a clear message to the Greek and Armenian population that their status would not continue as before.[27]

As positive policy, the CUP initiated conscious measures of promoting Muslim businessmen through government contracts, monopolies, and the like. Although successful to some extent, the benefits of this policy were not fully realized until the war years, when the government's involvement in the economy rapidly grew because of military purchases and the need to provision urban areas.[28] Another significant change contributing to the growth of a Muslim bourgeoisie during the war years was the unilateral abrogation of the Capitulations, thus abolishing the fiscal and legal advantages enjoyed by foreigners and passport-holders. In addition, a ruling requiring the use of the Turkish language in business concerns had the practical effect of substituting Muslim clerks and other professionals for non-Muslims.[29]

Important as these positive measures were, it would be wrong to suppose that they were sufficient for the Muslimization of the economy. The greatest impetus for Muslimization proved to be the physical removal of the non-Muslim population. Starting in 1909, when they were conscripted to the army for the first time, there had been a steady out-migration of Greeks and Armenians. During the war this trend accelerated: in 1915 the Armenian population of most of the interior regions was officially deported, leading to the well-known tragedy. During the War of Liberation a civil war ensued where Armenians and Greeks were driven out of their homes; when Turkish forces defeated the Greek army in 1922 almost a million Greeks fled to Greece. Finally, in the Exchange of Populations agreed on in Lausanne, the remaining Greek Orthodox population, except those who could prove their legal residence in Istanbul dating from the prewar period, were forced to emigrate.[30] By 1924 only one tenth of the non-Muslim population of 2.5 million in 1908 remained in the new republic.[31] This considerable population movement meant the disappearance of most of the prewar bourgeois class, especially in the provinces.

Unlike in Egypt there was not much of a native bourgeoisie in Turkey to take over from the departing Christians. A social vacuum resulted, which the state attempted to fill by a voluntaristic creation of a business class. In Egypt, the success of the native bourgeoisie meant that the gradual departure of many foreign capitalists (during the interwar period and afterward) did not leave a similar vacuum in the social fabric.[32]

Stages in the Development of the Turkish Bourgeoisie

1. The 1920s were years of reconstruction when Turkish merchants captured the business opportunities arising from the departure of the old bourgeoisie. They were successful in partially regaining the prewar levels of business activity.[33] While the internal bourgeoisie of the Ottoman period had attained the strength to defend its autonomy against foreign capitalists by the end of the previous century, the republican bourgeoisie was yet inexperienced and new to the accumulation game. Partly for this reason, the departure of the Greeks and the Armenians, who had functioned as the native bourgeoisie of the previous period, left the field open to foreign capital.[34] Especially in the Aegean arena, Turkish businessmen did not object to accepting a subordinate role vis-à-vis foreign capital in order to accelerate their own maturation. The situation was somewhat different in Istanbul in that the non-Muslim population had survived to some degree; although they had to relinquish some of their preponderant position, they continued to control the business of the old capital. They were, however, totally alienated from the new political power. On its part, the new republican government in Ankara treated all Istanbul businessmen with some coolness. The new bureaucrats identified the old capital with the defeated empire; Mustafa Kemal, symbolically, did not visit the city until the 1930s.

There was one new and distinct group of people in Istanbul who could boast a capitalist tradition and who were willing to put themselves forth as candidates for a Turkish bourgeoisie: these were the Salonicans. Salonica had been captured by Greece in 1912, and some Muslim and Jewish businessmen had migrated to Istanbul then. During 1923–24, under the ruling of the Exchange of Populations Treaty, all the remaining Muslims of Salonica arrived in Turkey; most of the wealthy settled in Istanbul. Salonica had been the third largest economic center in the empire and the part played by Muslim businessmen in its prosperity had been relatively larger than in Istanbul or Izmir.[35] The Salonicans were the largest urban group to migrate to Turkey. Some Salonicans enjoyed one more advantage in special cohesiveness: membership in a religious sect. They were followers of Sabbatai

Zevi, the Jewish 'false prophet' of the seventeenth century, who apostatized and ostensibly accepted Islam when threatened with execution.[36] His followers, commonly known as *Dönmes*, had settled in Salonica, and had become important businessmen in the nineteenth century, especially active in the textile trade. These businessmen continued to invest in textiles and related manufacturing after arriving in Turkey. More than their counterparts in other cities of the empire, Muslim and Dönme businessmen in Salonica had adopted bourgeois lifestyles. Upon their arrival in Turkey, they sought to reproduce some of the institutions of this lifestyle by establishing a daily newspaper in Izmir, two secondary schools in Istanbul, various clubs, and Masonic lodges. They were, however, understandably timid in the political field.[37]

The initial years of the republic witnessed a minimum of bourgeois presence in the political scene. There are, of course, sound reasons why exchangees and other Muslim businessmen did not assert themselves politically. First, as already mentioned, the period could be considered an era of plenty, since the field had been left wide open with the departure of the old bourgeoisie. Hence, economic reconstruction consumed all the available energy, and the bureaucracy was willing to oblige in facilitating this. Second, although the republican state was ostensibly new, and could have been supposed to be young and malleable; in fact it was composed of the same bureaucrats who had now made the geographical move to Ankara. The state personnel were the same functionaries who had carefully nurtured the Muslim businessmen before and during the war. Moreover, this state had acquired a politically intolerant dimension during its transformation by coup. Even in the 1920s, the single-party regime was unflinching in its nationalist vigilance, hence it was costly to incur the wrath of the ruling clique whose power was yet to be legitimized. Third—and most important—not only the immigrants but probably every single wealthy Muslim in a position to make the transformation to bourgeois status had acquired some property from the departing Greeks and Armenians. Some of the best land in the Aegean and in Cilicia, and the best urban property in virtually all the cities (warehouses, workshops, oil presses, etc.) had been appropriated during and in the aftermath of the wars. Not all was put to use. The irrigation canals and the terraced vineyards in the east, which the Armenians had cultivated, lay in ruins. In many Aegean cities houses remained empty, mulberry plantations were uprooted, warehouses and workshops were left to crumble. This was because the population in the 1920s, compared with the pre–World War I population, was smaller, less urban, less commercialized, and certainly poorer.[38]

Not suprisingly, the process of appropriating the abandoned property had been somewhat random and had depended on political connections and social power. Legally, all the property had first been nationalized, to be distributed later to new settlers, war-widows, and local notables who had participated in the War of Liberation. The latter group probably received the best of the land devoted to commercial agriculture. In the case of the population arriving in Turkey through the Exchange, the allocation of property was to follow the principle of equivalence. The evaluation was in most cases based on personal declaration, which was often disputed by others. In fact, in all these cases the ratification of the ownership of newly acquired property was a politicized affair, finally resting on the approval of the Ankara government.[39]

2. Had the economic expansion of the 1920s continued for another decade, Turkish merchants might have come of age and reproduced some of the economic, social, and cultural accomplishments of the non-Muslim bourgeoisie in the prewar era. It should be remembered that a major difference between the two periods was that the uprooting of the Greek and Armenian population in Anatolia had deprived the country of a significant petty-commodity-producing commercialized stratum, which constituted the background for the development of the mediating bourgeoisie. The newly arriving population contributed more than its share to market-oriented agricultural production, but its members could not establish a comparable context in which peasant mentality would be transformed in the direction of market rationality. The advent of the economic crisis and its impact on export agriculture arrested the development both of the marketized segment of the agrarian population and the evolving bourgeoisie of the urban areas.

The economic crisis meant that a large number of enterprises dealing in foreign or domestic trade and finance suffered immediate losses and went bankrupt.[40] Smaller merchants in the provincial centers who had replaced the non-Muslim bourgeoisie were especially sensitive to price fluctuations and to the availability of commercial credit. Such credit had been abundant in the 1920s, deriving as much from foreign sources as from the proliferating domestic banking sector.[41] With the break in lines of credit, overextended importers, exporters, and producers rapidly became insolvent. Another immediate casualty was foreign capital. Inflow of foreign capital ceased with the collapse of the world market; foreign businessmen disappeared from the scene. The free-trade regime which had prevailed since the 1923 Lausanne Treaty also came to an end in 1929 and was replaced by a relatively protectionist one.[42] All these new conditions favored local manufacturing, leading to rudimentary import substitution whereby former importers turned to the finishing of imported raw materials.

Within three years of the 1929 balance-of-payments crisis and the onset of bankruptcies, the Ankara government had prepared an interventionist economic program and had adopted an antiliberal rhetoric.[43] The objective was the creation of a public-private nexus of enterprises which would not have to compete either in the internal market or against imports. A small number of state enterprises would be coordinated by a state bank (Sümerbank); and a large number of privately owned, smaller manufacturing, assembly, and commercial enterprises would be held under the umbrella of an ostensibly private bank (İş Bankası), on whose board sat high state officials.[44] It was difficult to ignore the fact that the emerging national economy would be regulated by the new government. Accordingly, the aspiring bourgeoisie began to gravitate to Ankara, which emerged as the focus of the formation of the new business class. Under CUP governments the bureaucracy had concentrated on creating a Muslim bourgeoisie out of provincial merchants; during the etatist period of the 1930s the central bureaucracy itself became involved in the economy—not only because of state enterprises, but also directly. Most deputies became businessmen investing for personal gain.[45]

In a majority of today's peripheral countries, political nationalism has underpinned the process of state formation. During this process, a previously disparate population of diverse affiliations had to be fashioned into a new community with allegiance to the new state. Nationalism provided the justification for changing the form and substance of government, education, and even the language—all for the legitimation of the new polity.[46] Nationalist elites leading the new states were not content to maneuver in the political space liberated by the waning of formal or informal empires; they also wanted to exercise power over the economy. Under conditions characterized by the 1930s disarray in the world economy, antiliberalism became the political economy counterpart of 'nation-building'. During the Great Depression, merchants of the entire world lost face, the market came to be distrusted universally, and the fascist model, with its declared aim to forge national unity, became an attractive way to build strong states. Freed from the test and sanction of the world market, industrialization emerged as the natural prescriptive formula to nurture the bourgeoisie and consolidate the political rule of nationalist cadres.

3. Although the etatist alliance dominated the economy, there were three identifiable streaks which managed to survive while remaining relatively distant from the center. One was the already described Salonican group in Istanbul engaged in manufacturing, mostly of textiles. They remained socially aloof from the recently emerging alliance. The second consisted of Jewish, Greek, and Armenian businessmen who continued to be active, although on a much reduced scale, in foreign and internal commerce, in representing foreign firms, and also in some manufacturing dating from Ottoman times. Some featured a nineteenth-century colonial look, complete with dark offices in tall-ceilinged buildings near the port and shipping forms in various languages. Fancier retail shops on the former Rue de Pera in Istanbul catered mostly to the same community. Others were distinguished by their superior education, contacts, and worldliness.[47] In the imperial economy, the politics of the minorities had been at least indirectly significant and their social orientation had provided a modernizing example. Now, both from the point of view of the direction that the economy had taken, and in terms of their social and political impact on the rest of the population (due to the simple material fact of the displacement of their co-religionists from Anatolia), this group had become thoroughly marginal.

The third group of businessmen who remained essentially independent from state intervention and favoritism comprised the wealthy landlords of Çukurova (Cilicia). They mostly grew cotton and invested in the traditional forward linkages associated with cotton agriculture: ginning, cottonseed-oil-processing, and textiles.[48] After having argued that Turkish agriculture was small-owner-dominated, the assertion that there were large landlords accumulating sufficient surpluses to make the transition to industry requires explanation. The Adana area was closest to Egypt in its agrarian structure; its contours, in fact, had much to do with Ibrahim Pasha (Muhammad Ali's son) introducing cotton cultivation and seasonal labor to the region, then under occupation.[49] Subsequently, the 1858 Ottoman Land Legislation allowed the consolidation of private property and the registering of land in the name of individuals, and the cotton boom of the 1860s contributed to the accumulation of wealth and land. Towards the end of the century, wetlands were reclaimed and new settlements progressed. Land came to be appropriated on a large scale by former nomadic tribes, urban notables, and wealthy Christian (mostly Armenian) merchants.[50]

Çukurova witnessed Muslim–Armenian conflict during the 1890s, and again during the war. There had been some land accumulation by wealthy Armenians during the first decade of the century, contributing to the Muslim resentment.[51] Armenians and Greeks fled to Syria and beyond during the hostilities; Armenians came back under French occupation but departed in haste in 1921 when, after many bloody fights and massacres, the Turkish army repossessed the region. When the Christian landlords and businessmen departed, land, abandoned merchant houses, and manufacturing establishments were taken over by Muslims. During the 1920s and 1930s Adana appears to have been an active business center which attracted immigration, especially of enterprising men.[52] The original accumulation permitted by cotton agriculture and by the appropriation of manufacturing plants created a regional economy which turned away from exports and toward the national economy in the 1930s and after. The business developing there was relatively immune to the rule by fiat which characterized the Ankara-dominated public–private nexus. Çukurova businessmen made the transition to the national arena after World War II, siring some of the giant family 'holding companies' which later came to dominate the modern sector in Turkish economy.

4. While ordinary people suffered shortages and declines in real income during World War II, it was not an entirely inauspicious time for the aspiring bourgeoisie. The government increased its purchases and contracts; imports declined even further, creating opportunities for manufacturers; an inept policy of compulsory agricultural sales and price controls led the way to profiteering by provincial merchants.[53] The war years also witnessed a more ominous development: a Wealth Levy which, according to its preamble, had been designed in order to tax extraordinary profits obtained due to wartime conditions. Similar wartime prestation existed in many countries, but the

Turkish Wealth Levy seemed to aim at solving a social problem: nationalizing the economy. Arriving in 1942, at the height of German influence, its application was left to local commissions, with the guideline that non-Muslims would be taxed ten times as much as Muslims, and Dönmes twice as much.[54] Local tax authorities applied the tax quite subjectively: most Greeks—even professional employees who were not in a position to make profits—were assessed at large sums equal to several years' earnings.[55] Few could pay. Businesses, residences, and movables were sold, and some non-Muslims were sentenced to a labor camp in eastern Anatolia where they were supposed to work in order to pay their debts to the tax authorities. At the wage rate of one lira a day most would have had to work for several lifetimes. The Wealth Levy was abolished after one year, but the damage had been done and its message was clear.

Those non-Muslim Istanbul businessmen who had been stricken by the Wealth Levy were the first to leave the country. The foundation of the Israeli state in 1948 attracted some of the Jewish population, although many of the wealthier families remained. The extraordinary tax and anti-Dönme campaigns of the war period took their toll on the Salonican groups, which also lost their relative standing. Dönmes adopted a low profile and generally forfeited the chance to expand into new fields; they remained within the confines of their initial business undertakings. By the 1960s they only supplied small niches in old markets. Of the entire non-Muslim group of businessmen only a small number of Jewish families retained their relative status in the economy, and even they did not regain a confidence in the political situation until the mid-1950s.

For the Greek minority, the period between the Exchange of Populations in 1924 and the Wealth Levy had been relatively uneventful. During World War II, however, various nationalist currents began to exercise a not-too-subtle pressure on the Greek population, and the Wealth Levy constituted a strong economic mechanism of exclusion. In the 1950s the Cyprus issue led to a confrontation between the Greek and Turkish governments, and the consequence was borne by the Greek minority of Istanbul. A lumpen mob, which might have been incited by the government, set out to destroy a large number of Greek-owned businesses in September 1955. The absence of police protection and the relative inaction and thinly veiled approval of the authorities made many in the Greek minority extremely insecure, and a large number of them subsequently departed. The flight continued into the 1960s; in 1964, again on the occasion of incidents in Cyprus, all Greeks who carried Greek passports (although born and living in Turkey) were expelled. The Greek Orthodox population, which exceeded 125,000 in 1927, had declined to fewer than 5,000 by 1975.[56]

At the end of the war, two of the three 'independent' streams identified above (the remaining minority population and the Dönmes) were no longer in a position to make an impact on the evolution of the bourgeoisie.

5. Businessmen connected with the state-dominated economy of the previous era were apparently the group best-positioned to reap the benefits of the post-war era of reconstruction. They had allied themselves closely with managers and engineers who had gained experience in the public sector, offered them partnerships, and thus prepared themselves for a post-etatist future by safeguarding their access to the higher echelons of the bureaucracy. Nonetheless, it was provincial merchants, the profiteers benefiting from war shortages, who gained the most in the circulation of business elites. They were anxious to invest their newly acquired wealth in cities, especially in Istanbul, which had lost a good proportion of its wealthy population. The end of the war witnessed a massive migration of provincial merchants and aspiring industrialists to the old capital.[57]

As American funds through the Marshall Plan began to arrive in Turkey, one of the principal tenets of US policy was the active pursual of economic measures favoring the private sector. Accordingly, the greater part of the official transfers went to constructing highways and importing agricultural machinery, with the intention of correcting the urban and public-sector bias of the etatist period.[58] Investment in agriculture created boom conditions for the private economy, and a domestic market for manufactures began to develop. Initially, the new bourgeoisie confined itself to commerce (this was a period when foreign exchange hoarded during the war was channeled towards imports of manufactures) and to government contracts. It was only after the mid-1950s that profits in import substitution became high enough to induce them to invest in production.[59]

The atmosphere of optimism that American ascendance incited was such that, as early as 1948, the bourgeoisie had gained sufficient confidence to call a congress in which they asked for liberation from the fetters of etatist policies.[60] Workers whose real incomes had declined since the 1930s, commercialized peasants who had suffered the consequences of forced sales in the war, and the members of the public–private alliance who now felt ready to emerge from under the burden of state tutelage, formed a wide opposition front against the ruling republicans. The leaders of the new Democrat Party had mobilized a coalition of discontents, whose principal economic demand was the reduction of etatist intervention. Policies in consonance with greater autonomy for the market translated to the elimination of special privileges which had previously been accorded to the public–private nexus centered in Ankara.[61]

Elections in 1950 brought the antietatist Democrat Party to power and the bourgeoisie of provincial origin became the most favored clients of the new government. In turn, the political preferences of the new party were partly responsible for the rise of the provincial bourgeoisie. Among the provincial businessmen, those from Çukurova figured prominently. Landowners in Çukurova, more than their counterparts elsewhere in Turkey, had experienced rapid accumulation after the war. They had first benefited from the arrival of tractors and expanded cultivation, and then from the increase in cotton prices during the Korean War boom. The prosperity of the cotton-related economy was eventually translated to finance and manufacturing capital, and the rapid growth of Çukurova and other provincial capitalists became one prominent element of the postwar business scene.[62]

As I argued above, the impact of the world system becomes crucial at turning points. The post–World War II conjuncture was such a turning point, when newly forming American hegemony presented a set of opportunities at an unprecedented scale. Whether these opportunities would be seized depended on the presence of social forces adequate to the task. Liberal economic policy in the 1950s was successful precisely because there was a structural fit between the social transformation desired by dominant social forces in Turkey and the agenda set by the world hegemonic power. American hegemony, complete with its international institutions, was not in and of itself determinant of particular outcomes as they occurred in individual countries. Yet the set of opportunities it created was a powerful inducement toward a specific type of development. The members of the Turkish bourgeoisie, who were now mobilized against etatism, were aware of the new opportunities and conscious that new policies were required to seize them: they called for a political regime that could accommodate the US willingness to underwrite capitalist development in Turkey.

Once again, the contrast with Egypt is telling, where the postwar environment did not lead to a discernible change in state policy or social balances. As a result, the opportunities offered by American hegemony were not seized. The reasons for this lie in both the external and internal arenas. One reason was that Egypt was still entangled in the old colonial relationship with Britain. Consequently, American experts and agencies could not freely dispense policy advice and financial inducement as they could in Turkey. Second, compared with its Turkish counterpart, the Egyptian bourgeoisie in 1946 was less factionalized, considerably more developed, and much more in control of the state apparatus. Since it was sufficiently unified and enjoyed enough power over the state, it could prevent radical change in policy. Finally, the fundamental difference in the agrarian structures of the two countries was important. The liberalization of the Turkish economy proceeded on the basis of massive support by the middle peasantry, which appreciated the promise of market freedom and the chances of enrichment through commodity production.[63] There would be no such popular acclamation of any policy change in the Egyptian context—unless it involved land reform legislated against the wishes of the ruling class.

American aid agencies and experts were closely involved in Turkish economic policy-making in the 1950s. They counseled limits on public investment and encouraged the private sector. For this reason the World Bank organized the establishment of an Industrial Development Bank in 1950, which would extend foreign funds to the private sector.[64] In a world where foreign exchange was scarce and every manufacturing undertaking required imported machinery, technology, and inputs, these dollar credits became the sine qua non of successful investment. Those manufacturers deemed worthy of credit gained an immediate advantage; the American connection gave them the wherewithal to accumulate rapidly in modern technology and established their autonomy vis-à-vis the state. It was no longer desirable to be identified with the Ankara bureaucracy. Those businessmen favored by the new investment bank were generally of a newer vintage compared with the republican bourgeoisie.

The 1950s constituted a break in the formation of the Turkish bourgeoisie; accumulation was now directed by new groups and new types of entrepreneurs. Compared with the former republican bourgeoisie, the businessmen of the 1950s were far more independent of the state, their sources of accumulation more closely connected with the provincial economy and with foreign credit. In addition to the prominent Çukurova families, whose initial wealth came from landownership, there were a number of entrepreneurs who had made their earlier fortunes as Anatolian merchants, and some whose capital consisted of technical expertise earned through public employment. The earlier urban elite of bureaucratic and metropolitan origin had been relegated to a minority presence.

Industrial Structure and Business Groupings

1. After the break of the 1950s, the successive stages of transformation and accumulation were smoother, and the circulation of groups less discontinuous. Although beset by the usual cyclical problems in the economy and frictions within the political process, the development of capitalism in Turkey took a predictable course. Once the euphoria of liberalism had dissipated, foreign-exchange problems forced a policy of protectionism and the prospect of high returns in manufacturing became concrete.[65] The process of import substitution was underway by the early 1960s, requiring a greater involvement of the state in economic policy-making and a greater degree of bureaucratic autonomy.[66]

In most countries of the world, industrialized and raw-material-producing alike, antiliberalism had been the appropriate response to the Great Depression. Post–World War II evolution, however, had different impacts on developed and developing countries. While in Europe under American domination a liberal trade regime was quickly re-established, in the developing world the same American hegemony reinforced the industrializing state's involvement in the economy.[67]

In Turkey, as in many other countries of similar levels of development, protectionism and import substitution were adopted as policies of industrialization. In most cases of import substitution, the economy that emerged found it very difficult to generate foreign exchange, basically because the manufacturing structure had evolved in a particularly inefficient manner, and it could not possibly compete in the world market.[68] The lack of foreign exchange led to a centrality of the state in the economy, because both the procurement of additional dollars and the allocation of scarce foreign funds became political problems. Successive Turkish governments tried to bargain for foreign exchange on the basis of Turkey's geopolitical position. The obvious source of such extra funds was the American government, in its capacity as the international redistributor of purchasing power.[69]

Import-substituting industrialization did not initially require the creation of new markets. As it succeeded, however, it necessitated not only an expanding labor force but also a growing domestic market to purchase the products of industry. Concomitantly, developmentalism evolved into a more broadly based populism in order to ensure the incorporation of the rural population into the previously restricted national fabric.[70] The promise of nationalism to create a single population with a unitary principle of cohesion seemed to come true with the construction of a national labor market. State policy ensured that migrants to the cities would be accommodated at some level—through consumption subsidies, permissive regulations concerning shanty-town settlement, or through other social policies. At a more instrumental level, the state was also responsible for regulating the growth of the market. As most of the products of import-substituting industrialization were consumables (at first light consumer goods but gradually durable ones as well), the purchasing power had to be dispersed to growing ranks of urban dwellers, most of whom were becoming workers. Since industrialists did not face any competition from abroad, they could determine their prices by what amounted to a cost-plus method; thus, the raising of wages in exchange for industrial peace was a bargain they were willing to make.[71]

The social balances already described contributed to the formation of a national consensus around the principle of developmentalism during the 1960s and the 1970s. The prevailing ideology as propagated by the politicians and the bureaucrats (and even shared by most of their 'left' critics, whose vision was often circumscribed by planning and industrialization) coincided perfectly with the activities of the business circles. Manufacturing investment was privileged; agriculture was mostly ignored; shielded by protectionist duties and an artificial exchange rate, the industrial sector was not encouraged to worry about cost-efficiency or world-market competitiveness. Such a consensus was viable because the industrial bourgeoisie, for the most part, had no landowning entanglement and therefore would not be averse to trade-discouraging policies that penalized exporting farmers. The second dimension in this consensus was that neither the bourgeoisie nor the bureaucracy wanted foreign capital to be excessively involved in the industrialization effort. As far as the ownership of the assets was concerned, Turkish capitalism remained overwhelmingly 'national' during this period. Foreign loans and grants tied to specific ventures were welcomed, and the private sector often established links with multinationals through licensing arrangements and the like, but direct foreign investment was minimal.[72] Compared with the bourgeoisie of the Liberal Age in Egypt, or with most examples in Latin America, the Turkish industrial bourgeoisie was distinguished by its lack of ties both to landowners and to foreign capital.

Another characteristic of the Turkish bourgeoisie which distinguishes it from its counterparts in interwar Egypt, or in most of Latin America, was its willingness to tolerate the sharing of ideological hegemony, and to yield a rather large space to state (bureaucratic) autonomy. The bourgeoisie never had full control over the economy. In addition, it lacked a rural clientele which could be mobilized for political ends. Its only social power came from the knowledge that it was indispensable in a capitalist economy. Hence, until the 1980s, it never attempted to rule in its own name, correctly assessing its inability to legitimize itself. Besides, the fact that the dominant current in public opinion remained populist and developmentalist—if not actively anticapitalist—led to an uneasy coexistence between the political and economic classes. It was quite unthinkable for a prominent capitalist to bid for political position, and rare to find one openly declaring liberal views. Although these constraints were reinforced by the nature of the accumulation model, and the behavior of the state managers could justifiably be seen as promoting the general and long-term interests of the bourgeoisie, the result was that businessmen remained outside the corridors of power and the dominant ideology of the period was not even remotely liberal. As Buğra also concludes in this volume, the political and ideological maturation of the bourgeoisie took longer than its early success in economic development.

2. Given the conditions of its development, it may be argued that the economic coming-of-age of the Turkish bourgeoisie was relatively rapid. One important factor leading to this success was the internal organization of the modern sector in the economy: all the major enterprises were closely linked to groups of other enterprises and one or more bank, under the legal umbrella of 'holding companies'.[73] By the late 1970s, a dozen or so of these holding companies came to control the commanding heights of the economy, undertook most of the investment in the modern, import-substituting sector, and allocated among themselves the direction of the major business organization of the industrialists, TÜSİAD.[74]

Starting in the 1920s the republican bourgeoisie had found security in congregating around the centralized planning function assumed by the largest 'private' bank of the time, the İş Bankası.[75] This identification had not only set a precedent, but had also made it incumbent on aspiring groups to emulate the İş Bankası example if they were to challenge the supremacy of the republic-nurtured bourgeoisie credibly. Accordingly, a structural innovation of the 'provincial invasion' of the 1950s had been the formation of a number of smaller banks, which subsequently became the nuclei of holding companies. Yapı ve Kredi, Garanti, Akbank, and Pamukbank, which evolved into the largest private banks in Turkey, were products of these formative years.

Each holding company represented a typically diversified portfolio, ranging over financial, commercial, and real-estate sectors, as well as various industrial undertakings. The advantages gained through this framework permitted the grand bourgeoisie of the industrial sector to establish dominance over the entire modern economy. During the 1970s there were often struggles between large and small capitalists, manifested in conflicts to establish control over various businessmen's associations, such as chambers of commerce and industry and employers' associations.7[6] In the crisis-ridden period of the late 1970s, the holdings emerged victorious out of this struggle. They clinched their success during the subsequent decade, which witnessed a rapid transformation of industrial organization, culminating in the concentration of economic power.

In tandem with this polarization, a corporate social structure began to develop, where the large holdings took on, in smaller scale, some of the appearance of Japanese and Korean holding companies.

One of the aims of the military coup of the 1980s was the dismantling of the national developmentalist and populist equation of the previous decades. This shift was principally instigated by the crisis of the economic model and the ensuing debt situation, which brought the IMF and its package into the picture. In conjunction with the experience of the entire capitalist world, the policy-makers of the 1980s attempted to instill a new ethic of market supremacy through various liberalization schemes. The large holding companies once again emerged as the candidates most favorably positioned to enter the world economy successfully. Accordingly, holding companies were given new privileges and policies were designed to respond to their demands.

During the entire national developmentalist stage, economic development was supposed to proceed through antiliberal tenets; it was to be a solidaristic engagement proving the desirability of the nationalist model. The new bureaucrats of the 1980s repudiated the populist rhetoric and practice of the previous period, and tried to eliminate its inclusionary social policies. Working within the constraints of austerity programs, they accepted the test of the world market—at least in principle—as the criterion of efficiency. All the factors which had precluded the ideological coming-of-age of the bourgeoisie were gradually eliminated, as market liberalism came to be accepted as a valid principle regulating social life. Liberalism, which started as external imposition, carried the promise of ideological emancipation for the bourgeoisie; it held the promise of rationalizing the capitalist model on the basis of the market ideal. This constituted a genuine break with the previous period, when ideological dominion was shared with nationalists, bureaucrats, populists, and the like. For these reasons, the ambivalence of the bourgeoisie towards the restructuring of the economy yielded to warm reception as it perceived the long-term promise consisting of no less than ideological hegemony. The bourgeoisie was willing to gamble away the economic security of the national model (which, in any case, seemed beyond healing) for the promise of risk-ridden restructuring and ideological coming-of-age.

The strength deriving from its inner structure made it easier for the grand bourgeoisie to make the choice to accept a difficult economic transition. In terms of economic orientation, the internal diversification of the holding companies provided them with a ready structure with which they could attempt to orient their production to world markets. In cases when they themselves did not produce for export, they organized large trading companies to claim a share in the new markets. Second, their size, diversity, and knowledge of the local situation made them ideal partners for foreign capital, which was invited to participate in Turkey's restructuring. The arrival of foreign capital in unprecedented amounts allowed the holding companies to break out of their internal-market-oriented mold, and gain access to new technology, design, and world markets.77 The Turkish economy's internationalization was carried out by means of links established between multinationals and Turkish holding companies. It therefore progressed more rapidly and farther than in Egypt where business units ready to form the linkage with foreign capital were lacking. Thus the relative standing of the holding companies and the grand bourgeoisie of Istanbul was strengthened during the difficult decade of the 1980s.

In the political and ideological realm, the striking feature of the 1980s was the increasing willingness of the grand bourgeoisie to get involved in both short-term discussions of economic policy and in the longer-term questions of political model, international relations, and civil rights. This intervention seemed to target what used to be called a 'bourgeois democratic' order, complete with checks and balances at both the internal political and the world-systemic levels. TÜSİAD, the organization which the grand bourgeoisie securely controls, increasingly seemed to specialize in creating and propagating a political and ideological platform, occupying itself with the institutional requirements of the desired transformation.

3. It is possible to interpret the history of Turkish capitalism as a success story, mostly because the development of the productive forces has been rapid, and because a confident bourgeoisie has been created. In addition, following the transformation of the 1980s, when etatism and national developmentalism were discredited, the business elite has convincingly bid at political and ideological power. This is quite unique in this part of the world. I have argued in this essay that there were several reasons for this success. First, the creation of a Turkish bourgeoisie was seen to be an integral part of the anticolonial and anti-Christian struggle; hence, development of capitalism became a national project and the bourgeois class was nurtured by the republican elite. Second, since the newly emerging bourgeoisie had no

links to a landowning class, the goals of capitalism did not clash with existing class balances. As a corollary, when capitalist development found etatist intervention in the economy dysfunctional, the potentially market-oriented peasantry came to their assistance. This made for a smooth transition toward the autonomy of the capitalist economy. Third, the political transformation of the post–World War II period coincided with the establishment of American hegemony and allowed the Turkish economy to benefit from the potential opportunity offered by US and international agencies. This early link gave the bourgeoisie an indispensable impetus, which was put to use in the later import-substitution period.

Finally, the combination of rapid market growth during the 1950s and successful import substitution in the 1960s and early 1970s led to the emergence of a number of 'holding' companies with a diversified grip on a spectrum of commercial, financial, and industrial activities. The holding companies controlled the commanding heights of the modern economy; the polarized structure of capital allowed for the emergence of a rather small and cohesive group of capitalists that came to enjoy prestige and influence in the society. This status made an easy transition to the very different world of the 1980s possible. Turkish capitalists successfully linked up with international capital, opened to world markets, and managed an ideological transition whereby the new liberalism received widespread support. It is now possible to argue that temporary setbacks in economic performance will not reverse the course of bourgeois ascendance which has characterized the past decades.

Notes

1 For a debate on the methodology of such explanations see T. H. Aston and C. H. E. Philpin, eds., *The Brenner Debate* (Cambridge: Cambridge University Press, 1985); for the application of similar issues to the Middle East context see Ç. Keyder and F. Tabak, eds., *Landholding and Commercial Agriculture in the Middle East* (Albany: State University of New York Press, 1991).

2 For the nineteenth century background, see Alan R. Richards, "Primitive Accumulation in Egypt, 1798–1882," in *Review*, vol. I, no. 2, Fall 1977; Kenneth Cuno, "The Origins of Private Ownership of Land in Egypt: A Reappraisal," *International Journal of Middle East Studies*, vol. 12, no. 3, November 1980; Gabriel Baer, "Social Change in Egypt: 1821–1962," in P. M. Holt, ed., *Political and Social Change in Egypt, Historical Studies from the Ottoman Conquest to the United Arab Republic* (London: Oxford University Press, 1968).

3 See Çağlar Keyder, *State and Class in Turkey: A Study in Capitalist Development* (London: Verso, 1987); on the uniqueness of Turkish agrarian structure, see Haim Gerber, *The Social Origins of the Modern Middle East* (Boulder: Lynne Rienner, 1987).

4 See Halil İnalcık, "Centralization and Decentralization in Ottoman Administration," in T. Naff and R. Owen eds., *Studies in Eighteenth-Century Islamic History* (Carbondale: University of Southern Illinois Press, 1977); Andrew G. Gould, "Lords or Bandits? The Derebeys of Cilicia," in *International Journal of Middle East Studies*, vol. VII, no. 4, October 1976.

5 See Helen Rivlin, *The Agricultural Policy of Muhammad Ali in Egypt* (Cambridge: Harvard University Press, 1969).

6 Alexander Schölch, *Egypt for the Egyptians* (London: Ithaca Press, 1981).

7 V. J. Puryear, *International Economics and Diplomacy in the Near East, 1834–1853*, Stanford University Press, Palo Alto, 1935; see also the discussion in the articles contained in Çağlar Keyder and Donald Quataert, eds., "The Impact of 1838 on Anatolia and Egypt," special issue of *New Perspectives on Turkey*, no. 7, 1992.

8 The classic reference is D. C. Blaisdell, *European Financial Control in the Ottoman Empire* (New York, 1929).

9 Roger Owen, *Cotton and the Egyptian Economy, 1820–1914* (Oxford: Oxford University Press, 1969); David S. Landes, *Bankers and Pashas: International Finance and Economic Imperialism in Egypt* (Cambridge: Harvard University Press, 1958).

10 Roger Owen, *The Middle East in the World Economy, 1800–1914* (London: Methuen, 1981), chapter 5. See also Cuno, "The Origins of Private Landownership," and Richards, "Primitive Accumulation."

11 Robert Tignor, "The Economic Activities of Foreigners in Egypt, 1920–1950: From Millet to Haute Bourgeoisie," in *Comparative Studies in Society and History*, vol. 22, no. 3, July 1980; Robert Vitalis, "On the Theory and Practice of Compradors. The Role of Abbud Pasha in Egypt's Political Economy," *International Journal of Middle East Studies*, vol. 22, no. 3, August 1990.

12 The Chilean case is paradigmatic. See M. Zeitlin, *The Civil Wars in Chile or the Bourgeois Revolutions that Never Were* (Princeton: Princeton University Press, 1984); also F. H. Cardoso and E. Faletto, *Dependency and Development in Latin America* (Berkeley: University of California Press, 1978).

13 An instance of this difficulty is the short-lived experiment of land purchases by foreigners (especially the British) in the Izmir region. The would-be plantation-owners could not find cheap wage labor or sharecroppers, and the land reverted to small peasant property in a short time; *cf.* Orhan Kurmuş, *Emperyalizmin Türkiye'ye Girişi* (Istanbul: Bilim, 1974).

14 See the articles in Keyder and Tabak, eds., *op. cit.* The contributions of İslamoğlu-İnan and Arıcanlı are especially relevant.

15 See Şevket Pamuk, "The Ottoman Empire in Comparative Perspective," in Ç. Keyder, ed., *Ottoman Empire: Nineteenth-Century Transformations*, special issue of *Review*, vol. XI, no. 2, Spring 1988.

16 See Şevket Pamuk, *The Ottoman Empire and European Capitalism, 1820–1913* (Cambridge: Cambridge University Press, 1987).
17 For a full version of the argument see Keyder, *State and Class*, chapters 1–3.
18 See Reşat Kasaba, *The Ottoman Empire and the World Economy* (Albany: SUNY Press, 1988); also R. Kasaba, "Was There a Comprador Bourgeoisie in Mid-Nineteenth Century Western Anatolia?" in Keyder, ed., *Ottoman Empire: Nineteenth-Century Transformations*.
19 Not only did they acquire the cultural attributes of a bourgeoisie, but there also grew, from within their ranks, a large group of middle-class professionals. This was mostly due to the superior educational opportunities available to the non-Muslim minorities; *cf.* Alexis Alexandris, *The Greek Minority of Istanbul and Greek–Turkish Relations, 1918–1974* (Athens: Center for Asia Minor Studies, 1983).
20 *Cf.* A.J. Sussnitzki, "Ethnic Division of Labor," in C. Issawi ed., *The Economic History of the Middle East* (Chicago: University of Chicago Press, 1966).
21 Nasim Sousa, *The Capitulatory Regime of Turkey* (Baltimore: Johns Hopkins University Press, 1934).
22 There is an extensive literature on such passport holders. See R. Davison, "Nationalism as an Ottoman Problem and the Ottoman Response," in W. W. Haddad and W. Ochsenwald, eds., *Nationalism in a Non-National State: The Dissolution of the Ottoman Empire* (Columbus: Ohio State University Press, 1977).
23 See Çağlar Keyder and Donald Quataert, eds., *Port-Cities in the Eastern Mediterranean*, special issue of *Review*, winter 1993.
24 See Vedat Eldem, *Osmanlı İmparatorluğunun İktisadi Şartları Hakkında Bir Tetkik*, T. İş Bankası Kültür Yayınları, Istanbul, 1970; and Gündüz Ökçün, ed., *Osmanlı Sanayii: 1913, 1915 Yılları Sanayi İstatistiki* (Ankara: SBF, 1970).
25 See Çağlar Keyder, "Creation and Destruction of Forms of Manufacturing: the Ottoman Example," in Jean Batou ed., *Between Development and Underdevelopment: the Precocious Attempts at Industrialization of the Periphery, 1800–1870* (Geneva: Droz, 1991).
26 Paul Dumont, "A propos de la classe ouvrière Ottomane à la veille de la révolution Jeune Turque," in *Turcica*, vol. IX, no. 1, 1977.
27 See Feroz Ahmad, "Vanguard of a Nascent Bourgeoisie: The Social and Economic Policy of the Young Turks 1908–1918," in O. Okyar and H. İnalcık, eds., *Social and Economic Policy of Turkey, 1071–1920* (Ankara, 1980); also Erdal Yavuz, "1908 Boykotu," in *ODTÜ Gelişme Dergisi*, special issue, 1978.
28 Zafer Toprak, *Türkiye'de 'Milli İktisat,'* (Ankara: Yurt Yayınları, 1982).
29 Harry Stuermer, *Deux ans de guerre à Constantinople* (Paris, 1914); Ahmet Emin (Yalman), *Turkey in the World War* (New Haven: Yale University Press, 1930).

30 Dimitri Pentzopoulos, *The Balkan Exchange of Minorities and its Impact upon Greece* (Mouton, Paris, 1962). See also Alexandris, *The Greek Minority.*

31 Justin McCarthy, "Foundations of the Turkish Republic: Social and Economic Change," in *Middle Eastern Studies*, April 1983; Kemal H. Karpat, *Ottoman Population 1830–1914, Demographic and Social Characteristics* (Madison: University of Wisconsin Press, 1985).

32 Robert Tignor, *State, Private Enterprise, and Economic Change in Egypt: 1918–1952* (Princeton: Princeton University Press, 1984).

33 Çağlar Keyder, *The Definition of a Peripheral Economy: Turkey 1923–1929* (Cambridge: Cambridge University Press and Maison des Sciences de l'Homme, 1981).

34 Gündüz Ökçün, *1920–1930 Yılları Arasında Kurulan Türk Anonim Şirketlerinde Yabancı Sermaye Sorunu* (Ankara: SBF, 1971).

35 See the article on Salonica by Basil Gounaris in Keyder and Quataert, eds., *Port-Cities*, and also A. Vacalopoulos, *A History of Thessaloniki* (Salonica, 1963).

36 See İbrahim Alaettin Gövsa, *Sabatay Sevi, İzmirli Meşhur Sahte Mesih Hakkında Tarihi ve İçtimai Tetkik Tecrübesi* (Istanbul: Semih Lütfi Kitabevi, 1940).

37 The newspaper is *Yeni Asır* and the schools are Şişli Terakki and Işık; all three institutions are still in existence.

38 Total population within Turkey's borders was 13.6 million according to the 1927 census, while the prewar figure probably exceeded 15 million. Urban population might have been 25 percent of the total before the war, this proportion declined to 18 percent in 1927. See also Frederic C. Shorter, "The Population of Turkey After the War of Independence," in *International Journal of Middle East Studies*, vol. 17, no. 4, 1985.

39 This episode remains uninvestigated in Turkish historiography. Official documents are not available, all information concerning the appropriation of abandoned property is anecdotal.

40 These bankruptcies signaled the real death of Istanbul. See H. Tahsin, and R. Saka, *Sermayenin Şirketlerdeki Hareketi* (Istanbul: Hüsnütabiat Matbaası, 1929), and their *Sermaye Hareketi* (Istanbul, 1930).

41 See Keyder, *Definition of a Peripheral Economy*, chapter 4.

42 İlhan Tekeli and Selim İlkin, *1929 Dünya Buhranında Türkiye'nin İktisadi Politika Arayışları* (Ankara: ODTÜ, 1977).

43 İlhan Tekeli and Selim İlkin, *Para ve Kredi Sisteminin Oluşumunda Bir Aşama: T.C. Merkez Bankası* (Ankara, 1981) and *Uygulamaya Geçerken Türkiye'de Devletçiliğin Oluşumu* (Ankara, 1982).

44 The literature on etatism is vast. See Korkut Boratav, "Kemalist Economic Policies and Etatism" in Ali Kazancıgil and E. Özbudun eds., *Atatürk. Founder of a Modern State* (Hamden: Archon Books, 1981); Faruk Birtek, "The Rise and Fall of Etatism in Turkey, 1932–1950," in *Review*, vol. 8,

no. 3, 1985; and Afet İnan, *Devletçilik İlkesi ve Türkiye Cumhuriyetinin Birinci Sanayi Planı* (Ankara: Türk Tarih Kurumu, 1975).

45 This trend had in fact started in the 1920s, *cf.* Gündüz Ökçün, *1920–1930 Yılları*.

46 Two essays particularly relevant to the Turkish experience are Ernest Gellner, *Nations and Nationalism* (Ithaca: Cornell University Press, 1983); and Benedict Anderson, *Imagined Communities* (London: Verso, 1983).

47 *Cf.* Alexandris, *The Greek Minority*; similar judgements can be found in most travel writing on Istanbul.

48 Sadun Tanju, *Hacı Ömer* (Istanbul: Apa Ofset, 1983); Sakıp Sabancı, *İşte Hayatım* (Istanbul, 1985).

49 The regulations that Ibrahim Pasha introduced concerning the employment conditions of seasonal labor still constituted the basis of custom in Çukurova cotton cultivation during the 1930s. *Cf.* "Memleketimizde Mevsimlik Ziraat İşçisi Meselesi," in *Ülkü*, June 1936.

50 This is, of course, similar to the case of Syria. See Gerber, *Social Origins*, for the impact of the 1858 Land Legislation on the modes of land appropriation.

51 *Cf.* W.J. Childs, "Armenia," in *Encyclopedia Britannica*, twelfth edition, vol. 30, 1922 (supplementary volume to the eleventh edition, published in 1909).

52 There was a large number of immigrants from Kayseri who subsequently became important businessmen, among whom were Sabancı, Has, Sapmaz. They were shareholders in the largest financial concern to emerge out of Adana, Akbank, whose name apparently derived from "Adana'da Kayserililer," that is AK, meaning Kayseriots in Adana. For the appropriation of Christian-owned ginneries and textile concerns by Muslims (from Kayseri and elsewhere) see İlhan Tekeli and Selim İlkin, "Savaşmayan Ülkenin Savaş Ekonomisi: Üretimden Tüketime Pamuklu Dokuma," paper presented at Türk Tarih Kongresi, Ankara, 22–26 September, 1986.

53 For the impact of wartime policies on agricultural production, see Şevket Pamuk, "War, State Economic Policies and Resistance by Agricultural Producers in Turkey, 1939–1945," in *New Perspectives on Turkey*, vol. 2, no. 1, 1988.

54 Faik Ökte, *Varlık Vergisi Faciası*, Istanbul, 1951; Edward C. Clark, "The Turkish Varlık Vergisi Reconsidered," in *Middle Eastern Studies*, May, 1972.

55 Ibid.; also Alexandris, *The Greek Minority*, chapter 8.

56 Ibid., p. 142.

57 There is a rich Istanbul-based literature on the interaction between the wealthy newcomers and slick urbanites. See Sabancı's disarming account of how he purchased the mansion of an impoverished Istanbul family, in Tanju, *Hacı Ömer*.

58 There are many expert reports on the Turkish economy of this period. See e.g. Max Thornburg, *Turkey, An Economic Appraisal* (New York, 1949).

59 Some, like Koç, started manufacturing investment early, as an extension of import trade. Import shortages led to rudimentary substitution in the 1950s, when fortunes accumulated through government contracts during the infrastructural expansion of the early 1950s, were invested in manufacturing. See Vehbi Koç, *Hayat Hikayem* (Istanbul, 1973); also Erdoğan Soral, *Özel Kesimde Türk Müteşebbisleri* (Ankara: AİTİA, 1974).

60 This congress constitutes the first initiative of the would-be leaders of the civil society in Turkey. Its proposals were almost fully adopted by the republican government, but this acquiescence did not prove sufficient to postpone the demise of the single-party regime.

61 For this all-important transition, see Keyder, *State and Class*, chapter 6.

62 In addition to the Sabancı, Has, and Sapmaz families and their Akbank, the Karamehmet and Eliyeşil families and their Yapı ve Kredi and Pamukbank banks also originated in cotton. For the relationship between holding companies and banks, see Öztin Akgüç, *Türkiye'de Bankacılık* (Istanbul: Gerçek Yayınevi, 1987).

63 The middle peasantry have continued to play a crucial role in Turkish politics, and have usually given their support to center-right parties. See Keyder, "The genesis and structure of small peasant ownership in agriculture," in *Review*, vol. VII, no. 1, 1983.

64 Mustafa Sönmez, *Kırk Haramiler* (Ankara: Arkadaş, 1990) (fourth printing), chapter 3. This is a useful history of the large holding companies in Turkey. See also Korkut Boratav, *1980'li Yıllarda Türkiye'de Sosyal Sınıflar ve Bölüşüm*, Gerçek Yayınevi, Istanbul, 1991. Boratav argues that there are thirty holding groups of 'large capital,' each one controlled by a family, pp. 66–67.

65 For a good economic history of the period, see Morris Singer, *The Economic Advance of Turkey, 1938–1960* (Ankara, 1977).

66 For the planning period, see Oktar Türel, ed., *Two Decades of Planned Development in Turkey*, a special issue of *METU Studies in Development*, 1981.

67 The American government actively encouraged the adoption of import-substitution policy in a number of countries. See, S. Maxfield and J. H. Nolt, "Protectionism and the Internationalization of Capital: U.S. Sponsorship of Import Substitution Industrialization in the Philippines, Turkey and Argentina," in *International Studies Quarterly*, vol. 34, March 1990.

68 This inability to generate foreign exchange was the principal criticism that neo-classical economists leveled against import substitution. Taiwan and South Korean experiences show that different class balances coupled with more far-sighted policy-making might have avoided the foreign-exchange bottleneck. See the essays in Frederic Deyo, *The Political Economy of New Asian Industrialism* (Ithaca: Cornell University Press, 1987).

69 See Keyder, "The American Recovery of Europe: Aid and Hegemony," in Giovanni Arrighi, ed., *Semiperipheral Development: The Politics of Southern Europe in the Twentieth Century* (Beverly Hills: Sage, 1985).

70 Populism functioned as the peripheral counterpart to social democracy. Given national developmentalism and the inability of the bourgeoisie to establish its hegemony, populism emerged as a feasible balance assuring some social harmony via etatist promises without challenging capitalist development.

71 Workers' organizations benefited from this mutual accommodation; the promise of union membership became self-fulfilling because unionized workers and especially the members of select unions could ask for and obtain high wage increases. It was thus that privileged workers in the modern industrial sector evolved as a labor aristocracy, as a socially distinct stratum within the much larger working class.

72 The total amount of direct foreign investment in manufacturing between 1961 and 1975 was only $200 million, which corresponded to approximately 3 percent of the total manufacturing capital formation. This figure is very low in comparison with Latin American magnitudes ($1,480 million in Argentina, $6,900 million in Brazil, $3,670 million in Mexico), but probably higher than Egypt. See Keyder, *State and Class*, pp. 182–83, for calculations.

73 By the late 1970s there was a large number of these holding companies which dominated the modern sector of the economy. See Sönmez, *Kırk Haramiler*. The economic crisis and subsequent transformation took their toll, however, and there was considerable consolidation. By the end of the 1980s fewer than a dozen of these holding companies enjoyed real economic clout. See Boratav, *1980'li Yıllarda.*

74 Robert Bianchi, *Interest Groups and Political Development in Turkey* (Princeton: Princeton University Press, 1983); Ayşe Öncü, "Chambers of Industry in Turkey: An Inquiry into State–Industry Relations as a Distributive Domain," in E. Özbudun and A. Ulusan, eds., *The Political Economy of Income Distribution in Turkey* (New York: Holmes and Meier, 1980).

75 For a history of the foundation of this bank see Turgut Bayar, *La Türkiye İş Bankası* (Montreux, 1938).

76 Bianchi, *Interest Groups*; A. Öncü, "Chambers of Industry,"; M. Sönmez, *Kırk Haramiler*, chapter 6.

77 Legislation concerning foreign capital was changed in the early 1980s. More importantly, bureaucratic attitudes towards foreign investment were transformed. By the late years of the decade foreign capital inflow reached $1,000 million per annum.

State Formation, Transformation, and Legitimizing Ideologies

3

Ideology and Legitimacy in Egypt: The Search for a 'Hybrid Formula'

Ali E. Hillal Dessouki

Introduction

The question of legitimacy lies at the heart of political inquiry. Legitimacy and stability are interdependent, and therefore political regimes seek to enhance their legitimacy using different strategies and ideologies. Ultimately, the less successful a regime and the fewer its achievements, the more it resorts to ideological and symbolic legitimation.

Ideological change constitutes a subset of the general development of society and polity at large. It reflects the interests of different social groups and classes. Ideas and ideologies are instruments through which social conflicts are waged and their conclusions are legitimized. Researches in the field of sociology of knowledge have taught us that a positive correlation exists between interests, broadly defined, and ideologies. A change in the former can render a particular ideology irrelevant. The history of social and political thought shows that the endorsement of an ideology is not contingent merely upon the intrinsic merits of the ideas that make up its principles. Rather the ideology must correspond to the wants and needs of a given society or a group within it. Thus, modes of thought cannot be adequately understood as long as their sociohistorical origins and context are obscured.[1]

This essay argues that ideological legitimation in Egypt is achieved through a 'hybrid formula.'[2] Social differentiation, class formation, and elite fragmentation have been encountered by the more stable elements of unity and cohesion in society. Eventually, ideological polarization tends to be diluted through the adoption of a middle-of-the-road solution emphasizing unity and solidarity.

In the twentieth century, Egyptians have revealed a pattern of identifying themselves with broad political movements which have been a function of social unity on one side and the imperatives of anticolonial struggle on the other. For instance, in 1919 the Wafd ('Delegation') was established to negotiate Egypt's independence. And again, after a period of ideological polarization in the late 1940s, Nasser was able to reinforce the theme of unity in the context of noncompetitive politics. In 1992, and after some fifteen years of party politics, there was a dominant ruling party and no likelihood of its being voted out of power. The opposition continues to suffer from its inability to establish a coalition or to maintain a sustained unified position.

Both geography and ethnicity account for the unity and cohesion of Egyptian society. Egypt's geography is simple but extremely significant; a line of water that runs between two deserts and widens near the Mediterranean Sea. Because the geography of the country has dictated the settlement of the population, Egypt has been an easy country to control, resulting in a tradition of centralized rule and the absence of long-standing regional loyalties. Dependence on the Nile for irrigation has called for central administration and enabled the government to extend its authority to the most remote parts of the land.

The population is characterized by social cohesion. Historically, Egypt is one of the oldest continuously settled communities in the world and Egyptians long ago acquired the sense of being one people. All Egyptians speak Arabic, with the exception of the Nubians (less than 1 percent) and an insignificant number of isolated Berber-speaking groups in the Western Desert. More than 90 percent are Muslims, and the indigenous Copts constitute the other largest religious group. The Copts speak Arabic and there are hardly any racial or ethnic differences between them and the Muslims. In contrast to the situation in many developing countries, the population of Egypt shows a high degree of social and national integration.

These features of the geographic–demographic make-up of Egypt interact with, and indeed reinforce, a mass culture that encourages indifference and discourages political participation. For a long time, the average Egyptian viewed authority as power maintained by force and injustice. It represented taxes and corvée work, rather than specific services of public welfare. It has always been a 'they'. Inherited from the past, there is a lack of trust causing a sense of insecurity towards the government.

So when the educated elites seek to mobilize the support of the masses they have to reckon with this harsh reality. Thus, elite politics are not usually linked to mass activities; this explains, for instance, why the enthusiasm of the elite for specific events such as the Camp David Accords or for certain more abstract and general issues like liberal freedoms has not been reflected at the mass level. On the other hand, when the matter relates to basic economic needs or Islam, popular feelings and actions can be mobilized. Thus, elite political pluralism/fragmentation is no reflection of the society at large, a fact which weakens opposition parties and limits their influence.

At different points in its modern history, Egypt has experienced freedom of expression and has constrained political pluralism, in particular in the period 1923–52 and subsequently from 1977 until now (1992). The first period is usually considered 'the liberal age' in Egyptian politics. Alas, it was marred by a despotic king who refused to confine himself to constitutional power or accept in good faith the results of elections. He was too ready to dismiss majority cabinets (1924, 1928, 1930, 1937, 1942, and 1944), to dissolve parliaments (1924, 1928, 1930, 1934, 1938, and 1948 twice) and to suspend the constitution (1930–34). The British occupation authorities made sure that party politics should not threaten their interests, and intervened accordingly.[3]

Competitive politics, however, possess their own dynamics and suffer (not necessarily hardship) their own consequences. They have produced a number of protest organizations, chief among them the Young Egypt Party, which became the Egyptian Socialist Party, the Muslim Brotherhood, which emerged as a major political force in the late 1940s, and a range of communist organizations which suffered from internal infighting and organizational fragmentation. The 1948 military defeat in Palestine gave impetus to these system-challenging organizations by alienating an increasingly large section of the army from the king and his regime.

This alienation was further compounded by the growing imbalances and problems in society. Egyptian cities, particularly Cairo, experienced massive rural immigration. The people who migrated to the cities did so "with no home, attended no school, did no work, got no cash, and bought no goods."[4] As the cities lacked the facilities to absorb such a floating urban mass as nonparticipants, those people simply increased the nation's potential for population explosion.[5] Workers went on the streets calling for social justice. Also in the cities, the new middle class, comprising university graduates, civil servants, and professionals, became the motive force behind and the articulate voice calling for social change. It demanded more political participation and a greater share in economic gains. As employment opportunities failed to keep pace with the expansion of educational opportunities, these people became discontented.

The multiplication of these political and social contradictions was accompanied by ideological polarization and a resorting to violence and assassinations as a vehicle of political action. Almost all major political groups established their para-military organizations. An interesting example of the tendency towards ideological polarization is the fate of Islamic modernist thinking. Islamic modernism, which was heralded by Muhammad Abduh at the turn of the century, took on a more orthodox character at the hands of his biographer, Rashid Reda, whose disciple Hassan al-Bana founded the Muslim Brotherhood. The modernist position was besieged from almost every corner. The secular elite which assumed power did not welcome a role for Islam, other than that of legitimizing its own policy. Other ideologies and persuasions, nationalism and socialism in particular, attracted the attention of large numbers of young people. New concerns and questions were advanced, primarily on the subject of social justice, for which the modernists had no adequate answers. On the other side, the traditional *'ulama* and fundamentalist groups accused the modernists of sacrificing Islamic principles for the sake of Western ideas. With the rise of the Muslim Brotherhood within Egyptian politics, thoughts of social welfare were measured against the needs and requirements of political expedience.

The political and ideological polarization caused stalemate. No single party or group could muster enough strength to impose its own will. Nor was any able to establish coalitions or fronts capable of challenging the king and the British. A breaking of the stalemate had to come from a different source; the army moved in July 1952 to end the polarization and initiate a new era of national solidarity and noncompetitive politics.

Attempts at Ideological Legitimation

The new era represented a break with the institutions, ruling elite, and ideology of the old regime. The members of the new ruling elite were primarily military, young, and from middle-class backgrounds. They had little love for the old pashas and the liberal ideas of the Wafd. They were obsessed with the problem of national unity, which they considered the cornerstone for any progress. Lacking a clear ideological commitment or a social doctrine, they developed their ideas in an eclectic and pragmatic manner. For the following eighteen years (1952–70), President Nasser experimented with a number of ideological and organizational formulae.

As will be demonstrated later, the regime's primary concern was unity, cohesion, and solidarity. The military elite discouraged competitive politics and equated them with weakness and disunity. The image of Egypt in the late 1940s haunted them—an image of a divided society and polarized politics. So they sought to combine in their thought the different ingredients that would legitimize the regime and make it acceptable to the masses.

The development of a new ideology for the 'Revolution' proceeded in a gradual and piecemeal fashion. The evolution of the elite's ideas, particularly of Nasser's, took place in conjunction with changes in socioeconomic policies and developmental strategy. Four stages can be recognized. First, the 'etatist' phase from 1952 to 1956, which was one of stabilizing the new regime and maintaining law and order in the face of diverse opposition. Second, there was the 'populist' phase from 1956 to roughly 1961–62, which witnessed 'the philosophy of the National Union.' From 1962 to roughly 1973, a third phase emerged, which has been variously described as state socialism, state capitalism, or simply the takeover of economy by the governmental bureaucratic apparatus in the name of socialism. And finally, with the death of Gamal Abd al-Nasser in 1970, a new phase started which involved major reconsideration of ideological commitments and social preferences.[5]

The Etatist Phase

This period is described as 'etatist' because the primary objective of the regime was law and order. The immediate goal was to consolidate power and mobilize mass support. The new regime sought discipline and loyalty. The officers punished severely violent demonstrations by both left and right. In order to consolidate their power, the army, the police, and the civil service were purged of opposition elements. The press was censored and eventually the press syndicate was dissolved, to be replaced by a pro-regime group in 1954. Political parties were requested to purge themselves of corrupt elements, and on 16 January 1953 a law banned political parties in the interest of national unity.

In the midst of power struggles, elite rifts, and consolidation of power, there was not much time for the development of ideology. The regime issued the famous six principles: the liquidation of colonialism, the liquidation of feudalism, the ending of domination of power by capital, the establishment of social justice, the establishment of a strong national army, and the establishment of a sound democratic life.

The two major themes in Nasser's speeches during this period were democracy and national unity. On 9 April 1953, he said in al-Mansura that the Liberation Rally (established in January 1953 after the banning of political parties and continuing until 1957 as the sole legitimate political organization) "is not a political party. It is a means to organize popular strength for the restructuring of society on a sound new basis."[6] Another statement by Nasser concluded that the "Liberation Rally is the school where People will be taught how to elect their representatives."[7]

The basic argument against political parties was that Egypt needed all the energies of its leaders, and that it would be highly unwise to allow them to dissipate those energies in parliamentary debates and political opposition. Unity was badly needed, the officers urged. Thus, the prevailing idea was that the dissolution of parties was a temporary measure and that sooner or later a multiparty system would be re-established. "Our ultimate aim is to provide Egypt with a truly democratic and representative government. We want to make sure that in the future the senators and deputies will serve all the Egyptians rather than the few," wrote Nasser in January 1955.[8]

These ideas were incorporated into the platform and programs of the Liberation Rally. Its motto was unity, order, and work. "The masses that came [to the support of the army movement of 1952] were disunited, divided groups of stragglers. The picture that emerged on that day looked dark and ominous. It embodied danger. We needed order but we found nothing behind us but chaos. We needed work but we found behind us only indolence and sloth. It was from these facts, and no others, that the revolution coined its slogans," Nasser wrote.[9]

The Populist Phase

On 16 January 1956 President Nasser announced the end of the three-year transitional period and presented the Egyptian people with a new constitution.[10] The authors of the constitution did not consider Egypt ready for a parliamentary democracy, and political parties were still banned. Instead, a new organization, the National Union, was set up as a successor to the Liberation Rally to represent all segments of society. Nasser and his associates consistently emphasized the 'uniqueness' and 'originality' of the National Union formula. It did not, according to them, fit into the categories of either the multiparty system or a single-party one, as neither system had proven adequate to Egypt's real needs. Egypt, it was argued, could not afford a multiparty system. Political parties were regarded as a disruptive force and a source of disunity. Nasser noted that "parties cooperated with colonialism and represented reaction and opportunism." [11] As he viewed them, parties tended to be agents of external forces.[12] Nasser firmly believed that a return to party politics without first educating the masses would be a return to the chaos and corruption of the prerevolution epoch. "A period must pass during which independent free thought shall crystallize and become deep-rooted in our land," he said.[13]

Nasser defined the National Union as "a national forum which includes all the members of the nation except reactionaries, opportunists, and agents of colonialism because it is they who controlled us in the past and proved to be traitors."[14] According to him, the functions of the National Union included filling the vacuum created by the banning of political parties, mobilizing the efforts of the people to realize the objectives of the revolution, training leaders at different levels, and studying local problems and solving them.

Western scholars had different views of the National Union. For instance, Simon Jargy, writing in 1959, observed that, "it is difficult not to regard it as a political organization functioning in the service of the political regime."[15] P. J. Vatikiotis referred to the goal of the National Union as "the development of a homogeneous citizenry and a homogeneous political culture through the control of all aspects of popular activity."[16] The same contention led the Lacoutures to view the National Union as not "so much of a single party as of a censor of political activity, a kind of crucible in which the whole public life of Egypt would be remolded." [17]

The official ideology of the ruling elite, which was reflected in the establishment of the National Union, was predicated on two main concepts: social democracy and national unity. As to social democracy, Nasser seemed to believe that political democracy required certain social and economic prerequisites. Before political freedom could be established, there must be social and economic democracy, which involves the removal of class barriers and the ensuring of more social mobility in society. As for national unity, Nasser envisaged the stage that Egypt was currently passing through as one of national construction and economic development out of which would evolve a new socialist, democratic, and cooperative society. For him, the fulfilling of that vision required the highest degree of national unity, the minimizing—if not the elimination—of existing class differences, and the development of a functional citizenry dedicated to the creation of a viable country and a strong nation.[18] Thus, the goal must be the achievement of a national consensus transcending class differences. All Egyptians "have one goal and one aim—to work for the welfare of the nation with no individual, no group or party working for its own benefit but all of us working together for the benefit of this nation," Nasser asserted.[19] The idea of reconciling class differences was embodied in the 1956 Constitution. Part II, entitled "Basic Constitutents of the Egyptian Society," made social solidarity the cornerstone of society. The government viewed itself as a neutral body operating between conflicting social classes. It disclaimed any intention of favoring one class over another; rather it would check the struggle between classes by molding all Egyptians into one *shaab*.[20]

We must emphasize that Gamal Abd al-Nasser believed deeply in the need for national unity. According to him all the previous failures of Egyptians could be attributed to differences and disunity between them.[21] The National Union was to be the vehicle for implementing this populist ideal.[22] By calling Nasser's ideas 'populist', we refer to an orientation of thinking characterized by, first, a rejection of class struggle, second, a view of society as one organism with a sense of oneness transcending all class differences, and third, the development of society as the function of harmonious coordination of the efforts of all the people. But soon, Nasser was to recognize the shortcomings of these views.

In a mood of self-criticism after the Syrian secession in September 1961, Nasser made the first official critique of the National Union scheme. According to him, one shortcoming had been the lack of an adequate guide to revolutionary action, i.e., ideology. The absence of ideology meant, for Nasser, the absence of intellectual commitment to the movement. In November 1961, Nasser complained that intellectuals were not cooperating fully with the regime. He had been disappointed at the paucity of academic writing on the new economic and political system of the country. He singled out for special criticism the law schools which were still teaching Adam Smith. He concluded that Egypt was undergoing an experiment in which practice preceded theory.[23] The pragmatic nature of the regime made it possible to benefit from the National Union's experience. The announcement of the National Charter and the establishment of the Arab Socialist Union reflected the regime's new outlook.

The Socialist Phase

The Syrian Secession in September 1961, and the fact that its leaders held key positions in the National Union, had a profound effect upon Nasser and his associates. It seems clear that in 1962 Nasser was obsessed by the necessity of having an ideological document which would define the objectives and means of the Egyptian Revolution. He thought that the lack of such an ideological guideline had been one of the main defects of the National Union. The Charter, a document of ten chapters setting forth the principles of the revolution, was to fill this gap. In Nasser's terms, it contained "the principles and the ideas of development in our society and our culture."[24]

The Charter emphasized socialism,[25] which was seen as the instrument by which a society based on justice rather than profit would be established, planning rather than following market forces, and industrialization as opposed to the production of raw materials for export. In effect, socialism was perceived as a means of mobilizing the resources of society and stimulating the masses to increase production. The basic principle of Nasser's Arab socialism was "sufficiency and justice," i.e., an increase in production and justice in its distribution. The government should interfere to ensure equitable distribution of wealth and income. The objective was to resolve class conflict through the reduction of socioeconomic disparities, the elimination of exploitation, and the extension of social services and educational opportunities. Nasser was keen to distinguish his brand of socialism from Marxism. He established that distinction on three grounds: rejection of the dictatorship of one class, respect for the principle of private property, and belief in religion. In fact, Nasser referred frequently to the compatibility between Islam and socialism.

The Charter asserts that economic or social democracy is no less fundamental than political democracy. True democracy can be achieved only on the basis of social democracy. Thus, the Charter concludes that parliamentary institutions could not function properly in a distorted socioeconomic environment. From the writings of many intellectuals, it appears that social democracy entailed three recurring ideas. The first is the rejection of bourgeois democracy; for the first time, the rejection of political parties in Egypt was based on a general view of classes and democracy. Second, Egyptian society was seen as undergoing a process of transition from a kind of feudal-capitalist structure to socialism. Consequently, Egypt needed a profound revolution in its legislation, values, and social relations. Third, socialist democracy can be achieved only through the continuous supervision by the people over the state apparatus.[26] M. Kerr discusses this 'radical' notion of democracy in terms of J. L. Talmon's totalitarian democracy. He observes that it is characterized by a moral preference "for maintaining the maximum degree of unity of purpose and action at all political and social levels; by an emphasis upon virtues of group solidarity and the evil of individual self-absorption and self-seeking, by mistrust of competition, bargaining, and the promotion of special interests; and by a vision of strong government as a liberator rather than a danger of liberty."[27]

The stress on the 'uniqueness' of the Egyptian political experiment continued. The Arab Socialist Union, it was repeatedly emphasized, was not a political party because it did not represent any one class; on the contrary, its very aim was to prevent class domination. And it was not a front because it did not include different political parties and organizations. What was it then? It was, we are told, the people's alliance aiming at the realization of national liberation and socioeconomic development.[28] A professor of law wrote that the Arab Socialist Union was a political authority transcending the three branches of government and representing the alliance of the working forces of the people.[29]

Nasser thought that issuing the Charter would solve the ideological problems of his regime. He was soon to discover his mistake; the Charter was interpreted differently by people of different ideological persuasions.[30] Indeed, the Charter is a loose ideological document in which the ideas of Lenin, Laski, and liberal democrats coexist in some sort of intellectual compromise. A Marxist commentator described Egyptian socialism as "a conglomeration of scientific and utopian socialism, petit bourgeois ideas, narrow nationalism, religious prejudices, and subjective idealism."[31]

The Crisis of Ideological Legitimation and its Consequences: The Reconsideration and Retreat Process

The political views of Nasser and his group were predicated on a deep belief in national unity. They had a nationalistic vision of a strong independent state. Social and class struggles were not welcomed since they tended to weaken, or at least threaten, national cohesion.[32] The rationale for the absence of political competitiveness was the need for unity. Similar to many Third World countries, the single party claimed to be a Gemeinschaft party, an integrative mass movement which consolidates social solidarity, moral unity, and popular consensus. The party emanated from the Volksgeist and represented le Volonté Général.

Behind the establishment of the three political organizations (the Liberation Rally, the National Union, and the Arab Socialist Union), there was a firm belief in populism, in the unity and oneness of the people. Unity becomes an all-consuming value, an almost religious obsession. The notion of unity, as understood by the regime, precluded organized opposition; the differences between various segments of society were seen as marginal and insignificant and the party was viewed as the living symbol of the unity of the nation.

This concept was based on the assumption that diversity generates disintegration and disunity. It categorically denied that diversity may indeed stimulate creative competition or that the diversity of modern society, as

Durkheim suggested, is a source of cohesion.[33] On the contrary, the vision of the ruling elite encouraged uniformity; unanimity not heterogeneity.

Instead of openly recognizing the conflicts resulting from the disagreements over the allocation of scarce resources, they stressed political organization as a means of creating solidarity and an expression of integration.[34] Karl Mannheim suggests that "conformity is desired, firstly, because it is simpler to govern people who are identically conditioned, and secondly, because those at the top are often narrow-minded and primitive in their outlook, being frequently the product of petite bourgeoisie, and primitivism is characterized by its intolerant treatment of deviation."[35]

The ruling elite's approach to economic development also shows its obsession with the notion of unity. For them, socialism was not so much a matter of ideological commitment as it was a pragmatic way of solving the problems of development. The aim of socialism was to minimize and avoid conflict as much as possible by means of rational planning.[36] Politics were approached primarily as an instrument of serving economic activity. The objective of political action was to increase production. Like economics, politics can—and must—be planned and administered. In both spheres it is denied that pluralism can produce any better state of affairs. Indeed, a planned economy and the single-party political system were perceived as two sides of the same coin. If socialism is the ideology of economic development, and the single party is the ideology of political development, then both constitute the strategy of national development.

In a sense, the Nasserite regime had a nonpolitical conception of politics. Politics were perceived as a vehicle for economic development. It rejected the definition of politics as the resolution of conflict. Herbert J. Spiro suggests that while the basic requisite for a community is consensus, the basic requisite for a political system is dissensus, and politics arise out of disagreement about public issues within the community. Thus, the existence of conflict among groups and classes should be genuinely recognized, though there must necessarily be a sphere of consensus within which political conflicts are carried out.[37]

The regime in Egypt rejected the ideas of diversity, pluralism, and conflict as elements of the political process. It resisted the notion of organized opposition and political competitiveness, and it suppressed political differences through the search for imagined homogeneity and uniformity.

This problem was accentuated by the essential eclectic, compromising, and pragmatic nature of the ruling elite's thinking.[38] Their ideas were derived from Arab nationalism, socialism, revolutionism, and reformist Islam, resulting in a system of ideas lacking internal coherence. In his late days, Nasser increasingly recognized the inability of this system to provide a legitimizing basis of his regime.

Nasser's death in 1970 marked the beginning of a new era in Egypt. Bit by bit, Sadat started to introduce a series of new ideas and policies which eventually led to a radical alteration of Nasser's Egypt. Changes affected both the political and economic fabric of society as well as its foreign policy. Indeed, Sadat sought to constitute his regime on new sources of legitimacy. The change was not abrupt and in fact had its genesis in the late days of Nasser.

Following the 1967 defeat, Nasser reshuffled the Arab Socialist Union in 1968 and made promises for democratization (the 30th of March Declaration) which actually achieved very little. After his death in 1970, and the subsequent Sadat–Sabri rift in May 1971, the regime started to reexamine its strategy. Greater skepticism was now called for concerning the assumptions underlying its patterns of political behavior.

The process of reexamination advanced slowly but steadily. When Engineer Sayed Marei was appointed First Secretary of the Arab Socialist Union in 1971, he issued a 'Guide for Political Action' which included steps for realizing a certain amount of political liberalization. Discussions ensued, arguments flared up, and eventually nothing practical was achieved. During this period, Sadat legitimized his rule on the basis of three slogans: rule by law, government by institutions, and political freedom.

In the post–1973 war period, with the official adoption of a policy of economic and political Infitah, Egypt witnessed a new political climate. Sadat himself led the criticism of the Arab Socialist Union by issuing a paper on the need to restructure it. A national debate took place, in which discussions were not confined to the political structure of the country, but ranged over all aspects of political and social life since 1952.[39] The result was a restructuring of Egypt's political system and economic policies; and Sadat legitimized his regime on new grounds. While Gamal Abd al-Nasser symbolized revolution, anticolonialism, social equity, and socialism, Anwar Sadat emphasized the symbols of love, peace, and faith. The regime's constituency also underwent a noticeable change. Nasser's constituency consisted primarily of the middle and lower-middle classes. Sadat's policies, on the other hand, appealed to the upper-middle class and those elements of the old bourgeoisie that resurfaced.[40]

On the whole, Sadat was much less interested in ideological legitimation than Nasser. The key concept in his thinking was *Infitah* ('opening' or Open-Door Policy). The basis of Egypt's new economic policy was laid out in November 1974 in the October Paper, which called for a vigorous program that would mobilize Egyptian domestic capital, and Arab and foreign resources. In a major speech on the occasion of his re-election as president in 1976, Sadat articulated the main features of his policy. Private initiative was to be encouraged, and individuals could earn freely as long as they paid due taxes.[41] The socialist ideas and policies of Nasser were strongly criticized as sacrificing individuals for the state.[42] They had led to inhuman and illegal practices such as torture, confiscation, and sequestration of property for political reasons.[43] Hence Nasserite socialism had failed completely.[44] Instead,

Sadat called his brand of ideology 'democratic socialism' and identified it with European social democratic experiences.

Democratic socialism is a vague system of ideas that was not taken seriously by the regime itself. In a basic document, attributed to Dr. Sufi Abu Talib, the former president of Cairo University and in 1980 the speaker of parliament, the key concept was balance: between society and individuals, between material and spiritual considerations, between public and private sectors, and between planning and individual initiative.[45]

Democratic socialism does not recognize nationalization or sequestration as legitimate policy options.[46] It emphasizes the importance of individual initiative, free enterprise, and foreign investment.[47] Its main instrument of social justice is progressive taxation. In a statement on 4 February 1975, Sadat emphasized the importance of taxes as an instrument to achieve three objectives: a) sharing public responsibility, b) imposing a ceiling on large incomes, and c) reducing luxury consumption. The real problem for this line of thinking is the inefficiency of Egypt's taxation system. It is hard on salaried people and lax on private activities. Hence it was doubtful that existing taxation policy could be used effectively as the main instrument of income distribution.

The Infitah is not merely an economic policy. It is rather an orientation, a guiding principle. It has implications in all spheres of society, such as government, administration, political organization, migration, employment, and foreign policy. In Egypt, economic liberalization has been accompanied by a corresponding process of political liberalization. How much divergence between economic and political liberalization will continue to exist in the future is yet to be seen.

There is enough evidence however, to show that the economic liberalization has already outpaced the political one. The new political environment enabled different political groups to express themselves and challenge the official ideology. For instance, the Infitah policy was criticized on many grounds. According to these critiques, first of all, the policy has tended to be consumer-oriented rather than product-oriented. Egyptian markets were filled with all kinds of goods that enhanced a consumerist spirit in society. Second, the policy created an environment conducive to bureaucratic corruption and parasitic activities. Some flagrant examples of corruption came to the public eye, such as those related to the Pyramids' plateau project and the Ameriyya project.[48] Third, the Open-Door Policy could have been very useful had Egypt defined its priorities and needs. Not only did a set of priorities not exist, but government agencies made little effort to develop one. For instance, in the debates on the Ameriyya textile project, ministers of planning and industry used different statistics to defend different positions, a clear example of elite fragmentation. Another instance can be shown in the contradictory views held by the ministers of economy and trade in 1975 on the controversial policy of own-import.[49] Finally, a number of critics discussed the impact of the Open-Door policy on the widening gap between the many poor and the few rich.

The most organized political opposition to the policy has come from the left, led by the National Progressive Unionist Party (NPUP). The party demands the protection of the Egyptian economy from foreign domination and insists on the importance of planning and the role of the public sector. It is highly critical of the Infitah policy and its consequences for the poor. According to the party, the policy leads to inflation, the concentration of wealth in only a few hands, excessive foreign influence, and the development of parasitic capitalism.

The real challenge to the regime, however, has come from a different source: Islam and militant Islamic groups. They have questioned the legitimacy of the regime and presented Islam as the ultimate source of legitimation in society. The genesis of this development can be traced back to the social consequences of the 1967 defeat. The defeat of that year was not merely a military one, for it represented a challenge to what Nasser symbolized for Arabs and Egyptians, i.e., the semi-secular revolutionary nationalist option. Nasser resorted to Islam to rationalize and explain the completely unexpected defeat. He referred to it in his speeches as Egypt's fate, God's will, and a destiny from which there could be no escape. The government encouraged religious activities as a diversionary technique. In December 1967, *al-Ahram* reported the longest march of Sufi orders ever organized in recent history. Christians had their share as well. The Virgin Mary allegedly continued to appear over Cairo for more than a week. People flocked to Cairo from all parts of the country, and the Arab Socialist Union had the responsibility of seating and maintaining order while people awaited the appearance of the Virgin Mary.

Islamic groups wasted no time, seized the opportunity to offer an Islamic interpretation for the defeat. Their message was simple: we were defeated because we are no longer good Muslims. It was imported Western ideologies, such as socialism, nationalism, and secularism, which defeated us, they argued. The only solution lay in a return to Islam. It would provide Egyptians with a cause to fight and die for and thereby cultivate a new sense of dignity and courage among them. Later, they compared the performance of Egyptian soldiers in the 1967 and 1973 Wars. Egyptians fought better in 1973 because, they argued, they were convinced that it was an Islamic War. It was fought in the month of Ramadan and its code name was Badr. A number of sheikhs volunteered the story that Allah sent his angels to fight on the side of the Muslims. Sadat also flirted with religion, and projected an image of himself as a good believer. In fact, he was introduced occasionally in public appearances as the 'believer–president'. In his pursuit of legitimacy after liquidating his opponents, in May 1971, Sadat manipulated religion for his own purposes. The government encouraged Islamic associations in the universities as a counterweight to Nasserite and Marxist ones.

In contrast to Nasser and Sadat, President Mubarak (1981–) is the pragmatist par excellence. He has paid far less attention to ideological legitimation. Unlike his predecessors, Mubarak did not issue ideological documents summarizing the objectives of his regime. His party platforms in the 1984, 1987, and 1990 elections addressed down-to-earth problems rather than delving into ideological and philosophical discussions. The decline of ideological legitimation under Mubarak can be attributed to three factors: first, Mubarak's personal dislike of abstract concepts; second, the failure of explicit ideological formations as evidenced by the developments in the Soviet Union and East Europe; and third, the reaction towards Nasser's and Sadat's ideological constructs and a growing sense of pragmatism in Egypt's political culture.

Retrospect and Self-Criticism

Some twenty years ago, in 1970, I wrote about the tendency towards polarization or fundamentalism in the Arab world. The thrust of my argument was that, in contrast to many European countries where the major issues of development were faced successively, in the Arab world they are posed simultaneously. Thus, Egypt, for instance, faces the problems of economic development, distributive justice, democratization, technological and social change at the same time. "Our hypothesis is, therefore, that what is probably to dominate Arab thought is a total view of the universe, a view which is both consistent and emotionally satisfying since it reduces all social ills to one cause and then proposes an overall remedy. It is a view based on a fundamental principle or concept which makes it easy to be understood by the masses. Finally, it reduces intellectual tensions and doubts since it has ready answers for almost every issue."[50]

In the 1970s and 1980s Islamic fundamentalism presented itself as an alternative source of legitimacy. The new wave of fundamentalist Islam signifies the failure of Egyptian intellectuals to formulate a functioning synthesis between Islam and modernism or to define the role of Islam in modern society. A continuous state of confusion surrounded this issue. This remark can be placed within the larger context of Egyptian development. A characteristic feature of this process has been the peculiar relation between the old and the new. New elements have not replaced or substituted old ones but coexist with them, thus creating a kind of complex and intricate dualism.

The 'old' does not wither away but rather tends to redefine and reproduce itself in the context of the 'new'. Also, to acquire legitimacy and credibility the 'new' tends sometimes to cast itself in the image of the 'old'. In the realm of thought, two societies continue to survive with their different intellectual universes and collective consciousness, each having its own educational systems, journals, masters, and symbols. The dualism can be explained by the pattern of development which took place in Egypt in the nineteenth century.

The two prominent modernizers of the last century. Muhammad Ali and Ismail, followed a strategy of establishing new structures and institutions without abolishing the old ones. Accordingly, modern legal codes and court systems were introduced alongside Sharia law. New schools were established alongside the old *kuttabs* and *madrasas.* This strategy might have been a practical solution to avoid the opposition of the *'ulama* but, in Daniel Crecelius' terms, "it led to a painful cultural bifurcation in all fields. Two societies, the one modernizing around imported institutions and concepts, the other clinging tenaciously, but often in bewilderment, to traditional values and habits were now locked in constant competition."[51]

The social, economic, and political changes in Egypt led to the emergence of three schools of thought. For some intellectuals, Islam was the key element of their thinking and they conceived of *al-nahda* (renaissance) in Islamic terms. They regarded Islam as important not only for individual salvation but also as a cohesive social force and the source of moral solidarity, which gave unity to the nation. Their goal was thus to strengthen religion and to prove its worth in the face of Western cultural encroachment.

Within the context of the Islamic school of thinking, there have been a number of trends. At one extreme we find those who are concerned with a passionate defense of Islamic traditions and orthodoxy. Others were more preoccupied with a reinterpretation of Islam in order to bring it more in harmony with modern ideas and realities. They tried to regenerate Islam by cleansing it of those corrupting and hindering alien accretions which had clung to it in the course of time.

A second major group of intellectuals reflected the transitional nature of the society. Janus-faced, they combined in their ideas both the traditions of Islamic Arab culture and the new concepts of Western culture. Islam was, so to speak, the national cultural heritage but it could not be accepted as the source of legislation and policy in society. The members of this group were aware of the crisis taking place within themselves, of the duality of their ideas and general outlook. They knew they belonged to two different worlds, the world of traditional Islam and the world of Western civilization. Unable to decide between the two, their contribution was primarily in the area of reconciliation between the new and the old, reason and faith, and finally, tradition and modernity.[52]

A third group representing yet another intellectual stream consisted of the bearers of the secular-rational trend. Their point of departure was Western culture and civilization. Its members believed in the scientific spirit and rational reasoning, and their aim was the establishment of a modern society, similar to those of Europe and North America, a society which retains tradition as long as it does not impede change and progress. This trend encompassed a multiplicity of views extending from laissez-faire liberalism to Marxism.[53] Clearly for this group, the purpose of the introduction of Western values and structures was not to perfect tradition, but to replace it.

Each of the three trends had its limitations. As mentioned earlier, Abduh's religious efforts were to end at the hands of Rashid Reda, who affirmed an orthodox social and political thought. On the other hand, the representatives of the rational-secular trend were basically non-Egyptians and Christians, which posed a limitation on their influence regarding the issue of Islam. Their ideas appeared abstract and foreign. Those who attempted to reconcile the two cultural traditions also failed to produce the much-needed synthesis.

These three schools and perspectives provide the intellectual context within which the issue of political legitimacy is debated or decided. The situation favored an eclectic middle-of-the-road view. Because of its pragmatic and reconciling stance it appeals to a wide stratum of society. Due to its hybrid nature, different groups find its interests and ideas represented in its formula.

Conclusions and Prognostications

Twenty years ago, I thought that this 'middle-of-the-road' was destined to bankruptcy, and that Arab thought would move towards polarization between holistic ideologies. History proved that my thinking was not entirely wrong (though not entirely correct, either). Indeed, fundamentalist Islamic groups represent that holistic ideology. What did *not* happen is the emergence of a nationalist holistic ideology or the downfall of 'middle-of-the-roadism'. The eclectic perspective proved its resiliency, perseverance, and ability to survive. The official ideology of Egypt today is a combination of political liberalism, Islam, social justice, nationalism, and free-market economy. The main slogans of the ruling party are development, stability, and peace. These are general objectives which can be achieved through various means.

The ruling elite in Egypt does not perceive the need for an ideological document or blueprint to legitimize its position. Rather, it employs a broad array of ideas and thoughts derived from diverse sources. Its political discourse is political and pragmatic rather than ideological and symbolic. The ideological challenge of Islamic and other groups is countered by a network of interests, coalitions, and bargaining processes. Thus, there is an asymmetry between the ways the ruling and competing elites seek legitimacy.

Notes

1 Karl Mannheim, *Ideology and Utopia* (London: Routledge and Kegan Paul Ltd., 1952), pp. 2–3; and W. C. Runciman, *Social Science and Political Theory* (London: Cambridge University Press, 1965), pp. 162–75.

2 For analysis of this period see my *Politics and Government in Egypt* (in Arabic) (Cairo: Dar al-Sharq, 1977), pp. 248–72.

3 Daniel Lerner, *The Passing of Traditional Society* (New York: The Free Press, 1964), pp. 87–88.

4 Ibid., pp. 218–19.

5 On this development from political–institutional perspective, see my paper and other contributions in Ali E. Hillal Dessouki, ed., *Democracy in Egypt: Problems and Prospects,* Cairo Papers in Social Sciences, vol. 1, monograph no. 2, (Cairo: The American University in Cairo Press, 1978)

6 P. J. Vatikiotis, *The Egyptian Army in Politics* (Bloomington: Indiana University Press, 1961), p. 83.

7 Keith Whealock, *Nasser's New Egypt* (New York: Frederick A. Praeger, 1960), p. 33.

8 Gamal Abdel Nasser, "The Egyptian Revolution," in *Foreign Affairs*, vol. XXXIII, no. 1, January 1965, p. 208.

9 Gamal Abdel Nasser, *Egypt's Liberation, The Philosophy of the Revolution*, translated by Dorothy Thompson (Washington, D.C., 1953), pp. 32–33; the same idea in Mohamed Naguib, *Egypt's Destiny* (New York: Doubleday, 1955), pp. 187–88

10 See the text in Mohamed Khalil, *The Arab States and the Arab League*, vol. I, (Beirut: Khayat, 1962), pp. 499–520; analysis can be found in M. Fathalla al Khatib, "Egypt's New Constitution. An Appraisal in the Light of Past Experiences," *Review of Economics, Political and Business Studies*, vol. IV, no. 3, pp. 21–24, published by the Faculty of Commerce, Cairo University, October 1956; and Don Peretz, "Democracy and the Revolution in Egypt,' *Middle East Journal*, vol. XIII, no. 1, pp. 26–40, winter 1959.

11 Nasser's speech, published in *al-Ahram,* 2 June 1956.

12 Nasser's interview with representatives of the Columbia Broadcasting System, published in *al-Ahram*, 8 June 1958.

13 Ibid.

14 Quoted in Ronald Segal, *Political Africa* (New York: Frederick A. Praeger, 1961), p. 468.

15 Simon Jargy, "La Syrie à la veille d'une nouvelle expérience," in *Orient*, no. 10 (1958), pp. 28–29.

16 Vatikiotis, p. 105.

17 Jean and Simone Lacouture, *Egypt in Transition* (New York: Criterion Books, 1959), p. 273.

18 On 15 December 1957, Nasser addressed the following words to the Third Congress of Arab Writers: "We need unanimity of thought in order to strengthen our solidarity." Quoted in G. E. von Grunebaum, *Modern Islam* (Berkeley: University of California Press, 1962), pp. 139–40.

19 Nasser's speech, published in *al-Ahram*, 14 November 1958.

20 Nasser expressed this idea in an early speech at Mansura on 19 July 1954, published in *al-Ahram*, 20 July 1954, by saying, "This is the government of the whole nation, the government of farmers and workers, of officials and students, of financiers and businessmen, of the rich and the poor, of the weak and the strong, and of the mere beginners and those who have

attained success. It is government that looks to all Egyptians as one big family and is working for the common good." Cited in Hassan Khedr and Amin Hassouna, *Egypt's Republic in its First Year*, published in English by the Department of Public Relations of the Egyptian Armed Forces, Cairo, 1957, p. 84.

21 Nasser's interview with the daily newspaper *al-Gumhuriya*, 30 May 1956.

22 See S. N. Eisenstadt, *Modernization Protest and Change* (Englewood Cliffs: Prentice Hall, Inc., 1966), pp. 34–35; *Encyclopedia of the Social Sciences under Agrarian Movement*, vol. I–II, pp. 289–315, and (under "Russian Revolution") vol. XIII–XIV, pp. 474–93; Peter Worsley, *The Third World* (London: Weidenfeld and Nicolson, 1964), pp. 127–28, 165–74; and Seymour M. Lipset, *Political Man* (New York: Doubleday, 1963, pp. 169–73. On populism in Middle Eastern countries see Manfred Halpren, *Politics of Social Change in the Middle East and North Africa* (Princeton: Princeton University Press, 1963), pp. 290–91. For populism in Turkey see Niyazi Berkes, *The Development of Secularism in Turkey* (Montreal: McGill University Press, 1964), pp. 461–63.

23 Nasser's speech, published in *al-Ahram*, 25 November 1961.

24 Quoted in Robin Buss, "Wary Partners. The Soviet Union and Arab Socialism," in *Adelphi Papers*, no. 73, p. 15, International Institute for Strategic Studies, London, 1970.

25 On this question see Fayez Sayegh, "The Theoretical Structure of Nasser's Socialism," in Sami Hanna and George Gardner, eds., *Arab Socialism* (Leiden: E. J. Brill, 1969), pp. 98–141.

26 See articles by Kamal Riffat, in *al-Iqtisadi* ('Economist'), 15 February 1963; Mohamed Anis, in *al-Ahram*, 18 December 1964; Ibrahim Abu Auf, in *al-Ahram*, 11 February 1965; and Adel Ghoneim in *Tali'a*, vol. 11, no. 10, October 1966, pp. 45–55. See also Nasser's 16 May 1965 speech in the National Assembly.

27 Kerr, *op. cit.*, pp. 10–11.

28 Mohamed al-Khafif, "Tahaluf quwwat al-sha'b" (The alliance of people's forces), paper written for the Higher Institute for Socialist Studies, which was the Arab Socialist Union Cadre School, memo, pp. 3–4.

29 Muhammed Hafez Ghanem, "al-Ittihad al-ishtiraki al-'arabi, dirasa muqarrana," *Egyptian Journal of Political Sciences*, no. 24, March 1963, p. 56.

30 See article by Ihsan Abdul Qudus on the unity of the intellectuals in *Ruz al-Yusif*, no. 1906, 21 December 1964.

31 *Peace, Freedom, and Socialism*, vol. V, no. 9, September 1964, p. 52.

32 Maxime Rodinson, "The Political System," in P. J. Vatikiotis, ed., *Egypt Since the Revolution* (London: George Allen and Unwin, 1968), p. 87.

33 Douglas E. Ashford, "The Challenge of Diversity to the Single Party States," paper delivered at the 1963 Meeting of the American Political Science Association, p. 22.

34 James Heaphy, "The Organisation of Egypt," *World Politics*, vol. XV, no. 3, January 1966, p. 187.

35 K. Mannheim, *Essays on Sociology and Social Psychology* (London: MacMillan, 1953, p. 257.

36 Isiah Berlin remarks that "it is populist ideas which lie at the base of the socialist economic policy pursued by the emergent countries today." Cited in Worsley, *The Third World*, p. 172.

37 Herbert J. Spiro, "The Primacy of Political Development," in Spiro, ed., *Africa: The Primacy of Politics* (New York: Random House, 1966), p. 158.

38 On eclecticism as an orientation among Arab thinkers, see Abdullah Laroui, *The Crisis of Arab Intellectuals* (Berkeley: University of California Press, 1976), pp. 153–55.

39 On these changes see John Waterbury, *Egypt: Burdens of the Past/Options for the Future* (Bloomington: Indiana University Press, 1978); Raymond William Baker, *Egypt's Uncertain Revolution Under Nasser and Sadat* (Cambridge: Harvard University Press, 1978), pp. 88–173; and Mark N. Cooper, *The Transformation of Egypt* (London: Croome Helm, 1982), pp. 35–125.

40 The major work outlining and analyzing the two regimes from a political economy perspective is John Waterbury, *The Egypt of Nasser and Sadat* (Princeton: Princeton University Press, 1983).

41 Sadat's speech, published in *al-Ahram*, 17 September 1976.

42 Sadat's speech, published in *al-Ahram*, 2 May 1977.

43 Sadat used the term 'centers of power' in reference to a number of senior associates of Nasser's with whom he had a power struggle in May 1971.

44 Sadat's speech, published in *al-Ahram*, 27 June 1977.

45 Sufi Abu Talib, *Democratic Socialism* (in Arabic) (Cairo, 1978).

46 Sadat's speech, published in *al-Ahram*, 20 January 1977.

47 Sadat's speech, published in *al-Ahram*, 2 March 1978.

48 *Ruz al-Yusif*, 18 December 1978 and 22 January 1979.

49 This system permits Egyptians to import goods by means of foreign exchange from their earnings abroad, without requiring license.

50 Ali E. Hillal Dessouki, "Arab Intellectuals and al-Nakba: The Search of Fundamentalism," *Middle Eastern Studies*, vol. IX, no.2, 1973, p. 193.

51 Daniel Crecelius, "The Course of Secularisation in Modern Egypt," unpublished paper, p. 18.

52 The major study on this group is that of I. I. Ibrahim, "The Egyptian Intellectuals between Tradition and Modernity: A Study in Some Important Trends in Egyptian Thought: 1922–1952," unpublished Ph.D. dissertation submitted to the University of Oxford, 1967.

53 Anouar Abdel Malek, *Anthologie de la littérature arabe contemporaine*, (Paris: Editions de Seuil,1965), pp. 15–17.

4

The Politics of State Interventionism in 'Populist' Egypt and Turkey

İlkay Sunar

In May of 1950, a new project was launched in Turkey: its aim was to establish and practice popular-democratic capitalism. In Egypt, July 1952 proved eventually to be the beginning of a new project as well: to found a populist-socialist order. Although both projects were hegemonic in intent, they never became so in reality. Egypt in 1973 and Turkey in 1980, each in its own fashion, officially inaugurated the politics of *Infitah* entailing a new discursive strategy, a new accumulation regime and a new set of state institutions. The purpose of this essay (and it is an *essai* in the French sense of the word) is to ask why these projects failed to reproduce themselves and to propose a framework for possible answers.

One possible paradigmatic answer, which I shall pose only to reject and exploit for my own strategic purposes, is crudely Hegelian: in the case of both Egypt and Turkey, this thesis would go, we are not really confronted with cases of reversals or failures but cases of *aufhaben*. Populism failed in both countries because it succeeded. In other words, populism in Egypt and Turkey (in its country-specific variants) performed its historical mission and completed its transitional functions only to be superseded by higher forms of hegemony. This super-functional answer, I submit, will not do. It will not do because it presumes that populism was a phase in the realization of a historical telos destined toward the Infitah. More crucially, it will not do because it ignores the very substratum of historical process: human conflict. Are conflicts among actors superfluous to historical outcomes? The persistent difficulty of the super-functionalist perspective (and its many variants) is to account for the reasons why conflicts among specific actors under specific historical circumstances would regularly result in 'history', or 'the system', in performing its function regardless of human interventions and conflicts. And, if political actors are not the passive victims of 'history' or 'the system', then we need to incorporate these actors and their conflicts into our explanatory account of outcomes.

The State as the Object of Political Conflicts

Conflicts occur not in a vacuum but under specific conditions. Historical changes occur (or fail to occur) as outcomes of political struggles that are rooted in the structure of preestablished state practices. More specifically, the impasse of popular-democratic capitalism in Turkey was the effects of political struggles that failed to negotiate a coherent popular-democratic state out of the old, preestablished bureaucratic-authoritarian one.[1] In the case of Egypt, populist struggles failed to extract a unified developmental state out of the old oligarchic one.[2] Before I proceed further, however, I should explain why I see state structures and practices as the key variables in my explanatory account of Egyptian and Turkish populism.

All populist projects, of whatever variety, entail the intervention of the state for their consolidation.[3] The distributive policies on which the formation of populist coalitions and constituencies depend require an interventionist state. But not all interventions have the same size, shape, and direction. Populism in Turkey was a postbureaucratic phenomenon; in Egypt, it was postoligarchic. Hence, while the discursive intervention, the coalitional basis and strategy of Turkish populism, and its economic objectives, were defined in juxtaposition to an etatist, bureaucratic power bloc, in Egypt such populism took a different course since it confronted not a bureaucratic bloc but an oligarchic one made up of (domestic and foreign) commercial urban and landed rural classes.

Populism is ultimately a strategy for acquiring and retaining power. The ideological, organizational, and the human bases of populist struggles are all defined in reference to the characteristics of the preestablished dominant power coalition. This dominant power in Turkey was bureaucratic, etatist, and secularist, and the basis of its power was the monopoly control it exercised over the means of civil and military administration. The popular classes, in turn, were the urban and rural producers: the workers, the urban and rural petit-bourgeois groups, and the commercial-industrial bourgeoisie—all shared being on the other side of the power tracks. The Democratic Party (DP) appealed to these groups and mobilized them against the bureaucratic alliance.

Power divided prepopulist Egyptian society differently: on the one side were the oligarchic commercial and landowning groups, and on the other were the urban and rural petite bourgeoisie and labor. Although the Egyptian 'landed-bourgeoisie'[4] had made some headway toward national autonomy, the military, as the 'native sons' of Egyptian society (and its 'new middle class') appealed to the 'national' classes as 'the people', acted as their vanguard and mobilized them against the 'landed-bourgeoisie', the monarchy and the British. (See the essay by Dessouki in this volume.)

Thus, while the Turkish populists mobilized the economic power of producer groups against the bureaucratic state, the Egyptian revolutionaries mobilized the power of the state against the economic power of the upper classes. This is also why the ideological discourse of the Turkish populists was consistently antibureaucratic, antietatist, liberal, and capitalist, while the Egyptian discourse was initially antioligarchic and antiliberal, and eventually anticapitalist, etatist, and socialist.

The Turkish populists were bent on shaping state interventionism for the enhancement of private capitalization. The Egyptians, on the other hand, tried to forge a bureaucratic state that would enlarge etatist nationalization. State interventionism in Turkey was caught in the contradictory logic of the populist project: compelled to enhance private capitalization and populist distribution simultaneously, the Turkish populists had to intervene once and then intervene again, once to enhance private market production, and a second time to counteract the effects of market distribution that would have divided their basis of popular support. The whole project required a social compromise: the popular sectors would be induced to concede to private production if the capitalists would agree to public distribution. It was left to the state to coordinate the terms of this compromise.

For the Egyptians, the problem was posed differently: the revolutionaries had to intervene once to dispossess upper classes of their economic power, and they had to intervene again to forge a strong state that could appropriate for itself both the accumulation and distribution functions. The Egyptian project was premised on forging a popular-socialist coalition for a strong state in control of economic resources. The 'noncapitalist' state would deliver both dynamic growth and equitable distribution.

Clearly, then, while the Egyptian project required a strong state that would control the 'commanding heights' of both sides of the economy (i.e. production and distribution), the Turkish project relied on a state that could induce class compromise on private production and public distribution. A penetrative, regulative state was a must for the production and reproduction of popular-socialism in Egypt; an engaged, coordinative state was required for Turkish populism. It is no wonder then that scholars studying Egypt have been obsessed with the autonomy and the power of the Nasserite state and those studying Turkey with the development of civil society and an appropriately supportive state.

State–Society Relations as the Object of Analysis

What I have proposed so far also implies that economic failures and crises require political and social explanations. The recent debates on the Egyptian case have been conducted within terms that are attentive to this issue of political and social underpinnings of economic development and decay.

John Waterbury, for instance, has argued that the Nasserite state was too 'soft' to undertake the socialist reconstruction of Egyptian society.[5] In other words, it was not that social classes asked or resisted too much, it was the state that asked too little. Beset by a savings crisis and the inefficiency of the public sector, Nasser was compelled to choose between capitalism and fundamentalist socialism, and he chose capitalism because it was the easy way out. For Waterbury, Sadat's Infitah, however, suffered from the same ailment that afflicted Nasser's populism: namely, the Infitah state was also too 'soft' to undertake a capitalist reconstruction of Egyptian economy.

Concealed within the idiom of a political economy approach, Waterbury is really giving us a cultural explanation: it is the lack of puritan will that condemns Egypt to failure. Neither international nor domestic constraints are insurmountable; what Egypt lacks is puritanism either of the left or the right variety. If you are deprived of a puritan society, then, you must at least have a puritan state.

Other scholars, however, have argued for the class constraint theory of failure but have nominated different classes as the main suspect. Leonard Binder, for instance, has nominated the rural middle class, while Hamied Ansari has argued for the traditional landed classes.[6] Did state incompetence or class constraints obstruct Egyptian socialism? And, which among the classes was the primary culprit: the rural middle class, the traditional landed interests, or the excessive demands of the popular sectors?

If these scholars have not given us definitive answers, at least they have looked in the right places. In the Turkish case, we have yet to raise similar questions about the populist Second Turkish Republic and its trials, tribulations, and demise. The scholarship on Turkey has yet to establish a framework in which political actors and their struggles, constraints, and opportunities matter in the shaping of outcomes. What we have so far are attempts that are either purely descriptive or mechanically theoretical. Classes, states, their conflicts and compromises—in short, what we have called societal and state actors, their discursive and political strategies, and their organizational characteristics—continue to be conspicuous in their absence. And, if societal actors appear at all, they appear as automatons that act out their structurally determined fate with no capacity to exercise effects upon historical outcomes. Or, interestingly enough, they appear in these structuralist accounts in purely descriptive fashion. I suspect that when actors are not theoretically appropriated, they are empirically and superfluously tacked onto a structuralist frame that otherwise has no space for them.[7]

The incorporation of the Turkish case into the terms in which the Egyptian debate has been conducted would not only lay the basis for a productive comparison, but it would also help us tackle the case of Turkish populism.

To restate, in these terms, what I have proposed so far: the constraints on Turkish populism did not stem from the structural characteristics of an import-substituting peripheral capitalism, as some Turkish scholars have argued. Peripheral import-substituting industrialization (ISI) was not intrinsically incompatible with democratic-capitalist development. Rather, the proximate constraints exercised on Turkish political economy stemmed from the structural characteristics of the populist state. The fate of popular-democratic capitalism was sealed by the development of an irresolute state that had neither the coherence nor the capacity to elicit the class coordination and compromise necessary for its reproduction.

By the same token, the demise of popular noncapitalism in Egypt was due neither to public-sector inefficiency, nor to peripheral dependence or regional embroilments, but to the absence of institutionalized links between state and society. In the absence of these organized intermediaries, loyalty to the state was procured through economic distribution handed out by the state. Since societal actors were deprived of effective political and functional representative organizations, they exercised a variety of strategies to influence the state. They used their 'voice' option by clientelist penetration of the bureaucracy; their 'exit' option was to disengage from the state and to constitute an 'informal' economy and society. And, if all failed, they 'boycotted' the state through such diffuse actions as riots, mass demonstrations, rallies, etc.

In Turkey, the shifts in the relative power of contending forces were related to electoral alignments and military interventions. Elections and military interventions brought to power new political coalitions with new designs on the state. In Egypt, state politics was primarily intra-bureaucratic: the shifts in the relative power of class-laden bureaucratic factions were related to the power calculations of the Egyptian inner ruling circles and Nasser.

What was needed in Turkey as well as in Egypt, but was lacking in both, was the organized and cooperative engagement of state and societal actors. When such a state could not be built, protracted struggles became the source of enfeeblement for both state and society. When the state in both countries failed to become the site of an organized system of policy concertation and mutual accommodation, it became instead the center of conflicts that kept it suspended in a state of irresolution.

The Origins and the Impact of Political Conflicts: A Sequential Analysis

I have tried to elaborate the nature of political struggles that centered on the reorganization of state and society in Turkey and Egypt. I also mentioned, at the beginning, that the impact of these struggles was mediated by the conditions that existed when they emerged. It is important to relate the struggles to the attendant conditions of their birth, and illuminate the way in which past conditions were linked to subsequent outcomes.

In an insightful article, Martin Shefter has suggested that the way in which the first popular mobilization takes place in a country is a 'critical experience' with 'character-forming' consequences.[8] He further suggests that such an experience is shaped by the sequence of bureaucratization and popular participation. If a strong constituency for bureaucratic autonomy has formed before popular mobilization is undertaken, the outcome is programmatic parties that appeal to interests and dispense benefits on universalist, collective bases. Otherwise, in the absence of a strong, autonomous state bureaucracy, popular parties turn out to be coalitions for patronage, appropriating state resources for clientelist purposes.

Shefter's article is interesting not only because it is excellent reading on why political parties turned out be programmatic in Germany and Britain, and clientelist in Italy, but also because the cases of France and the United States do not conform to his predictions. The type of state that preceded political participation in France defies Shefter's thesis, because in France the prior formation of a strong, autonomous bureaucratic state was followed by the popular challenge of patronage politicians and parties. In the United States, it was the reverse: after the prior formation of party-machine politics, a successful progressive coalition became the basis for bureaucratic autonomy.

The French case is particularly relevant to and illuminating of the Turkish experience. Just as in France, the prior existence of a constituency for bureaucratic autonomy in Turkey did not engender universalist, programmatic parties, but rather a protracted struggle for the control of the state between the constituency for bureaucratic autonomy and a constituency for clientelist populism. Shefter claims that the 'expected' outcome was reversed in France at the cost of a profound crisis of the state, since the transition from universalist politics to popular clientelism required a "total reorientation of the nation's politics—perhaps even a revolution—to succeed." The key to the crisis of the Turkish state during the populist Second Republic lies, I believe, in these lines.

In Shefter's terms, the case of Egypt entailed a different sequence but a similar problem. Following the modernizing reforms of Muhammad Ali's absolutist alliance, Egypt had fallen into the hands of an oligarchic coalition. The upper commercial/landed upper classes, the monarchy, and the British were the pillars of this alliance, whose inner coherence as well as external support were contingent upon the dispensation of patronage for loyalty. Hence, in Egypt as well, when the Free Officers attempted to reverse the expected, again a 'total reorientation' or 'revolution' was required.

Shefter contends that in the European experience, there have been two types of constituencies for state autonomy: 'absolutist coalitions' and 'progressive coalitions'. The former were led by modernizing monarchs who sought to create modern, centralized states "to replace the decentralized, patrimonial *standestaat* of the earlier era." In progressive coalitions, on the other hand, the leading role was played by a 'rationalizing bourgeoisie'. Shefter's points are well taken, but the two types of coalitions for state autonomy that he proposes do not exhaust other possible types of such coalitionary alliances. In Turkey, for instance, the absolutist coalition led by modernizing monarchs initiated at the beginning of the nineteenth century evolved eventually into an 'etatist coalition' led by the modernizing civilian–military bureaucracy. This coalition included the whole range of the state-affiliated salaried 'new middle class': the military and the civilian administration proper, the university, the secondary-school teachers, the judiciary, the state-employed intelligentsia and artists—all were a part of this etatist coalition for bureaucratic autonomy.

In the case of Egypt, neither an absolutist nor a progressive coalition immediately preceded the onset of Nasserism. As I have noted above, the prior formation of an absolutist coalition by Muhammad Ali was followed by the formation of an oligarchic alliance among the British, the monarchy, and the Egyptian landed bourgeoisie before an etatist constituency led by the military began to develop in the early twentieth century. The coalition for state autonomy in Egypt was led by the state-affiliated, salaried middle class that mobilized the market-engaged rural and urban petite bourgeoisie and the rural and urban working classes. These 'national-popular' classes constituted the core of the coalition for state autonomy forged against the 'non-national' classes. Both the Kemalist and Nasserite revolutions were supported by these etatist coalitions. While the Kemalists made no attempt to enlarge this coalition through incorporation of the popular sectors, the Nasserist elite, after an initial period of indecisiveness and vacillation, tried by half-measures to do so: while Nasser incorporated them economically through redistributive policies, he excluded them politically by eschewing organizational engagement with the popular classes. The outcome was 'populism without participation'. The early republican elite in Turkey used the rhetoric of populism but did not incorporate the masses either economically or politically. The outcome was 'populism without incorporation.'

In the light of these conceptual revisions, let me restate my case: political conflicts over the nature of the state in Turkey were primarily between supporters of bureaucratic autonomy (of one kind or another) and the coalition for patronage. The crisis of the Second Republic stemmed from the fragmentation of Turkish politics into constituencies for patronage and etatist rule, and eventually from the decomposition of both constituencies into subgroups propelled by distributive and ideological conflict. In Egypt, the state became the victim of its conception of autonomy. Autonomy was conceived by the Nasserist elite as the distribution of economic resources for political acquiescence without the mediation of organized, civil society. The outcome, in the absence of organized access to the state, was the emergence of particularist strategies of influence that fragmented the state into bureaucratic factions, clientelist networks, and personalist cliques. Nasser, as the occasion warranted, sided with one or the other, played them against each other, or condemned them as 'power centers' and viewed them with suspicion and distance.

The Case of Turkey

Let me be more specific about the Turkish case. The patronage coalition that coalesced around the Democratic Party (DP) was shaped by the sequence and timing of historical change in Turkey.[9] Before democratization, Turkey underwent bureaucratization but did it in the absence of substantial industrialization. When, therefore, the DP burst forth upon the stage of Turkish politics, it confronted a yawning gap between state and society. There was, on the one hand, a ruling, modernist bureaucratic alliance, and on the other, a nonindustrial society steeped in tradition. The prior formation of an etatist alliance compelled the DP toward program and universalism, but the logic of a traditional, state-disassociated, and a class-underdetermined society pulled it toward particularism and patronage. Under these circumstances, the trick was to fabricate electoral majorities without offending the state-affiliated, bureaucratic minorities. The dilemma was to incorporate the 'people' without re-traditionalizing the state, and to uphold modernization without getting isolated from the people. Ultimately, the strategy which the DP adopted was to underplay cultural modernization, emphasize economic development, and hitch the hitherto disengaged (and frustrated) energies of social groups to the party through patronage. The cultural strategy of appeasement, the political strategy of state intervention through patronage, and the developmentalist strategy of state-assisted capitalism all became the bases of a sharp confrontation between etatist and patronage coalitions, and paved the way for the military intervention in 1960.

The military attempted to replace the electoral alignment of popular-clientelist groups forged in 1950 with an urban, productivist coalition forged among opponents and dissidents of patronage. The social bases of this new alliance would be composed of managerial bureaucrats, big business, and organized labor. Planning instead of patronage, social democracy instead of populism, and an urban, suave universalism instead of rural parochialism would constitute the platform of this new governing coalition. Its economic strategy would be a planned, import-substituting industrialization married to Keynesian demand management, and structural (industrial) and income policies.

The critical electoral realignment required to support this envisaged governing coalition never took place. A bourgeois–labor alliance, backed by the military but without the support of the vast majority of the urban and rural petty producers (accustomed to clientelist supports under the DP regime), did not have much of a chance of survival in any case. And, when the coalition partners failed to engage in the necessary cooperation and compromise required for policy concertation, the antipatronage front collapsed after a brief and uneasy existence under various coalitionary governments between 1961–65. In 1965, with the accession to power of the Justice Party (AP), the old multiclass alliance among business, market-based urban and rural lower-middle classes, and labor coalesced once again into a populist constituency for state patronage.

When a new, progressive, and productivist alliance failed to materialize, the initial outcome was the re-formation of the patronage front and the decomposition of the old etatist alliance. Without belaboring the point, we should note that the struggles unleashed within the etatist coalition were basically defined by the institutional position of each group. As the most coherent, professional, and strategic actor, the military was powerful enough to defend its corporate interests under changing conditions. This was not true, however, of the other partners of the etatist coalition: the civilian administration was subject to erosion of its political power, income, and social status, and was the object of clientelist penetration by party partisans. The Republican Peoples' Party (CHP), as the party of the etatist bureaucracy, would be condemned to permanent minority status under democratic conditions if it lacked the courage and the capacity to undergo electoralizing changes. The old partners were compelled to go their different ways under the challenge of the populist-clientelist coalition; they went in directions defined by their institutional position and functions.

The military, after purging the radicals amongst its ranks, was able to consolidate the power of the moderates who reserved their veto power but were not averse to coexisting with a popular-democratic-capitalist-patronage state. The state-affiliated intelligentsia was radicalized and splintered into various factions. It sought constituencies and spread radical political culture among students, workers, and the urban marginals. A faction of the intelligentsia even attempted to forge a Nasserite, Baathist type of coalition among the nationalist-radical wings of the civilian and military bureaucracies. The third pillar of the old etatist front, the CHP, after being suspended in a state of confusion and intra-party struggles, moved toward a kind of left-radical populism.

If the decomposition of the etatist bloc was provoked by the challenge of patronage politics, the effects of bureaucratic fragmentation and radicalization were to split the patronage alliance. The two most radical wings of the bureaucratic alliance gave up on electoral politics. I have already mentioned the military–civilian wing of Nasserites and Baathist nationalists; they were purged once after the 1960 military takeover and once again after the 1971 intervention by the moderate wing of the military officers. When the advocates of 'revolution from above' were greatly weakened after the 1960 intervention, the strategy of 'revolution from below,' bent on capturing civil society, gained influence. The major object of radicalization was the labor movement, whose market power grew in leaps and bounds, but without a commensurate increase in its political power, for the other effect of radicalization on labor was to divide it into ideological factions.

When the new CHP, with its new left-populist leadership and policies, began to make advances toward labor, the union movement had already been divided into clientelist and socialist camps. As the arrival of the new CHP to fill the vacuum on the center-left divided the partisan left, this division was soon reproduced within the labor unions, thus further fragmenting labor. Add to this the later penetration of the labor movement by the fundamentalist nationalist and Islamicist parties, and what emerges is an escalating struggle for higher wages fueled by an intense competetion for membership and ideological hegemony.

The growing radicalization and market power of the union movement had critical consequences for Turkish politics in the 1960s and 1970s. The radicalization of the labor union movement not only split labor ideologically, it also had divisive effects upon the multiclass clientelist-populist coalition as well. The patronage coalition fragmented in the face of growing distributive conflicts that were engendered by the growing market power of the labor unions. The union movement was strong enough to strain the clientelist coalition to the breaking point, but too divided to service a populist-social democratic realignment. The outcome was a political deadlock: populist options of either the clientelist or the social democratic variety were constrained by the existing (and fragmented) balance of forces.

The viability of the patronage coalition in Turkey was premised on the political support of the petite bourgeoisie and the economic performance of the industrial bourgeoisie. Whereas the protection of the urban and rural petite bourgeoisie was necessary for electoral success, the protection of the industrial bourgeoisie was necessary for economic growth. The reconciliation of these two necessities rested on a political compromise: the petite bourgeoisie would consent to state capitalization of the corporate-industrial sector so long as the state would also subsidize small business and the smallholding peasantry. The political necessity of protecting an increasingly unproductive petite bourgeoisie was costly but possible, so long as the working class was weak and did not threaten the state-mediated distribution of available resources. But as the labor union movement began to acquire growing organizational and market power, its demands for wage increases (which surpassed productivity growth) began to strain the patronage coalition. Resources had to be distributed away from either the big or the small bourgeoisie. Thus the clientelist Justice Party was caught in the conflicting policy requirements of its policy base: economic growth was increasingly contingent on state encouragement of corporate–industrial investment, but electoral power required the protection of the inefficient petit-bourgeois sectors.

In the absence of adequate resources and growth, the upshot of these developments was, on the one hand, the radicalization of the urban petite bourgeoisie as it abandoned the patronage coalition for nationalist and religious fundamentalist movements, and, on the other hand, the disenchantment of industrial–corporate capital with the Justice Party as it began to search for other political options. As for the Justice Party, in a last-ditch effort to hold on to power, it resorted not only to governmental coalitions with fundamentalist nationalist and religious parties, but also to short-term foreign borrowings. The outcome, however, was not social peace but severe exchange shortages, fiscal crisis, spiraling inflation, and escalating political turmoil.

To overcome the impasse, a more fundamental solution was needed: in the face of the disintegrating clientelist alliance, a coalitionary realignment was necessary. This was the populist-social democratic option. This option required important sacrifices from the working class and a new social contract from corporate capital. The fundamentalist radicalization of the urban petite bourgeoisie could be prevented if the working class would agree to an incomes policy that would serve as the basis of a new compromise among social classes. The social democratic realignment, in other words, hinged on the internal structure of the classes in general, and labor in particular. Neither the internal structure of social classes nor that of the state, however, was coherent enough to forge a new consensus that required mutual concessions. The labor movement was ideologically fragmented and would not support the social pact proposed by the CHP. Corporate capital was too wary of radical labor to seek accommodation with it. The small peasantry and urban small businesses were too disorganized to discipline their constituencies and too powerful electorally to be dropped by political parties.

The major point here is that the limits of the populist state to manage popular-democratic capitalism stemmed from the limits of its own internal structure and that of social classes. Both the state and social classes were too fragmented, inchoate, and divided to commit themselves to and uphold compromises necessary for the survival of the populist Second Republic. Compromises were possible, and the outcome was not predetermined.

What I have tried to show so far is that the populist challenge in Turkey, launched in the aftermath of World War II, instead of leading to a virtuous cycle of compromises and cooperation led to a vicious cycle of state and societal fragmentation. The challenge of the populist right led to the fragmentation of the etatist coalition which, in turn, led to the fragmentation of the labor movement. The fragmentation of labor begat the fragmentation of the patronage coalition, and the incapacity of fragmented classes to forge a new compromise led to an intense scramble for the further parcellization of state power, and so on.

The options to build a popular-democratic state in Turkey were blocked not simply by the balance of forces, but more fundamentally by the organizational incapacity of the state and social classes to manage the diverse interests of their constituencies and to engage in mutual cooperation and compromise. The outcome was the formation of a coup coalition that opted for the 'neo-conservative' project. The aim was to reduce the state economically and to strengthen it politically. The populist state was to be exchanged for a small but strong neo-utilitarian one.

The neo-conservative/liberal project, however, did not follow the expected orthodox path in Turkey. Particularly after the military interlude and the redemocratization of politics, the neo-conservative leadership was caught between the orthodox demands of its international constituency and the distributive demands of its domestic allies. As I have suggested elsewhere, the results were pragmatic stop-and-go politics of accumulation and distribution, and vacillation between clientelist particularism and market universalism, that have satisfied neither the international support community nor the domestic constituency of the neo-conservative Motherland Party.[10]

The Case of Egypt

In the Egyptian case, neither a progressive nor an absolutist coalition for state autonomy existed when the Free Officers took power in 1952. The formation of an absolutist coalition under Muhammad Ali in the nineteenth century was followed by the emergence of an oligarchic-clientelist coalition that presided over an economy that was neither 'nationally controlled' nor of an 'enclave' type.[11] During the interwar period in particular, Egypt was ruled by an uneasy alliance of the monarchy, the landed bourgeoisie, and the British. The inter-elite relations within this oligarchic alliance were marked neither by severe conflicts nor by a stable peace. Among the ruling trio, the landed bourgeoisie was the most 'progressive' and nationally oriented. It was also the major actor and architect of the Egyptian Liberal Age. In politics, it was the leading force in the establishment of a parliamentary party system; in economics, it led the banner for national economic development and industrialization. In ideology, it was liberal and secular. Despite these progressive characteristics, however, the Egyptian landed bourgeoisie was never able to forge a stable progressive coalition for national and state autonomy. It was more willing to compromise with the British and the monarchy than to mobilize a middle- and lower-class constituency. This is why despite the progress toward the formation of a national state and economy, during the entire interwar period Egypt remained at best a semi-independent country.

In the absence of a modernizing absolutist coalition and a rationalizing bourgeoisie, the ruling oligarchic alliance held together and elicited support through transformist politics based on patronage. When the economy failed to expand at the pace necessary for clientelist inclusion of middle and popular sectors, the discontended groups became available for antipatronage politics. And, when the crisis of transformism and liberal discourse was compounded by a national crisis with the 1948 defeat, the outcome was the demise of the oligarchic rule at the hands of the Egyptian military.

Antipatronage, antioligarchic politics in Egypt, during the interwar period, found widespread support among two major groups: the traditional middle and lower classes mobilized by Islamic fundamentalist leadership, and a state-affiliated new middle class whose vanguard was the military. The ideological discourse of both groups was anti-oligarchic, anti-imperialist, and populist. The state-affiliated middle class, however, was secular–nationalist, in constrast to the religious–nationalist orientation of the fundamentalists.

This background helps us to understand better the postoligarchic politics that followed the military takeover in 1952. In particular, it helps us to understand better the evolution of the strategies of coalition formation under the new leadership. The interwar period was marked by the advance of the so-called Liberal Age (1922–52) in Egypt. Ultimately, the Liberal Age failed: it failed to forge a lasting coalition for national and state autonomy, it failed to consolidate a parliamentary party regime, and it failed to sustain a process of economic development. There were, however, notable advances in all of these fronts: even if partial, national independence was achieved; even if unstable, a parliamentary party regime was established; and even if weakly and intermittently incorporated, the middle and popular sectors were mobilized for national autonomy. Furthermore, again although uneven and dependent, a national industrialization effort was initiated. All of these efforts were led predominantly by the landed bourgeoisie of Egypt during the Liberal Age.

When the Free Officers took power in 1952, what they confronted, therefore, was not a typical enclave society dominated by foreign capital and its collaborators in its capitalist enclave, and by a landowning oligarchy in its feudal backwater. Nor, of course, was Egypt during this period a society that was altogether dominated by a capitalist economy and national bourgeoisie. This is why when the Free Officers took power, they did not immediately pursue a strategy of coalition formation that was anticapitalist and pro-socialist as was the case with radical movements in the enclave societies of Latin America. In fact, during 1952–56, the project of the Revolution Command Council (RCC) can, at best, be characterized as the pursuit of 'national capitalism' under the auspices of an authoritarian regime. Its main thrust was antifeudal, aiming to eliminate large landowners, encourage the formation of an industrial bourgeoisie, and to gain the suppport of the middle peasantry. Hence, what the RCC and Nasser initially envisaged was the formation of a bourgeois–petit-bourgeois alliance for national and state autonomy.

Let it suffice to say that the formation of such a partnership failed to materialize, partly because the commercial and industrial bourgeoisie was largely one and the same class as the landowners. Threatened and undermined by the redistribution of their land, the landed bourgeoisie was not willing to invest. But, the partnership failed also because of international complications that propelled the RCC leadership toward Third Worldism and alliance with the Soviet bloc.

By the end of the 1950s, the Nasserist project shifted from national capitalism toward national populist-socialism. The new populist strategy of coalition formation was based on the 'alliance of the national working classes,' meaning the elimination of the bourgeoisie and the formation of a coalition between the (rural and urban) petite bourgeoisie and the workers as a base of social support for the regime.

Populist-socialism for Nasser and his colleagues turned out to be as much a strategy for state autonomy as it was a strategy of coalitionary support. The RCC leadership wished to win the loyalty of the masses without engaging them politically. The Liberation Rally and the National Union were more efforts to preempt the organizational space that others might occupy than genuine efforts of organizationally linking the popular sectors to the state. The Arab Socialist Union (ASU), on the other hand, did seek to structure state-society relations through a corporatist design. Its failure stemmed from the same fears which had led Nasserist leadership to eschew organizational engagement in the first place: the ASU was suspected of undermining the autonomy of the state by becoming the site for conflicting 'power centers' that would penetrate the state and Balkanize it.

The Nasserist dilemma was how to forge a support coalition without getting organizationally entangled with the popular sectors. The solution was to form a coalition that would mobilize the popular sectors ideologically and include them economically, but exclude them politically. The strategy, in other words, was to uphold state autonomy by keeping the masses unorganized. As John Waterbury has put it, "The Nasserist state enhanced its autonomy only by denying itself organized support."[12] Waterbury's point is that in the absence of organizational linkages with societal actors and classes, the Nasserist state was able to accumulate boundless autonomy for itself. There is, however, another side to autonomy that is won at the expense of organizational support. The state becomes hooked on distributive politics and deprives itself of much of its capacity to manage and reconcile the competing claims of distribution and economic development. This is precisely what happened in populist Egypt.

The populist state was the distributive state par excellence; its strategy was to couple distributive incorporation with political exclusion. Thus, a politically insulated state became dependent on its capacity for distributive delivery. In the absence of commensurate economic development, autonomy based on distributive delivery becomes precariously balanced between foreign aid and borrowing (and dependency) and the constraining of domestic distributive demands. But, in the absence of the constraints that can be exercised through organizational disacipline, both state and societal actors become 'hyper-politicized' and governed by the logic of survival. Societal actors, organizationally underdeveloped and excluded, seek other more informal and personal means of meeting their needs and demands: the result is the formation of clientelist networks that penetrate the very heart of the state, bureaucratic corruption, and the emergence of a parallel, informal economy, as well as demonstrations, boycotts, etc. The last resort of the state leadership is also to the repertoire of survival: co-opt to procure loyalty, shuffle and divide to weaken opponents, and use 'dirty tricks' if necessary. This was the scenario played out by state and societal actors in Egypt. Its performance deprived the state of much of its coherence and regulative capacity, and proved ultimately to be too costly to carry out.

The difficulties of the Nasserist-populist state, I have suggested, were inherent in its conception of autonomy. Autonomy that is not sustained by the support of organized constituencies in civil society makes the state almost entirely dependent on its unity and distributive capacity. The distributive emphasis not only reduces incentives to develop a coherent and stable state administration, but also makes the organizationally underdeveloped state the sole target of societal demands. Since the state in Egypt was omnipresent (but hardly omnipotent), the competition for state favors was intense both inside outside the state administration. Thus, omnipresence in the absence of organizationally mediated state-society relations led, on the one hand, to a society that sought particularist means of access to state-controlled resources, and on the other, to an overloaded bureaucratic apparatus that was shot through with divisions, incoherent policies, and patrimonial practices.

By 1967, the capacity of the populist state to manage a 'noncapitalist' economy had reached its outer limits. To overcome the impasse required what populist Egypt lacked: an organizational revolution. There were three options: the first was to set state-society relations in a corporatist frame of mutual cooperation and forge a productivist coalition in support of it. The second alternative was to mobilize for socialist transformation and create an omnipotent state apparatus to bring it about. And the third was to opt for the neo-utilitarian state of the neo-conservative variety. The Egyptian Infitah, I believe, showed that there was in fact a fourth alternative: what emerged in Egypt in the 1970s was neither a neo-utilitarian nor a socialist or corporatist state, but a pragmatic state with a pragmatic constituency that pursued opportunities wherever it found them, made the necessary international, political, and economic adjustments without ever facing the radical reorganization the three options required. But then, the (at best) mixed record of the Egyptian Infitah raises the question of whether the pragmatic option has proved to be more of a problem than a solution.

Concluding Remarks

The consensus that formed after World War II on the inescapable role of state intervention in socioeconomic development came to be seriously challenged in the 1980s by the neo-liberal conservatives. These advocates of the neo-utilitarian state condemned state intervention *tout court* and held it responsible for the economic crises of the 1970s. What failed in Turkey and Egypt was not the interventionist state but its populist version. Underlying my analysis of these two cases was the hypothesis that effective state intervention is premised on the corporate coherence of the state and the way it is linked with societal actors. Corporate coherence requires some degree of insulation and autonomy from the surrounding society. But, although state autonomy is a necessary for state capacity it is not sufficient. An absolutely autonomous state might overwhelm society but it will not be able to tap its energies, trigger initiative, and elicit cooperative action for very long. A developmental, entrepreneurial state requires more than insulation and corporate coherence, it also demands sufficient external engagement with organized societal actors so as to involve them in the pursuit of collective and developmental goals. I am suggesting, in other words, that a capable state is characterized by 'engaged autonomy' which joins well-organized state bureaucracies with well-organized societal groups.[13]

In the light of these remarks, let me review the evidence presented by the cases of Egypt and Turkey. In neither country was the state able to develop the capacity to manage and reconcile the competing claims of distribution and accumulation. In neither country was the state able to engage societal actors in cooperative action for public ends. In Turkey, the state became the object of prey for a populist–clientelist party system that had the effects of particularizing and segmenting not only the state but also social classes. In Egypt, state autonomy conceived as the absence of institutionalized engagement with society led ultimately to a heteronomous and incoherent state.

The incapacitation of the populist state does not mean that no development took place in populist Egypt and Turkey; despite their ultimate failure to reproduce themselves, the populist states in Turkey and Egypt were effective and made considerable progress in a variety of areas. The Egyptian and Turkish states were neither of the 'predatory' Zambian type, nor, however, were they of the 'developmental' variety of states that came into existence in the newly industrializing countries of the Far East.[14] Rather, confined to 'pockets of efficiency,' their effectiveness was partial rather than global, and isolated rather than cumulative.[15] These pockets of efficiency were surrounded by a mass of patronage ties and personalist networks. The state, therefore, was in both countries too fragmented and particularized to be transformed by rare examples of efficiency and universalism. But whether the postpopulist states in Egypt and Turkey have transcended these limitations constitutes, of course, another story to be told at another time.

Notes

1 For a more extensive analysis of Turkish democracy and its periodic breakdown at ten-year intervals during 1950–1980, see İlkay Sunar and Sabri Sayarı, "Democracy in Turkey: Problems and Prospects," in Guillermo O'Donnell, Philippe C. Schmitter and Laurence Whitehead, eds., *Transitions From Authoritarian Rule: Experiences in Southern Europe and Latin America* (Baltimore: The Johns Hopkins University Press, 1986).

2 My analysis and intepretation of the Egyptian case relies predominantly on the following sources: John Waterbury, *The Egypt of Nasser and Sadat* (Princeton: Princeton University Press, 1983); Raymond Hinnebusch,

Egyptian Politics Under Sadat, Lynne Rienner Publishers, New York, 1988; Derek Hopwood, *Egypt: Politics and Society: 1945–1984* (London: Allen and Unwin, 1985); Leonard Binder, *In a Moment of Enthusiasm* (Chicago: University of Chicago Press, 1978); Hamied Ansari, *Egypt: The Stalled Society* (Albany: State University of New York Press, 1986); Robert Springborg, *Family, Power and Politics in Egypt* (Philadelphia: The University of Pennsylvania Press, 1982); Ira Lapidus, *A History of Islamic Societies* (Cambridge: Cambridge University Press, 1988), ch. 24; Joel Migdal, *Strong Societies and Weak States* (Princeton: Princeton University Press, 1988), chs. 5 and 6; Saad Eddin Ibrahim, in this volume; Guilain Denoueux, "State and Society in Egypt," in *Comparative Politics*, April 1988; Robert Springborg, "Approaches to the Understanding of Egypt" in Peter Chelkowski and Robert J. Pranger, eds., *Ideology and Power in the Middle East* (Durham: Duke University Press, 1988); and Yahya Sadowski, "Is there a Civil Society in Egypt?," paper presented at the New York Social Science Research Council Conference, 1989.

3 The best treatments of populism are found in Torcuata Di Tella, "Populism and Reform in Latin America" in Claudio Veliz, ed., *Obstacles to Change in Latin America* (London: Oxford University Press, 1970); Ernesto Laclau, *Politics and Ideology in Marxist Theory* (London: New Left Review Books, 1977), ch. 4; Nicos Mouzelis, *Politics in the Semi-Periphery* (London: Macmillan, 1986), ch. 2.

4 See Ibrahim, in this volume.

5 See Waterbury, *The Egypt of Nasser and Sadat.*

6 See Binder, *In a Moment of Enthusiasm,* and Ansari, *Egypt: The Stalled Society.*

7 This approach is best exemplified by an otherwise informative study by Çağlar Keyder, *State and Class in Turkey* (London: New Left Review Books, 1987), especially chapters VII and VIII.

8 Martin Shefter, "Party and Patronage: Germany, England, and Italy," in *Politics and Society*, vol. 7, no. 4, 1977.

9 For further elaboration on the consequences of such sequencing in Turkey, see İlkay Sunar, "Populism and Patronage: The Demokrat Party and its Legacy," in *Il Politico*, LV/4, October-December 1990.

10 Ibid.

11 For the analysis of Latin American development from the viewpoint of 'enclave' and 'nationally controlled' economies, see Fernando H. Cardoso and Enzo Faletto, *Dependency and Development in Latin America* (Berkeley: University of California Press, 1979).

12 See Waterbury, *The Egypt of Nasser and Sadat.*

13 Provoked by the neo-corporatist literature on Western Europe, I coined the term 'engaged autonomy' to characterize the nature of effective state intervention only to find out, however, that Peter Evans used a very similar concept as 'embedded autonomy' in his "Predatory, Developmental and

Other Apparatuses: A Comparative Analysis of the Third World State," in *Sociological Forum*, no. 4, 1989.

14 See note 9.

15 For the elaboration on the concept of 'pockets of efficiency,' see Barbara Geddes, "Building 'State' Autonomy in Brazil, 1930–1964," in *Comparative Politics*, vol. 22, no. 2, January 1990.

Economic Policies and Regime Performance

5

Evolution and Shifts in Egypt's Economic Policies: In Search of a Pattern

Galal A. Amin

Introduction

In any review of the modern history of Egypt's economic policy, it is difficult not to note certain common features between the economic policies of the two best-known of Egyptian leaders: Muhammad Ali (1805–48), and Gamal Abd al-Nasser (1952–70).[1] Though different in many other respects (their origins, the length of their periods in power, let alone the great differences between the economic and demographic conditions of the two periods), both leaders adopted strongly interventionist economic policies which, towards the end of their respective rules, turned the state into virtually 'the sole manufacturer, the sole trader, and the sole farmer.' Of course, this last phrase contains some exaggeration, especially in the case of Nasser, but it is true that, in both experiences, the bulk of manufactured output, and of new investments in all sectors, came to be realized by the state, in addition to the very tight control by the state of prices, incomes, and of the composition and marketing of agricultural output. It is worth noting however, that this predominance of the role of the state under Nasser was achieved to a large extent through nationalization, whereas under Muhammad Ali it was achieved mainly by creating what had not existed before, including the introduction of new and highly successful varieties of cotton.

This overwhelming role of the state in running the economy, and indeed in shaping political and social life, was associated in both cases with three important economic features which, to a large extent, explain why these two periods stand out as constituting two of the most important turning points in Egypt's modern history. These three features are: a) a radical transformation of economic structure in favor of manufacturing, b) the achievement of a high degree of economic independence, and c) a distinct rise in the level of living of lower-income groups.

Although these three statements should be interpreted cautiously and understood in relative terms, they seem to provide correct descriptions of some of the most important characteristics of these two periods. In all three respects—economic structure, economic independence, and income distribution—there was a clear deterioration during the two periods following the Muhammad Ali and the Nasserist eras respectively.

During most of the period falling between the end of Muhammad Ali's reign and the outbreak of World War I (1848–1914), Egypt was ruled by weak, unambitious rulers who were strongly influenced or dominated by the representatives of foreign powers, even before the beginning of the British occupation in 1882. More important for our purposes is the fact that during the greater part of this long period, Egypt was forced to follow an open-door policy with regard to both foreign trade and foreign investment.

The same thing could be said about the two decades which followed the death of Nasser in 1970. In both respects—the weakness and lack of vision of the rulers, and the nature of the economic policy they followed—these two periods were in direct contrast to those of Muhammad Ali and Nasser. So it was in the case of the three major features referred to above.

The aim of this essay is to provide evidence for this claim of striking contrast in these three respects between the Muhammad Ali and Nasser experiences, on the one hand, and the two periods of Open-Door Policy which immediately followed them, on the other, and to present an explanation of this contrast. A separate section dealing with the interwar period (1918–39) lends additional support to the argument, and a final section, which draws some parallels from the Turkish experience, may make the argument more widely applicable and hence of some theoretical interest.

Economic Consequences of Etatist Policies

Economic Structure

The most obvious and least controversial of the economic consequences of the interventionist policies of both Muhammad Ali and Nasser was the radical change in economic structure. There are of course no national income statistics for Egypt under Muhammad Ali, but there is enough evidence that Muhammad Ali not only attempted but in fact succeeded in launching an industrial revolution in Egypt, through what Crouchley calls "an almost incredible effort of development."[2] Egypt was transformed from a country that produced hardly any manufactured products other than the simplest kinds of textiles, pottery, straw mats, and sugar, to a country that produced, apart from textiles, spinning machines, weaving looms, armaments, and every kind of ironwork. The modern factory system was introduced, and by

1837 there were as many as twenty-nine such factories all over the country. In the 1820s, the cotton factories alone employed no fewer than 30,000 workers,[3] a stunning figure for a country of no more than 2.5 million people.

A similarly incredible and successful effort at changing Egypt's economic structure in favor of manufacturing was made by Nasser 130 years later. During the period of Nasser's and Egypt's first five-year plan (1959/60–1964/65), investment in industry and electricity was about 37.3 percent of total investment, compared with 21 percent for agriculture (including the High Dam). Industrial output grew at 8.5 percent annually, compared with 3.3 percent for agriculture, and employment in industry grew by 6.5 percent, compared with only 3.3 percent for agriculture and 4.1 percent for total employment.[4] The share of manufacturing in GDP increased, therefore, from 17 percent in 1956 to 23 percent in 1965 and the share of industry, electricity, and construction in employment from 13 percent in 1959/60 to 16 percent in 1964/65.

'Economic Independence'

One is on less solid ground arguing that there was a high degree of 'economic independence' under both Muhammad Ali and Nasser, but only because the concept of economic independence is more elusive. Muhammad Ali certainly caused Egypt to be more integrated in the world economic system than it was before him, and as a result Egypt came to be more 'dependent' on external sources of goods than previously. However, in spite of the great increase in the variety of goods available in Egypt under Muhammad Ali, imports were reduced to a minimum. To give one example, "a complete arsenal was erected with foundry, workshops, rope factory, etc., which could turn out everything required to make and fit out a complete ship-of-war except for the finer nautical instruments, brass nails, and cannons, all of which were brought from England."[5]

Needs had certainly multiplied, and so had imports; what is most impressive is the degree to which the growth of the former had exceeded the growth of the latter. The point will become clearer when the degree of economic independence under Muhammad Ali is compared, not with the almost complete isolation of Egypt before 1800, but with the degree of dependence on imports that characterized the period following his reign, to which I will return later. If to this is added the fact that, with all his efforts for development, Muhammad Ali left Egypt completely free from external debt, the statement about "a high degree of economic independence under Muhammad Ali" would probably be considered true in more than one sense.

A similar statement could be made of the Nasserist era, and there are more statistics available to support this thesis. Table 1 provides twelve indicators of different aspects of what could be called 'economic independence,' related to foreign trade, including food imports, and the financing of investment. The figures show that, with regard to almost all indicators related to foreign trade, in the period 1957–67, which is the most representative period of Nasserist policies, Egypt achieved a higher degree of economic independence than in the previous period (1952–56). With regard to some of these indicators, the effect of Nasser's policies seem to appear more clearly in the following five years (1968–73), which constitute a transitional period between Nasser's period of tight state control and Sadat's period of open-door policies.

The labeling of the Nasserist period as a period of economic independence seems, however, to need clarification in terms of the dependence on foreign capital. As table 1 shows, the period 1957–67 witnessed some dependence on foreign borrowing, in contrast to the previous period. During the decade preceding the Suez War, Egypt was in fact a net creditor country, as a result of the accumulation of sterling balances during World War II. During the Nasserist years of 1957–67 what remained of these balances was used up, and significant foreign debt started to accumulate. It is possible to argue, however, that when Nasser's borrowing is examined as a part of his overall economic policy, the rise of Egypt's foreign indebtedness between 1957–67 may not necessarily be regarded as a step away from greater independence. It may indeed have been a step towards it. This view may gain support from certain facts related to the nature of Nasser's debt, and the use to which the proceeds of the loans were (to be) put, as well as the conditions under which the loans were obtained.

With regard to utilization, it may be argued that almost all the proceeds of the loans obtained during the Nasserist period were directed to productive use. The loans from the Eastern Bloc went to finance industrial products as well as the High Dam. But even the food aid provided by the United States can be regarded as having been largely used for 'productive' purposes rather than as merely an addition to consumption. Food can legitimately be regarded as 'capital goods' when its increased supply is used to employ a greater number of people in productive activities rather than in raising the level of consumption of those already employed. And this is precisely what happened during the Nasserist period, in contrast to what happened in the 1970s. The level of employment increased (1959/60–1974/75) at a rate 50 percent higher than that of the increase in the labor force, and the highest rates of increase were for employment in the construction, electricity, and manufacturing sectors, in that order.

As for the conditions of the loans, it can safely be stated that they were among the best that Egypt has ever obtained, if not actually the very best conditions. For, as far as political conditions are concerned, the decade from the mid-1950s to the mid-1960s was characterized by a relatively high degree of tolerance on the part of the two superpowers, and of Third World neutrality between East and West. This was a period, reminiscent of that of Muhammad Ali, during which each of the two superpowers could accept the relative independence of a small country from its own sphere of influence, provided it did not fall under the domination of the other superpower. Egypt could thus

Table 1 Egypt: Some Indicators of Economic Independence

Period	Exports as % of imports	Concentration of exports[1]	Geographical concentration of exports[2]	Imports as % of GDP	Imports of consumer goods as % of total consumption expenditure	Imports of capital goods as % of gross domestic investment
1952–56	70	86	47	21	8	24
1957–67	70	75	39	20	5	22
1968–73	60	58	57	12	2	19
1974–80	80	69	58	24	9	26
post-1980	90[a]	84[b]	73[c]	35[d]	19[e]	32[f]

Period	Imports of consumer goods as % of total imports	Geographical concentration of imports[3]	Debt service ratio[4]	External debt as % of GDP[5]	Foreign financing as % of gross domestic investment	Food imports as % of food consumption[6]
1952–56	47	47	--	--	--	4
1957–67	38	58	10	26	15	4
1968–73	31	40	35	25	19	5
1974–80	35	62	26	48	32	34
post-1980	34[g]	79[h]	41[i]	53[j]	53[k]	41[l]

Notes

a average of 1981 and 1983–84
b 1981–83
c 1983
d average of 1981–82 and 1983–84
e 1982
f average of 1981–82 and 1982–83

g average of 1981 and 1982
h 1983
i average of 1982 and 1983
j average of 1981–83
k average of 1981–82 and 1986–87
l 1983–84

1 percentage of primary commodities in total community exports
2 share of most important geographical bloc in total exports
3 share of most important geographical bloc in total imports
4 percentage of debt service to total exports of goods and services
5 does not include military debt
6 refers to eight major food items: wheat, rice, maize, beans, lentils, edible oil, sugar, and meat

Source: Compiled from various tables in Ibrahim el Issawi, *The Measurement of Dependence in the Arab World*, pp. 138–201, Center for Arab Unity Studies and UN University, Beirut, 1989.

obtain a large amount of economic assistance from each of the two superpowers so long as it showed itself to be quite independent of the other.

Income Distribution and Relative Poverty

Several writers have drawn a picture of increased suffering under Muhammad Ali, in both the countryside and the towns, and of a deterioration in the standard of living. Not only do they refer to his incessant wars—in Arabia, Sudan, Greece, Syria, and in Turkey itself—but also to the forced labor of hundreds of thousands of peasants driven to work on his irrigation schemes. Muhammad Ali's monopoly system is said to have been too harsh and exploitative, with the peasants being paid far less than international prices for their crops, which they were forced to deliver to the *Wali*. The peasants lacked incentives to grow cotton, which was particularly unpopular as it required more work than other crops and brought little reward.

Another source of complaint was the system of 'solidarity' in tax payment. According to this system, if one farmer failed to pay his taxes, his neighbors would be collectively responsible, as was one village for the failure of another. Crouchley even refers to "the apathy and discontent" of industrial workers who were "dragged from their fields and workshops to labor in the factories."[6] Roger Owen's assessment of the conditions of Muhammad Ali's industrial workers is that "working conditions were bad, hours were long, and there was every encouragement for the workmen to commit various acts of sabotage. St. John reported that there was not one of Muhammad Ali's mills which had not been accidentally or designedly set on fire."[7] Even if all this did not contain some element of exaggeration, it is quite likely that the living conditions of most Egyptian peasants and industrial workers actually improved under Muhammad Ali. The change in this respect, brought about by Muhammad Ali as compared with what happened under the Mamluks, is probably analogous to the changes brought about by the Industrial Revolution in Britain as compared with living conditions of the eighteenth century.

Writers who describe the sufferings brought about by the Industrial Revolution tend to forget the horrors of life before it. Even if Muhammad Ali did not pay the farmers the international prices of their crops, he allowed the country to make any benefit at all out of these crops, the most important of which were introduced by him. We also know that "the production of wheat, beans, and barley remained fairly steady during Muhammad Ali's reign," and that in the 1840s, "cereal production rose to three or four times above its 1821 level."[8] People were almost certainly eating better, which, in those times at least, was the most important measure of the standard of living. Demographic data lend support to this conclusion, since the population, which remained more or less constant during the first two decades of the century (at about 2.5 million), increased by no less than 75 percent between 1821 and 1847, to 4.5 million.[9] This increase occurred in spite of the high death toll resulting from the plague of 1835, which killed one quarter of the population, and in addition to the frequent wars.

Table 2 The Share of Wages in Agricultural and Industrial Income in Egypt (1960–1974)

Year	Share of wages in agricultural income (%)	Share of wages in industrial income (%)
1960	25	27
1961	31	29
1962	30	36
1963	29	35
1964	29	35
1965	32	33
1966	33	32
1967	31	35
1968	31	33
1969	28	32
1970	29	31
1971	27	
1972	25	
1973	24	
1974	22	

Source: Galal Amin, *The Arab East and the West,* (in Arabic) p. 147, Center for Arab Unity Studies, Beirut.

Table 3 Development of Average Annual Real Wages in Agriculture and Industry in Egypt (1959/60–1970/71)
(1959/60 = 100)

Year	Agricultural wage	Industrial wage
1959/60	100	100
1960/61	91	84
1961/62	108	91
1962/63	118	119
1963/64	126	119
1974/65	134	112
1965/66	136	101
1966/67	136	96
1967/68	134	98
1968/69	135	97
1969/70	132	91
1970/71	129	

Source: Galal Amin, *The Arab East and the West,* (in Arabic) p. 148, Center for Arab Unity Studies, Beirut.

The improvement in the standard of living of the lower-income groups and the narrowing of income gaps during the Nasserist era is less controversial. Those were the years (1956–65) of the great expansion of the free or greatly subsidized social services of education, health, and housing, and of the application and extension of land reform, which put a ceiling on land ownership and land rents and provided valuable security for tenant farmers. Large industrial firms were nationalized, tax rates greatly increased on high incomes, profit sharing for industrial workers introduced, and prices tightly controlled. Statistics show a significant increase in the share of wages in both agricultural and industrial incomes between 1960 and 1966 *(see table 2)*, a very big increase in real agricultural wages during the same period and in the real industrial wage between 1959–60 and 1964–65 *(see table 3)*, and an improvement in the distribution of consumption expenditure in rural areas as measured by the Gini coefficient.[10]

Economic Consequences of Open-Door Policies

Although the term 'Open-Door Policy' was introduced to describe the shift in policies brought about by Anwar Sadat in 1974, the label can just as aptly be used to describe the shift which occurred in the mid-nineteenth century, particularly under the reign of Said Pasha (1854–63), towards freer trade, greater foreign investment, and less government control. This earlier experience of 'open-door' policy lasted for almost a whole century, until the revolution of 1952, but the interwar period (1918–39) witnessed some important deviations from the open-door principle which warrant a special discussion later in this essay, making it more appropriate to confine our present discussion of that experience to the period 1848–1914. In all the three aspects discussed in the previous section, the two periods following Muhammad Ali and Nasser respectively witnessed remarkable deterioration.

Economic Structure

It is not an exaggeration to say that Egypt was a much less industrialized country in 1914 than it was in 1848. Rapid growth did occur in agricultural output and infrastructure was greatly developed, as indicated by the length of railway and telegraph lines introduced, the construction of roads and bridges, the digging of new canals, the expansion of sea ports, and the opening of new schools. Most of this effort was made, however, to serve foreign trade, foreign merchants, and foreign investors, and contributed little to the diversification of the economy.

This was a period that can be described as one exhibiting 'growth but little development.' Although income statistics are lacking, the growth of agricultural production and international trade undoubtedly imply a substantial increase in average income, but also an even more unbalanced economy in 1913 than that which existed in 1848.

The similarity with the post-Nasser period is striking. Between 1975 and 1985 the annual rate of growth of GDP in Egypt was 8.5 percent in real terms, a rate which has been rarely experienced in Egypt's modern history, and was surpassed only by very few countries during the same period. As a result, real per capita income more than doubled, from $334 in 1975 to $700 in 1985. Gross domestic investment was increasing at an unprecedented rate, reaching 25 percent in 1984, a rate 50 percent higher than the already respectable rate achieved during the period of comprehensive planning in the early 1960s. The most striking results of this high rate of investment are evident in the progress of infrastructure: transport and communications, electricity and natural gas, water, and sewage systems.

Behind these successes however, lies a much bleaker picture of failures and imbalances. In many ways, the most serious failure, simply because it explains much of the rest, is the imbalance in the economic structure. During the fifteen years following Nasser's death, agriculture grew at a rate below that of population and well below that of GDP. Manufacturing industries grew at a much slower rate than service industries and crude petroleum extraction. Thus, while the share of the two major 'productive' sectors in GDP tended to decline, the share of extractive industries tended to rise. Between 1972 and 1985, the share of agriculture in GDP declined from 25 percent to 17 percent, that of industry (excluding petroleum) from 28 percent to 20 percent, while the share of petroleum rose from 5 percent to 16 percent and that of services remained more or less the same at about 47 percent.

The deterioration in the structure of employment was more serious, for while the share of manufacturing in the total labor force remained virtually constant at about 12 percent during that period, the decline in the share of agriculture was almost totally matched by the rise in the share of services in the labor force, which increased by about 50 percent (from 30 percent to 45 percent) and this is where 'disguised unemployment' is most evident.[11] The government sector, in particular, acted as the 'employer of last resort,' where those failing to find remunerative jobs in agriculture or manufacturing are employed for very low pay in return for little or no work.

This serious imbalance in economic structure was quite effectively covered up for a considerable amount of time, until it was dramatically revealed in the mid-1980s by the sudden collapse of oil prices. Between the mid-1970s and mid-1980s, the drastic increase in oil prices and in the oil revenues of the Arab oil-surplus countries opened up new opportunities for work for hundreds of thousands of Egyptian laborers, both skilled and unskilled, who migrated to the Arab Gulf countries and to Libya. Their earnings were sent back to Egypt during what, in the early 1980s, became the largest single source of foreign exchange, surpassing even oil. However, the collapse of oil prices in 1986 revealed how fragile the economic structure has been, and how the rapid growth of income and infrastructure since the mid-1970s had been merely the result of regularly injecting the economy with external sources of income or capital, whether in the form of foreign aid, labor remittances or higher oil prices, all of which had little relation to an increase in productive activity at home.

The bleakness of the economic picture during the last four or five years, therefore, constitutes a bitter but, to my mind, just judgment of Egypt's economic performance since 1975. Since 1986, Egypt has been suffering from 'stagflation' and severe unemployment, both of which are directly related to the weakness of the economic structure. The real rate of growth of GDP has been barely above the rate of population growth since 1986, and was accompanied by a rate of inflation in the neighborhood of 20 percent. What was also fairly new to Egypt was the high rate of overt unemployment since 1985. This rate exceeded 12 percent of the labor force and is now as high as 25 percent among university graduates.

Economic Dependence

According to virtually all twelve of the indicators of economic dependence/independence contained in table 1, Egypt became much more economically dependent during the period 1848–1914 than it was under Muhammad Ali. Foreign financing came to constitute a handsome proportion of domestic investment, while it played virtually no role under Muhammad Ali. Foreign debt emerged and grew until it constituted about 100 percent of national income at the turn of the century. Exports became even more dominated than ever by cotton, and both exports and imports became more concentrated on Britain. With the growth of the middle class and the increasing extravagance of the ruling elites, imports of consumer goods increased as a proportion of total consumption, and with the complete abandonment of capital-goods industries, the imports of these goods must have grown as a proportion of total investment. The degree to which imports were covered by exports varied between the first half of this period (1848–82), during which the deficit in current account tended to grow and was covered by increased borrowing from abroad, and the second half (1882–1914), during which one of the main aims of the colonial administration was to realize a surplus on current account so as to service the foreign debt. Even with regard to self-sufficiency in food, the situation deteriorated in spite of the very rapid growth in agricultural production. With the growing profitability and popularity of the cotton crop, cotton increasingly replaced wheat, and this, together with the increase in population, made the locally grown wheat insufficient, by the turn of the century, to meet the needs of the country. Imports of wheat and flour started to grow, in turn encouraged by the increasing availability of cheaper wheat from Canada, Australia, and South America. By 1914, Egypt had become a British Protectorate, had been under British occupation for over three decades, and was as dependent politically as it was economically.

Table 1 provides data on the change in a number of indicators measuring 'economic independence' since 1974. It clearly points out the tendencies towards an increase in the concentration of exports, both with regard to their composition and their geographical destination, an increase in the geographical concentration of imports, an increase in the percentage of food imports in total food consumption, in the proportion of foreign financing in domestic investment, in the percentage of total imports in GDP, in the percentage of imports of consumer goods in total consumption expenditure, and in the percentage of imports of capital goods in domestic investment.

Particularly striking is the growth of external debt. On Nasser's death in 1970, Egypt's public external debt, both long- and medium-term. but excluding military and private debt, was $1.7 billion. If one adds to that the estimated public short-term debt, the military debt and the private debt, the total would probably not exceed $5 billion. Compared with the total debt on the death of Sadat in 1981, of $30 billion, it is clear that Egypt's external debt was multiplied six times during the 1970s. It increased again by about 50 percent during the first nine years of Mubarak's term in office to reach $45.7 billion at the end of June 1989.[12] Of this, military debt constitutes slightly under 25 percent *(see table 4).*

Table 4 Egypt's Outstanding External Debt ($ million at end of period)

Year	83/84	84/85	85/86	86/87	87/88	88/89
Supplier's credit	4,260	4,650	5,562	6,160	7,518	8,509
IBRD and IDA loans	1,554	1,752	1,903	1,963	2,011	n/a
GODE*	2,269	2,381	2,406	2,449	2,529	n/a
Other multilateral loans	413	42	603	682	685	n/a
Bilateral civilian loans	9,740	10,365	10,759	12,012	12,756	
Military loans	7,330	9,380	8,936	9,447	10,495	
Total medium- and long-term public and public guaranteed debt	25,566	28,956	30,169	32,713	35,994	38,591
Short-term debt	5,655	5,637	4,929	4,388	4,321	4,344
Private sector debt	1,849	1,807	2,750	2,750	2,826	2,818
Total debt	33,070	36,400	37,848	39,851	43,141	45,753

(*) The Gulf Organization for the Development of Egypt
Source: International Monetary Fund, *Report on the Egyptian Economy, 1990.*

Table 5 Egypt's Balance of Current Accounts (1984/85–1988/89) ($ million)

Year	84/85	85/86	86/87	87/88	88/89
Trade balance	-6,588	-5,681	-5,688	-6,567	-7,533
Exports (f.i.b.), of which					
- petroleum	3,928	3,576	2,264	3,274	2,546
Imports (c.i.f.)	-10,516	-9,256	-7,952	-9,841	-10,079
Service Balance	434	-232	778	1,941	1,836
Receipts, of which	3,505	3,450	4,016	4,575	5,044
- Suez Canal	897	1,028	1,148	1,269	1,307
- Investment Income	568	533	614	624	729
- Tourism	410	321	380	886	920
Payments, of which	-3,072	-3,683	-3,238	-2,634	-3,208
- Interest	-	-	-	-	-
- Payments	-981	-1,321	-1,094	-785	-1,016
Transfers	4,593	4,183	3,986	4,081	4,240
Governmental Workers	1,097	1,210	974	698	710
Remittances	3,496	2,973	3,012	3,384	3,530

Source: American Embassy in Cairo: *Egyptian Economic Trends,* March 1990.

Needless to say, this rapid growth of external debt is largely the result of the very poor performance of agricultural and manufactured exports when compared with the growth of imports, a fact which is again a reflection of the weakness of the economic structure, manifested mainly in the poor performance of the two major commodity sectors: agriculture and manufacturing. Egypt's external debt today is high by any standard, even when compared in relative size with the famous Egyptian debt of a little over a century ago (about 100 percent of GDP), which led to the dethronement of Khedive Ismail and to the British occupation. Today, the servicing of the debt has gone beyond Egypt's capacity to pay. According to a recent report by the US embassy in Cairo, Egypt's total debt-service obligations during the year 1989–90 exceeded $6 billion, or 54 percent of the total value of all Egypt's exports of goods and services of the year before (1988–89) *(see table 5).*

Such obligations, like all those of the last few years, cannot be met and the result was the accumulation of debt-service arrears exceeding $10 billion at the end of June 1989. According to the same US report, "both commercial and official sources of external credit tightened. . . . At the beginning of 1990, the government was experiencing difficulties in financing high-priority food imports."[13]

Income Distribution

One can also confidently argue that income distribution worsened between 1848 and 1914, even though conclusive statistics are lacking. There are several indicators for this. First, there was the emergence and growth of ownership of agricultural land by foreigners. While under Muhammad Ali this was confined to uncultivated land so as to encourage bringing new land into cultivation, in 1858, under Said Pasha, foreigners were allowed buy already cultivated land, and this was confirmed under Ismail by a decree from Constantinople in 1867. Such foreign ownership of agricultural land continue to increase as small cultivators failed to repay their debts to mortgage banks. Second, the burden of land tax became excessively high on small cultivators. What the small cultivator gained under Said, as a result of the abolishment of the 'solidarity' principle in the collection of taxes, was lost under Ismail, as a result of an excessively high burden of taxation to which Ismail was driven by his own heavy burden of foreign debt.

The growing gap between the poor and rich under Ismail is vividly illustrated by Janet Abu-Lughod's description of the development of Cairo during his reign. She calls this development "a tale of two cities," the two cities being the modern part of Cairo, which grew under the name of 'Ismailia' between the Nile and the Azbakeya gardens, and was inhabited mainly by foreigners and the newly rich Egyptians, and the 'oriental' city, which occupied roughly what is now called 'Old Cairo,' and in which the bulk of lower-income Egyptians dwelled. While this 'old city' was left practically untouched, the 'new city' was built in French style, with pavements and boulevards lined with trees. This can be contrasted with the Cairo of Muhammad Ali, the physical features of which were virtually the same when he died as when he came to power, except for the factories, iron foundries, and the schools he built.[14]

The trend of growing inequality continued under the British occupation. The British can indeed boast of a significant increase in agricultural production, in the productivity and profitability of agriculture, in the security of land ownership as well as a reduction in the burden of taxation. But along with this went a subtantial increase in foreign ownership of agricultural land until it covered no less than one seventh of total cultivated land by the turn of the century. The process of depriving small landowners of their land, which started under Ismail, also accelerated. The burden of land tax became indeed lighter and lighter, but only for a progressively smaller proportion of the population. By 1917 no less than 53 percent of the population of Upper Egypt and 36 percent of the population of the Delta was landless.[15] More and more landowners were therefore forced to become either tenants of other people's land or merely agricultural laborers. For tenants, conditions became increasingly difficult with the growing scarcity of land as agricultural rent tended to soar, to the benefit of landlords. As for agricultural laborers, although they benefited from the abolition of corvée labor, the more rapid growth of supply of labor compared with demand, especially with the migration every year of some 500,000–800,000 laborers from Upper Egypt to the Delta, worked to hold the wage rate down close to subsistence level.

The development of income distribution following what we called the 'Nasserist era' (1956–67) is less straightforward than that of the change in economic structure or in the degree of economic dependence. Reviewing the variety of information and statistics available, one is left with a strong impression that income distribution deteriorated slightly or remained more or less the same between the mid-1960s and the mid-1970s, in relation to both the size of the gap between the rich and the poor and relative size of the population in absolute poverty. There are signs of significant improvement in the latter, but a steep deterioration in the former between 1975 and 1985, and of deterioration in both after 1985. The conclusion with regard to the period 1965–75 is based on data on the Gini coefficient,[16] on the development of real agricultural and industrial wages *(see tables 2 and 3)*, as well as on the nature of economic policies undertaken during this period, which did not witness any important redistribution measures. This was also a period of economic stagnation following the 1967 war. The allegation of a widening gap between rich and poor in the decade following 1975 is strongly supported again by the nature of economic policies followed during this period, the laxity of government efforts in collecting taxes and fighting corruption, and the very rapid growth of national income and external revenues.

The suggestion that the proportion of people falling under the poverty line has declined in the decade following 1975 is supported by the International Labor Organization (ILO) sample survey of rural Egypt in 1977, by statistics on the movement of real wages in both the rural and construction sectors,[17] as well as by the study of the impact of the migration of Egyptian labor abroad after 1975 on low-income groups.[18] The suggestion of a deterioration in income distribution since 1985, particularly in the sense of an increase in the proportion of people falling under the poverty line, is based mainly on the very large rise in the rate of inflation and in the rate of unemployment, and on the big reduction in government expenditure on food subsidies and social services following the dramatic fall in oil prices, particularly since 1986. Looking at the period of the last twenty-five years (1965–90) as a whole, it seems clear that the gap between rich and poor in Egypt has widened significantly since 1965, although the lower-income groups, especially in rural areas, may be living significantly better now than they were in the mid-1960s.

An Attempt at an Explanation

If one is at all correct in suggesting that certain economic features tend to be associated with a state-controlled economy and that the opposite features tend to be associated with open-door policies, one is naturally tempted to look for an explanation. It is of course possible that such associations may merely be coincidence, with no causal relationship involved. But one presumably should not dismiss the matter as pure chance, unless no causal relationship seems to be at all plausible. What follows is an attempt to find such a relationship.

Both Muhammad Ali and Nasser were committed to what may be called an 'ambitious national project of independent development' to which they were wholeheartedly dedicated and for which they made a heroic effort to mobilize the nation's material and human resources. Each was 'ambitious' since the goals went far beyond what the nation had achieved for a very long time before their rule, 'national' in the sense that it revolved around the image of the nation's future rather than the ruler's own personal ambitions, and involved almost every aspect of the country's development, and 'independent' in the sense that it was not inspired or motivated by the interests of foreign powers, but rather was often in conflict with these interests. The two experiences may indeed have been 'tolerated' by these powers but they were not 'dictated' by them.

The nature of the two projects, though quite similar in many respects, was of course not identical; military strength may have been the dominant element in the case of Muhammad Ali, in contrast to rapid industrialization and social justice in the case of Nasser. But in both cases, the fact that the project was highly ambitious and often came into conflict with the interests of foreign powers seemed to require a high degree of consolidation of political and economic power in the hands of the state. The rapid change in economic structure was itself an essential element in Nasser's national project and was at least a necessary condition for the fulfillment of that of Muhammad Ali, since a strong army capable of fulfilling independent military targets required an ambitious industrialization program. To increase the country's resources to an extent which would make possible the fulfillment of national goals required a greater integration of the national economy into the international economic system, as was manifested by the growth of foreign trade under Muhammad Ali, and of foreign aid under Nasser. However, very clear and strict limits were drawn to this integration by the determination to preserve the ambitiousness and independence of the national project, hence all the elements of 'economic independence' to which we referred in describing both Muhammad Ali's and Nasser's experiences.

The implementation of this national project was bound to have important consequences, in both cases, for the standard of living and the way of life of the masses, both in the cities and the countryside. In the case of Muhammad Ali, the new irrigation projects, the introduction of new crops, the change in the system of cultivation and of tax collection, as well as the never-ending mobilization of new recruits for the army, radically changed the way of life of the peasants, and not always for the better. In the city, the introduction of the monopoly system, the massive industrialization program, the restrictions imposed on merchants and artisans, the great expansion of education, and the improvement of medical facilities—in addition to the successful maintenance of law and order—have also radically changed the way of life of the urban population, mostly for the better, and this involved a growing proportion of total population. In the case of Nasser, life in the countryside was transformed by land reform and the various forms of government intervention in the production and distribution of agricultural output and agricultural income. In the city, life was transformed by redistribution measures, industrialization, the growth of the bureaucracy and the army, and the expansion of education, medical, and other services. In both experiences, economic progress was achieved at the cost of political authoritarianism. This probably did not entail great sacrifices in the earlier experience, except for the human sacrifices exacted by Muhammad Ali's military campaigns. The political price was much higher in the Nasserist experience, and the controversy will probably continue about whether or not the economic benefits of Nasserism were greater than its political cost.

In both cases, the transformation of the way of life of the masses, more often than not for the better, was not dissociated from the high degree of independence, attempted and achieved, from foreign pressure. Lacking a permanent and reliable source of foreign support, Nasser had no alternative but to rely on a domestic source which, given his attack on the old ruling elite of big landowners and urban bourgeoisie, could only be provided by the lower ranks of the middle class, industrial workers and small landowners. In this way, a relationship can be seen between the commitment to an independent national project and the third feature of the Nasserist era: the improvement in the standard of living of the lower-income groups. One may note a similar relationship between Muhammad Ali's pursuing of an independent project and his new reliance on a purely 'Egyptian' army consisting, for the first time in centuries, of Egyptian peasants.

It is important to emphasize that this commitment to a 'national project of independent development' was conspicuously lacking in the two extended periods that followed the two experiences of tight state control under Muhammad Ali and Nasser. Successive rulers between Muhammad Ali and World War I were mostly weak and unambitious, and/or severely manipulated by foreign powers. I contend that the same thing could be said of the rulers following Nasser. Whether this was merely a historical accident or the inevitable result of the prevailing international or domestic conditions is a highly controversial point, and I have already expressed my position on it elsewhere.[19] Very briefly, I believe that a very strong case can be made for the view that changing international conditions were the dominant factors behind the shift in Egypt's economic and foreign policies after 1840 and again after 1970. Although domestic conditions obviously play a role, including the personal inclinations of individual rulers, not to mention the underlying economic, social, and demographic conditions, the decisive factor in the case of countries like Egypt seems to lie in the international context.

In studying the economic, political, or cultural development of a country which is truly independent it may be perfectly legitimate to have as one's starting point the nature of the country's natural or human resources, its technological development, the changing balance of power among its own social classes, or even the personal characteristics of its political leadership. The same approach might, however, be seriously misleading when applied to a country which is desperately dominated by another, and in such a case, it may be much more fruitful to have as one's starting point whatever developments that might have occurred within the dominant country itself.[20]

I have traced these developments as well as their impact on the Arab world in an earlier work,[21] so it is unnecessary to pursue the argument any further here. One point, however, may deserve some elaboration, namely the role played by the political nature of the system, particularly in relation to the degree of democracy and mass participation in determining the nature of economic policies. This issue of the relation between democracy and economic policy and economic performance has come to attract much greater attention since the recent dramatic changes in Eastern Europe. Unfortunately, the lessons which are often drawn for Egypt and the Arab world from these events seem to me to be faulty in logic, even when they are nobly motivated.

As I have discussed earlier in this essay, many of the economic successes of Muhammad Ali and Nasser were based on their tight control of the state and economy. An apparent decline in people's motivation and weakening in their private incentives seems to have done little damage to the country's economic performance, whether in the first four decades of the nineteenth century or in the 1950s and 1960s. When economic decline started after 1840 and again after 1967 it was sudden and abrupt, and was clearly associated not with a sudden decline in people's participation or support but with sudden and severe external shocks. It seems to me that we tend here to commit an error of logic by thinking that if two things are desirable, (e.g. democracy and economic development) then they must come together or one must be a condition for the other. The real world does not clearly lend support to this view.

The Special Case of the Interwar Period

In many ways, the interwar period in Egypt lies somewhere in between the two models outlined above: that of far-reaching interventionist policies and that of an unrestrained laissez-faire system. No state-monopoly system of the type introduced by Muhammad Ali or Nasser was applied, but the tariff system was dramatically changed in order to provide a much greater protection for domestic industry. Industry remained in private hands, but the state did not make deliberate efforts to stifle it, as happened during the first three decades of the British occupation. Agricultural production was subject to little control, but the state interfered to provide some protection for small landowners from the impact of the world depression.

Politically, the interwar period also shows some parallel characteristics. Egypt was still under British occupation, but achieved nominal political independence in 1922 and a measure of freedom by the Anglo–Egyptian Treaty of 1936. No absolute ruler of Muhammad Ali's or Nasser's type could be expected to emerge, but nor did Egypt completely lack effective nationalist leaders, as it did in the second half of the nineteenth century or in the two decades following the death of Nasser. Saad Zaghloul and Talaat Harb provided, respectively, the models of political and economic leadership. These two men may not have demonstrated the degree of ambition of Muhammad Ali and Nasser , but they probably had as much of it as circumstances could allow. Interestingly enough, some success was achieved during the interwar period in changing the economic structure and in gaining economic independence, but here again, the success was less notable than that achieved under strict government control.

Agriculture did quite badly between 1918 and 1939, but manufacturing grew rapidly, thanks mainly to the establishment of Bank Misr in 1920 and to the contribution of its companies under the leadership of Talaat Harb. The result was that the share of industrial output (including manufacturing, mining, electricity, and construction) in GNP doubled between 1927 and 1937, though still not exceeding 8 percent in the latter year.[22] The rate of urbanization during this period was probably the highest rate experienced by Egypt either before or since, with the proportion of urban population doubling between 1913 and 1947 (16 percent and 33 percent, respectively). By 1939, the degree of self-sufficiency in several manufactured products—sugar, soap, cigarettes, shoes, cement, and furniture—exceeded 90 percent, while the share of manufactured consumer goods in total imports declined heavily in favor of imports of industrial raw materials and intermediate goods.[23] Cotton continued to dominate exports and, even here, notable progress was achieved in the form of diversification of export markets. Britain's share in Egyptian exports fell from 43 percent in 1913 to 32 percent in 1938, and that in imports from 31 percent to 23 percent, respectively.[24] The interwar period also witnessed a very significant reduction in Egypt's external debt until it was completely liquidated in 1943, and Egypt quickly became a creditor rather than a debtor of Britain.

Behind all these developments it is not difficult to discern the primary importance of the international environment. Egypt's economic and political development, including the shifts in economic policies between 1914 and 1945, was largely the result of the two world wars and the Great Depression of the 1930s. It is difficult to imagine the establishment of Bank Misr, the rise of the Bank Misr companies, the great progress in manufacturing, the decline of agriculture, the very rapid urbanization, or the repayment of the external debt, in the absence of the accumulation of savings during World War I, the fall in agricultural prices as a result of the World Depression, the difficulties facing importation of manufactured goods, and the huge expenditure of foreign troops during the two wars. The interwar period may indeed seem to be neither the replica of the two periods of 'etatism' of Muhammad Ali and Nasser, nor of the laissez-faire periods of their immediate successors, but still lends support to our main theses, namely that there are certain important economic features that tend to be associated with one or the other of the two types of economic policy, and external factors seem to play a primary role in determining the nature of this policy.

Parallels With Turkey?

In Turkey, as well, one can make a strong case arguing that the two periods of etatism (1933–39) and economic planning (1963–73) were much more successful than the following periods in diversifying the economic structure, in achieving economic independence, and in reducing income disparities. During the etatist era of Atatürk, the share of agriculture in national income declined in favor of industry and services from 50 percent in 1929 to 38 percent in 1939.[25] This was achieved "without any loss of economic and political independence."[26] Only two foreign loans were received during the 1930s, one of 8 million gold dollars from the Soviet Union to be repaid without interest over a twenty-year period, and the other of 10 million gold dollars from a Swedish–American firm at 6.5 percent interest in return for a grant of the matches and briquette monopoly, but this latter loan was repaid within a short time and the monopoly returned to Turkey. During this period, Turkey also managed to repay a good proportion of its external debt, and to reduce its dependence on the imports of textiles and foodstuffs, while its imports of capital goods increased from 14.5 percent to 37.2 percent of total imports between the beginning and the end of the 1930s.[27]

During the period 1963–72, the diversification of economic structure was also impressive, with the share of industry in GNP rising from 17.3 percent in 1963 to 22.7 percent in 1972, and that of agriculture falling from 34.8 percent to 25.9 percent during the same period.[28]

In contrast to these two periods of the 1930s and the 1960s, the 1950s show a big increase in dependence on Western aid, with Turkey's total foreign indebtedness reaching $1,011 million in 1957, or about three times its export earnings, while the remaining years of the 1970s (1973–79) again show a striking increase in foreign indebtedness, in spite of the great increase in labor remittances.[29] This is strongly reminiscent of Egypt's experience during the same years: a rapid growth of borrowing when the country is least in need. Income distribution seems to have deteriorated in Turkey in the two periods of the 1950s and 1973–79, while the economic structure stagnated in the latter period.[30]

The liberalization policies of the 1980s were supposed to correct all this, but there are already signs that, at least with regard to income distribution, there has been further deterioration, with real wages in 1988 at less than half their level in 1979, compared with the development in real-interest income which is estimated to have multiplied more than sixteen times during the same period (see Boratav in this volume).

Thus, in spite of all their differences, the consequences of the major shifts in economic policies in Egypt and Turkey demonstrate a strikingly similar pattern.

Notes

1 An excellent book on the political history of Egypt under Muhammad Ali is H. Dodwell, *The Founder of Modern Egypt: A Study of Mohamed Ali* (Cambridge, England: The University Press, 1931), and the best economic history is probably still A. Crouchley, *The Economic Development of Modern Egypt* (London: Longman Green Ltd., 1938). For the nineteenth century as a whole, an excellent source on Egypt's economic history is Roger Owen, *Cotton and the Egyptian Economy 1820–1914* (Oxford: Oxford University Press, 1969). It is not as easy to select two works on Nasser. Arabic sources on Nasser are probably indispensable, and good books written on him in English tend to be more specialized than those dealing with earlier periods of Egyptian history. The most balanced works on the political economy of Nasserism seem to me to be those of Charles Issawi, Bent Hansen, Patrick O'Brien, John Waterbury, and Robert Mabro.

2 Crouchley, p. 41.

3 Owen, p. 45.

4 B. Hansen, "Planning and Economic Growth in the UAR 1960–1963," in P. J. Vatikiotis, *Egypt Since the Revolution* (London: Allen and Unwin, 1968), pp. 22–35.

5 Crouchley, p. 69.

6 Ibid., p. 72; see also Crouchley, *op. cit.*, p. 25.

7 Ibid., p. 45.

8 Ibid., pp. 49–59.

9 Crouchley, p. 51.

10 International Labor Organization, *Employment Opportunities and Equity in Egypt* (Geneva, 1982), p. 95.

11 G. Amin, "Adjustment and Development: The Case of Egypt," in S. el Nassar, ed., *Adjustment and Development Strategies in the Arab World* (International Monetary Fund, 1987), p. 93.

12 G. Amin, *The Story of Egypt's External Debt* (in Arabic) (Cairo: Ali-Mukhtar Publishing House, 1987), pp. 71–72.

13 American Embassy in Cairo, *Egyptian Economic Trends*, March 1990, p. 2.

14 Janet Abu Lughod, *Cairo: One Thousand and One Years of the City Victorious* (Princeton: Princeton University Press, 1971).

15 Owen, p. 240.

16 ILO, *op. cit.*, pp. 93–96.
17 Ibid., pp. 96–127.
18 G. Amin, and E. Awny, *International Migration of Egyptian Labour*, (Ottawa: International Development Research Center, 1985), pp. 130–45.
19 G. Amin, "External Factors in the Reorientation of Egypt's Economic Policy," in M. Kerr and S. Yassin, *Rich and Poor States in the Middle East* (Boulder: Westview Press, 1982).
20 Ibid., p. 285.
21 G. Amin, *The Arab East and the West* (in Arabic) (Beirut: Center for Arab Unity Studies, 1979).
22 Charles Issawi, *Egypt in Revolution* (London: Oxford University Press, 1963), p. 44.
23 Egyptian Economic Society, *Proceedings of the 50th Anniversary* (Cairo, 1960), p. 455.
24 Issawi, p. 39.
25 Z. Y. Herschlag, *Introduction to the Modern Economic History of the Middle East* (Leiden: Brill, 1964), pp. 190–91.
26 Ibid., p. 193.
27 Ibid., p. 198.
28 W. Hale, *Political and Economic Development of Modern Turkey* (London: Croom Helm, 1981), pp. 130–31.
29 Ibid., pp. 106, 230.
30 Ibid., pp. 111, 131.

6

Political Regimes and Social Performance: The Case of Egypt

Nadia Ramsis Farah

Is there a relationship between types of political regime and patterns of social equity? The weight of historical evidence suggests an inverse relationship between social equity and the extent of democratization during the process of development. Social equity, it seems, can only be obtained at the price of democracy. There are, nonetheless, notable exceptions to this generalization. In Latin America, for instance, populist regimes have often been both democratic politically and equitable socially, while the bureaucratic military regimes which followed them increased social inequities. In Egypt, the latter half of the twentieth century has been broadly characterized by authoritarian political systems. But the Nasserist regime is usually identified with populism, whereas the regimes of Sadat and Mubarak have been depicted as bureaucratic–authoritarian.

The central theme of this essay is that social equity is a function of prevailing political alliances which differentiate between different types of political regimes, within the broader parameters of an authoritarian state. After a brief theoretical discussion of relationship between regime types and patterns of social equity in Third World countries, the concrete manifestations of these relationships will be examined in the Egyptian context since the end of World War II.

Phases of Development and Power Relations

The dependent and fragmented economic and social structures of peripheral dependent societies enhances the relative autonomy of the state, enabling it to assume a strongly interventionist role in the economy. This has often resulted in systems of distribution of economic resources wherein political rather than pure economic criteria are paramount. Such distributive systems, especially in the Arab world, are geared towards the requirements of regime security, rather than the fulfillment of targets of social justice or the achievement of certain economic goals.[1]

Development in the Third World has been described in terms of three broad historical phases:

1. A primary-product export-oriented growth phase, and hence a certain internationalization, often coinciding with periods of colonization;

2. An industrialization phase, based upon an inward-oriented import-substitution strategy, often involving massive state intervention in the economy;

3. A re-internationalization phase, in which industrial growth becomes contingent upon foreign capital and technology provided by multinational corporations, and the state actively intervenes to restructure the power relations that prevailed during the previous regime.

Most Third World countries have been through these phases, the change from one phase to another triggered by transformations in the international economic system dominated by core countries. However, the configuration of internal political relations and the way they are modified and restructured in response to international economic constraints show significant variations among peripheral countries, as will be discussed in the special case of Egypt.

The broader phases of development outlined above are generally associated with particular distributive policies and outcomes. The first phase of development has been often characterized by exclusionary social policies where the benefits from development accrued mostly to the colonialist powers and the thin layer of national elites. The import-substitution stage was frequently associated with populist regimes which adopted inclusionary socioeconomic policies. Benefits were better distributed across the social stratification system. The current phase of re-internationalization is accompanied by exclusionary policies and the use of coercive power to exclude the previous populist coalition from the benefits of growth.

This essay focuses on two types of peripheral political regimes which have dominated Third World social formations after independence, i.e., populism and traditional bureaucratic-authoritarianism. Before taking up Egypt as a special case study, the salient features of these regime types will be briefly outlined below.

Populism and Social Equity

Populism is an ill-defined concept. There is, however, a more or less general consensus that populism at least means a) a noncapitalist form of state industrialization with a marked concern for a more equitable distribution, b) advocacy of a non-class type of social evolution, and, c) an attempt to combine capitalist development with anticapitalist rhetoric.

Populist regimes were a natural outcome of the social movements which emerged in the Third World as it threw off the yoke of colonialism and attempted to gain both political and economic independence. In order to mobilize the national population in the fight against colonialism, it was necessary to use an ideology which emphasized national unity and articulated the hopes and ideals of major social forces. An alliance of the nationalist elites, the middle classes, and the powerful sectors of the peasantry and urban workers emerged in response to the needs of this struggle against colonial power and its domestic allies, the big industrial and landed bourgeoisies. These national alliances, which were populist in nature, proclaimed the sovereignty of the people, and sought to improve the living standards of the masses through development driven by rapid industrialization.

The victorious new populist regimes soon realized, however, that the state was the only institution capable of achieving their developmental goals, through direct economic intervention, involving the control of national resources, the promotion of investments, and the ensuring of an equitable distribution of income. To facilitate this massive intervention by the state, the new ruling elites resorted to a restructuring of the political power relations that had prevailed till then. Moreover, to ensure the stability of the nationalist alliances which had brought them to power, each new regime sought to broaden its social base by adopting inclusionary political and economic policies. A large public sector, therefore, served to expand the middle class (in the form of technocrats and bureaucrats) and to enlarge the labor force, while land reform measures bound large sections of the peasantry to the regime.

Populist regimes depended on a developmental model—that of 'import substitution'—to stimulate internal industrialization, coupled with welfare measures such as land reform, free education, and subsidized health care, etc., designed to effect a more equitable distribution in the interest of political stability.

These economic and social policies usually led to high rates of economic growth in the first few years of their implementation, coupled with a substantial improvement in the distribution of economic assets and benefits in favor of the lower-income groups. However, in the process of industrial and economic expansion, the inherent contradictions within the nationalist alliance deepened, threatening the political hegemony of the new elites.

The intersection of the now substantial public sector with the private sector allowed administrators of the former to appropriate a substantial part of the economic surplus and enrich themselves, either through their direct control of public projects or through dealings with private entrepreneurs.

Through the spread of such practices among the top echelons of the bureaucracy, a new social class emerged: a bureaucratic bourgeoisie. Depending on its financial ability to achieve its own ends, this bureaucratic elite was split into two; one faction that strongly favored private capital (usually the top echelons of the administration) and another that wished to further strengthen state capitalism at the expense of the private sector. The rising need for capital and the increasing difficulty of providing employment for a rapidly increasing workforce driven by a high rate of population growth plunged the economy into serious difficulties which signaled the end of the import-substitution phase. As that policy began to show signs of exhaustion, the split between the two above-mentioned factions of the bureaucracy widened.

There are two ways out of such economic difficulties: either an infusion of massive amounts of capital to maintain the same socioeconomic policies, or the elimination—or at least the drastic reduction—of the state's welfare program.

The first option is usually unavailable. And the state is reluctant to adopt the second, for fear of undermining the populist regime's social base and political stability. The way out of this impasse is usually sought in the adoption, by the state, of inflationary methods. But since such methods have disproportionate negative impact on the underprivileged, their net result is to effect a redistribution from low-income to high-income groups, thereby increasing once more the inequality of distribution. Mounting popular pressures and political agitation tend to drive the nationalist alliance into disarray, with the private economic elites, allied with the top echelons of the bureaucracy, blaming the public sector for inefficiency and economic waste, and attributing current economic difficulties to the regime's populist policies. This leads to a demand for a liberalization of the economy, and the elimination, or at least a considerable reduction, of the public sector. The intensification of the conflict between the proponents of a free-market economy and those favoring increased state intervention tends to create high political instability.

Bureaucratic Authoritarianism and Redistribution

The second phase usually led to the ascendancy of a regime that espoused liberal economic policies and a reintegration into the international capitalist system. To curb inflation and rescind the previous welfare policies, the only alternative was to cut wages and/or drastically reduce government expenditures on social welfare services. To implement such a strategy, however, required the use of drastic repressive measures to deactivate labor politically and tame it economically.

The major results of economic liberalization and the adoption of the so-called export-oriented industrialization strategy have, whenever applied, generally led to the following results:

a) deterioration in social equity

b) marginalization of a growing proportion of the population

c) dependence on a high level of repression and coercion to maintain political stability

d) reliance on foreign capital and markets to maintain economic growth rates

e) growing foreign debt and greater deficits in the balance of payments, due to reliance on an unstable foreign demand and the heavy burden of profit-repatriation required by foreign capital.

Egypt's Populism and Social Equity

While the case of Egypt conforms in general terms with the above analysis, it departs from it in two main ways. First, while most populist regimes, especially in Latin America, were democratic, Egypt's populist regime was highly repressive. Contrary to the above model, Egypt experienced a degree of political liberalization during the economic liberalization period; this experience differed from the general trend of repressive and highly coercive regimes usually associated with the implementation of the export-oriented industrialization strategy. Second, available data for Egypt do not show a huge deterioration in income distribution during the shift from import substitution to economic liberalization, as posited by the above general analysis.

These departures from the general model are significant. There is, therefore, a need to examine carefully the special conditions which allowed for these kinds of differences in the Egyptian case from the generally observed trends in other areas of the Third World.

The following factors account for the specificity of the Egyptian experiment: a) the special articulation of power relations prior to 1952 and after 1970; b) the oil-price revolution in the mid-1970s, and the subsequent massive labor migration from Egypt to oil-rich Arab countries; c) the strategic political situation of Egypt, on the international and regional levels, which allowed massive inflow of foreign aid, alleviating the need to adopt drastic measures in order to redistribute income from the low-income to the upper-income groups; and d) the massive resistance of the population to drastic measures designed to eliminate the welfare state of the 1960s or to engineer a substantial contraction of the role or the size of the public sector in the economy.

Import-substitution strategies for industrialization did not start with the populist regime of Gamal Abd al-Nasser (1952–70). They were first adopted, in the 1930s, by the Egyptian landed bourgeoisie and emerging industrial elites in an attempt to diversify—and thus avoid—the hazardous pattern of economic growth that relied almost solely on the production and export of cotton (see Ibrahim in this volume).

The industrialization drive of the Egyptian bourgeoisie was accompanied by an effort to supplant the British and Circassian–Turkish interests, or at least share in the dominant power alliance. To that end, they utilized a nationalist ideology.

The national economic and political gains ensuing from the popular revolt of 1919 were further augmented when the Egyptian bourgeoisie succeeded in 1930 in imposing tariffs to protect the infant domestic industries, and then again in 1937 in abolishing the Capitulations, which gave privileges to foreign nationals. By then, the landed bourgeoisie, in alliance with the industrial elites, had succeeded in restructuring the Egyptian economy by establishing three major institutions that were intended to promote capital accumulation and industrialization: the Misr Bank, the Egyptian Federation of Industries, and the Egyptian General Syndicate.

These developments resulted in the launching of a major import-substitution industrial program in the 1930s. While industrialization proceeded, the economic policy of the 1930s acted mainly to the benefit of the landed and industrial elites. The industrial elites, direct descendants of the agricultural elites, benefited from the Customs Law of 1930 and the cancellation of the Capitulations. The landlords were assisted by loans from the newly established 'Crédit Agricole,' and high increases in the price of main food crops. Inequalities increased. While the upper classes became richer, the peasants and workers suffered under low wages and successive waves of inflation. Industrialization was restricted by the small internal market and the lack of access to foreign markets. By the end of the 1930s, 65 percent of the working population was still absorbed by the agricultural sector.[2]

Industrialization under the auspices of private entrepreneurs resulted in the establishment of basic consumer-goods industries, mainly textiles and food industries. The industrial labor force was restricted, and the trickle-down effects from economic growth did not materialize. The political system was dominated by the economic elites, who appropriated most of the benefits while keeping the majority of the working population at barely subsistence levels by paying very low wages and concentrating the ownership of agricultural land in their own hands. Before the 1952 Revolution, only 0.1 percent of landowners appropriated around 20 percent of agricultural land, while almost 95 percent of owners controlled 35 percent of total land *(see table 1).*

World War II added to the economic hardships of the Egyptian people. Recession and high inflation resulted in deep stagnation and an increase in income inequalities. The nationalist question, which was the cement of the alliance between elites and the rest of the population, could no longer hide the increasing social contradictions. The middle classes, which became more disillusioned with the pattern of semi-parliamentary regimes and high economic inequalities started to form organizations as alternatives to the nationalist alliance of the Wafd Party. During the 1930s, other alternative political organizations, such as the Muslim Brotherhood, Young Egypt (the radical right), communist and socialist splinter groups (a radical left), etc., started to emerge. Political instability reached previously unknown heights in the period 1945–52. The whole system would have collapsed, and a bloodbath would have ensued, if it had not been for the intervention of the army on 23 July 1952.[3]

Table 1 Patterns of Landownership in Egypt

Size of land-holding	1950 % owners	1950 % land	1953 % owners	1953 % land	1961 % owners	1961 % land	1965 % owners	1965 % land	1975 % owners	1975 % land
feddans										
>5	94.3	35.4	95.8	46.6	94.1	52.1	94.5	57.1	95.0	49.7
5–10	2.8	8.8	2.0	8.8	2.6	8.6	2.4	9.5	2.7	11.1
10–20	1.7	10.7	1.1	10.7	2.1	10.7	1.9	8.2	1.3	10.5
20–50	0.8	10.9	0.7	13.6	0.8	13.4	0.9	12.6	0.7	12.2
50–100	0.2	7.2	0.2	7.2	0.2	7.0	0.2	6.1	0.2	9.3
100–200	0.1	7.3	0.1	7.2	0.2	8.2	0.1	6.5	0.1	7.1
200+	0.1	19.7	0.1	5.9	-	-	-	-	-	-

Source: National Center for Criminological and Sociological Research, *Comprehensive Sociological Survey of Egypt: 1952–1980: On Stratification,* (in Arabic) NCCSR, Cairo, 1985, pp. 103, 106.

The ruling officers came to power with a nationalist orientation and a vague program of political and economic reforms. In response to popular sentiments, the program included the target of achieving social equity. To achieve this, the new ruling elites had to contend with the old powerbrokers and their representatives within the newly established revolutionary council.

After a short power struggle in 1954, the ruling officers suspended all forms of parliamentary democracy and established a single-party system. This step was necessary to establish the hegemony of the ruling military elites and to maintain the stability of their regime. The re-establishment of a parliamentary democracy would have meant the re-integration of the old political and economic elites in the dominant ruling alliance. This would have meant the defeat of the new reformist economic program, which aimed at rapid development through a deepening of the industrial process, with a concomitant lessening of Egypt's dependence on the production and export of cotton—still its main economic asset at the time. The re-integration of the old elites would have prevented the new ruling elites from forming their own social base, favorable to their policies and programs. A return to the old parliamentary formulae would also have prevented the new regime from the freedom of action it sought to guarantee Egypt's international political independence. If the new military elites had opted for parliamentary democracy, it would have meant their surrender to the old elites and their eventual elimination from the dominant ruling alliance.

To achieve their own program, the military elites had to reshape the old power relations and to get rid of any contending social forces, seeking hegemony over the state. The first step towards the restructuring of power relations was to remove the old elites and induce internal industrialization, which was effected through the implementation of the first land-reform law, issued in September 1952. The land reform program dealt a serious blow to the traditional landowning elites, undermining their basis of economic and political power. It also led to the redistribution of the confiscated lands to the poorest peasants. The implementation of the first land-reform law, restricting maximum ownership of land to two hundred feddans, resulted in reducing the share of the large landowners from around 20 percent of total land to only 6 percent; while the share of the poorest and largest group of owners (around 95 percent of total owners) increased from only 35.4 percent to 46.6 percent *(see table 1).*

The Land Reform Law of 1952 did not just improve the distribution of landownership in the countryside. It also brought a substantial group of the poor peasantry into the social coalition supporting the new regime. At the same time, the 1952 law was thought by the revolutionary council to be an incentive for channeling private capital from agriculture to industry. This was complemented by the adoption of a liberal economic policy to attract foreign capital for financing national industrialization programs.[4]

The reliance on private Egyptian and foreign capital to deepen the industrialization process did not, however, result in any substantial investments in the industrial sector, for several reasons. First, while the land reform act was thought by the revolutionary council to benefit the industrial elites, the private industrialists took it as a sign of the ability of the new state to nationalize their capital. Second, the elimination of the industrial elite from the dominant power alliance reinforced its members' perception of their inability to protect their interests. Third, international capital was not forthcoming. While the United States was not hostile to the new regime, the strident nationalism of the free officers, and their resolve to build a strong state by strengthening the army and the industrial sector, was a hidden threat to foreign powers' interests in the Middle East. Foreign capital and foreign states preferred not to support the new regime too openly until they could gauge its intentions quite clearly.[5]

A test of the Western powers' willingness to support the new regime came in the simultaneous refusal of the United States to sell sophisticated arms to Egypt, and its withdrawal of financial support to the High Dam project. In doing so, Western powers were trying to prevent the emergence of a strong army and economy that was hostile to the state of Israel. Gamal Abd al-Nasser reacted by turning to the Soviet block for armaments and substantial economic aid. The nationalization of the Suez Canal in 1956 marked a serious turn in Egypt's foreign relations and signaled a change in its internal orientation.

The ensuing hostility of Western powers to Nasser's regime, and the reluctance of the Egyptian elites to invest in Nasser's developmental schemes, forced the regime to adopt more radical policies. A nationalization process, which started in the mid-1950s, reached its climax in 1961 with the seizure

Table 2 Shares of Wages and Profit in Gross Domestic Product

	1950	1964/65	1967/68	1975	1981/82
Wages in LE (millions)		890.30		2,180.90	7,449.10
Profits in LE (millions)		1,084.70		2,597.90	12,122.00
GDP in LE (millions)		1,975.00		4,778.90	19,571.10
% Wages to GDP	38.00	45.08	50.00	45.64	38.06
% Profits to GDP		54.92		54.36	61.94

Source: CAPMAS *Annual Statistical Reports 1969, 1977, 1989.*

of many existing industrial and financial assets. At the same time, a strong industrialization program was implemented. To ensure that large sections of the population supported the new policies, the economic benefits of these measures were dramatically extended. Besides the institution of more radical land-reform laws and tighter rent controls over land and real estate in 1961, the public education program was expanded and public health programs initiated. In addition, measures ensuring low-cost food supplies and a state commitment to full employment and more stringent labor laws contributed to a substantial decrease in income inequalities. The share of wages in gross domestic product increased from 38 percent in 1950 to 50 percent in 1967–68.[6]

The share of the poorest landowners of total land increased from around 47 percent in 1953 to 57 percent in 1965 *(see table 1);* and the percentage of families living under the poverty line decreased from 35 percent in 1958–59 to around 27 percent in 1964–65 for the rural areas, and from 30 percent to 27.8 percent in the same years for the urban areas *(see table 3).*

All these economic inclusionary policy measures strengthened the social base supporting the regime's policies, regardless of its authoritarian character. As a matter of fact, the political authoritarianism of the state and the elimination of the traditional economic elites from dominant power relations gave the state a large degree of autonomy from all social classes and groups, which allowed it to act swiftly in reshaping power relations so as to ensure the regime's security and stability.

The strengthening of the state role in the economy led at the same time to the emergence of a new social class to manage the growing public sector: the bureaucratic elites. This new class evolved from the ranks of the bureaucracy. Through their administrative posts, their collective monopoly and effective possession of public assets, the members of this new class acceded to political power, and thereby increased their own economic worth. Many of the members of the new class managed to amass extensive wealth, using both legal and illegal means.[7]

The policies of the Nasserist regime promised postive results at the beginning of the 1960s. The first five-year plan (1960/61–1964/65) resulted in rapid economic growth, estimated at an average annual rate of 6.4 percent. However, the years 1965–70 saw a drastic decrease. The average rate of growth did not exceed 3.3 percent annually during the latter period.[8]

The import-substitution strategy seemed exhausted as a means of deepening the industrialization process. However, the blockage cannot only be attributed to purely economic factors. First, the drainage of the system through the corruption of some bureaucratic elites, coupled with the major public-sector deficiencies of gross administrative inefficiency and a lack of accountability, can all be attributed to the lack of any attempt to democratize the system. The power of the bureaucratic elites reached new heights, which allowed the formation of strong power centers within the state, immune from any public pressures. The inclusionary economic policies of the regime, in addition to the repressionary policies, effectively eliminated any strong popular opposition to the growing power and corruption of the bureaucratic elites.

Second, Egypt's involvement in two external political events brought the economic system to a standstill: the Egyptian military intervention in the Yemen War (1963–67) and the Arab–Israeli war of 1967. Both wars caused substantial financial drain, paid through a reduction of investment funds; the regime was reluctant to cut down on consumption so as to avoid not to alienate the broad masses—especially after a brief experiment in raising prices (1965) that proved to be politically undesirable.[9]

These changes in the socioeconomic structure did not go unchallenged. With the economic strains created by the early exhaustion of import substitution in the late 1960s, the differences between factions of the bureaucratic elites widened and resulted in the polarization of two main groups: a left-wing faction, which was later identified as Nasserist, and a new right. The Nasserists thought that the only way to solve Egypt's economic and political

Table 3 Percentage of Households Below Poverty Line

Area	1958/59 (1)	1964/65 (1)	1974/75 (1)	1981 (2)	1984 (2)
Rural	38.00	26.80	44.00	43.00	47.20
Urban	30.00	27.80	34.50	44.40	51.10
National				43.70	49.10

Sources: (1) Robert Aliboni, et al., *Egypt's Economic Potential,* Croom Helm, London, 1984, p. 191 (2) Karima Korayen, *The Impact of Economic Adjustment Policies on Vulnerable Families and Children in Egypt,* Unicef, Cairo, p. 46, tables 1–2.

problems was to deepen state capitalism and strengthen Egypt's ties to the Soviet bloc. This policy was intended to regenerate growth through a complete centralization of the economic process, maintaining Soviet economic and military aid, and enlisting Soviet support to end Israeli occupation of Sinai, either through military action or a comprehensive diplomatic settlement of the Arab–Israeli conflict. The right wing of the bureaucratic elite was averse to any policy which would eliminate the private market, the main conduit of wealth and power for this group. Egypt's problems, according to the right wing, stemmed from the inefficiencies of the public sector, and the reliance on the Soviets, who had very little power to affect Israel's behavior. The solution, then, would be to strengthen the private sector, restrict the role of the state to more or less indirect forms of intervention in the economy, and encourage foreign capital to play the crucial role of deepening the industrial process. In order to implement this strategy, Egypt would have to seek a rapprochement with the United States, make peace with Israel, disengage itself from Arab politics and concentrate its efforts on the internal problems of economic development.[10]

This power struggle came to a head with the death of President Nasser in September 1970. Led by the new president, Anwar Sadat, the right wing managed to dismantle the Nasserists' leadership in May 1971, when the vice president, Ali Sabri, and top Nasserist officials were ousted from power.

By gaining complete control of the state with this swift and dramatic act, the Sadat regime embarked upon the implementation of its policies. However, the new elites had a major task to perform if they were to ensure their hegemony: weakening the Nasserist social base, which constituted large sections of the middle class, the peasantry, and the labor force. The fulfillment of the Sadatists' plan required far-reaching changes in dominant socioeconomic power relations in order to move from a populist regime, relying on economic inclusionary policies of social and economic equity, to a regime favoring a new social alliance formed of top bureaucratic elites, the traditional wings of the old bourgeoisie, the captains of the private market. and foreign capital. This change in dominant power relations required massive redistribution policies from the lower- to the upper-income classes and therefore a new political formula to ease the transition. The Sadatists found the formula in the slogan of democracy and, as part and parcel of democratic rights, the restoration of the ultimate right to private property and the reintroduction of market mechanisms. If this political formula failed to effect the transition peacefully, then the state could resort to coercive powers to restrain opposition to the new policies.

Infitah and Redistribution in Egypt

The proponents of *Infitah*, or the Open-Door Policy, had a specific model for economic growth, that of the internationally supported strategy of an export-oriented industrialization. According to the supporters of this strategy, the deepening of the industrial process can no longer depend on internal capital accumulation. Economic growth can only be promoted through heavy reliance on foreign capital and technology. Local capital is encouraged to participate in the new strategy, either through joint ventures with foreign capital or by diversifying into areas of no particular interest to the multinational corporations. But many economic and political factors weigh in the multinationals' investment strategies. On the economic level, multinational corporations will only invest in those industries which either have a substantial internal market or which are geared mainly toward export markets large enough to make production more profitable than in similar industries in the companies' home bases. A cheap and skilled labor force is necessary to maintain high returns. Taxes and regulations on production and profit repatriation have to be at a minimum. In all cases, a risk-free environment is considered necessary for the multinationals. Among those risks which should be strictly avoided are nationalization measures and, above all, a politically activated labor force.[11]

To implement this strategy in Egypt in the 1970s, the Sadatists had to provide the conditions required by foreign and internal private capital. To achieve these desirable conditions, they had to alter quite drastically the existing political power relations established by the Nasserists. They were partially successful in their attempt, although—because of factors explained later—they could not implement all the following conditions:

1. To create an internal market for multinational companies' products, which are mainly consumer-durables requiring an income large enough to afford them, income has to be redistributed from the lower- to the upper-income groups.

2. Workers' wages have to be low enough to ensure the high profitability that would attract the multinationals.

3. The small-scale agricultural system has to give way to large-scale capitalized farms. Land-reform laws have to be downgraded until it is possible to eliminate the small farms completely.

4. The state also has to restore the free-market mechanism. This requires a) the elimination of state subsidies to industries and welfare programs, especially food subsidies, and b) the streamlining of the bureaucracy and the elimination of overemployment in the public sector, in order to increase productivity and reduce economic inefficiencies. In fact, the state's commitment to full employment must at the very least be drastically reduced in order to restore the free-market mechanism.

The implementation of such a program in Egypt meant a frontal attack on the Nasserist populist alliance, i.e., the workers, the peasants, and the salaried government and public-sector employees, who formed a substantial proportion of the middle classes. To effect this transition, the Sadatists had to undertake two major tasks: constitute a new dominant class alliance and defeat the nationalist/populist alliance of the 1960s.[12] In order to constitute a new dominant class alliance, the regime had to form a power-block under the hegemony of the bureaucratic elites, overcome the internal contradictions within the new power-block, and create a social base for the new dominant alliance by forming a distinct social base that supported its policies. In order to defeat the populist coalition, the regime resorted to reshaping the political system so as to deprive the populist alliance any effective influence. They attempted to appease the populist social base through the regime's economic and political performance, and used coercive measures in cases of open resistance.

The regime used a specific ideology—that of politicized religion. This religious-ideological interpellation aimed to a) mold the different factions of the new dominant alliance into a cohesive block, b) broaden the basis of support, c) build a distinctive political platform, and d) discredit and isolate the opposing forces by implying that their acts and attitudes were inspired and motivated by atheist ideologies, thereby alienating the rest of society from their perspective.

This frontal attack on the Nasserist policies was led under the banner of restoring democracy to the Egyptian political system. While the regime acted swiftly in realigning the dominant power relations, it moved at a snail's pace on democratization. Even now, democracy in the Egyptian system is restricted. A few opposition parties, marginally represented in parliament, are tolerated, and a certain degree of freedom of expression in the opposition press is allowed. At the same time, the regime has armed itself with a whole array of laws, such as the 'permanent' so-called emergency laws which allow it to curb and even restrict this margin of democratic rights at the first threat, real or imaginary, to the regime's stability and security. Such laws were used harshly in the aftermath of the massive bread demonstrations which erupted in January 1977, and again after the assassination of President Sadat in 1981. This is not to deny that the present political regime in Egypt does not possess a degree of liberalism which exceeds by far the freedoms guaranteed under the previous populist regime. Nevertheless, economic liberalization did not proceed as smoothly or as quickly as conceived by its proponents.

The slow pace of economic liberalization can be explained by the resistance of substantial parts of the middle classes, the workers, and the peasants to economic measures which would reverse the economic rights they gained under the populist regime. Investment by foreign and private capital, especially while the political system is still under the complete hegemony of the bureaucratic elite, has been hesitant and slow, and the dominant section of the bureaucratic elite has opposed the liquidation of the public sector, which is their main source of economic, and therefore political, power.

The attempts of the postpopulist regime at income redistribution from the lower- to the high-income groups in a direct manner through the elimination of subsidies (especially subsidies of strategic food items) have met strong resistance. The Egyptian population erupted into massive riots when the regime announced the elimination of subsidies in January 1977. To maintain the regime's stability, the government had to rescind its decisions and restore the subsidies. Attempts at increasing the rent on agricultural land and housing units have led to great political controversies. While rents on agricultural land have been slightly increased, legislation to increase rent on housing was paralyzed in lengthy debates in the People's Assembly with no decision taken on the issue. More important is the inability of the postpopulist regime to reverse the iron-clad laws of tenure on rented land and housing units, which give tenants the rights of real possession, if not that of formal ownership. Owners of old agricultural land and housing units have the right to charge only a fixed rent. Other rights relating to termination or reversal of tenure lie completely in the hands of the tenants, not the formal owners. This inability of the postpopulist regime to alter the tenure systems and to restore market mechanisms in agriculture and housing is due to the regime's fear of massive resistance by the tenants, who form a substantial majority of middle-income peasants and urban dwellers.

However, although the government could not alter rent regulations on the lands and housing units that had been set up under the previous populist regime, they could formulate more liberal regulations concerning the new forms of investment in new housing and new lands. To avoid the strict tenure laws, new legal forms emerged, such as cooperative condominiums, etc.

This policy of appeasement towards certain sections of the population, by maintaining the Nasserist laws in some sectors of the economy while allowing private entrepreneurs to take advantage of the free-market laws in new investments, has led to the creation of two economies in Egypt: one that is still ruled by the populist laws, and another that abides by the free-market rules.[13]

The coexistence of these two economies has resulted in a whole set of price distortions, and opened wider the channels of corruption. A new class taking advantage of these distortions, and amassing huge wealth through its access to channels of decision-making and authority, has emerged: they can be called the 'parasitic bourgeoisie'.

While the postpopulist regime proceeded slowly in its economic liberalization program, so as to avoid massive political discontent, it also counted on substantial private investments, both foreign and domestic, to promote economic growth in a sluggish economy. Successive (and very generous) investment laws, starting with the famous Law 43 of 1974, were intended to attract foreign, Arab, and domestic capital. Nevertheless, private capital was, and is still, very slow to take advantage of these new investment incentives. Gross fixed investment averaged around LE7 billion per year for the period 1983/84–1987/88, and 75 percent of that is still supplied by the public sector.[14]

Foreign investments, from either the capital-rich Arab countries or Western countries, never materialized on the scale expected by the ruling elites. Moreover, the foreign capital that has been invested is concentrated in the service and financial sectors of the economy, i.e., those sectors which promise quick returns but do not add much to industrial or agricultural productive capacities. From 1974 to the end of 1982, total investments committed under Law 43 did not exceed LE5 billion. From that total, 24 percent were invested by the Egyptian public sector, 37 percent by the Egyptian private sector, 23 percent by Arab investors, and only 16 percent by Western investors. Egyptian capital, both public and private, contributed 80 percent of all agricultural investments, 72 percent of all industrial investments, 52 percent of financial investments, 75 percent of construction investments, and 57 percent of investments in the service sector. The bulk of Arab investments went to the free-zone areas (72 percent of the LE1,952 million of committed projects), 40 percent of financial investments, followed by construction (16 percent) and services (10 percent). Western capital did not represent more than 16 percent of internal investments and 12 percent of free-zone investments. Most foreign investments were concentrated in the service sector (33 percent of total investments in that sector). Worse still is the fact that of all investments committed for the period 1974–82, only 32 percent of total capital was actually invested. Another 28 percent was invested in projects under implementation, while 40 percent of the capital was tied to projects that were yet to be implemented.[15]

The method of industrialization using foreign capital failed miserably in the Egyptian case. It is usual to blame the failure to attract substantial foreign capital on the obstinacy of the Egyptian bureaucracy, current labor laws, the cowardice of private capital, etc. While some of these factors are undoubtedly relevant, the most significant reason to be found for the small inflow of foreign capital and the reluctance to invest by private capital is rather political.

The hegemony of the bureaucratic elites on the political system and the very narrow margin of democracy have prevented private capital from having a real and effective presence in the political system. The subordination of the private economic elites to the bureaucratic elites has made them very hesitant to invest substantially in a system they do not dominate politically. Private investments under these conditions carry the substantial risk of being expropriated by the bureaucratic elites at any sign of threat to the dominant position of these elites. The swift collapse of the economic empire of the Islamic financial companies after state intervention, in the second half of the 1980s, demonstrates the political weakness of the private entrepreneurs and their inability to compete effectively with the politically dominant bureaucratic elites.

Another related factor in the slow progress of economic liberalization is the resistance of the dominant bureaucratic elites themselves to attempts at privatizatizing the public sector. For while the bureaucratic elites do not, of course, privately own the public sector, they do in fact control the public sector's resources and determine the ways and means of their exploitation in the manner normally associated with real titled ownership. In this way, the bureaucratic elites can be said to own the public sector, collectively if not privately. This kind of economic power, over a substantial proportion of Egypt's economic resources, consolidates the political hegemony of the bureaucratic elites over the system. The resistance of the bureaucratic elites to privatization measures urged by foreign donors and private entrepreneurs is usually couched in terms that appeal to the majority of the population. One of the main reasons for preserving the existing structure of the public sector is to maintain low prices for the low-income groups through direct government subsidy of the public-sector goods' prices. In this way, the bureaucratic elites defend their monopoly of public-sector resources by mobilizing large sectors of the population in its defense.

While the argument for a large public sector leading the development process is valid, there could be measures to rationalize its performance by allowing more direct intervention of the people in decision-making processes. In a democratic and free system, the public sector could be geared toward satisfying the development and distributive needs of the population, while eliminating the monopoly of the bureaucratic elites, which use the public sector to ensure their political and economic hegemony.

The flow of foreign funds to Egypt after the 1973 Arab–Israeli War allowed the government to finance its investments and expenditures without undue recourse to drastic measures, which would have redistributed income substantially from the lower- to the upper-income groups. Since 1979 Egypt has become a major recipient of American aid. In 1989 Egypt received a total of $2.6 billion from the United States. This aid was divided as follows: $930 million in economic grant aid, $1.3 billion in military aid, $170 million in food aid, and $200 million in commodity-export credit guarantees.[16] At the same time, Egypt became one of the main recipients of foreign loans. In 1988 Egypt's total external debt stood at around $50 billion, the bulk of which (over $42 billion) is publicly guaranteed.[17]

Constraints on the availability of foreign exchange have been greatly relaxed since the mid-1970s. The boom in oil prices has resulted in a substantial flow of foreign exchange to Egypt, either through direct revenues from the export of Egyptian oil, or through remittances of migrant workers. In the first half of the 1980s, Egypt's revenues from the sale of oil, remittances of workers, Suez Canal dues, and tourism averaged $7 billion per year. The drop in oil prices in the second half of the 1980s led to a substantial drop in revenues from the export of oil. However, remittances did not decrease. In the fiscal year 1987–88, Egypt received $1,563 million for oil exports, $1,269 million from the Suez canal, $884 million from tourism, and $3,385 million from workers' remittances.[18]

This flow of foreign funds has alleviated the pressures on the government to proceed quickly in the economic liberalization process. They have also helped maintain the large system of subsidies which are an important factor in the regime's ability to maintain political stability.

For all the above reasons, which have slowed the quick implementation of economic liberalization, income distribution has not been drastically skewed. Available data on income distribution in Egypt demonstrate that by 1981 the lowest 40 percent of the population have managed not only to maintain their share of income, but to improve it. The relative share of the lowest 40 percent increased from 18.8 percent in 1974–75 to 20.3 percent in 1981 for the rural areas, and from 18.3 percent to 21.3 percent over the same time period for the urban areas *(see table 4).* Patterns of landownership demonstrate that the share of the poorest 95 percent of owners decreased from 57 percent in 1965 to around 50 percent in 1975. This decrease was mainly compensated for by the increase in the owners' share from five to ten feddans. This does not seem to indicate a major redistribution of land assets from the poorest to the highest-income groups *(see table 1).*

Other, but less reliable, estimates of income distribution seem to indicate that there was a substantial redistribution of income from the lower- to the upper-income groups. The share of wages in gross domestic product (GDP) have decreased from 50 percent in 1967–68 to only 38 percent in 1981–82 *(see table 2).* Estimates of the percentage of the population at or below the poverty level show a great deterioration, from 26.8 percent for the rural areas and 27.8 percent for the urban areas in 1964–65 to 47.2 percent and 51.1 percent, respectively, for 1984 *(see table 3).*

Despite these contradictions, the decrease of the share of wages in GDP and the deterioration of poverty levels do not seem to affect the relative shares

Table 4 Relative Shares in Rural (R) and Urban (U) Household Expenditures with Gini Coefficients, 1958–1981

Relative shares of income	1958/59[1]		1964/65[1]		1974/75[1]		1981[2]	
	R	U	R	U	R	U	R	U
Lowest 40%	17.6	16.4	19.0	16.5	18.8	18.3	20.3	21.3
Lowest 60%	34.2	30.9	35.2	31.2	35.5	34.4	37.7	39.2
Middle 30%	37.7	38.7	37.2	38.0	37.8	38.0	36.8	37.7
Top 10%	28.0	30.4	27.4	30.8	26.7	27.6	25.9	23.0
Gini coefficient	0.37	0.40	0.35	0.40	0.35	0.37	0.32	0.29

Sources: (1) John Waterbury, *The Egypt of Nasser and Sadat,* Princeton University Press, Princeton, 1983, p. 211. (2) Karima Korayen, *The Impact of Economic Adjustment on Vulnerable Families and Children in Egypt,* UNICEF, Cairo, 1987, p. 41, table 1.1.

in rural and urban household expenditures *(see table 4)*. These kinds of discrepancies might be due to the use of different criteria to assess the extent of income inequalities, especially if the data generated are built on certain estimates that are biased to some degree.

This does not mean that social inequalities did not increase in the postpopulist regimes. However, the new forms of inequalities are rather unconventional. As a matter of fact, the real inequalities in income occurred within different sections of the same class, rather than between classes as a whole, i.e., between those who had access to foreign exchange through migration and those who did not. Inequalities between sections of the same class also occurred between those who are still dealing within the Nasserist sector of the economy, i.e., the recipients of fixed income and wages; and those who rely for the derivation of their income on the free-market dynamics of the open-door sector.[19]

This might explain the contradictory sets of data which try to measure income distribution in Egypt. However, this situation requires a massive survey to estimate actual income distribution in Egypt, an exercise that has yet to materialize.

Conclusion

In this essay, I have tried to demonstrate the specificity of the Egyptian experiment in effecting the change from the populist to the postpopulist regime. While the postpopulist regime had attempted economic liberalization, it managed at the same time to maintain the populist income distribution, without affecting dramatically the lower-income groups. This was facilitated by external conditions, either in the Arab region, or in the international arena. The important question is, how long can Egypt remain in this condition of half-hearted liberalization? Only future developments can tell us if Egypt will be able to maintain the delicate social balance, or be forced to use coercive measures to redistribute income drastically for the benefit of the customers of Infitah.

Notes

1 N. R. Farah, "Science, Ideology and Authoritarianism in Middle East Economics," in E. L. Sullivan and J. S. Ismael, eds., *The Contemporary Study of the Arab World* (Edmonton: The University of Alberta Press, 1991).

2 Z.Y. Hershlag, *Introduction to the Modern Economic History of the Middle East* (Leiden: Brill, 1964).

3 M. Hussein, *Class Conflict in Egypt: 1945–1970* (New York: Monthly Review Press, 1973).

4 R. Mabro, *The Egyptian Economy: 1952–1972* (Oxford: Clarendon Press, 1974).
5 N. R. Farah, *Religious Strife in Egypt: Crisis and Ideological Conflict in the Seventies* (New York and London: Gordon and Breach, 1986).
6 National Center for Criminological and Sociological Research, *On Stratification*, NCCSR, Cairo, 1985.
7 R. Baker, *Egypt's Uncertain Revolution Under Nasser and Sadat* (Cambridge: Harvard University Press, 1978).
8 R. Mabro and S. Radwan, *The Industrialization of Egypt, 1939–1973* (Oxford: Clarendon Press, 1976).
9 G. Amin, "External Factors in the Reorientation of Egypt's Economic Policy," in M. Kerr and S. Yassin, eds., *Rich and Poor States in the Arab World* (Boulder: Westview Press, 1982).
10 Farah, "Science, Ideology, and Authoritarianism."
11 P. Evans, *Dependent Development: The Alliance of Multinationals, State, and Local Capital in Brazil* (Princeton: Princeton University Press, 1979).
12 Farah, *Religious Strife in Egypt.*
13 A. Hussein, *The Egyptian Economy from Independence to Dependency, 1974–1979* (in Arabic) (Cairo: Dar al-Mustaqbal al-'Arabi, 1982).
14 US Embassy in Cairo, *Economic Report of Egypt*, Cairo, 1990.
15 Ministry of Investment and International Cooperation, *Annual Report*, Cairo, 1983.
16 US Embassy in Cairo, *Economic Report of Egypt*, Cairo, 1990.
17 World Bank, *Development Report*, 1990.
18 US Embassy in Cairo, *Economic Report.*
19 Farah, "Science, Ideology, and Authoritarianism."

7

Contradictions of 'Structural Adjustment': Capital and the State in Post-1980 Turkey

Korkut Boratav

Introduction

This essay studies the so-called 'structural adjustment' operation which Turkey experienced during the 1980s, within the context of its distributional impacts and the chains it created within the domain of state–bourgeoisie relationships.

Before engaging in this theme, it will be useful to place the 1980s in a historical setting and compare some of its specificities briefly with other periods of the republican era. Table 1 provides a framework for such a comparison. Eight periods from 1923 up to the end of the 1980s—including the crisis years of the late 1970s which immediately preceded and led to the stabilization/structural adjustment operation of the 1980s—are covered, and a few indicators, which are also relevant for the central theme of the essay, are incorporated in the table.

The first three columns of table 1 show, for each period, the direction of changes with respect to the rates of surplus extraction from the two major classes of direct producers, i.e., the working class and the peasantry. The first column is based on distributional tradeoffs between wage-labor and capital within industry. A plus sign (+) indicates declining trends in wages/value-added ratios estimated either directly or on the basis of comparisons between real wage, productivity, and employment movements. Vice versa for a minus sign (–).

The second column is based on agriculture's terms of trade with respect to industrial prices. A positive sign indicates falling terms of trade and vice versa. This is interpreted as reflecting the distributional tradeoffs between peasants and industrial capital within the context of a peasant-based agrarian structure.

The third column reflects the direction of changes in commercial margins based on a comparison of prices paid by final users/consumers and prices received by farmers for agricultural (agriculture-based) commodities. A positive sign indicates widening commercial margins and vice versa. This indicator is considered to reflect distributional tradeoffs between the peasantry and merchant (commercial) capital. These indicators will be explained more fully when I investigate the 1977–89 years.

Columns 4 and 6 present the average figures on the contribution of the external world to capital accumulation during different periods. Because we lack comparable and reliable balance-of-payments/current account series for the republican era as a whole, trade deficit figures were used instead as the basis for these columns. Columns 4 and 6 give trade deficits as a proportion of GDP and of capital formation, respectively, as period averages.

Columns 5 and 7 present investment/GDP ratios and average growth rates for industry, respectively. A comparison of these columns with the others gives an idea of how far changes in internal rates of surplus extraction and external sources have contributed to capital accumulation and industrialization. In this context it should be pointed out that higher internal rates of surplus extraction and increases in external sources (deficits) improve merely the potential for overall (or industrial) capital formation. There always exists a wide area for nonproductive patterns of surplus utilization. The internal division of the surplus—a theme which will be discussed later—is an important variable in this context. Columns 1–4 and 6 in table 1 indicate how far conditions have been suitable in terms of this potential. Columns 5 and 7, on the other hand, show how far this potential has been realized in terms of accumulation rates and industrial growth.

As can be observed from the table, of all the periods of the republican era, the 1980s should be considered as the period creating the most appropriate conditions in terms of accumulation and growth potentials: there is no other period in which all three indicators of internal rates of surplus extraction as well as external deficits show definite improvement. The outcome, however, in terms of accumulation and industrialization, is disappointing; investment/GDP rates during the 1970s had increased significantly, and the table shows that it was impossible to sustain the pace of capital accumulation reached by the end of the 1970 during the 1980s. The other indicator, industrial growth, declines significantly between the precrisis period of 1962–76 and the 1980s. It should be pointed out that industrial growth during the 1980s owes much to increased rates of capacity use following the very high levels of excess capacity reached during the crisis of the late 1970s. Potential industrial growth, in terms of additions to existing capacities, declined even more significantly: the share of industry within total investments—in constant (1987) prices—was 46.3 percent in 1977, but a mere 22.7 percent in 1989.

Table 1 Indicators of Accumulation, Distribution, and Industrialization by Major Periods, 1923–1989

		Direction of changes in rates of surplus			External deficits	Accumulation		Industrialization
Periods	Characterization	Intra-industry	From agriculture to industry	From agriculture to commerce	(M-X)/Y[1] (%)	I/Y[2] (%)	(M-X)/I[3] (%)	Industry growth rate Period average (%)
1923–29	Open economy; state power used to facilitate private accumulation	?	-	?	3.8	9.1	41.2	8.5
1930–39	Protectionism and etatism	+	+	?	Surplus	10.1	Surplus	11.6
1940–45	War economy	+	-	?	Surplus	8.3	Surplus	-6.5
1946–53	External and internal liberalization	+,-	+	+	1.90	10.50	18.10	9.20
1954–61	Interruption and readjustment	-	+	?	1.40	14.00	10.00	4.30
1962–76	Domestic market-oriented industrialization	Stable	-	+,-	3.70	17.90	20.80	9.40
1977–79	Crisis	-	+	+,-	5.90	23.50	24.90	3.70
1980–89	Counteroffensive of capital and a new mode of regulation	+	+	+	5.9*	21.00	33.1*	5.40

Notes: (+) and (-) signs represent rising and declining rates of surplus appropriation during the relevant period.
(+,-) represents lack of a definite trend with respect to the same rates.
* 1980–88
1 trade deficit as % of national income 2 investment as % of national income 3 trade deficit as % of investment expenditures

Sources and methods: See Boratav (1988b). The quantitative findings there have been updated on the basis of Boratav and Türel (1990) and Uygur (1990).

The 1980s, on the basis of the foregoing findings, emerges as a period of missed opportunities for growth and industrialization for the Turkish economy. Although this problem per se is not exactly the central theme of this essay, it is impossible to understand the dismal accumulation/industrialization performance for the economy under such ideal preconditions without analyzing internal contradictions of capital and capital–state relations. The present essay, in investigating these contradictions and relations, may also provide significant clues for understanding the wider dynamic macroeconomic issues of the 1980s.

A bird's-eye view of the 'structural adjustment' operation of the 1980s within the context of the present essay's paradigm will be useful here. As it will be seen in more detail further on, a dramatic decline in the relative and absolute economic positions of the workers and peasants took place in the 1980s. This is the usual and expected outcome of an orthodox stabilization/structural adjustment package, although the magnitude and duration of these changes in Turkey has probably exceeded what had happened in similar experiences elsewhere. Our investigation, however, emphasizes another and rather neglected distributional impact of the structural adjustment program as implemented in Turkey, namely the radical changes which occurred within different subgroups of the bourgeoisie. These latter changes within the domain of secondary relations of distribution, or of the redistribution, of the surplus, have affected the balance of forces within the ranks of the bourgeoisie.

Concomitantly with these changes, significant transformations took place within the bureaucratic and political layers of the state with respect to the mechanisms shaping and implementing economic-policy decisions affecting individual business groups. The Turkish bourgeoisie, therefore, faced radical changes on three fronts during the 1980s, all of which affected different segments of the class in different ways: changes occurring within primary relations of distribution (i.e., vis-à-vis the working class), changes occurring within secondary relations of distribution of the surplus, and changes occurring in the mechanisms of the state's economic decision-making. Towards the end of the 1980s, the last two categories of changes started to create contradictions and tensions within the ranks of the bourgeoisie vis-à-vis their links with the state.

This essay will discuss these issues without depicting and analyzing the overall framework and components of the structural adjustment operation of 1980s—this has been done elsewhere.[1] The policies followed throughout the 1980s in Turkey share most of the common features of orthodox stabilization/adjustment recipes implemented in many semi-industrialized countries during the past decade. It may be useful, however, to emphasize the specificities of the Turkish experience, which, to a limited degree, distinguish it from similar cases in a number of other countries.

First of all, income policies distinctly played the most crucial role in the Turkish version of stabilization and structural adjustment. It must be noted that this policy component could be executed effectively thanks to the extra economic measures of the military regime established following the coup of September 1980. Second, the program benefited from substantial financial support from abroad—a factor which explains the fact that there was practically no GDP decline throughout. Third, there was a striking continuity throughout the 1980s: the Motherland Party (MP) government, from 1984 onwards, adopted and developed further the policy orientations of the military regime. If we leave aside the frontal assault on labor incomes during the early 1980s, it was a gradual policy: stabilization preoccupations and liberations of the internal commodity and money markets characterized the first five years; liberalization of external transactions dominated the post-1984 phase. There were no erratic reversals—as observed in certain Latin American experiences. It is partly due to this continuity that we can now speak of a new mode of regulation in the Turkish economy. In other words, certain components of the policies of the 1980s have now been transformed into structural features of the Turkish economy, thereby giving a strong element of permanence to the new policy model.

Changes in Primary Relations of Distribution: Capital versus Labor

Table 2 presents most of the significant indicators on income distribution covering the period from 1977 up to the late 1980s.[2] With respect to changes in the primary relations of distribution—which essentially represent the distributional tradeoffs between classes of direct producers and certain segments of capital—the following observations can be made.

1. A striking feature of the period is the drastic regression of labor incomes, represented essentially by indicators on wages and agriculture's terms of trade, both in relative and absolute terms, as observed specifically under rows 1–3. Indicators covered in rows 4 and 5 corroborate these observations. It is significant to note that both the magnitude and duration of the relative regression in worker and peasant incomes are without precedent during the republican period.[3]

2. The dramatic regression in real wages, in both relative and absolute terms, has been the outcome of an ongoing process throughout the 1980s. (rows 1–3). This trend has been shaped by:

i) the suspension of trade-union activities and of collective bargaining under the martial law period until 1985;

ii) the dismantling and enforced elimination of the militant wing of the Turkish trade-union movement by the military authorities, leaving behind a large traditionally moderate and 'collaborationist' Turkish Trade Union Confederation—demoralized and paralyzed during most of the period—practically monopolizing the trade-union movement;

iii) the authoritarian reorganization of labor-market institutions within the framework of the 1982 constitution and the labor legislation in the same spirit which accompanied it;

iv) the anti-trade-union orientations of MP governments from 1984 onwards; and

v) the fact that mark-up rates in manufacturing industries have been raised, possibly in response to regressing real wages during the 1980s.

Two qualifications are in order in this context.[4] First, it should be noted that the deterioration of wage levels and shares does not correctly reflect changes in household incomes of urban workers. Within the Turkish urban economy there exist possibilities for a number of economic and social adaptation mechanisms through which working-class families have managed to make up for the regression of wages, albeit by leading to deteriorations in their quality of life. Secondly, although MP governments have been extremely tough vis-à-vis unions' wage demands, they have, at the same time, followed a deliberate policy of reaching out to the poor through a mixture of municipal and social policies, thus alleviating some of the adverse impact of wage movements, or at least creating expectations in that direction.

3. Relative prices received by farmers, as represented by agriculture's terms of trade (representing the distributional tradeoff between peasants and local or external industrial capital) (row 3), or by commercial margins for agriculture-based commodities (representing the distributional conflict between peasants and commercial capital) (rows under 4) have deteriorated throughout the period. The deterioration for the former indicator is particularly striking and continuous. The gradual scrapping of the elaborate system of agricultural support policies, which had evolved through the three decades from the late 1940s onwards, was the major policy factor leading to the adverse terms of trade movements for farmers during the 1980s: the ratio of support purchases by public agencies of agricultural output to agricultural value-added had declined from 20.4 percent in 1976 to an annual average of 12 percent during 1980–86.[5]

The peasants' reaction to the process of price deterioration seems to have been to engage in increasing degrees of self-exploitation of family labor and suppression of household consumption so as to sustain the level of current inputs, which explains the realization of modest rates of productivity increases throughout the period. Increasing productivity has not, however, prevented real declines in peasant incomes.[6] These particular adaptation mechanisms have led to deteriorations in the 'quality of life' in peasant households as well.

It should be noted that the repression of relative prices for farmers was not a major demand of the Turkish bourgeoisie during the early 1980s. It is mainly the textile lobby which benefits directly from lower prices for agricultural raw materials in Turkey; other processed crops are either channeled to state-owned enterprises (tea and sugar, for example) or have traditionally been excluded from support policies (canned vegetables and fruits). The Ricardian effect of 'lower wheat price leading to lower nominal wages' was not relevant for the Turkish scene of the early 1980s, since the elimination of price controls and subsidies on wage goods led to a state of affairs in which lower relative crop prices for farmers were accompanied by higher relative retail prices for necessities (rows 4a–4d). When wages are significantly above subsistence level and when direct mechanisms for repressing wages can be operated, there is no need to have recourse to the indirect Ricardian route for realizing a higher profit share. I believe that the antifarmer policy stand was mainly a 'transplanted commodity' originating from external architects of the structural-adjustment models, and implemented by their fanatical followers in the state, who were committed to a 'free-market solution,' regardless of the consequences.

4. The late 1970s have been referred to by V. Koç, the doyen of Turkish big business, as "years of nightmare." Profit-squeeze, caused by effective trade-union action under economic-crisis conditions, was one of the factors behind this characterization of the period. But these were also years of an increased degree of grassroots workers' militancy. Industrialists were feeling more and more unable to control and manage their enterprises because of continuous struggles with workers, not only on economic and social issues, but occasionally on political issues as well. 'Disciplining the labor market' and 'disciplining the working class movement' became the urgent demands of bourgeoisie during 1978–79.

The mechanisms leading to the military regime's full commitment to these demands by the bourgeoisie is a story which has been told elsewhere.[7] It should only be re-emphasized that the post-1980 operations on the labor front were the crucial element in the bourgeoisie's assessment of economic policies of the early 1980s, a factor which explains the almost unqualified support extended to the military regime by the prominent representatives of the class.

Elements of internal conflict within the ranks of the bourgeoisie and strong reservations on certain policy elements and 'style of government' started to come to the surface much later during the late 1980s. It is necessary to investigate the transformations taking place within the domain of secondary relations of distributions to understand these changes in attitudes.

Changes in the Redistribution of the Surplus: Contradictions within the Bourgeoisie

An anatomy of the bourgeoisie is required to investigate intra-class contradictions. The most suitable scheme of internal division for the bourgeoisie as a starting point should be based on the well-known functional differentiation: industrial, agrarian, functional, and commercial segments of capital, plus rentiers, provide the essential components of such a division. It is possible to quantify changes in distributional shares of these groups by the use of conventional statistical data, as witnessed by table 1, and this possibility provides an advantage of using this scheme. It is, moreover, based on a consistent and theoretically sound conceptual framework. One should note,

Table 2 Indicators of Primary and Secondary Relations of Distribution

	1977	1979	1980	1983	1984	1985	1986	1987	1988	1989
Real wages (1977=100)										
Manufacturing, Turkey	100.0	93.8	84.7	84.0	72.6	71.6	73.8			
Overall, Turkey	100.0*	99.9	81.1	74.5	68.2	58.2	54.0	53.5	4.5	
Wages/value added in industry (%)										
Private/Turkey	34.6	31.8	27.6	26.0	23.8	22.8	18.2			
Largest private				42.7	38.2	39.4	32.6	29.5	31.8	
Private/Eskişehir		62.7	60.6	50.5	45.0	47.0	43.9			
Agriculture/industry terms of trade (GDP)	100.0	66.6	57.2	49.6	51.2	47.5	46.7	48.9	43.8	47.7
Commercial margins for agriculture										
Bread/wheat	100.0	111.8	115.5	123.0	115.3	113.7	110.2			
Sugar/sugar beet	100.0	108.2	207.3	129.4	129.4	122.5	126.4			
Cloth/cotton	100.0	77.0	76.8	108.6	105.4	130.0	116.0			
Margarine/sunflower	100.0	105.7	134.9	129.5	214.7	161.1	142.6			
Tobacco (export/farm)	100.0	106.9	230.3	307.6	316.3					
Cotton (export/farm)	100.0	129.2	89.6	169.3	185.2					
Real civil service salaries (1977=100)	100.0*	91.3	68.0	58.6	46.7	42.9	45.4	48.8	45.7	

Table 2 contd.

	1977	1979	1980	1983	1984	1985	1986	1987	1988	1989
Interest payments/industrial surplus (%)										
Largest private				52.6	54.1	60.4	67.6	50.1	56.3	
Private/Eskişehir		13.4	22.1	53.7	42.0	46.0	39.0			
Trade and finance in GDP										
Finance/GDP (%)	2.5	1.8	1.8	1.9	2.7	2.9	2.9	2.8	2.8	3.1
Trade/GDP (%)	13.5	15.0	15.9	17.6	18.1	17.2	17.1	17.6	17.6	17.5
Real bank profits, index		100.0	247.3	329.0	636.7	617.6	968.8	1310.4		
Rentier incomes										
Deposit interests/GDP (%)	0.3	0.8	1.4	5.6	7.7	10.8	9.2	7.7	10.6	
Real deposit interest rate (%)	-16.9	-47.9	-80.8	14.4	-7.0	15.0	21.3	8.0	0.4	
Interest (domestic) from budget/GDP	0.5	0.5	0.5	0.7	1.0	1.0	1.8	2.4	3.5	
Total interest income/GDP (%)	0.8	1.3	1.9	6.3	8.7	11.8	11.0	10.1	14.1	
Real interest incomes, index	100	172	246	938	1357	1919	1978	1939	2775	

* Average 1976–77

Sources: Rows 1b and 5 are from Celasun (1989). Row 8c on budgetary interest payments is taken from an unpublished study by Aykut Eksen. For detailed explanation on data sources and methods of calculation of the findings in other rows, see Boratav (1990a). The findings there have been updated in this paper.

Notes: Rows 1a and 2a are based on surveys and censuses of manufacturing industry undertaken by the State Institute of Statistics. Real wages series in 1a and 1b are based on wholesale price and GDP deflators respectively, thereby representing real wage costs rather than incomes. Rows 4a–4d are index numbers of the ratios between the index numbers of the relevant consumer prices and prices received by farmers. Rows 4e and 4f are index numbers of the ratios between the index numbers of the relevant unit export prices and the prices received by farmers. Rows 6a and 6b are percentage shares of interest payments made by the relevant group of industrial firms within value-added minus wages. Row 7c is calculated from balance sheets of commercial banks as published by the Union of Banks. Row 8a covers only time deposits within the banking system and foreign-exchange accounts, and annual average interest rates for the relevant category are used in calculating total deposit interest. Row 8c covers consolidated domestic interest payments from the public budget and excludes state enterprises. Row 8d = rows 8a + 8c.

however, that the rentier group does not fall strictly within the functional division of capital.

On the other hand, the functional division loses some or most of its relevance in those cases where vertical integration on the basis of different functional layers shape the economic structure, i.e., where the economy is dominated by single conglomerates incorporating the productive, commercial—internal and external—and financial functions within the same organizational entity. In the absence of vertical integration the same division becomes economically insignificant in those cases where capital does not suffer from rigidities and can change its domain of operation from one 'function' to the other with ease.

In the Turkish case,[8] we observe eight conglomerates which operate simultaneously in industry and trade (including export houses), and have their own banks. Although these are large economic groups, it would be an exaggeration to assert that Turkish industry and trade are under the control of these groups. On the other hand, all private commercial banks—except a single one—are integrated with one of the conglomerates, and it follows that distributional indicators with respect to the profits of financial capital should be interpreted as accruing to large holding-type conglomerates. As for the rentier category, consisting of economic agents whose revenues are derived from returns on nonproductive assets, this is a conceptually and functionally clear-cut group. But it is also heterogeneous in its social composition, unpredictable its political attitudes and difficult to delineate in practical empirical terms. It should also be noted that within the economic policy framework of the late 1980s, banks have started to operate partly as 'institutional rentiers'. A final observation is related to the de facto absence of a strong, significant, and influential agrarian bourgeoisie in Turkey: the Turkish agrarian structure can realistically be depicted as a predominantly peasant agriculture (i.e., petty commodity production) and the past decade's policy orientations towards agriculture have not been suitable for inducing capital of nonagrarian origin to invest in the sector.

On the basis of the foregoing observations on the anatomy of the Turkish bourgeoisie, we can now start to interpret the changes observed in table 1 (rows under 6–8, and partly under 4 as well) with respect to redistribution of the surplus during the 1977–89 period. The following set of interpretations seems valid:

1. It is clear that the 1980s have been far from neutral with respect to the redistribution of the surplus. These changes have been on such a large scale that it would have been anomalous if deep-seated internal conflict between different sub-groups of the bourgeoisie had not surfaced.

2. The internal division of the surplus has shifted in favor of rentiers (rows under 8) and of financial capital (rows 7a, 7c) and definitely against net industrial profits (rows under 6). Extremely high interest rates have prevented industrial capital from preserving the superprofits which could have accrued

to it via depressed wages: the largest private industrial corporations have allocated between a half and two thirds of gross profits to their interest obligations (row 6a). Rentier incomes from time and foreign-exchange deposits and government bonds have risen from around 1 percent in the late 1970s to reach the spectacular ratio of 14.1 percent. There is definitely something wrong in an economy where interest incomes have practically reached the level of value-added in agriculture—a sector which provides a livelihood for more than half of the active population. There is also evidence that commercial margins have widened, reflecting improvement in the relative economic position of commercial capital (row 7b, rows under 4, especially 4e and 4f), although higher interest rates have created similar burdens on gross commercial profits as well.

3. These transformations are clearly linked with economic policies of the period with respect to the so-called 'liberalization' of the financial system and the obsession of policy-makers with the need to offer positive interest rates to 'savers'. There have also been policy components favoring commercial activities over productive activities, particularly with respect to the privileged status of large and specialized export corporations.

4. It is interesting to note that these policies leading to far-reaching changes in the redistribution of the surplus were not the outcome of systematic pressures emanating from certain subgroups of the bourgeoisie; rentiers, the major beneficiaries of the new policy model, have never been a well-defined, organized lobby within the business community. On the other hand, specialized industrial capital organized outside the large conglomerates, i.e., the major losers within the business community, had, during the preceding decades, developed into a well-organized group keenly aware of its short-term interest, and it would be very difficult to perceive a 'rentier lobby' prevailing over the industrialists, considering the balance of forces within the bourgeoisie during the 1980s. Although business groups organized in large and vertically integrated conglomerates have been more receptive to the new patterns since they have been allowed much more flexibility to shift their resources from disadvantaged activities to the newly emerging and privileged ones, they did not openly campaign for financial liberalization and higher interest rates. I think it is safe to say that the new model, with respect to the redistribution of the surplus, has essentially been a transplantation from abroad, i.e., originating in international capital.

On the other hand, once major operations on the labor front were completed, and once the optimism emanating from the pro-business discourse of the MP government eroded as the 1985–87 boom came to an end, the pro-rentier orientations of the structural adjustment policy came under strong attack from representatives of specialized industrial capital. The most vocal critics belong to large specialized and influential (e.g., in textiles) industrial companies which do not have their own banking extensions. It interesting to note that during the 1980s, that is, long after the essential 'disciplining' of the labor market was completed, these groups started to blame the deterioration in labor's share as an outcome of financial liberalization and of the government's obsession with high interest rates.9 Industrial groups which were unable to establish their own export corporations with privileged status were also severely critical of the tendency to transform Turkey into a mainly 'trading society'.[10]

Political and Bureaucratic Layers of State Structure: Changing Patterns of State–Class Relations

The 1980s have witnessed another important change affecting the patterns in which the relationships of the bourgeoisie with the state structure are articulated. This is closely related to those aspects of economic policies which, by their very nature, create positions of advantage and superprofits for individual business establishments. Although I am not satisfied with the terminology and the underlying theory, I will follow the convention of referring to this phenomena as 'rent-seeking and rent-creating activities' of the bourgeoisie.

'Rent-seeking' behavior has usually been depicted as specific to protectionist, import-substituting developing economies. The Turkish experience of export promotion/liberalization of the 1980s produced ample evidence for repudiating this shallow view. There is a widely held opinion within the business groups that, particularly under MP governments, the state's power to create and destroy positions of advantage for individual business groups has been used much more extensively and in a much more 'arbitrary' fashion then the preceding periods, and that the magnitudes (i.e., the 'spoils') involved during the 'liberal' phase have been substantially larger than those observed under the 'protectionist/interventionist' phase.[11] Export subsidies, import surcharges, government tenders, fiscal incentives, subsidized credit, building licenses, 'salvaging operations' for insolvent firms, tax inspections, and amnesties on 'economic crimes' are some of those areas in which decisions by public authorities have continued to create huge gains or losses for individual business groups. The persistence of these areas of 'rent-creation' in a self-proclaimed 'liberal' regime demonstrates limits of liberalization in a under-developed economic structure.

On the other hand, businessmen's references to 'arbitrariness' in the allocation of these 'rents' or 'positions of advantage' on the aforementioned areas and activities point to a relatively new development which has been occurring within the state structure during the 1980s. Decision-making and implementation on 'rent-allocating' activities have gradually been shifting to become the prerogative of the political layer of the state structure, with the bureaucratic layer being relegated to an increasingly passive position. In practical terms, this means that the decision on such diverse questions as, 'which company will get the government tender on a particular infrastructure investment?'; 'will a building license for a vacant plot at the center of Istanbul be given to A and for how many square meters?'; 'should surcharges on imported item X competing with the same item produced locally by firms A and B be lowered or raised?'; 'should the case against exporter A on charges of invoicing be lifted or not?' are now being taken by the relevant minister and in some cases directly by the prime minister. And the scope for independent action by the bureaucracy on all these issues has been narrowing drastically.

This is a relatively new phenomenon. The potential conflict between the political and bureaucratic layers of the Turkish state has been present particularly since 1945, when the bourgeoisie gradually managed to establish undisputed control over the political 'class'. In the meantime, the traditional Turkish bureaucracy managed to preserve autonomous positions within a number of strategic state agencies, and true to the typical petit-bourgeois illusion of being the real 'protectors of the state', kept an eye on the mechanisms of 'rent distribution'. The basic function of the bureaucratic layer during the phase of import-substituting industrialization was not the elimination of 'rents'; but rather the guaranteeing of conditions of equality among rival claims with respect to the distribution of rents. Detailed regulations, on government tenders, import licenses, urban land use, etc., usually produced by the bureaucracy had aimed at establishing the guidelines for creating equality on the distribution of the spoils. In this endeavor they were helped by the overall democratic atmosphere of most of the 1960s and 1970s, in which a sensitive public opinion had developed against the use of economic layers in favor of individual business interests.

During the same period, the strengthening of the organic link between the political layer and the bourgeoisie was essentially taking the form of individualized, clientele-type relations. The bureaucracy's aforementioned functions were creating impediments to fully reaping the benefits of these links for the political party in power, as well as for their constituencies within the business community. The pattern in which the political layer reacted to the bureaucratic/democratic challenge was (a) to keep intact the bureaucracy's traditional decision-making authority in economic issue, but (b) to establish a 'partisan bureaucracy', particularly within the decision-making echelons of public administration. This was a long and tedious process, with each new government changing the handful of top-level civil servants in the ministries of its predecessor. Most of the strategic economic agencies, however, such as the Ministries of Finance and Trade—despite partisan appointment at the highest level, usually from within the relevant agency—managed to preserve their autonomy to a significant degree up till the early 1980s.

Although this state of affairs was never fully satisfactory for the political class, or for its constituencies within the business community, it was nonetheless instrumental in creating a significant degree of stability for the bourgeoisie as a class. There were always complaints of bureaucratic high-handedness, slowness, narrow-mindedness, etc., and unhappiness with the presence of a relatively incorruptible and efficient tax-collection system which represented the generalized sentiments of the bourgeoisie vis-à-vis the bureaucracy. On the other hand, the presence of a mechanism of 'having access to equal conditions in sharing the advantages emanating from public policies' created a strong sense of stability within the ranks of the bourgeoisie, and led to the prevalence of a modus vivendi between the individual business groups, the bourgeoisie class, the bureaucracy, and the political cadres. The bureaucracy benefits from 'rents', provided that nobody is specifically privileged or discriminated against. It was a curious modus vivendi, which created the appearance of a mature form of state–class relations, somewhat in the European fashion, although the two principal actors, namely the political layer of the state structure and the individual elements of the bourgeoisie, never willed such an outcome deliberately.

This modus vivendi was destroyed by MP governments during the second half of the 1980s. The operation was preceded and accompanied by an antibureaucratic campaign linked with the ideological slogan of 'less government' emanating from international capital. Under the pretext of "eliminating the bureaucratic fetters in economic issues," a number of functions traditionally allocated to the bureaucracy shifted to the political layer (e.g., to the ministries and the prime minister) along the lines described above. The 'partisan appointment' in this case took the form of 'importing' experts (usually from the United States, and usually with no prior experience in Turkish public administration) who acted as channels of transmission from international capital to the decision-making units. The bureaucratic layer of decision-making and implementation on economic issues was thereby gradually paralyzed.[12]

These new orientations created acute tensions and inner conflicts within the bourgeoisie and between certain business groups and the state, particularly after the 1985–87 boom was exhausted. These arose in addition to the tensions already accumulating due to the industry-finance-rentier-commerce contradictions discussed in the preceding section. The top-level political cadres of MP had origins in the business community—a factor which initially determined which business groups were to have privileged treatment. A second factor in choosing 'the select few' was the attitude of different businessmen during the period when MP was being established as a rival to the pro-military Party of Nationalist Democracy (PND) before the 1983 elections. MP leaders never forgot or forgave those business groups that supported PND in 1983. Credit squeezes, reduction or elimination of surcharges on imported rival products, heavy ministerial inspections and delays on tax-rebate claims on exported commodities and on tax evasions, advertisement bans and distribution restrictions on the particular commodity (e.g., on beer producers), refusal to grant building permits or incentives on touristic metropolitan real-estate investments, and rejection of government construction tenders (even in those cases when the most economical offer was made) were some of the means used to discriminate against and penalize the 'dissident' or non-favorite business groups. Since, by definition, all segments of the business community could not have equal access to the political centers, and since the 'excluded' would always be more numerous than the 'favorites', it was natural that such orientations created more adversaries than supporters and led to the emergence of a strong sense of uncertainty within the bourgeoisie at large.[13]

Concluding Notes

On the basis of transformations in state–class relations in Turkey's experience with structural adjustment during the past decade, the following conclusions seem to be relevant and interesting:

1. 'Disciplining the labor market' was the major objective of the post-1980 economic model, and the Turkish bourgeoisie was unanimous in approving an operation to attain this objective through state repression under military rule.

2. After the operation on the labor front was completed and after the 1985 boom was exhausted, certain components of the structural-adjustment program affecting the redistribution of the surplus in a non-neutral fashion created tensions within the ranks of the bourgeoisie. These elements of the structural-adjustment operation were not responses to demands and needs coming from certain segments of the local bourgeoisie. Instead, they were implantations originating from international capital. Specialized industrial capital emerged as the main loser; rentiers and vertically integrated big business turned out to be the major winners.

3. There are limits to liberalization within the structural features of an underdeveloped capitalist economy. While certain mechanisms of 'rent creation' are undermined, state power is used to create positions of advantage in other, and sometimes new, areas. The scale of alteration involved in Turkey recently seems to be no less than in preceding decades.

4. There emerged a pattern of disarticulation in the state structure during the 1980s. The bureaucratic layer was paralyzed under the pretext of 'less government' when the political layer took over most of the functions the bureaucracy used to perform.

5. This transformation created acute tensions within the bourgeoisie as MP political cadres used state power to extend privileged or discriminatory treatment to individual business groups.

6. It seems that even to reduce the economic role of the state effectively, what is needed is a well-paid, dedicated bureaucracy with a strong historical tradition and without ideological illusions regarding its mission in society. Turkey was lucky enough to have such a bureaucracy; but the developments during the 1980s have gone a long way towards destroying its presence as an

independent economic actor. Turkish society will probably pay the price of this evolution in the coming years.

7. The 1980s can also be interpreted as a period when the degree of maturity of state–class relations has regressed. Different business groups have turned out to be prisoners of short-term, segmented, and individualized interests, and their possible transformation into a mature bourgeoisie as a 'class for itself' has not taken place. With respect to the state structure, the disarticulation of its political and bureaucratic layers has led to the emergence of a more backward pattern than that observed in an 'oligarchic' state: it is not towards the realization of the interests of well-defined segments/sub-groups of the economically dominant class(es) that state power is being exercised. On the contrary, that power is being manipulated for the accommodation of the interests of individual business groups and businessmen not necessarily representing sectoral or functional interests. This creates a state of affairs in which one can hardly speak of generalized or even oligarchic class rule. We therefore conclude that the class nature of the Turkish state has taken a step backward—even taken on a primitive shape—during the past decade.

As outlined in the introductory section of this essay, the 1980s emerge as a period in which conditions for accumulation and growth were extremely favorable, but this potential has hardly been realized. The foregoing observations on the internal contradictions of capital and on capital–state relations throw some light on the relatively dismal performance with respect to accumulation, industrialization, and growth during the post-1980 period. It is our contention that the redistribution of the surplus in favor of rentiers and the financial and commercial bourgeoisie is also a redistribution against those business groups with high propensities to invest, i.e., those segments of capital with strong 'animal spirits'. Moreover, the qualitative deterioration in business–state relations and the transformations within the state apparatus, i.e., undermining the role of the traditional bureaucracy, created instability, uncertainties, and pessimism, particularly within the ranks of the industrial bourgeoisie—further factors that explain stagnant rates of industrial accumulation.

Other major factors, such as the external economic environment and the so-called 'fiscal crisis of the state', have also contributed to the macroeconomic performance of the 1980s. They fall, however, within the domain of more conventional economic analysis. This essay is an attempt to highlight some phenomena which, despite having significant implication for the growth path of the economy, have usually been neglected by economists.

Notes

* Research support by the Ford Foundation within the context of the Middle East Research Competition is gratefully acknowledged. Thanks are also

due to my research partner, Galip Yalman, and to participants of two workshops in Cairo and Istanbul for their contributions, criticisms, and suggestions.

1 See, *inter alia*, K. Boratav, *Stabilization and Adjustment Policies and Programs, Country Study 5: Turkey* (Helsinki: Wider, 1987); and K. Boratav, "The Medium-Term Prospects for the Turkish Economy," in F. Desmond McCarthy, ed., *Problems of Developing Countries in the 1990s, Volume 2: Country Studies* (Washington, D.C., The World Bank, 1990). For a recent and interesting contribution, see also E. Uygur, *Policy, Productivity, Growth and Employment in Turkey, 1960–1989 and Prospects for the 1990s*, mimeo, 1990.

2 For a detailed discussion of the choice, construction and interpretation of the quantitative indicators used in the table, see K. Boratav, "Intra-class and Inter-class Relations of Distribution under 'Structural Adjustment': Turkey during the 1980s," in T. Arıcanlı and D. Rodrik, *The Political Economy of Turkey: Debt, Adjustment and Sustainability* (London: Macmillan, 1990); see also M. Celasun, "Income Distribution and Employment Aspects of Turkey's Post-1980 Adjustment," in *METU Studies in Development*, vol. 16, no. 3–4, 1989.

3 For a quantitative overview of various indicators of income distribution between 1923–1980, see K. Boratav, "Birikim Biçimleri ve Tarım," (Patterns of Accumulation and Agriculture"), in Ş. Pamuk and Z. Toprak, eds., *Türkiye'de Tarımsal Yapılar: 1923–2000*, (Agrarian Structures in Turkey, 1923–2000), (Ankara: Yurt Yayınları, 1988).

4 For changes in manufacturing mark-up rates, see K. Boratav, "Intra-class and Inter-class Relations," *op. cit.*; for a detailed investigation of the compensation mechanisms with respect to working-class households, see K. Boratav and G. Yalman, " A Study on the Political Economy of Structural Adjustment: Workers and Peasants during a Major Reorientation of Economic Policies: Turkey, 1980–1987," research paper prepared for IDRC, Canada, mimeo, 1989.

5 Since the widening of the price gap between retail and on-farm prices (rows 4a–4d) represents both loosening price controls and elimination/reduction of consumer subsidies, the distributional trade-off involves farmers versus general tax-payers (via the Treasury) as well. For a quantitative analysis of the policy determinants behind the adverse changes in agriculture's terms of trade, see K. Boratav, "Intra-class and Inter-class Relations."

6 For macro-level and sociological evidence on these points, see Boratav and Yalman, *op. cit.*

7 For a detailed analysis of the bourgeoisie's position-taking during the late 1970s, and the mechanisms leading to the adoption of the bureaucracy's economic programme by the military, see K. Boratav, "The Turkish Bourgeoisie and the State during a Major Reorientation of Economic

Policies," paper presented to the Conference on Dynamics of State and Societies in the Middle East, Center for Political Research and Studies, Cairo University, 17–19 June 1989.

8 Ibid., for more detail on these issues.

9 Here are a few examples on the antirentier position-taking of the industrial bourgeoisie: "Under the present circumstances the share of interest charges has reached almost twice that of the wage share. If the value of labor has declined to one half of the cost of finance and enterprise, there must be an imbalance there. In order to survive, we industrialists are repressing wages and transferring the resulting savings to the increased cost of money. We can bargain with our workers, but we have no bargaining power vis-à-vis interest, energy and raw material costs." (E. Faralyalı, leather industrialist, former chairman of the Turkish Union of Industrial and Commercial Chambers, as quoted in *Milliyet*, 10 December 1987).

"Thanks to the present monetary policy, the idle middle class is getting richer merely by investing in bank deposits and government bonds whereas workers, civil servants, farmers, artisans, and industrialists are getting poorer. Banks charge 120 percent interest to the productive sector so as to transfer this return to [the rentiers]." (S. Yaşar, chairman of a major industrial group in Izmir, as quoted in *Ekonomik Panorama*, 7 August 1988).

"This system will bust . . . . All factories will first be taken over by banks and then banks will be taken over by the government. And then, you know that . . . " (T. Ercan, industrialist in the automotive sector, quoted in O. Ulugay, *Kim Kazandı, Kim Kaybetti?* (Who Won, Who Lost?), p. 206, (Ankara: Bilgi, 1987).

"The Government shifted resources considerably to the rentier class . . . [and] . . . The industrialist moved his resources away from industry and into rentier-type activities . . . this is why employment has not improved . . . in recent years." (C. Boyner, textile industrialist, then the chairman of the prestigious 'club of big business,' i.e., Turkish Association of Industrialists and Businessmen, as quoted in *Cumhuriyet*, 5 November 1989).

10 A few examples of critical statements by industrialists on the pro-mercantile orientation of the current policy model:

"We do not want to be a nation of merchants or a [people] who carry their money in their pockets. . . . We want a Turkey in which every penny is invested in business." "It is to be regretted if the present government wants Turkey to become merely a trading society." H. Narin, textile industrialist former chairmen of the Turkish Union of Employers, as quoted in *İşveren*, September 1987 and *Kapital*, December 1986, respectively.

U. Garih of the big industrial group Alarko, which started a gradual movement out of industry in the late 1980s reflects, "If I were to start as a businessman today, I would not go into industry: I would prefer to go into export trade." as quoted in *Cumhuriyet*, 19 August, 1989.

11 Numerous interviews with prominent businessmen undertaken during our joint research with G. Yalman provide almost undisputed evidence in this score.

12 See B. Çetin, *Soygun: Hayali İhracatın Boyutları*, (Robbery: Dimensions of Fictitious Exports), (Ankara: Bilgi, 1988), for a vivid account of the struggle between the traditional bureaucracy and MP Ministers including the then Prime Minister Özal around the 'fictitious exports' issue. It is interesting to note that the traditional economic bureaucracy lost the initial battle, but it turned out to be pyrrhic victory for the political class, when certain members of the judiciary, influenced by an outraged public opinion used their own initiative—through a disputable interpretation of legislation—and started criminal proceedings against exporters involved in false documents and overinvoicing of exports.

13 Edes, a businessman whose contracting firm ESKA was for some years one of the 'rising stars' of the MP period, observes that "companies cannot survive in Turkey unless they establish good dialogues with those in power," as quoted in *Ekonomik Panorama*, 19 November, 1989.

The industrialist H. Narin, one of the 'losers' of the same period (see also note 10 above), is in full agreement, but understandably in a bitter mood: "For the business community to be against the party in power is suicidal. . . . We are unable to criticize [because] . . . when we talk adverse things happen." "A few privileged companies emerged recently and we see their representatives at every official ceremony. . . . It is wrong that most government tenders should accrue specifically to these privileged groups . . . who claim to monopolize all activities. We, the representatives of the free enterprise, belive that . . . everybody should benefit from the opportunities created by the state equally." Statements in *Kapital*, March 1989 and in *Ekonomik Panorama*, 12 March 1989, respectively. It is significant to note that Narin's aspiration to "benefit equally from opportunities created by the state" conflicts fundamentally with the campaign for 'less government' imposed from abroad on Third World governments under structural adjustment programs.

International Contexts and Developmentalist Strategies

8

The International System and State Policies: The Case of Egypt

Abdel Monem Said Aly

Introduction

The focus of this essay is the impact of the broad contextual characteristics of the international environment on the state policies of Egypt. This is based on the perspective that as aspects of the international system change, there will be changes in the policy behavior of the individual states comprising that system. More precisely, the international system functions as an input into the making or unmaking of policy, and defines the broad external limits and opportunities within which states operate.

The propositions that will be advanced in this essay are that the more the international and regional environment is characterized by tension and poses a threat to the state, the more state policies will tend to be centralized. And as the external environment becomes less tense and threatening, more interdependent, and as transnational forces have more influence in the international system, the more state policies will be decentralized and greater opportunities will open to civil society and private initiative.

The thesis of this essay, therefore, is that the post–World War II international system seems to have influenced Egyptian politics in two directions: the first started in the 1950s and 1960s and was characterized by state-centered policies. The second developed from the mid-1970s onward and was characterized by more liberalized policies. External factors have contributed to both directions. For the first, the bipolar world of the postwar era, the decolonization trend in the Third World, the rise of socialist ideas in the world developmental plans, and the Arab–Israeli conflict, have each had their impact. In the second, the decay of the bipolar world, the rise of transnationalism, the alteration to world developmental plans, the oil revolution, and the deescalation of the Arab–Israeli conflict have affected the liberalization trend.

Operationally, political and economic policies of members of the international system have been influenced by a mixture of variables which pushed along a continuum of centralized-decentralized state systems. One can envisage the following variables:

a) the degree of nation-statehood or independence in the world system, in which political and economic nationalism is an important outcome;

b) the networks of international alliances and threats with dominant world and regional powers;

c) the links with the world-dominant international, transnational and regional orders; and

d) the dominant international developmental ideology (state-centered import substitution, export-oriented growth, privatization and deregulation).

In the case of Egypt, the phase of national independence, the growing alliance with the Soviet bloc, the adversarial relations with the West and the conflict with Israel, the weak links with the world economic order (one-crop-oriented economy), and the dominant state-centered import-substitution developmental strategies of the 1950s and 1960s made it imperative for Egypt to move toward the centralized pole of the continuum. The consolidation of nation-statehood, the alliance with the United States, peace with Israel, growing Egyptian–Arab interdependence as a result of the oil boom, the increasing links with the world transnational economy, and the shifts in the international developmental strategies towards export-oriented privatization plans have moved Egypt away from the centralized politics and economy. In both phases, the international and regional factors and the interplay between them acted as both incentives and disincentives for a certain package of economic policies.

It is axiomatic to understand these two phases dialectically. The choice of the mid-1970s as the moment when Egyptian politics changed direction is so designated only for analytical purposes. Elements of centralization and decentralization are always present at any given point of the continuum. Consequently, this essay will be divided into four sections: the first will focus on the changing global and regional environment; the second will concentrate upon the contributions of the external factors to the centralization trend in Egypt in the post–World War II era; the third will emphasize the impacts of these factors on the decentralization of Egyptian politics from the mid-1970s onward; and the fourth will conclude by showing the contradictory forces in Egypt which may indicate the direction of the country in the future. There is no claim in this essay that only external factors explain Egyptian behavior. Domestic and cultural factors have their roles.

The Changing Global and Regional Environment

Egypt's geographical position, at the southeast corner of the Mediterranean Sea, and at the crossroads of the three continents of the old world, has led, almost automatically, to the need for Egyptian politics and economics to be sensitive to factors and ideas generated in the global and regional environment. In the post–World War II era, this environment has been changing rapidly in a way that has posed threats as well as providing benefits to Egypt.

First, the structure of power distribution after 1945 reflected a largely bipolar world divided into two major blocs. International politics were dominated by a political and ideological conflict in Europe between the Soviet Union and the United States. These two superpowers organized their power through collective alliances in which they each, respectively, had the advantage both politically and militarily. Ultimately, the conflict spread from Europe to Asia, the Middle East, Africa, the Caribbean, and Latin America. The superpowers adapted their competition to the heterogeneous and fluid regional and local patterns of politics emerging out of the destruction of the colonial system. Not only was the world divided along territorial, military and strategic lines, but also along politico-socioeconomic frontiers. Each bloc's perception of the other reflected such divisions. In the Cold War period, such dichotomous phrases as 'imperialistic' and 'democratic', or 'socialist' and 'capitalist', or 'totalitarian' and 'democratic', on the American side, were condensed symbols of that bipolar world. In practice, the Cold War was essentially a zero-sum contest between the two superpowers who surmised that an aggression by any small state, or a change in its political system, would shift the world balance of power toward one of the two blocs.[1]

By the end of the 1960s, the era of détente had become increasingly evident. Détente has come to mean a pattern of interactions between the superpowers, with the purpose of avoiding nuclear war and establishing a modus vivendi based on a network of agreements (particularly in arms control) and understandings held together by a process of bargaining and the linkage of mutual accommodations. In that sense détente was a superpower strategy of managing adverse relationships in the international system.[2]

By the late 1970s the adversarial relationships between Washington and Moscow posed serious pressures upon the politics of détente. East–West tensions escalated and dominated the international situation. Gone were the détente days of the North–South dialogue, the new international economic order, and the politics of world interdependence that obscured the 'high politic' of global power interactions. The international system once more came into another period of intense Cold War characterized by a higher level of armament acquisition. The doctrine of 'mutually assured destruction', which was thought to prevent the unthinkable nuclear holocaust, was replaced by the doctrine of flexible response made possible by the creation of intermediate nuclear forces, e.g., SS-20s and Pershing and cruise missiles, which might achieve military and political advantages. Strategic parity between the United States and the Soviet Union, which, with the help of arms-control agreements, was to ensure world peace, was finally replaced with policies of achieving strategic superiority on earth and space.[3]

As of 1985, an incremental change started to take place in Soviet–American relations. Following a radical change in Soviet leadership, signals of mutual accommodation started to pass between the two superpowers. Not only were arms-control negotiations resumed, but summit meetings were also rapidly convened in Washington and Moscow. An agreement on intermediate and short-range nuclear forces was reached in 1987, and agreements on strategic and chemical weapons became possible. By the end of 1989, Eastern European communist states had collapsed one after the other. The process of German unification started. The Warsaw pact collapsed. The Soviet Union started to disintegrate. By 1990, the West, not the meek, had inherited the earth.

The second important and relevant factor was that the two superpowers were heavily involved in the Middle East regional crises, thus increasing the magnitude of conflicts and insecurities in the area. A study published by the Brookings Institution in 1978 found that during the period 1945–75, the United States used its armed forces as a political instrument in 215 incidents around the world. The Middle East's share was 17.7 percent of these incidents. However, among the thirty-three most intense incidents in the same period, the Middle East's share rose to 27.3 percent, surpassing all world regions including Europe, the Caribbean, and Southeast Asia.[4] Another study published by the same institution in 1981, this time about the Soviet use of armed forces as political instrument, shows almost the same results. In the top ninteen incidents in terms of Soviet intense use of coercive action between 1956 and 1979, four (more than 21 percent) were related to 'The Middle East Crisis'. In the post-1945 era, the Strategic Nuclear Forces of the two superpowers were involved in nineteen incidents, four of which were related to the Arab–Israeli conflict—in second place after Berlin (five incidents). On only two occasions was there an explicit American threat of using strategic nuclear forces: the Cuban Missile Crisis and the October 1973 Arab–Israeli War. In one incident (the 1956 Suez Crisis) the Soviet Union explicitly threatened to use nuclear forces.[5]

This high level of superpower desire to deny one or more Middle Eastern country access to the other superpower has made the region one of the most highly penetrated regions of the world.[6] As the countries of the Middle East relied on the superpowers for military and economic aid, regional politics have corresponded to the international escalations and deescalations of conflicts.

In the Middle East, regional politics corresponded to the Cold War climate of the 1950s and 1960s. "The Arab Cold War," as Malcolm Kerr called it, was in fact a reflection of the international system.[7] The battle of the Baghdad Pact of 1955, the Arab–Israeli conflicts in 1956 and 1967, the

Lebanese Civil War of 1958, and the Yemeni Civil War of 1962, were examples of regional tensions and conflicts which were partially an extension of worldwide tensions and conflicts.[8]

The Middle East states were not less responsive to the détente politics of the 1970s. Intra-Arab conflicts were at their minimum. Their disagreements over the Palestinian question were reduced and when the civil war erupted in Lebanon in 1975, the Arab states covered the Syrian presence in Lebanon by forming an 'Arab Deterrent Force' to de-escalate the conflict among the Lebanese warring factions. The Arab–Israeli conflict was brought to the bargaining table, and three disengagement agreements were concluded in 1974 and 1975, even before the Camp David Accords in 1978. Military means were no longer used in a 'life or death struggle' in this conflict, but they were used to improve bargaining positions, e.g., the October 1973 War. In 1975, Iran and Iraq were able to reach a settlement, with the help of Algerian mediation, for their long-lived border dispute.[9]

The Second Cold War was no less contagious in the area. The Arab coalition of 1973 was fragmented between those who supported the Camp David Accords and those who stood against them, and between those who supported Iraq and those who chose to stand by Iran in the Gulf War. Israel struck down the Iraqi nuclear reactor in 1981, invaded Lebanon in 1982, and strengthened the hold it had gained in June 1967 on the occupied Arab territories. The Lebanese Civil War escalated throughout the 1980s.[10]

President Mikhail Gorbachev's new cooperative international politics era was reflected on the Middle East. Although the Arab–Israeli conflict still shows no signs of resolution, tensions in the area have been reduced. Egypt returned to the Arab fold. The Iran–Iraq War stopped. The Arab League managed to take control of the Lebanese conflict through the Ta'ef Agreement. The Arab Cooperation Council and the Arab Maghreb Union were created. North and South Yemen were united.

The Second Gulf War in 1991 shattered some of these developments. However, it seems that the war did bring into the open the links between the Middle East regional system and the new global order. Although the Arab world was divided over the process of liberating Kuwait, the postwar era witnessed an attempt to gather around the Arab League, to continue the Lebanese reconciliation process, and to start a new American-led initiative to settle the long-lived Arab–Israeli conflict. It is too early, however, to assess the full repercussions of the war on the regional system.

Third, the 1970s experienced a trend in the international system towards interdependence and transnationalism. As trade-flows, global investment, financial transactions, and technology transfers rose to unprecedented levels in human history, the nature of power politics in the system changed as well.[11] Multilateral functional arrangements and organizations such as the Organization for Economic Cooperation and Development (OECD), the International Monetary Fund (IMF), the International Bank for Reconstruction and Development (IBRD) (World Bank), and the General Agreement on Tariffs and Trade (GATT) have more influence over global policies than ever before. This global trend towards interdependence has been coupled with transnationalization which challenged the preeminence of the state in the international system. Transnationalism reflected the behavior of individuals and corporations in a way that bypassed the state in a shrinking world caused by modern technology and a revolution in communications.[12] As Joseph Nye has said,

> The changing technology of communications and transportations have had a revolutionary effect. A century ago, it took two weeks to cross the Atlantic; Lindbergh did it in thirty-three hours; the Concorde makes it in three; and telecommunications are instantaneous. Satellites and fiber optic cables have led to a tenfold increase in overseas calls in the last decade. Declining costs of transportation and communication have revolutionized global markets and accelerated the development of transnational corporations that transfer economic activity across borders.[13]

The Arab region came into this massive change in world affairs after the October 1973 War, which changed qualitatively the oil policies of the Arab oil-producing states. They had utilized the world's growing interdependence, the energy crisis, and the changes in the concept of power in the international system to get involved in the new world system.[14] Of particular importance was the policy of restricting production and increasing prices by Arab oil-producing countries. These nations were able to multiply their revenues to unprecedented levels. The oil returns of Arab OPEC members in 1965 were a mere $2.169 billion. By 1970, returns reached $51.5 billion and in 1980, they skyrocketed to $204.244 billion. Since then, revenues have declined annually to $182.9 billion in 1981, $134.7 billion in 1982, $101.7 billion in 1983, and $102.4 billion in 1984.[15]

Despite this dive in oil prices, two decades of accumulated revenues have motivated the colossal developmental plans of the Arab oil-producing countries. The oil era, in its rise and fall, has led to an extensive change in the Arab world. Interdependence with the world and in the Arab region intensified throughout the 1970s and 1980s. Petrodollars have drawn the Arabs securely into the world's financial markets. Labor migration has created waves of interdependence previously unknown to the Arab world.[16] The Arab world has become an integral element of the new changes in world politics.

Probably nothing proves this reality like the last Gulf War. The Iraqi invasion of Kuwait touched the energy nerve supply of world development. The world coalition against Saddam Hussein was, in essence, a stand against an attempt to cut away from the global economic system and thus destabilize world markets. On the other hand, the Gulf States' position in the world economy made them capable of mobilizing and financing the largest alliance since World War II. Kuwait, in particular, because of its international investments, was capable of running all the functions of the state even without a territory of its own during the seven months of Iraqi occupation.

Fourth, all these changes were accompanied by substantial changes in the prevailing world developmental strategies. In the early post–World War II years, there was a general belief that government had the leading role to play in the economy, and much faith was placed in the ability of governments to fine-tune the resource allocation process. Socialist ideas in the Eastern bloc and the welfare-state concept in the Western bloc called for different degrees of government intervention. It was believed that a degree of central planning and large public investment efforts would accelerate the rate of capital accumulation. Until the 1980s, state-owned enterprises (SOEs) had grown rapidly in importance in most of the less developing economies of Africa, Asia, and Latin America, while managing to hold their relative positions in the expanding mature economies of the developed world.[17] By the end of the 1970s this trend was reversed and throughout the 1980s calls for liberalizing market forces, deregulation and privatization became the prevailing developmental mood worldwide.[18]

The reasons for this shift are not of concern here, however. What is important is that the world donor institutions (IMF, World Bank, and aid agencies) have made this shift in their developmental strategies. Of particular importance to developing countries is the World Bank. The bank's attitude towards the role of the state in developing countries has evolved through three distinct phases. In the first phase, roughly between 1946 and 1960, its lending policies were marked by a strong bias in favor of market forces. In the second phase, the 1960s and 1970s, its operations were tilted towards enhancing state activity in the economy. During this phase, the bank poured billions of dollars into the creation of SOEs in developing countries worldwide. In the third period, the 1980s, the bank has changed course again towards consolidating market forces.[19] With the help of the IMF, other donor states and agencies, and 'the structural adjustment programs', the bank started to promote deregulation and privatization.[20] The trend towards privatization has become preponderant in developed (United Kingdom, France, Japan) and developing countries as well. The changes in Eastern Europe, the Soviet Union, and China by the end of the 1980s have given credence to this trend.

Egypt: The Centralized State

The keynote of Egyptian modern history is the steady growth in the state centralization and its control capabilities in political, social, and economic activities. The economic expansion inaugurated by Muhammad Ali, accelerated by Ismail, continued during the British occupation and intensified in the post-1919 era, was based on the state's public works and its regulation of the economy. The main contribution was in the form of dams, barrages, railways, communication, transportation, and land reclamation. For example, by 1909 the length of the Egyptian state railways was 3,200 kilometers. In 1949, it had reached 7,102. In that year, "Egypt . . . had some 14 kilometers of railway for every 100 kilometers of inhabited area, a figure which approaches the West European standard and is well above that of the other underdeveloped areas."[21] In 1950, Egypt had 5,500 post offices and 10,000 kilometers of telegraph lines, nine airports, and 105,000 telephone lines, (compared with 60,000 before the war).[22] In the field of education, from 1923 Egypt witnessed a steady expansion of state control over the educational process. Under the influence of Taha Hussein, by 1951 most preuniversity schools were free of charge, and private schools were completely under state regulations and control. Cairo University, which was established as a private university in 1908, became public in 1925.[23]

In the field of information, the Egyptian state was not going to let a new and influential innovation such as broadcasting fall into private hands. In 1924, Egypt had its first private broadcasting station. By 1932, there were eleven of them. In that year, the Egyptian government decided to abolish these stations, for "national reasons." A new 'national' station operated by the British Marconi Corporation was established in 1934. In 1947, again for "national considerations," the government ended the Marconi contract and broadcasting became completely Egyptian.[24] In the Liberal Age, economics could not escape the hands of the state. In 1930, because of the worldwide depression, Ismail Sidqi introduced tariffs to protect Egyptian products.[25] With the outbreak of World War II, state regulation and control increased substantially.[26]

Figures show that even before the 1952 Revolution, the state was more centralized than any 'liberal' state of the time. In 1951–52, Egypt had 350,000 public employees, constituting about 2.2 percent of the population.[27] In 1952, the public sector's share in GDP was about 13 percent, and in gross fixed capital formation (mostly infrastructure) about 28 percent.[28]

Even in politics, the Liberal Age was not really liberal. For almost three decades (1923–52) the Wafd Party, which always carried the majority of Egyptian voters in any free elections, was not able to rule for more than seven years. Minority parties took the rest.[29]

The 'golden age' of centralization, however, was in Nasser's Egypt (1952–70). Egypt was characterized by highly centralized political and economic systems. Over the 1950s and 1960s, Nasser brought the political system, including banking, the majority of industry, commercial activity, cooperatives, local councils, education, information agencies (press, broadcasting, and television), professional and labor unions, and even the religious institutions under state control.[30] The government imposed controls on virtually all private economic, political, and social activities. Towards the same end, it undertook a series of broad obligations to the Egyptian people: provision of basic human needs—food, health, and housing—at subsidized prices, free education up to university level, and guaranteed employment. "By the end of the 1960s . . . one out of every four Egyptians was directly or indirectly on the government's payroll.[31] Egyptians were living within "a larger context—the state."[32]

Nasser's regime was based on the most national and centralized of Egyptian institutions—the army. The 'Free Officers' Revolution of 23 July 1952 promulgated a law banning political parties. Up to 1970, Nasser created three political mass organizations. The first was called the Liberation Rally in 1954. It was followed by the National Union in 1956, and the third was the Arab Socialist Union (ASU) in 1961. The three organizations resembled many of the very loose one-party regimes of the Third World. They were in fact to act as a mobilization instrument for a limited ruling military group, headed by a single charismatic personality, who embarked on a large modernization and developmental program which led to an important shift in the socioeconomic makeup of the country. Political liberties were very much curtailed and political activities on the left and right were severely punished.[33]

Economics were to follow politics. Initially Nasser's regime opted to encourage foreign and domestic private investment during the period 1952–56. The land reform laws of 1952, however, gave the first indication of the extension of the role of the state in managing agricultural activities. The second came in 1956 with the nationalization of the Suez Canal, and was followed by the 'Egyptianization policy'. This policy expropriated the assets of nationals of the United Kingdom, France, and later Belgium.[34]

However, the radical shift towards centralization in the name of socialism only took place starting from 1960. Throughout the decade, large-scale nationalization of the private sector in all activities apart from agriculture was achieved. Central planning in the form of five-year plans was introduced. SOEs were to monopolize all of the former manufacturing sector, finance, and foreign trade, as well as the bulk of transportation and distribution working within the framework of centralized control. By 1970, the public sector held 74 percent of industrial production, 90 percent of total investment, and 35.2 percent of GDP. Private ownership and operation was restricted to agriculture, real estate, and the informal sectors, but even these were subjected to centralized control of pricing, marketing and the procurement of raw materials, and foreign exchange.[35]

External factors contributed to this centralized state policy. First, throughout most of its modern history, Egypt's development has occurred under the shadow of conflict with external powers. There was the Egyptian confrontation with revolutionary France when Napoleon's army invaded the country in 1798. Then, Muhammad Ali struggled to gain independence from the Turkish Ottoman empire. This was followed by the protracted conflict for independence from Great Britain which continued from 1881 to 1956. The conflict with Great Britain overlapped with the Arab–Israeli conflict, which started in 1948, accelerated in the mid-1950s, and became particularly significant for Egypt in 1967 when Egyptian territories came under direct Israeli occupation. The 'national question' has thus dominated the evolution of Egypt.

This security problem was compounded by the conflictful interactions of the bipolar environment. Superpower behavior in the Middle East had created more burdens for Egyptian national security. The global environment was reflected in regional conflicts which made Egypt part of highly destabilized environment. Therefore, there is no surprise to discover that building the Egyptian nation-state as an 'independent' and 'sovereign' actor in world affairs became the supreme concern of the Egyptian elite. Within this context of a conflictful world, mobilization of Egyptian human and material resources would not have happened without an increasing role for the state. It was the Suez War in 1956 that finally changed the direction of Nasser's regime towards further degrees of centralization. Pressures from the West, first on Egypt and later on the United Arab Republic, led finally to the socialist orientation of the 1960s with all the nationalizations and planning policies of the state, and the war of 1967 further consolidated the role of the state in the national economy.

Second, in the post–World War II era, Egypt has been one of the few lucky countries in terms of foreign aid. In the early 1950s, Egypt received American aid through the Four Point Program. From 1962 to 1966, \$500 million[36] worth of wheat aid was given to Egypt. In spite of all the tensions between Cairo and Washington, total American aid to Egypt (1946–72) was \$987 million, of which military aid added up to \$32 million.[37] From the mid-1950s to the mid-1970s, Egypt was able to tap Soviet resources to build and rebuild its army and to finance its industrial and developmental plans. Egypt alone received 30.9 percent of all Soviet economic aid and 49.1 percent of all military aid provided to countries in the Middle East.[38] Total Soviet economic aid to Egypt (1953–72) was \$967.4 million while military aid was \$2.7 billion.[39]

This large sum of foreign aid to Egypt was to help the centralization process. American and Western aid to Egypt was given in order to prevent Egypt from totally moving to the Soviet camp. This gave the Egyptian government more liberty to allocate aid resources to enhance state power. Further, the changing patterns of the world developmental strategies towards giving a wider role to the state was in harmony with Egyptian economic policies. Furthermore, Soviet aid to Egypt, although partially motivated by Cold War considerations, was also to be used to serve 'socialism' worldwide. Egyptian 'socialist' policies were in turn to give more justification to Soviet aid policies. Foreign aid worked as a catalyst to enhance the centralization of Egypt.

Egypt: The Decentralized State

After the October 1973 War, Egyptian civil society gained ground. The centralized and socialist legacy of the 1960s lost its glory and logic. The firm grip of the state was loosened in politics as well as economics. Different indicators show the erosion of state dominance over the economy and the reemergence of private sector initiative. New liberal legislation was enacted in the spirit of Infitah, including Law 43 of 1974, later amended by Law 32 of 1977, on the investment of Arab and foreign capital and free zones, and Law 159 of 1981 on joint-stock (Egyptian ownership) companies.[40] The more liberal Law 232 for investment came in 1989.[41]

The result of this policy has been the consolidation of the private sector. From 1974 to 1986, the private sector share of industrial output rose from 23 percent to 33 percent.[42] Joint-venture banks, Islamic Investment Companies (IICs), and private Egyptian banks have emerged and started to compete with government banks for investment, savings, and foreign exchange. The economic situation in Egypt, though not ideal, has nonetheless attracted business initiatives according to Law 43. As of 30 June 1987, the Investment Authority had approved 1,630 projects with a total capital investment of LE7.3 billion and an investment cost of LE14.3 billion.[43] The private sector has extended its activities into new areas, such as insurance and international trade, and intensified its share in industry, air transportation, agriculture, land reclamation, education, and housing.[44] Under Law 159, 830 companies were established up to 1988 with capital investment of LE1.1 billion.[45] This rise in the private sector of the Egyptian economy has breathed new life into

Table 1 Total Annual Dealings on the Alexandria and Cairo Stock Exchanges (LE million)

Year	Alexandria	Cairo	Total
1956	25	57	82
1958	45	67	112
1961	16	23	39
1963	1	5	6
1977	2	6	8
1982	1	8	9
1984	2.2	107.5	109.7
1985	11.2	114.5	125.7
1986	3.4	240	243.4
1987	26.3	330.5	356.8
1988	13	243	256

Source: For the years 1956–1982, *al-Ahram al-Iqtisadi,* 22 February 1988; and for the years 1984–88, Husni Khalil Ahmed, "The Development of Capital Markets in Egypt," paper presented to the conference on "Saving in Egypt," al-Mansura University, 4–5 April 1989, and published in the *Conference Record,* al-Mansura, 1989, p. 138.

activities that were moribund, such as the Cairo and Alexandria Stock Exchange Markets. Table 1 shows a notable increase in the total annual dealings of both markets in the 1980s compared with the 1950s, 1960s, and 1970s. In 1988, there were 484 joint-stock companies registered in both markets with a capital of LE5,397 million and 346.9 million shares.[46]

Not only are private-sector initiatives on the rise, but the government has also taken steps to deregulate private-sector activities and stimulate domestic capital formation as well as the inflow of foreign capital. Actual percentages of gross fixed investment in the public sector have been reduced from 79 percent in financial year 1983 to 70 percent in financial year 1986. While the Nasserist concept of economic planning in the form of five-year plans has been resurrected, the substance and direction of these plans in no way seeks to reestablish an exclusively state-run public sector as the major socioeconomic force in Egypt. Between the 1982/83–1986/87 five-year plan and the 1986/87–1991/92 plan, the percentage of GDP investment in the public sector has been scaled down, from 77 percent in the former plan with 23 percent going into the private sector, to approximately 50 percent investment in both private and public sectors for the latter plan.[47] The state share of GDP investment percentage remains high due to government involvement in oil production and the Suez Canal enterprises.

The state, however, has not conceded its economic powers easily. While it was generally willing to give room for the private sector, the state has been less willing to sell public-sector firms, and it has been unwilling to allow the private sector to control or dominate the more sensitive and strategic sectors of the economy. Up to 1989, there has been only one public firm sold, namely the Sheraton Hotel in Hurghada. When a second firm, the San Stefano Hotel in Alexandria, was offered for sale, the process provoked a politically charged controversy sufficient to stop the sale.[48] Another company, the Alexandria Transport and Engineering Company (TRENCO), was subjected to an Employee Share Ownership Plan (ESOP).[49] However, in 1990, it seems that the privatization trend was accelerated. In April, a cabinet committee was formulated for that purpose.[50] There are some indications that the government is willing to sell the small public projects in the provinces, the government share in the joint ventures under Law 43, and some tourist hotels.[51]

From the mid-1970s onward, decentralization in politics has been no less noticeable. The first step was in 1976, when President Sadat allowed for the establishment of three political forums within the framework of the Arab Socialist Union (ASU) to represent the right, the center, and the left. Three political forums were consequently formed, and after the 1976 elections, Sadat permitted them to become full political parties.[52] In 1990, Egypt had nine legal political parties, in addition to the quasi-legal Muslim Brotherhood. The dominance of the National Democratic Party (NDP), which continues to enjoy the legacy of the Nasserist ASU of the 1960s, has waned somewhat. The 1987 parliamentary elections led to one of the largest representations of the opposition in the history of the Egyptian parliament. The opposition gained 22.3 percent of the elected seats. Even in comparison with the Liberal Age before the 1952 Revolution, the opposition representation in 1987 was striking. The only exception was the 1950 elections, when the opposition share was 29.2 percent. Even in the 1990 elections, when opposition parties boycotted the election, the NDP share of the votes declined substantially. While the NDP gained 72.9 percent of the vote in 1984, the party share declined to 69.6 percent in 1987, and to 57 percent in 1990. This all-time low share of the NDP was basically a reflection not only of the influence of the opposition parties, but also of the growing contradictions within the NDP itself. Many party members ran as independents in the election against their own party. This development indicates increasing pluralization and differentiation in the Egyptian political process.[53]

In addition to political parties, the Egyptian civil society has grown.[54] 'Intermediate' organizations and associations have evolved to influence policy-making. The labor unions, professional syndicates, and business associations, which were timid under Nasser, have gained strength and influence within society and government. Their membership has increased, especially among the younger people. Increasing youth membership has prompted these interest groups to focus on their problems, particularly salaries, education, and housing. This, in turn, has led these groups to seek influence in both education and training.[55] At the same time, they have participated in formulating opinions and demands on most of the national issues: the role of the private and public sectors in the economy, subsidies, environment, and most important of all, politics.[56] In this latter area. particularly under Mubarak, human-rights associations have played an increasingly larger role in facing human-rights violations in Egypt. These institutions of the civil society use propaganda, the increasingly free press, meetings, strikes, and demonstrations to inform the public and pressure the government.

One important factor in the democratization of Egypt is the role the judiciary plays as a referee in Egyptian politics. Out of the nine legal parties in Egypt today, five were admitted to political life by court rulings. The judicial system was instrumental in readmitting the New Wafd Party (NWP) in October 1983, and its, leader Fuad Sirageddin, in February 1984, to Egyptian politics. Moreover, the judiciary was capable of deeming the election laws unconstitutional (concerning the People's Assembly in December 1986, the Consultative Assembly in April 1989, and the People's Assembly again in May 1990), a decision which was contested by the opposition. These election laws were made by the ruling NDP. The fact that the president and his party conceded the unconstitutionality of the election laws has placed previously unheard of constraints on presidential authority.[57]

These developments would not have happened without the changes which occurred in the external environment. First, the October 1973 War, which took place under the conditions of détente, was the prelude for changing Egypt's regional environment by paving the way for an Egyptian–Israeli reconciliation.

The Camp David Accords and the subsequent Egyptian–Israeli peace treaty have allowed Egypt to proceed under a new promise of peace. Political and socioeconomic restructuring of the country, formerly suppressed for the sake of unity needed to combat the external threat, was given a chance to evolve. The legacy of the 1960s has lost some of its luster and logic. The firm grip of the state has relaxed in politics as well as economics. Peace with Israel became a pillar of Egyptian politics, along with an alliance with the West, particularly the United States, the Open-Door Policy, or Infitah, and a degree of democratization.[58]

This 'package' of policies brought Egypt closer to the Western ideas of free-market economics. By the end of the 1970s, socialist ideas and New Deal policies lost the appeal they had enjoyed in the 1960s. Thatcherism and Reaganism became the order of the day in Western societies and international institutions.

Table 2 Total US Aid to Egypt:1975–1990
($ million)

Year	Military	Economic	CIP/PL480	Total Aid
1975		261,200	110,712	371,912
1976		794,900	191,671	986,571
1977		699,250	192,646	891,896
1978		750,760	189,093	936,853
1979		835,000	229,706	1,064,706
1980	1,500,000*	865,000	229,182	2,664,182
1981	550,000	829,000	298,353	1,677,353
1982	700,000	771,000	291,857	1,792,857
1983	900,000	750,000	257,542	1,907,542
1984	1,200,000	750,000	264,461	2,314,361
1985	1,300,000	1,065,000	236,248	2,601,248
1986	1,244,100	1,068,434	218,544	2,531,078
1987	1,300,000	819,558	171,394	2,290,952
1988	1,300,000	903,000	171,000	2,374,000
1989	1,300,000	1,130,000	170,000	2,600,000
1990	1,300,000	927,000	160,000	2,387,000
Total	12,694,000	13,219,000	3,452,409	27,405,611

* Included military assistance for 1979

Source: Compiled from US Embassy, *Egyptian Economic Trends,* March 1988, March 1989, March 1990.

Second, it was not the power of ideology alone that inspired Egypt to allow more freedom for the private sector. The Egyptian–Israeli peace treaty was linked to very generous American and Western aid. After the reestablishment of diplomatic relations between Egypt and the United States in 1974, the United States awarded Egypt $250 million in aid. In 1975, Egypt was included on the regular roster of US aid appropriations, receiving both loans and grants. The ratio of loans was tied to Egypt's movement towards peace with Israel. In 1975, loans represented 78.6 percent of all aid compared with 21.4 percent in grants. By 1983, loans were 21.2 percent of aid and grants were 78.8 percent. As of 1985, all US aid (economic and military) was in the form of grants. As shown in Table 2, in the period from 1975 to 1990, Egypt received over $27 billion. Direct investment by the United States at the end of 1987 was $1.7 billion, of which $1.4 billion was in the petroleum sector.[59]

The United States was not the only supplier of aid to Egypt. Europe and Japan contributed aid, both in loans and grants. Table 3 shows the increases in development assistance given to Egypt by the members of the Development Assistance Committee of the OECD (the United States excluded).[60] The Japanese grant-aid program alone up to 1989 cumulatively amounted to $340.7 million.[61]

Western aid in general, and US aid in particular, have targeted the Egyptian economy for transformation to a 'private-centric' one. A key

Table 3 Development Assistance to Egypt ($ million)

	1970-71	1980-81	1986-87
Australia		8.606	7.950
Austria		4.209	18.001
Belgium	134	2.950	
Canada		20.034	14.076
Denmark	2.814	8.190	20.194
Finland		2.583	7.087
France	9.080	52.884	103.322
Germany	9.192	92.972	144.960
Italy	22.080	4.278	30.480
Japan		96.984	133.480
Netherlands		19.572	28.084
Norway	.080		
Switzerland		2.223	17.451
United Kingdom		22.320	17.451
EEC	3.744	44.275	46.845

Source: Calculated from OECD 1988 Report,"Development Cooperation," December 1988, pp. 211–20.

element of the USAID mission growth strategy for Egypt has been to provide the incentives for production increases and an expanded role for the private sector.[62] Although direct US aid to the Egyptian private sector did not exceed 5 percent of the total economic aid to Egypt in the period 1975–89, it was intended that the investment infrastructure and other projects (about 42 percent) would facilitate the work of this sector.[63] Improvements during the 1980s in energy supplies, roads, and telecommunication have given the Egyptian private sector the opportunity to work in a much healthier productive environment than was the situation in the 1970s, when the Egyptian infrastructure reached its limits. Foreign aid has been instrumental in achieving these results.

Third, the IMF and the World Bank supported the decentralization of the Egyptian economy. After the debacle between Egypt and the World Bank over the Aswan Dam in 1956, the relationship between the two sides was almost nonexistent up to 1974.[64] As Egyptian–Western relations improved, and Infitah became formalized, the IMF and the World Bank became involved in the Egyptian economic policies. By the 1980s, and as the Egyptian debts mounted, both have been heavily involved in the process of economic reform. In 1987 the IMF signed an economic adjustment program with Egypt. In 1989 another round of negotiations was opened with the purpose of developing another program. The result of these negotiations has been to push Egypt towards further liberalization and privatization of the economy. In fact, the Egyptian government's declaration of privatization in 1990 has been a direct response to these pressures.[65] The Second Gulf War accelerated the process. The Egyptian position in the war was rewarded by another adjustment program, a 50 percent reduction to the Egyptian debt, and a guarantee of an annual $4 billion in development assistance. In exchange, Egypt accepted further liberalization of the economy and direct supervision by the IMF over its economic reform.

Fourth, the oil revolution has contributed vast resources to the Egyptians as a result of the growing Egyptian–Arab interdependence.[66] The well-known phenomenon of labor migration to the Arab oil-producing countries has provided extensive employment opportunities as well as capital to Egyptian individuals. According to conservative estimates for the decade 1974 to 1984, 3.3 million Egyptians migrated to work in the Arab oil-producing countries. They transferred $33 billion to Egypt in cash transfers, bank deposits, goods, and commodities—almost three times the US economic aid available to the Egyptian government over the same period.[67] The following years show that remittances seem to have continued at the same rate: in 1985–86, they were $3.063 billion, $3.012 billion for 1986–87, and $3.387 billion for 1987–88. The total 1974–88 reached $44 billion.[68] Less conservative estimates state these transfers at much higher levels. Nazli Chucri has put the figure for 1983–84 alone at $18 billion.[69]

Remittances are not the only source of income transferred to Egyptian society from its Arab connection. In 1982, 613,000 Arab tourists visited

Egypt, or about 43 percent of the total number of tourists. By 1987, Arab tourists approached 657,000, representing 36.6 percent of the total number of tourists. The Arab share in Egyptian tourism is so large because Arab tourists tend to stay longer, and so spend more than Europeans and Americans. In 1985, the Arab share of total tourist nights was 43 percent. By 1987, their share reached 48 percent.[70] The number of Arab tourists increased only slightly in 1988 (by 2.4 percent). However in 1989 the number grew by 44.3 percent, and their tourist nights grew by 26.2 percent.[71] Arab journalism, broadcasting, and television are dependent on Egyptians working in Egypt. Egyptian private-sector hospitals are preferred by the middle-income groups in the Arab oil-producing states. Consequently, it is not surprising that many Egyptians, even if they stay at home, have a source of income related to the Arab countries.

The result of this flow of capital to Egypt has been the consolidation of the Egyptian private sector. Foreign investment capital in Egypt as of June 1987 stood at LE7.3 billion, 65 percent of which was Egyptian (most of it generated from Arab countries), 18 percent Arab, and 17 percent foreign.[72] Furthermore, a study of small-scale manufacturing in Egypt found that remittances have a significant effect.[73]

Fifth, the revolution in the world capitalist market and communications technology has provided Egyptian society with transnational instruments to bypass the national government. The world stock, money, and commodity markets have given Egyptians the opportunity to invest, speculate, and transact with the world economy without being forced to deposit in public-sector banks or to abide by government exchange rates. Islamic Banks, Islamic investment companies, and Egyptian individuals are now able to circulate their money in and outside Egypt according to business opportunities, while their investment in Egypt is dependent on the government's ability to attract their capital by liberalizing the economy.[74]

Table 4 The Development of International Communications in Egypt

Communication System	1981	March 1990
International telephone lines	160	4,680
International telephone circuits	820	5214
Automated international telephone to Egypt	4	81
Automated international telephone from Egypt	29	171
Size of international telephone movement (million minutes)	28	263*
Telex lines	3,520	9,340
Fax participants		5,400

* For 1989

Source: The National Authority for Communication, *al-Ahrar,* 23 April 1990.

Interestingly enough, Egyptians would not have linked with transnational capitalism had it not been for the revolution in world communications and the state's growing communication capabilities. In 1952, Egypt had only ten international telephone circuits. By 1970, there were forty-four. Table 4 shows the development of international communications in Egypt in the 1980s. Certainly this large increase in transnational communications has minimized the government's ability to control and regulate.

State 'information sovereignty' is no longer absolute. Egyptian society has become capable of gaining information through transnational resources. As of the 1980s, the Arab world could claim 250 broadcasting stations that reached most of the region, including Egypt.[75] Many countries broadcast to the Arab world: the BBC, Voice of America, and Monte Carlo are the best known. Other countries as large as India and as small as Albania air Arabic programs. It has been reported that measured by the number of hours, the Arabic language is second only to English on the global airwaves.[76] In 1950, Egyptians had only 283,000 radios,[77] and in 1983 they had 8,843,330 (almost one for every family).[78] One study shows that 31.8 percent of university students in Egypt listen regularly to the BBC, Monte Carlo, and Voice of America. Since 1990, French television programs (up to four hours daily) and the American television network CNN broadcast in Egypt.[79] The state monopoly over information has been seriously curtailed, thus eliminating one of the main sources of political control.

Egypt: Prospects for the 1990s

The preceding section should not give the impression that Egypt has finally come of age and become a stage for decentralization, democracy, and private initiative. In politics the state still holds the significant cards. The ruling National Democratic Party dominates political life. The party continues to carry the legacy and legitimacy of the Arab Socialist Union. Its dominance over the bureaucracy and the security forces excludes complete neutrality and freedom in any election. The Egyptian Constitution of 1971 gave the presidential institution enough powers to overshadow and overrule the other legislative and judicial institutions of the country. Presidential powers, in the words of Tarek al-Bishry, are similar to those given to the caliphs and the Shi'ite imams.[80]

During the 1970s and 1980s, the Egyptian state might have lost some of its powers in relative terms. It has, however, continued to increase its capabilities. The Egyptian army expanded not only in numbers, excluding the high mobilization time of 1967–74, but also in the variety of its roles.[81] The public sector continued to be the backbone of the economy. The state was not only the largest employer, but also the largest educator, and enjoyed a monopoly over the expanding broadcasting and television networks.[82] As mentioned before, in 1952, 2.2 percent of the population were working for the government. At the end of the Nasserist era, in 1969–70, the figure grew to 1.2 million, or 3.8 percent of the population. In 1986, 4.8 million Egyptians were on the public payrolls, or almost 10 percent of the entire population, and some 35 percent of the labor force of 13 million.[83]

This discrepancy between the rising representative nature of the society and private initiative on the one hand, and the continued resilience of state dominance on the other, could not be understood without grasping the contradictory forces in the changing global and regional environment. First, the Second Cold War, Egyptian–Israeli peace, and the oil revolution have contributed massive resources to the Egyptian government and made it capable of ignoring major political and economic reforms. The Infitah policies to invigorate the economy through economic liberalization measures have not altered the basic controls on resource allocation and production, and price distortions and administrative regulations continue. External aid has provided the government with resources to penetrate, mobilize, and control the society. Even American aid to Egypt has been directed to the government. Out of $14.982 billion of economic assistance, only $751 million, or about 5 percent, went to the private sector from 1975 to 1989. In the same period, $1.150 billion, or about 7.6 percent, went directly to the industrial public sector alone.[84]

Second, the availability of externally generated resources, including foreign assistance, has made importing technology much cheaper than creating it. The weakness of the Egyptian base of research and development is one of the most serious structural problems of the Egyptian public and private economies. By the late 1980s Egyptian private-sector industries had started to suffer, or completely close down, because of their high reliance on foreign technology. As the country started to suffer from insufficient foreign resources, its ability to import became more limited. Ironically, out of the $14.982 billion of American economic assistance to Egypt, only 289 million, or 1.9 percent, was spent on science and technology.[85]

Third, the Egyptian–Israeli peace has opened the gates to the West, giving Egypt the opportunity to borrow and accumulate debts on a large scale. By 1987–88, Egypt owed $43.1 billion to Western states and institutions.[86] By 1990, Egypt was classified by the World Bank as one of the severely indebted states.[87] As the Egyptian government became increasingly constrained by its debt problem, and as foreign resources became less able to fill the empty state purse, its worries about the political as well as social consequences of its economic weakness became acute. The fear is that bold moves towards liberalization will not only undermine the state's political stand but also will increase the plight of the poor, thus contributing to social instability.

Fourth, in spite of the Egyptian–Israeli Peace Treaty, the absence of a comprehensive solution to the Arab–Israeli conflict has continued to justify substantial defense spending and legitimize the dominance of the military over the country. Egyptian perceptions of the Israeli threat have continued.

The Israeli qualitative advantage, not to mention quantitative advantage in certain areas, is a continued security threat for Egypt.[88] Consequently, in 1987, Egypt's direct military expenditure was 8.2 percent of GNP.[89] This does not include investments in military industry, which seems to monopolize Egypt's best resources in research and development.[90]

This high profile of the military in the national economy has become a strong disincentive for privatization in Egypt. As peace in the region remains uncertain, arms-racing becomes but one of the major results which tend to strengthen the hands of the military. Currently, Egypt is participating in this arms race.[91] Under the banner of national security, the Egyptian military establishment is less inclined to accept full liberalization in politics as well as economics.

Fifth, the transnational oil resources which contributed to the rise of the private sector in Egypt, have enhanced the Islamic movement in Egypt politically as well as economically. In the election of 1987, the Muslim Brotherhood became the largest single opposition group in the People's Assembly. Increasingly, Islamic banks and Islamic Investment Companies (IICs) control Egyptian savings. This is not exactly what the Egyptian government was hoping to 'open' the door to. The confrontation between the government and the ICCs in 1988 has increased the reluctance of the government to liberalize politics and economics.[92]

Sixth, the links with transnational capitalism have drained substantial capital from the Egyptian market. World markets have given Egyptians the opportunity to interact with the world economy without being forced to use public-sector banks or government exchange rates. Faisal Islamic Bank (FIB) has invested $500 million (about one third of total deposits) outside Egypt.[93] More importantly, the FIB practice is not an exception. As Mohamed Said demonstrated, "The most staggering feature in the operation of the banking system in Egypt is the contrast between its high reliance on mobilization of Egyptian savings on the one hand, and its tendency to 'invest' outside Egypt altogether on the other."[94] This feature is shared by commercial banks (Law 43 banks), which are majority-controlled by Egyptians, and investment and business banks established according to Law 43 (thirty-three banks, of which twenty-two are branches of foreign banks and eleven joint ventures and private banks). In 1984 and 1985, the net credit position of commercial and business banks in relation to banks abroad was slightly less than LE1.5 billion worth of foreign exchange. Since then, it has risen to LE2 billion for 1986, LE2.678 billion in 1987, and LE7.287 billion in 1988.[95] Even the public-sector commercial banks deposited an average of 13.25 percent of their total assets in foreign banks between 1981 and 1986. All this indicates that in fact "the banking system is a major channel for reverse transfer of money capital from Egypt to the developed world."[96]

All these factors might explain the slowness with which Egyptian decentralization policies were developed and instigated at the end of the

1980s. It seems, however, that the 1990s will see improvements in this direction. The end of the Cold War will enhance the ability of the Western donors of aid to pressure Egypt in that direction. The great volte-face towards democracy in Eastern Europe and the rest of the world is influencing the mood of Egyptian political life in this direction. And as oil prices increase during the coming decade, the government will be more willing to attract Egyptian and Arab capital for investment. The success of the government in curtailing the economic base of the Islamic movement in Egypt by issuing Law 146 of 1988, which regulates the ICCs, might open the door for more liberalization and privatization in the country.

Finally, the Second Gulf War has given Egypt a hand in this process. The war has put in doubt the wisdom of the Islamic forces in the country, allowed more resources for the avoidance of the social consequences of the reform, and installed mechanisms that counteract the government's penchant for reluctance and retreat. In conclusion, during the 1990s, it seems that decentralization, democratization, and privatization will continue at a more rapid pace. However, it seems also that full-fledged democracy and capitalism in Egypt will wait for some time to come.

The above presentation shows interesting comparisons with the Turkish case. The domestic, as well as foreign policies, of both Egypt and Turkey were influenced by their geography and history. Both countries tried to benefit from their geostrategic location, though in different directions. While Egyptian nationalism opted to disengage from Ottoman as well as Western yokes, Turkish nationalism went to join the West. This might be explained in the different historical contexts in both states. Egypt, a very-long-time colony under various types of colonialism, was determined to disengage from its former masters. Turkey, on the other hand, is but one of the consequences of a collapsing empire. A proposition could be made, for further investigation, that states which emerge from disintegrating empires tend to join their enemies, while states which emerge out of colonialism tend to independence. (Note the present case of the collapsing Soviet empire.) Another proposition will follow that those countries with important geostrategic position that opted for more independence have been more rewarded by the international system. Egypt has benefited much more handsomely from its regional and international policies than has Turkey (see the essay by Eralp in this volume).

In spite of these differences, both countries, however, seem to have had more or less similar developmental strategies in the last four decades. During the 1950s and 1960s, SOEs gathered momentum in both countries. State interference in politics, as well as economics, was notable. By the end of the 1970s and 1980s, both countries had ventured, in different degrees and with different results, into decentralization, liberalization, and privatization. This may indicate that the changes in the world developmental strategies, as well as the changes in the global economic system, are the more decisive external factors in shaping their domestic political as well as economic posture.

However, it seems that although Egypt was sensitive early to the changes in the regional and global environment (the shift in the Egyptian posture came in 1974), Turkey was much more forceful in its response. Economic, as well as political indicators, show that Turkey has a better record in liberalization and economic performance than Egypt. This may be understood in the light of the maturity of the bourgeoisie, the military–civilian relations, and the elite attitudes towards the West in both countries. Also, it could be understood in the light of the political culture as it pertains to violence and social unrest. These factors are embedded in the historical evolution of Turkey and Egypt.

In the last decade of the twentieth century both Egypt and Turkey are embarking on largely similar courses. Their regional policies are their pass for integration in the newly emerging world order. Their elites are more inclined to join a Western-dominated world with different degrees of pleasure and displeasure. Their masses, however, seem to be looking for varied degrees of authenticity in a world that is increasingly integrated. The widening or closing of the gap between the elites and the masses will shape the future of both polities and their relationship to the world system.

Notes

1 For a discussion of the Cold War see William A. Gameson and Andre Modigliani, *Untangling the Cold War* (Boston: Little, Brown, 1971); John L. Gaddis, *The United States and the Origins of the Cold War 1941–1947* (New York: Columbus Press, 1972); and Robert E. Osgood, "Introduction: Reappraisal of American Policy," in Robert E. Osgood et. al., *America and the World: From the Truman Doctrine to Vietnam* (Baltimore: Johns Hopkins University Press, 1970).

2 See Robert E. Osgood, et. al., *Retreat from Empire: The First Nixon Administration* (Baltimore: Johns Hopkins University Press, 1973); Coral Bell, *The Diplomacy of Detente, The Kissinger Era* (London: Martin Robertson, 1977; Henry Kissinger, *White House Years* (Boston: Little, Brown, 1979); and Henry Kissinger, *Years of Upheaval* (Boston: Little, Brown, 1982).

3 See Fred Halliday, *The Making of the Second Cold War* (London: Verso, 1984).

4 Barry M. Blechman and Stephen S. Kaplan, *Force Without War: US Armed Forces as a Political Instrument* (Washington, D.C.: The Brookings Institution, 1978).

5 Stephen S. Kaplan, *Diplomacy of Power: Soviet Armed Forces as a Political Instrument* (Washington, D.C.: The Brookings Institution, 1981).

6 Eugene V. Rostow, "America, Europe and the Middle East," in *Commentary*, February 1974, p. 41.

7 Malcolm H. Kerr, *The Arab Cold War: Gamal Abdel Nassir and His Rivals 1958–1970* (New York: Oxford University Press, 1971).

8 Michael Brecher, "The Middle East Subordinate System and Its Impact on Israel's Foreign Policy," in *International Studies Quarterly*, vol. 13, June 1969

9 Abdel Monem Said Aly, "The Superpowers and Regional Security in the Middle East: The Threat is Real," in Mohammed Ayoob, ed., *Regional Security in the Third World* (London: Croom Helm, 1986); and Abdel Monem Said Aly, "The External Factors in the Security of the Middle East," in *Europe and the Security of the Middle East* (Amman: Arab Thought Forum, 1986).

10 Ibid.

11 Robert O. Keohane and Joseph S. Nye, *Power and Interdependence* (Boston: Little, Brown, 1977).

12 The literature on transnationalism is extensive. See John H. Herz, "The Rise and Demise of the Territorial State," in *World Politics* , vol. 13, no. 3, April 1961; *The Nation State and the Crisis in World Politics*, (New York: McKay, 1976); Robert O. Keohane, "Transnational Relations and World Politics," in *International Organisation*, vol. 25, no. 3, Summer 1971; and John W. Burton, *World Society* (Cambridge: Cambridge University Press, 1981). For a review of the literature, see Michael Clarke, "Transnationalism," in Steve Smith, ed., *International Relations: British and American Prospectives* (New York: Basil Blackwell, 1985).

13 Joseph S. Nye, "The Transformation of American Power," in *Aspen Institute Quarterly*, no. 2, Winter 1990, p. 19.

14 Bahgat Korany, "The Crisis of Arab Society: A Research on the Premises and Consequences of the Contemporary Arab Political Economy," in *al-Mustaqbal al-'arabi*, no. 60, February 1984, p. 45.

15 Kiyotake Tsuji, *Forecast: OPEC's 1989 Oil Revenues and Current Account* (Toyko: The Japanese Institute of Middle East Economies, 1989), p. 8.

16 Abdel Monem Said Aly, "Back to the Fold? Egypt and the Arab World," *Occasional Papers Series* , Center for Contemporary Arab Studies, Georgetown University, September 1988.

17 Raymond Vernon, "Introduction: The Promise and the Challenge," in R. Vernon, ed., *The Promise of Privatization* (New York: Council on Foreign Relations, 1988), p. 3.

18 Ibid.; Steve H. Hanke, ed., *Prospects for Privatisation* (New York: The Academy of Political Science, 1987); Michael A. Walker, ed., *Privatization Tactics and Techniques* (Vancouver: The Fraser Institute, 1988); and Said al-Naggar, ed., *Privatization and Structural Adjustment in the Arab Countries* (Washnington, D.C.: International Monetary Fund, 1989).

19 Don Babi, "The World Bank and the IMF: Rolling Back the State or Backing Its Role," in Vernon, ed., *op. cit.*, p. 256.

20 Ibid., pp. 260–73; and Charles Vuylsteke, *Techniques of Privatization of State-Owned Enterprises* (Washington, D.C.: World Bank, 1988).

21 Charles Issawi, *Egypt at Mid-Century: An Economic Survey* (London: Oxford University Press, 1954), p. 181.

22 Ibid., pp. 186–88.

23 *The Comprehensive Survey of the Egyptian Society, 1952–1980* (in Arabic) (Cairo: The National Center for Sociological and Criminological Research, 1985), p. 703; and Lewis Awad, "The Dialogue of Generations," in *al-Ahram*, 13 May 1989.

24 Atif Adli al-Abd, *Egyptian Information: Past, Present and Future* (Cairo: Ministry of Information, 1988); *The History of Egyptian Broadcasting* (UAE Broadcasting Institution, February 1970); and Issawi, *Egypt at Mid-Century*, pp. 188–89.

25 John Waterbury, *The Egypt of Nasser and Sadat, The Political Economy of Two Regimes* (Princeton: Princeton University Press, 1983), p. 10.

26 Issawi, p.155

27 Robert Springborg, *Mubarak's Egypt: Fragmentation of the Political Order* (Boulder: Westview Press, 1989)

28 Heba Handoussa, Mieko Nishimizu, and John M. Page, "Productivity Change in Egyptian Public Sector Industries After "The Opening," 1973–1979, in *Journal of Development Economics*, vol. 20, no. 1, 1986, p. 54.

29 Abdel Monem Said Aly, "Democratization in Egypt," in *American–Arab Affairs*, Fall 1987, pp. 12–13.

30 Joel S. Migdal, *Strong Societies and Weak States: State–Society Relations and State Capabilities in the Third World* (Princeton: Princeton University Press, 1988), pp. 181–192. For the control of religious institutions, see D. Crecelius, "al-Azhar in the Revolution," in *The Middle East Journal*, vol. 20, no. 1, Winter 1966; and B. Borthwick, "Religion and Politics in Israel and Egypt," in *The Middle East Journal*, vol. 33, no. 2, Spring 1979.

31 Ghassan Salame, "Introduction," in Ghassan Salame, ed., *The Foundation of the Arab State* (London: Croom Helm, 1987), p. 2.

32 Iliya Harik, "Continuity and Change in Local Development Policies in Egypt: From Nasser to Sadat," in L. J. Cantori and I. Harik, eds., *Local Politics and Development in the Middle East* (Boulder: Westview Press, 1984), p. 85.

33 Aly, "Democratization in Egypt," p. 13.

34 Ibrahim Helmy Abdel Rahman and Mohammed Sultan Abu Ali, "Role of the Public and Private Sectors with Special Reference to Privatization: The Case of Egypt," in al-Naggar, ed., *op.cit.*, pp. 144–47.

35 Ibid., pp. 148–55; and Heba Handoussa, "Egypt's Investment Strategy, Policies and Performance since the *Infitah*," paper presented to the Seminar on Investment Policies in Arab Countries, Kuwait, 1989, p. 5.

36 Muhammad H. Heikal, *Years of Turmoil* (in Arabic) (Cairo: al-Ahram Center for Translation and Publication, 1988).

37 *Communist States and Developing Countries: Aid and Trade in 1972* (US Department of State, RECS-10, 1973); *US Overseas Loans and Grants: Military Assistance and Foreign Military Sales* (USAID, April 1973).

38 Iiana Kass, *Soviet Involvement in the Middle East: Policy Formulation, 1966–1973* (Boulder: Westview Press, 1978), pp. 42–48; See also Muhammad Heikal, *Sphinx and Commissar: The Rise and Fall of Soviet Influence in the Arab World*(London: Butler and Tanner, 1978), pp. 124–37.

39 See Note 37.

40 Egyptian National Bank, *Economic Bulletin*, no. 4, 1987, pp. 229–31.

41 Said al-Naggar, "On The New Investment Law," in *al-Ahram*, 31 May 1989.

42 US Embassy, Cairo, *Economic Trends Report*, December 1986, p. 8.

43 Egyptian National Bank, *Economic Bulletin*, no. 3, 1987, p. 211, Arabic version.

44 Amani Kandil, ed., *The Transfer Towards the Private Sector*(Cairo: Center for Political Research and Studies, 1989).

45 Husni Khalil Ahmed, "The Development of Capital Market in Egypt," paper presented to the Conference on Saving in Egypt, al-Mansura University, Mansura, 4–5 April 1989, p. 139.

46 Ibid.

47 "Foreign Investment: Making Participation Pay," in *Business Monthly*, October 1987, p. 6.

48 USAID, *Privatization in Egypt*, Cairo, September 1988.

49 Regina Soos, "The Alexandria Tire Company: An Experiment in Privatization," in *Business Monthly*, February 1989, pp. 28–29.

50 *Al-Ahram*, 3 April 1990.

51 *Al-Ahram*, 14, 24, and 30 April 1990.

52 Aly, "Democratization in Egypt," p. 14.

53 Ali E. Hilal, "Mubarak and the Completion of the Democratic March," in *al-Ahram al-Iqtisadi*, 20 April 1987, p. 92; and Aly, "Democratization in Egypt," pp. 18–23.

54 Osama al-Gazali Harb, "The Civil Society in Egypt,' in *al-Ahram*, 8 April 1988.

55 Center for Political and Strategic Studies, "Interest Groups," in *The Arab Strategic Report 1986 and 1987, al-Ahram*, Cairo, 1987 and 1988; and Amani Kandil, "Political Evolution in Egypt and the Making of Public Policies," in Ali. E. Hilal, ed., *The Democratic Evolution in Egypt: Issues and Discussions* (in Arabic) (Cairo: Maktabat Nahdat al-Sharq, 1986), pp. 87–114.

56 Amani Kandil, "Interest Groups in Egypt . . . Where are they Going?" in *al-Ahram*, 5 April 1988.

57 Aly, "Democratization in Egypt,"pp. 17–21.

58 Abdel Monem Said Aly, "Egypt: A Decade After Camp David," in William B. Quandt, ed., *The Middle East: Ten Years After Camp David* (Washington, D.C.: The Brookings Institution, 1988).

59 US Embassy, Cairo, *Egyptian Economic Trends*, March 1989, p. 19.

60 Calculated from *OECD 1988 Report: Development Cooperation*, December 1988, pp. 211–20.
61 Embassy of Japan in Cairo, *Japan Information Bulletin*, no. 42, 15 April 1989, p. 4.
62 USAID, Cairo, *Status Report: United States Economic Assistance to Egypt*, November 1989.
63 Ibid.
64 Ibrahim Shihata, *The World Bank and The Arab World* (Cairo: Dar al-Hilal, 1990), pp. 38–48.
65 Ibid., pp. 52–54; Rida Hilal, *The Making of Dependency* (Cairo: Dar al-Mustaqbal al-'Arabi, 1987); and The World Bank, "Egypt, Industrial Sector Momentum," *Report No. 7491-EGT*, 13 June 1989, pp. 70–80.
66 Aly, "Back to the Fold?," *op. cit.*
67 Nader Fergany, *Going After Salary: A Field Research on the Egyptian Migration to Work in Arab Countries* (Beirut: Center for Arab Unity Studies, 1988), pp. 80, 220.
68 Ahmad al-Naggar, "Temporary Migration From Egypt," unpublished research, Arab Research Center, Cairo, 1990, pp. 16–20.
69 Nazli Chucri, "Dimensions of National Security: The Case of Egypt," unpublished paper for the World Resource Institute, March 1987, p. 7.
70 Central Agency for Public Mobilization and Statistics, *Statistical Yearbook 1988*, pp. 213–16. It is estimated that the average Arab tourist spends $125 daily, compared with $90 for others, *al-Ahram*, 17 June 1990.
71 *Al-Ahram*, 22 February 1990.
72 General Authority for Investment and Free Zones. Figure reflects approved projects as of 31 March 1987. As found in "Foreign Investment: Making Participation Pay," in *Business Monthly*, vol. 3, October 1987, p. 6.
73 Gunter Meyer, "Employment in Small-Scale Manufacturing in Cairo: A Socio-Economic Survey," in *British Society for Middle Eastern Studies Bulletin*, vol. 14, no. 2, 1988, p. 6.
74 Abdel Monem Said Aly, "The Myth and The Reality: The Four Faces of the Islamic Investment Companies," in Louis Cantori, ed., *Democratization of Egypt*, forthcoming.
75 Hamdi Kandil, "Mass Communication and Integration in the Arab World," *al-Mustaqbal al-'Arabi*, no. 107, January 1988, p. 51.
76 Douglas A. Boyd, *Broadcasting in the Arab World* (Philadelphia: Temple University Press, 1982), p. 5.
77 Issawi, p. 189,
78 *Broadcasting and Television Annual Network, 1982/1983*, Cairo, 1983, p. 17.
79 Hamdi Kandil, "The Future of the Arab Television," in *al-Ahram*, 11 June 1990.
80 Tarek al-Bishry, *Democracy and Nasserism* (Cairo: Dar al-Thaqafa al-Gadida, 1975), p. 24.

81 Springborg, *op.cit.*, pp. 95–134.

82 Central Agency for Public Mobilisation and Statistics, *Arab Republic of Egypt: Statistical Yearbook 1988*, Cairo, 1988, p. 254.

83 Springborg, *op.cit.*, pp. 137–38.

84 USAID, Cairo, *Status Report 1990.*

85 Ibid.

86 US Embassy, Cairo, *Egyptian Economic Trends*, p. 21.

87 The World Bank, *World Debt Tables 1989–90: External Debt of Developing Countries* (Washington, D.C., The World Bank, 1989), p. 51.

88 Abdel Monem Said Aly, "Quality versus Quantity: The Arab Perspective of the Arms Race in the Middle East," paper presented at the Conference on Arms Control and the Proliferation of High Technology Weapons in the Near East and South Asia, Bellagio, Italy, 23–27 October 1989.

89 *The World Almanac 1990*, p. 706.

90 Aly, "Quality versus Quantity."

91 Ibid.

92 Aly, "The Myth and the Reality,"; and "Privatization in Egypt: The Regional Dimensions," in Iliya Harik and Dennis Sullivan, eds., *Privatization and Liberalization in the Middle East* (Bloomington: Indiana University Press, 1992).

93 Interview with Mahmoud al-Helw, Chairman of the Board FIB, in *al-Ahram al-Iqtisadi*, 5 May 1986, p. 34.

94 Mohamed al-Sayed Said, "The Political Economy of Migration in Egypt, 1974–1989," paper presented at the Seminar on International Worker Migration: Political, Economic and Social Change in Turkey and Egypt, Istanbul, Turkey, 28–30 June 1989, p. 55.

95 Ibid., p. 61.

96 Ibid.; and *The Arab Strategic Report 1986* (Cairo: The Center for Political and Strategic Studies, 1987), p. 434.

9

Turkey in the Changing Postwar World Order: Strategies of Development and Westernization

Atila Eralp

Introduction

Westernization and development have been the two grand projects embarked upon by the Turkish state and its bourgeoisie since at least the inception of the Turkish Republic. The postwar international system witnessed the establishment of organic links between these two projects, as the Turkish ruling elite opted to side with the West in the emerging East–West conflict. The members of this elite believed that Turkey would have an important strategic value for the West in the ensuing cold-war climate, and that this would ultimately prompt the inflow of external funds necessary for development. This essay will show how the flow of these external funds into Turkey has been closely linked to the escalation and relaxation of the East–West conflict.

The way in which the Turkish policy-making elite linked to the international system was rather critical in the provision of external assistance for its development strategies. After World War II, the international system was undergoing a dramatic change. The way the local forces perceived this change and the opportunities they saw in the new climate were quite decisive in forging a new coalition of forces within the country that would link with the international system in a special way. The convergence of interests between the US-led Western alliance and the local power-holders that emerged very quickly after the war showed a remarkable continuity. Although during the seventies and the eighties a number of internal factors and external events caused slight changes in the alliance between Turkey and the West, it could easily be maintained that the principal pillars of this alliance survived the dramatic changes in the Soviet block as well as the Gulf crisis.

This essay will trace the processes that have led to the creation and disintegration of a convergence between an internal consensus centering on Westernization and the postwar international order that has allowed the Turkish policy-makers to capitalize on Turkey's strategic value in the East–West conflict. I maintain that in the Turkish context, the Western orientation of the elite was critical in playing this strategic card. In comparison with some Middle Eastern countries, the Turkish elite's perception of the West was a strong factor leading to the establishment of close ties with the West in the East–West conflict. In contrast to many anticolonial Middle Eastern elites, Westernization for the Turkish elite meant a civilizing mission, embodying not only pragmatic economic concerns but a secular world view. Another difference between the Turkish elite and its counterparts in other Middle Eastern states was the former's consistency in its pro-Western stance.

For a long time, Turkey's position in the East–West conflict also determined Turkish perceptions of the Middle East as a region. Regional problems were considered in terms of the East–West conflict rather than in terms of specific regional concerns, as was the case among many Middle Eastern states. This perspective lent a rather unidimensional character to Turkey's approach to Middle Eastern matters. The analysis of Turco–Middle Eastern relations will show how, over a period of twenty-five years, Turkish governments tried to develop orientations that were increasingly autonomous from the West. Indeed, Turkish policies with regard to the Middle East embody the dilemmas of its Westernization project. As Turkey became embroiled in regional concerns it became increasingly difficult to keep the original Westernization project intact. The various shifts and turns that the Westernization project had to absorb resulted in a definition of Westernization that bore a higher degree of resemblance to that of other Middle Eastern states. The recasting of the Westernization project, mainly in pragmatic economic terms, was effected at the hands of a newly created technical elite in the 1980s.[1]

It is evident that the global events in Eastern Europe and the Soviet Union have posed a serious problem for Turkish elites: how to avoid the breakdown of internal consensus in the face of the transformation of the Western alliance. It is fair to say that, as a result of the removal of the 'Soviet threat' and the demise of the bipolar world order, the anti-Soviet basis of this alliance has increasingly given way to a definition of the West as the seat of democracy and humanistic values. For a while it looked as if the Turkish policy-makers faced a bleak future with regard to their relations with the West, which, in view of the events in the Eastern bloc, would remove all its backing and indeed interest in Turkey, leaving it to sweat its problems out alone (especially because of its human-rights record) in the international arena, as well as withdrawing funds for development.

Fears as to the loss of Turkey's strategic importance were quickly reversed in the subsequent Gulf Crisis. As in the aftermath of World War II, the dramatic changes in the international climate are allowing Turkey to develop new options for integration in the emerging international order. Efforts are now directed to the formulation of a new kind of strategic importance, one that would place that importance more in relation to Turkey's role in the region than in terms of the East–West dimension. This shift in definition of strategic importance signals an important novelty: Turkey is now trying to devise a more flexible notion of strategic importance, one that will be able to absorb shifts in the West's interests not only in the Middle East, but in the Balkans and Central Asia as well. In other words, Turkey's definition of 'region' now includes Eastern Europe, the Middle East, the Black Sea, the Caucasus, and the various Turco-Soviet republics. One aspect of the old policy remains: the effort to convert strategic importance into economic funds to sustain economic development policy as well as internal consensus. As Turkey seeks new roles in the affairs of its near and far regional neighbors, the various sections of the population seem to be involved in a centripetal movement in which are expressed conflicting identities and allegiances hitherto suppressed under the unifying banner of Turkish nationalism.

The Postwar Consensus

Since the early years of the Tanzimat period, the issues of development and modernization have involved a coming-to-terms with Westernization. The exact meanings that these terms would come to hold within Turkish society, and the ways in which these rather different projects came to be seen as part of the same baggage, have yet to be analyzed.[2] Nevertheless, it would not be unfair to say that the social order that the Turkish Republic depended on was based on a promise of bringing about what Gellner describes as "an industrial affluent society," a promise which he sees as forming the basis of what he calls "the new social contract."[3] For Atatürk, the 'liberator–developer' founding-father of the new nation,[4] development meant industrialization and Westernization. Atatürk defined what the new nation was to strive for as the creation of "a new country, a new society, a new state . . . respected at home and abroad."[5] The specific means of how to achieve this new nation which, so to speak, 'turned its back' on its Asian and Ottoman past, was more difficult to agree upon. Similarly, whether the West was prepared to accept 'the Turk' within its fold was also a moot question.

Reaching a consensus on the project of development-modernization-Westernization had not been easy, and the social breadth of this consensus was, if anything, rather narrow, excluding large sections of the urban and rural population. The political fortunes of the Republican People's Party (RPP) and its struggles with the Democrat Party in the late 1940s attest to the difficulty of establishing a specific type of development-modernization project. By the 1950s the parties to the struggle had reached something of a consensus. The active forces forming this consensus were, on the one hand, a rising bourgeoisie which was increasingly contesting state tutelage represented by the RPP, and on the other, a Western-oriented policy-making elite engaged in redefining the role of Turkey in the postwar system. While the former was motivated by the expectation of new trade links and an increased flow of funds from the West, the latter sought closer links with the West as a response to an increased concern for security matters prompted by what policy-makers perceived as the growing Soviet threat.[6] This convergence of interests created a coalition of forces among the elite, a coalition whose main parameters revolved around an anticommunism that favored pro-US tendencies.

On the international front, numerous factors, including the depression and the war in Europe, had prevented the forging of multiple exchange relations with the West until the end of World War II. For the first time, the postwar international system offered Turkish policy-makers a fertile ground for instituting organic links with the West. The division of Europe into two rival blocs and the position of Turkey as a 'front-line state' in the emerging cold-war atmosphere were the two factors which eased Turkey's entry into the nascent Western alliance. In the Cold War climate, the West was trying to create a united front from which Turkish policy-makers did not wish to be excluded. It is with such considerations in mind that Turkey's leaders applied for membership to almost all the institutions that were created in the process of forging the Western alliance: the Marshall Plan, the Organization for European Economic Cooperation (OEEC) (later the Organization for Economic Cooperation and Development, OECD), the Council of Europe, and NATO.[7]

Turkish policy-makers were specifically interested in two benefits they hoped to gain from inclusion in the Western alliance. First and foremost in their estimation came security considerations. They did not believe that Turkey could survive the Cold War alone, and hoped to enter into larger and more secure alliances. In support of their application to the Western military alliance, Turkish policy-makers emphasized the geopolitical importance of their country, a position which coincided with the US Cold War strategy of containment. The second benefit they hoped to gain from association with the West was the material resources necessary for the country's economic development. Indeed, the Marshall Plan and the economic and military aid received by Turkey after World War II did turn out to be important channels for the flow of credit as well as much needed agricultural machinery.[8]

Aid from the United States to Turkey was first channeled through the relief program, the military portion of which greatly exceeded economic assistance. As shown in table 1, the inclusion of Turkey in the Marshall Plan had the effect of substantially raising the proportion of US economic aid to Turkey. Both economic and military assistance were in the form of grants.

After the expiration of the Marshall Plan in 1952, the United States continued its aid program under the Mutual Security Act *(see table 1).*

In the four years following the end of the war, Turkey began to accede to the different organizations designed to increase economic cooperation between Europe and the United States. Inclusion in the Western military alliance did not come until 1952, after Turkey had displayed its allegiance by sending troops to fight in Korea.[9] In this atmosphere, relations with the European Economic Community (EEC) were seen as a logical extension of Turkey's inclusion in the other Western organizations, since these organizations were perceived as the economic dimension supplementing and cementing the Western alliance. The absence of the United States from the newly established EEC did not at this time conflict with Turkey's efforts to maintain intimate relations with the United States. Turkish policy-makers believed (and perhaps rightly) that the United States strongly supported the creation of an economic community in Europe as a way of buttressing Western unity. Such a community also suited the needs of Turkish policy-makers well.

Other groups within Turkey were also committed to the idea of closer ties with Europe. These included a small group of entrepreneurs organized in the Istanbul Chamber of Commerce and a few government functionaries working in the Ministry of Foreign Affairs. Both groups stressed not only the trade benefits, but also the 'civilizing mission' that association with the West would have. But rather than regarding membership to the EEC as posing the problem of how to establish relations with Europe, Turkish decision-makers adopted a holistic approach in which relations with Europe were considered as one strand of the more encompassing issue of relations with the West. Similarly, Europe too saw its links with Turkey (as well as Greece) mainly in terms dictated by the Cold War.

By the mid-1950s, the Middle East had become one of the arenas in which superpower rivalries were fought out. The strategy of containment developed by the United States acquired, after the Korean War, a more overtly military

Table 1 US Aid to Turkey: 1946–1961 ($ million)

Types of Aid	1946–1948 (Postwar Relief)	1949–1952 (Marshall Plan)	1953–1961 (Mutual Security Act)
Economic	44.5	225.1	1,000.2
Military	68.8	235.9	1,533.9
Total	113.3	461.0	2,654.1
Loans	44.5	85.0	333.1
Grants	68.8	376.0	2,320.9

Source: Agency for International Development, *US Aid to Turkey,* Washington, 1971, p. 13.

character, geared towards stemming Soviet expansion globally. In the Middle East, this policy meant undermining the rise of Arab nationalism, which in the mid-1950s was strongly flavored with socialist rhetoric. The Baghdad Pact signed between Turkey, Iraq, Pakistan, Britain, and Iran in 1955, and which was strongly opposed by Egypt and Syria, represented one of the first efforts in the region to establish a military alliance against the Soviet Union. This was followed by the promulgation of the Eisenhower Doctrine in 1957, designed to fill the gap left by France and Britain as a result of the Suez crisis. As Syria and Egypt increasingly shifted towards the Soviet Union, the United States emerged as the only power in the region to oppose rising Soviet influence.

The Iraqi coup in 1958 saw the implementation of this doctrine when Lebanon and Jordan asked for US assistance against hostile communist threats. In this crisis, the ruling Democrat Party deemed that Turkey's economic (external funds) and political interests (anticommunism) lay with the West. It is in this context that the NATO base at Incirlik was first used by the United States to intervene directly in the region.[10] The inclusion of Turkey in the Eisenhower Doctrine in 1958 allowed the Menderes government the necessary legal cover to allow the United States the use of the bases.

The effect of East–West rivalry was to create a strong rift between various Arab nations, a rift which immediately recalls the present-day division within the Arab world in the wake of Iraq's invasion of Kuwait. The main difference lies in the alignments of the actors involved as a result of the absence of the Soviet Union as an important actor, and the lack of a strong Western alliance, points which I shall return to later. Thus, in the 1950s, Turkey approached Middle East issues from a Western point of view and kept a distance from the nascent nonaligned movement among Third World countries. By contrast, Egypt had challenged the West (especially Britain and the United States) and found itself in a rather different configuration of forces in the international system.

The East–West rivalry defining the postwar world order goes a long way in explaining the character of multiparty democracy in Turkey ever since its establishment in 1946. Although the roots of Turkish democracy have been sought in its agrarian and urban class structure,[11] leaders of the ruling RPP saw multiparty democracy as a requirement for adherence to the West. Nevertheless, the intensification of superpower rivalry in the 1950s allowed Turkish democracy to be foreclosed to communist parties, as well as defining for years to come the anticommunist stance of the major governing parties. Anticommunism was, however, not a new introduction to Turkish politics. The belief in an integrated, classless nation fused on the basis of national identity marks the ideological position of the bureaucratic elite since the inception of the republic. This belief was enhanced during the 1930s and 1940s when this elite directed the country towards state-controlled industrialization on the basis of successive alliances with different sections of independent agricultural producers.[12] It was this anticommunist stance which allowed the Menderes government to take the steps described above with regard to the Eisenhower Doctrine. Anticommunism in a sense became the new basis of the social contract, linking modernization and development even more strongly to the Western model. By contrast, Egypt's political regime seemed to be more open to 'socialist' ideas, but in a more authoritarian, single-party context. Egypt had never been mobilized against the Soviet Union, and its anti-Western, more Third-Worldist stance can perhaps be explained in terms of the Arab–Israeli conflict, a regional conflict that has dominated Egypt's foreign policy. Thus, while Turkey played the strategic card by involvement in Middle Eastern affairs only as far as its membership of the Western alliance required, Egypt played the same card by standing firmly on regional ground, and in order to further its claim to leadership in the region. In Turkey, the break with the Ottoman past meant that Middle Eastern issues had little resonance in domestic matters, the latter being dominated by efforts at Westernization. By contrast, the recent colonial past in Egypt and the nature of Arab nationalism turned regional matters into important domestic issues.

It is in terms of the differences outlined above that one can perhaps best explain the ways in which a similar policy of economic development, import-substitution industrialization (ISI), was implemented rather differently in the two countries. In Turkey ISI was adopted after a brief attempt at liberalism. Compared with the Egyptian experience, the liberal phase in Turkey was very short, and the transition to ISI was comparatively smooth, and did not upset the internal coalition between state bureaucrats and private entrepreneurs. While in Egypt the adoption of ISI policies represented a sudden break with the liberal phase as well as with alignments in the international system, ISI in Turkey did not seriously affect the role of the state in industrialization, nor did it require a change in foreign-policy orientations. To the extent that state intervention in Turkey meant the buttressing of private initiative, the postwar coalition described above remained intact. The Turkish state eased the transformation of merchants into industrialists by protective policies and by creating the conditions for a flow of external funds into the country through a careful management of its geopolitical location.

The way ISI strategies operated in the Turkish case produced a rapprochement between nascent entrepreneurs and the state bureaucracy. Until then, most private business in Turkey was in the hands of merchants who dealt with international trading concerns individually. Towards the mid-1950s, the balance-of-payments difficulties faced by these merchants made it extremely difficult for them to continue trading on the previous basis. State backing was required in order to organize a more concerted effort to obtain foreign credit. Furthermore, as Turkey took decisive steps in commercializing and expanding its agricultural sector, efforts towards development turned to consolidating the internal market. Thus industrialization became the major thrust of development policy.

The main mechanism of ISI in Turkey, an import regime composed of quantitative restrictions and an overvalued exchange rate, was implemented by the state bureaucracy which, by deciding on the allocation of scarce economic resources, especially foreign exchange, came to occupy an increasingly important position in the regulation of industrial activities. This position also meant increasing the contacts between nascent industrialists and the state bureaucracy. Entrepreneurs actively sought state regulation of the economy, especially demanding the imposition of import restrictions when faced with competition from imported items that they had begun to produce locally. Thus, a coalition of mainly Istanbul-based industrialists and the state elite made it possible to minimize the risks associated with ISI. It was also through this process that merchants were smoothly transformed into industrialists. This transformation mainly took place between 1951 and 1960, and was greatly dependent on international collaborators. At the end of the 1950s, the bulk of merchants had become industrialists.

The convergence of interests between internal actors was further buttressed by, and in turn facilitated, another convergence: that between financial interests within Turkey and in the international economic system. This convergence depended first of all on the collaboration between the ex-traders/new industrialists and the foreign firms whose goods they had once imported into the country. This collaboration took the form of the joint production of previously imported items. This form of production proved to be quite profitable in a largely protected internal market. It is no coincidence that protective legislation regarding foreign investment was formulated at this time (the 1954 Law on the Encouragement of Foreign Capital). This invitation to foreign capital coincided with the phase of expansion of US capital as a result of the difficulties it faced in the exportation of goods. US firms increasingly turned away from a policy of free trade, and began to seek ways of promoting free investment in Third World countries. This policy required the collaboration of local actors. Thus, the industrialization drive in many Third World countries came at a time when the international economic system, dominated by US capital, was seeking investment outlets around the world.

The foreign aid program adopted by the United States after World War II was another factor aiding the expansion of US capital and industrialization attempts in the Third World. By creating a conducive environment for private investment, foreign aid was, in part, a way of overcoming the difficulties faced by the United States in exporting capital. Thus, foreign aid and foreign investment were seen as complementary processes. In the case of Turkish ISI, foreign aid rather than foreign investment proved to be the critical source of external finance, the latter making up about 2 percent of total foreign-aid inflows throughout the decade *(see table 2)*.

In spite of the rather limited amounts of actual investment to Turkey, the small amount that did take place was quite operative in giving a boost to the

Turkish private sector, which, in collaboration with foreign investors, directed their operations to the internal market. One of the factors that accounts for the high amounts of foreign-aid flow to Turkey was a convergence between the United States and Turkish policy-makers on the important strategic role of Turkey in the emerging Cold War context. Foreign aid also gave a boost to the domestic position of the Turkish bureaucracy, since its allocation within the country was completely under the control of the government. Since the Turkish government relied on a source of finance which had, so to speak, no strings attached to it, the Menderes government could afford to disregard the International Monetary Fund (IMF) and the International Bank for Reconstruction and Development (IBRD) (World Bank) pressures to change its economic policy.[13] Thus, the policy of containment greatly aided the flow of capital to Turkey, which, in turn, was the basis on which its ISI policy could continue during the decade.

The configuration making up the specific meaning of development in Turkey had largely emerged by the end of the 1950s. Development as the main 'glue' to national unity still meant, as it had in the early 1920s, progress, modernization, and Westernization. What was new was that Westernization was now firmly defined in terms of being part of the Western alliance, and development lost most of its autarchic overtones. Economic and political links with the West were therefore actively sought. In the process, the

Table 2 Inflows of Foreign Aid and Foreign Investment to Turkey: 1963–1973 ($ million)

Year	Foreign investment	Foreign aid
1963	10.16	413.33
1964	7.7	222.22
1965	10.62	451.67
1966	7.73	403.33
1967	7.53	431.67
1968	10.27	421.67
1969	6.82	365.00
1970	6.00	306.00
1971	7.35	337.50
1972	9.22	266.79
1973	5.29	166.79
Total	88.80	3785.97

Source: Calculated from OECD Economic Surveys: Turkey, Paris, 1976; and Korel Göymen and Gürel Tüzün, "Foreign Private Capital in Turkey: An Analysis of Capital Imported Under the Encouragement of Law 6224," in *METU Studies in Development,* no. 11, 1976, p. 66.

bureaucracy not only learned how to cooperate with the local economic actors, but by trading geopolitical importance for funds it increasingly came to occupy an indispensable position of mediation between the local industrializing bourgeoisie and international donors. Thus, in the 1950s, the Turkish bureaucracy and its elite was able to cash in on its geopolitical position in order to obtain the resources needed to industrialize, procure for itself a significant position in the international system and secure the means of creating internal order based on consensus.

The Breakdown of Internal and External Coalitions

During the 1970s the order described above came increasingly under threat, both by developments within the country and in the international system, and finally crumbled with the 1980 military coup. The main cause of this breakdown was the tension between the two components of Turkey's national modernization project that had hitherto seemed identical: Westernization and development. The internal catalyst was the ISI crisis that came to a head in 1973, a crisis which was mainly due to the difficulties in attracting external funding. Compounding the crisis were industrialists' attempts to produce intermediate goods rather than consumer durables, that is to pass to what Hirschman calls "the difficult phase of ISI"[14] at a time when the world was torn by a serious recession and the oil crisis. Increasing oil prices and the concomitant change in the international economic system affected the Turkish balance of payments negatively, and international funds were no longer so freely forthcoming.

Apart from changes in the international economic system, there were also important changes in the global political climate. An amelioration in the Cold War atmosphere and an, albeit slow, transition to a period of détente undermined to a considerable degree Turkey's ability to play its traditional strategic card. Furthermore, the decline of the importance of Turkey's position as a so-called "forward defense ally," after the withdrawal of Jupiter missiles following the Cuban crisis, was exacerbated by the development of intercontinental ballistic missiles.[15] Increasing difficulties in the US economy led to a revision of its global commitments and a reduction in the amount of aid it extended. As the United States put pressure on its European allies to "share the burden," the unity of the Western alliance, which Turkey had depended on in the 1950s and 1960s, gradually began to erode. During the 1970s, Europe paid less attention to strategic matters, and as its response to the application of Greece, Spain, and Portugal for membership in the EEC shows, European powers put a greater emphasis on issues of democracy, thus increasing the differences between the United States and Europe in their approach to world peace. These new considerations in Europe forced a change in its relations with Turkey, which continued to rely on strategic considerations in its dealings with Europe. Thus both Europe and the United

States found it increasingly more difficult to extend bilateral assistance to Turkey, albeit for different reasons.

The decrease in foreign funds resulting from the changed international context could not immediately be met by either the IMF or the World Bank. Firstly, the resources available to these institutions were not sufficient to meet the rising demand of oil-importing countries. Secondly, Turkey continued to try to avoid implementing the strict adjustment measures that the IMF stipulated before extending loans to meet balance-of-payments difficulties in Third World countries. Under these conditions, Turkey, in the 1974–77 period, turned to short-term loans obtained from international commercial banks, of which the infamous 'convertible Turkish Lira deposits' were the most important *(see table 3).* These short-term loans from commercial banks went a long way towards alleviating the problem of external funding, on which successful implementation of ISI depended, in an international context in which funds were increasingly difficult to obtain. However, they were also instrumental in aggravating Turkey's debt burden, which seemed manageable at the beginning of the decade. Two factors were largely responsible for the downturn in Turkey's external funding after 1973: the oil crisis and the decline in workers' remittances[16] *(see table 3).*

The state bureaucracy committed itself to solving the private sector's problem of finance by providing government backing for the short-term loans. Yet interestingly enough, it seems that the bulk of the funds flowing to Turkey in this manner were diverted by the bureaucracy to finance public investments.[17] Thus, the state not only managed to sustain growth in Turkey, but also found a way of keeping afloat the premises on which the social

Table 3 Composition of Turkey's External Debt: 1973–1980 ($ million)

Year	Total	Short-term (ST)	ST as % of total	Convertible Deposits (CD)	CD as % of ST debts
1973	3,263	279	8.6	225	80.6
1974	3,488	216	6.2	145	67.1
1975	4,734	1,155	24.4	999	86.5
1976	7,279	3,050	41.9	1,781	58.4
1977	11,405	6,191	54.3	2,267	36.7
1978	14,822	7,176	48.4	2,860	39.9
1979	15,932	3,556	22.3	617	17.4
1980	16,222	2,500	15.4	555	22.2

Source: Merih Celasun and Dani Rodrik, "Debt, Adjustment and Growth: Turkey," in Jeffrey D. Sachs and Susan M. Collins, eds., *Developing Country Debt and Economic Performance, Vol. 3: Country Studies, Indonesia, Korea, Philippines and Turkey,* University of Chicago Press, Chicago, 1989.

contract was based: the coalition of interests with industrialists could carry on as well as the redistribution of funds to the workers, peasants, and civil servants. It could very well be as suggested by Boratav[18] that it was the competition between the Justice Party and the Republican People's Party that kept these policies alive. And it was this policy of funding the social order on the basis of precarious finances (such as the short-term loans) that created the greatest debt crisis faced by a Third World country until then.[19]

And yet the event that perhaps most illustrates, as well as led to a deterioration of, Turkey's standing in the global context during the 1970s is the Cyprus crisis. Internally, the Cyprus question firstly led to a serious reconsideration of Turkey's relations with the United States, relations on which Turkey's economic as well as political stance had depended in the 1950s and 1960s. It was after the Cyprus crisis that Prime Minister Ecevit for the first time considered the formulation of an independent national security policy.[20] It was also with such considerations in mind that Turkish foreign-policy-makers began to seek closer ties with countries that were not part of the NATO bloc. Flirtations with the Soviet Union, the nonaligned countries, and even the Middle East, marked this wish for a more flexible Turkish foreign policy. But the greatest blow that Turkey sustained as a result of Cyprus was the arms embargo imposed by the United States in October 1974, which lasted until the summer of 1978. American economic as well as military assistance to Turkey declined from $300 million in 1971 to $125 million by 1978.[21]

At a time when Turkey's ISI policy was suffering badly from the oil crisis, the drastic decline in American military and economic aid forced Turkey to rely on short-term credits, thus exacerbating the domestic economic crisis. But apart from the directly military or economic consequences, one of the most important effects of the embargo was to undermine the Turkish elite's confidence in the United States, and created the first shreds of doubt regarding Turkey's Westernization project. Did this sort of 'punishment' dealt out by the United States indicate that the West did not after all accept Turkey as one of its own?

As a result of these doubts, Turkey began to concern itself with specifically Middle Eastern issues on its own terms rather than as a member of the Western alliance. In fact, many of the regional decisions Turkey took during the 1970s were in direct opposition to Western and especially American interests. Apart from increasing economic cooperation with Iraq, Saudi Arabia, the Gulf states, and Libya, Turkey recognized the Palestine Liberation Organization (PLO) in 1976 and allowed it to open an office in the capital in 1979. Furthermore, Turkey overtly sided with the Arabs in the 1973 Arab–Israeli War, tolerating Soviet overflights of Turkish airspace while at the same time refusing the United States refueling and reconnaissance facilities.[22] Thus it seemed that the reluctance of the West to sympathize with Turkey's sensitivity with regard to Greece and the Turkish minority in Cyprus put in jeopardy the Western identity that the Turkish elite had nurtured for such a long time. It could very well be said that the Cyprus issue drove Turkey for the first time towards a more Third-Worldist position both in terms of domestic rhetoric and in foreign-policy decisions.

Relations with the EEC also raised the same question. European powers did not seem to be as supportive of Turkey's efforts to become one of them as they could have been. This issue became especially relevant in the customs union problem in the mid-1970s. Turkey had applied for membership to the EEC in 1959, mainly for foreign-policy reasons. During the 1960s, the extension of financial supports by the EEC to Turkey and the unilateral removal by Europe of trade barriers had created the conditions for a smooth relationship between Turkey and the EEC. However, the controversial Additional Protocol, signed in 1971, whereby Turkey gradually undertook to lift import restrictions and customs duties, marked the beginning of a serious strain on this relationship. For many in Turkey, a customs union was detrimental to Turkey's development policy of ISI. Especially after the 1973 oil crisis, industrialists in Turkey started to complain that the transitional period specified by the Protocol was too short to achieve the necessary restructuring of industry. Opposition to the idea of a customs union began to be mounted even in originally pro-European institutions such as the Istanbul Chamber of Industry and the Economic Development Foundation.[23] But the EEC did not seem inclined to be lenient on this point.

As balance-of-payments problems worsened, the inability to import goods needed to sustain industrial production led industrialists to demand, in increasingly insistent voices, a revision by the government of the terms of association with the EEC. In October 1978, in an effort to gain time, Prime Minister Ecevit froze the tariff-reduction schedule stipulated by the 1971 Protocol. This measure, as well as the Cyprus issue, made it extremely difficult for the Ecevit government to secure the foreign credit necessary to run the economy. As Ecevit's bureaucrats flew from one European capital to another in an effort to find funds, relations between the government and the industrial bourgeoisie deteriorated to an all-time low. The bourgeoisie's mounting discontent was also exacerbated by what they perceived to be Ecevit's populist rhetoric, which served to spur rather than contain working-class militancy. In other words, as import capacity decreased to nothing, the bourgeoisie begun to consider that the terms of the social contract had been carried too far, and that the balance had been tilted against them.

By the end of the 1970s, tensions within the governing cadres had become increasingly acute. Conflicts tearing the state executive apart from the industrialists were also echoed within the bureaucracy itself. The Ministry of Foreign Affairs, the seat of the Westernizing elite representing the old state tradition in Turkey, and whose members were recruited from among the long-standing, established families of the country, argued for primacy of political rather than economic considerations in shaping Turkey's policy toward the outside world. They thus insisted on their policy of accession to the EEC at whatever cost, since, for them, becoming a part of the Western alliance was an overriding priority. By contrast, the State Planning Organization (SPO), in line with industrialists' demands, emphasized the detrimental effects of a customs union on Turkey's industrialization. SPO bureaucrats, whose ranks increasingly came to be dominated by the Ankara- or Istanbul-educated sons of provincial small traders and low-level civil servants, were under the influence of two rather different ideologies. On the one hand, industrialization and the rhetoric of economic autonomy meant that a customs union with Europe was viewed as a threat to independence. Moreover, increasing skepticism in Anatolian provinces regarding the payoffs of Westernization led to the strengthening of political forces that stressed Turkish nationalism and/or Islam as alternative identities for the Turkish population. The combination of these two views produced a rather specific notion of national economy that the SPO began to espouse.

Thus by the end of the 1970s, economic policy had become the main object of public controversy. A changed international climate in which Turkey found it increasingly difficult to play the strategic card in the same way, coupled with economic crisis, seriously curtailed the flow of foreign funds to Turkey, and upset the internal balance of forces. As the coalition on which social order had depended began to split at its seams, development and Westernization were decoupled for the first time, and alternative allies as well as identities began to be sought. Development remained the elusive national goal, it had always been. What was questioned was whether Westernization would bring about this goal or whether it would hinder it. It was to this dilemma that the numerous political movements within the country addressed themselves. Opposition to the project of Westernization was mounted from a wide spectrum of political positions, ranging from the parliamentary Islamist party (the National Salvation Party) to the various factions of right- and left-wing groups that gradually became entangled in a street war in the large cities of Turkey. What was common to this otherwise disparate lot was their insistence on 'a strong and independent' Turkey.

It is interesting that Egypt in the same global context should enjoy the smoothest period in its relations with the outside world. Opening its doors to foreign capital at a time when Turkey toyed with notions of national economy, and, starting on a peace process with Israel, Egypt began to patch up its relations with Western powers. As a result, the funds that Turkey was craving began to pour into Egypt. In a sense, Egypt seems to have anticipated many of the measures adopted by Turkey in the 1980s: revision of the state's role in development, dependence on private enterprise, 'liberalization' of the economy, and closer contact with its neighbors as well as the hegemonic powers.[24] Thus, at the end of the 1970s, Turkey found itself confronted with a series of problems that forced it to come to terms with its regional location, both in terms of foreign-policy issues and in terms of the domestic problem of national identity. Egypt, on the other hand, was beginning to solve its regional entanglements, making its peace with the United States and Israel, and ready to forge closer ties with the West.

The 1980s: Strategic Role Redefined

The 1980s were ushered in rather violently in Turkey. The military coup in September of that year was a serious indication of the breakdown of the internal coalition, which the military government tried to patch up. But already signs of a new understanding could be seen, especially in the attitude of the military rulers towards religion. The collapse of the social contract was a principal feature of the 1980s, and a new consensus is yet to be reached. By contrast, great fluctuations took place in the international context in the course of the decade. Turkey's strategic position received an unexpected boost towards the end of the 1970s, and for a time it seemed that the 'good old fifties' were back. It even seemed that the old internal alliances could be rekindled without the redistributive state policies. But the 'Second Cold War' lasted for only five years, and towards the end of the decade the well-known events in Eastern Europe and the Soviet Union shattered, until the breakout of the Gulf Crisis, the major premise on which foreign policy had been based.

The Soviet invasion of Afghanistan in 1979, the conflict in Lebanon, and events in Iran leading to war with Iraq all created an international climate that has been called the Second Cold War. The first undermined the process of détente, and both the United States and Turkey became extremely suspicious of Soviet expansionist intentions. Turkish foreign-policy-makers saw no option but to go back on their search for a flexible policy and so began to seek closer ties with the United States, which, in a similar vein, emphasized the importance of stability in the region, basically because of the Iranian revolution. Thus, once again, the strategic location of Turkey enabled it to effect a rapprochement with the United States, a rapprochement in the wake of which US funds began to flow back into Turkey. These events also led to a quick resolution of several issues that had soured US–Turkish relations. The arms embargo had already been lifted in 1978. After the Soviet invasion of Afghanistan, the US–Turkish Defense and Economic Cooperation Agreement (DECA) was concluded (March 1980), Turkey acquiesced to the Rogers Plan that enabled the return of Greece to NATO's military structure (October 1980), and the United States undertook the modernization of airfields in the eastern Turkey through the Memorandum of Understanding (November 1982) as well as agreeing to help Turkey modernize its air defenses. US assistance to Turkey quadrupled between 1978 and 1981, reaching an all-time high in 1985[25] *(see table 4).*

These changes in Turco–US relations had important positive effects on international lending agencies, and funds began to be available to Turkey from a multitude of sources. Two most important outcomes were the

Table 4 US Economic and Military Aid to Turkey: 1978–1989 ($ million)

Year	US Aid
1978	125.0
1979	250.0
1980	400.0
1981	450.0
1982	700.0
1983	685.0
1984	856.5
1985	878.1
1986	738.0
1987	590.0
1988	525.3
1989	500.0

Source: Duygu Sezer, "Turkey in the Western Alliance in the 1980s," in Atila Eralp, Muharrem Tünay and Birol Yeşilada, eds., *Socioeconomic Transformation in Turkey Since 1980,* Praeger, New York, 1993.

rescheduling of Turkey's debts and the availability of new loans from the OECD, the IMF, and the World Bank. Of the more important sources of assistance, the OECD provided $1 billion in 1980. It was also at this time that the World Bank extended Structural Adjustment Loans for five consecutive years (1980–85). For its part, in June 1980, the IMF entered into a three-year standby arrangement according to which it extended a total of $1.25 billion in SDR.[26] These advances constituted exceptional awards given to a single country, and exceeded by far the terms according to which these agencies extended credit.[27] It was on the basis of such loans that a new development policy gradually began to take shape in Turkey, that of export-promotion. The 1979–81 period is one in which economic funds from a multitude of sources began to flow into the country at a rate that is particularly striking when compared with the earlier period *(see table 5).*

In spite of the similarity to the situation in the 1950s with regard to Turkey's strategic standing in the international system, serious rifts between Europe and the United States no longer permitted a smooth unity in the Western alliance. Thus, contrary to Turkish expectations, amelioration of relations with the United States did not produce a similar outcome with regard to its relations with Europe, especially the Council of Europe and the EEC. The EEC froze all financial assistance to Turkey by refusing to free the 600 million ecus stipulated in the fourth Financial Protocol signed between Turkey and the EEC. Greater integration with world markets bypassed Europe, and the volume of Turkey's trade with the EEC, which had always retained a significant share of Turkish foreign trade, began to dwindle

Table 5 Flows of Medium- and Long-term Credit to Turkey: 1975–1981 ($ million)

Sources	1975–78 (Annual average)	1979	1980	1981
Official	623	1,131	2,683	1,799
Bilateral	360	659	1,671	988
OECD	226	596	1,138	491
OPEC	11	54	288	56
CPEs	124	9	245	441
Multilateral	263	472	1,012	811
WorldBank	224	306	616	570
Other	39	166	396	241
Private	494	634	299	249
Total	1,117	1,765	2,982	2,048

Source: Merih Celasun and Dani Rodrik, "Debt, Adjustment and Growth: Turkey," in Jeffrey D. Sachs and Susan M. Collins, eds., *Developing Country Debt and Economic Performance, Vol. 3: Country Studies, Indonesia, Korea, Philippines and Turkey,* University of Chicago Press, Chicago, 1989, p. 758.

dramatically *(see table 6).* The military intervention of 1980 and the suspension of democratic rights within the country led to a freezing of relations between Turkey and the EEC, which had by then begun to prioritize democracy and foreign-policy issues rather than economic and strategic ones. The inability of Turkish policy-makers to assess correctly the importance placed by the EEC on the question of democracy, even in view of the Greek, Spanish, and Portuguese examples, served to escalate tensions between Turkey and the EEC. Thus, undertaking relations with the EEC within a Cold War framework did not pay off, and could have well presaged the difficulties Turkey would later face with regard to its application for full membership to the European Community.

Strategic alliance with the United States at the turn of the decade brought Turkey in much closer contact with the Middle East rather than Europe. Initially, links between Turkey and the Middle East were security-oriented, activated, as they were, at the behest of the US government in response to the Soviet invasion of Afghanistan. While the 1982 Memorandum of Understanding was mainly concerned with the shoring-up of defenses against the Soviet Union, it also provided ground for speculation regarding the use of these airfields in the Gulf region, even if the Soviets were not directly involved. This memorandum also prompted questions regarding NATO's role in the region, the so-called 'out-of-area' problem. The task of delimiting NATO's area of legitimate activity still pending, Turkey has since the 1980s shown itself to be more ready to cooperate with the United States within the framework of NATO rather than under any bilateral arrangement. Thus, in the early 1980s, Turkey refused to take part in the Rapid Deployment Force

Table 6 Turkey's Exports: 1976–1989 ($ million)

Years	Total exports	To the Middle East	Middle East as % total	To the EEC	EEC as % total
1976	1960	238	12.1	960	48.9
1977	1753	220	12.5	868	49.5
1978	2288	323	14.1	1095	47.8
1979	2261	387	17.1	1097	48.5
1980	2910	630	21.6	1251	42.9
1981	4703	1895	40.3	1502	31.9
1982	5746	2543	44.2	1755	30.5
1983	5728	2447	42.7	2010	35.0
1984	7133	2768	38.8	2731	38.2
1985	7958	3188	40.0	3134	39.4
1986	7457	2571	34.5	3263	43.8
1987	10190	3010	29.5	4858	47.8
1988	11662	3530	30.3	5098	43.7
1989	11627	2874	24.7	5408	46.5

Source: Halis Akder, "Turkey's Export Expansion in the Middle East, 1980–1985," in *Middle Eastern Journal,* vol. 41, no. 4, autumn 1987, pp. 553–67; and State Planning Organisation, Main Economic Indicators, Ankara, January 1991, p. 56.

set up by the United States to ensure security in the Gulf region. Any operation undertaken jointly with the United States in the Gulf would seriously undermine Turkey's resolve after the Cyprus problem to further an autonomous policy in the region. It is with such considerations in mind that Turkey maintained a neutral position during the Iran–Iraq war. Thus, Turkey was increasingly drawn into the orbit of US activities in the region, and yet, past experience and domestic considerations cautioned Turkey not to make any specific regional commitment. An additional source of anxiety for Turkey was the everlasting Soviet presence. Any increased involvement with US regional plans outside the framework of NATO raised the possibility of a negative response from the Soviet Union. Turkey, therefore, in opposition to its European allies, favored an enlargement of NATO responsibilities to cover the Middle East, a position it has been able to hold with renewed fervor since the removal of the Soviet threat in 1989.

As security concerns in the Gulf increased Turkey's role in the region, Turkey turned towards reinforcing its economic ties with Middle Eastern countries. Although this policy had its roots in Turkey's financial and political problems after the 1973 oil crisis and the Cyprus debacle, the downturn in relations with the EEC in the 1980s gave an additional urgency to Turkey's search for new markets in the Middle East. One of the means by which Turkey has attempted to secure a steady supply of oil has been to build pipelines that would transport Iraqi oil and gas to Mediterranean ports. In this way, Turkey hoped to reduce its oil bill as well as ensure that dependence would cut both ways. Indeed, until the present Gulf Crisis, Turkey has been the most secure outlet for Iraqi petroleum since 1977. Turkey's exports to the Middle East also rose significantly after 1980, reaching 44 percent of total Turkish exports in 1982 *(see table 6).*

This increase in exports to the region was accompanied by a stepping-up of the activities of Turkish contractors in the region. One estimate puts the total value of contracts held by Turkish contractors in Libya, Saudi Arabia, and Iraq at $10 billion by the end of 1982.[28] Along with Turkish contractors in the region, the numbers of Turkish workers in the area have also increased. Finally, in 1981 Turkey instigated the establishment of a Standing Committee for Economic and Commercial Cooperation under the auspices of the Organization of the Islamic Conference, of which Turkey had hitherto been an inactive member.[29]

Greater involvement in the region at both private and state levels coincided with important changes in the ranks of the ruling elite. Compared with the staunchly secular, Western-oriented professionals of the 1960s and early 1970s, the technical elites of the 1980s in the bureaucracy as well as in the private sector were more concerned with integrating Islamic values with a pragmatic, policy-oriented approach rather than with the transmission of Western values and 'educating the people.'[30] Rather than upholding anti-Western, Third-Worldist views, as had the more Islamicist followers of the National Salvation party, this new elite tried to "reconcile (Muslim) cultural orientations with the requisites of economic growth and Western democracy."[31] Integration in Western financial and trade markets, and importing Western technology and know-how, became one of the most important 'fetish' goals of this new elite, a goal which they deemed themselves capable of accomplishing on the basis of their intimacy with the "universal language of science."[32] In this sense, one can argue that this new type of professional elite was more globalist and integrationist than the modernizing elite of the 1970s. It was among the ranks of this new elite that the Motherland Party (MP), the ruling party of the 1980s drew its leaders and membership. Thus emerged the "entrepreneurial politician" of the 1980s, at ease with numbers rather than words, ready to find a quick solution to immediate problems, and more inclined to act according to contingency rather than principle."[33]

It was this emphasis on economic and pragmatic matters that created a convergence of interests between the new technical elite and the traditional industrial elite. One of the effects of the crisis of ISI at the end of the 1970s was a prioritization of economic issues in the eyes of the latter. The industrial bourgeoisie tried to impress on the new military government the view that it could not sustain another shortage of external funds, and that the only way of avoiding such an eventuality was integration into world markets. This, in turn, required a restructuring of industry towards more international competitiveness. The increased tension between the private sector (at least between large industrialists) and the government towards the end of the 1970s had given rise to an increased demand by the former for less intervention by the state in the economy. The view that the bourgeoisie increasingly came to hold of the bureaucracy was of an antiquated state machine incapable of keeping up with changes in the world. Moreover, the street violence perpetrated by rival political gangs in the months preceding the military coup raised the issue of internal security. Thus, the grande bourgeoisie demanded less state visibility in economic matters but an increased presence in issues of law and order. This new definition of the state's role and a shifting of the terms of the coalition on which internal order had depended was endorsed by Özal, who pledged to meet demands on the strength of his links with the new technical elite.[34]

As argued by many observers, state regulation of the economy did not decrease in the 1980s, but merely changed form and direction. A rhetoric of liberalization was kept alive through the abolition of the quota system and import licensing, the main pillars of ISI, while at the same time import surcharges, tax exemptions, and rebates became the main mechanisms through which the economy was regulated. Most of these measures amounted to a system whereby the state continued to support the economy. But now, in line with the tenets of the export-promotion strategy expounded by Özal, state support was directed towards exporters. Once again, as was the case in the 1950s, the fact that these exporters were the very same people as the ISI industrialists meant that the transition to these policies could be effected without creating a major rift with the powerful sections of the bourgeoisie. At the beginning, exporters managed by using government backing to channel their unused capacity to external markets. But by the middle of the decade, the lack of new investments geared to exportation led to the disenchantment of the bourgeoisie.

As the economy and internal order became the main concern of the ruling elite, relations with the outside world also began to be viewed in the same light. The smooth economic performance in the Middle East, along with the strategic importance enjoyed by Turkey allowed, for a brief period, the decoupling of economic and security issues. While Özal and his policies took care of the former, it was up to the old bureaucratic elite to manage the latter. This rather economistic approach to foreign policy could continue as long as the Second Cold War lasted. But as the Western powers, including the United States, moved towards prioritizing human-rights issues, and as events in the Soviet Union demonstrated the value of such a policy, it became increasingly difficult for Turkey to obtain foreign funds on the basis of strategic importance alone. By the end of the decade, even strategic location—the last stronghold of Turkish claims to the Western order—had been seriously undermined as a result of the demise of the bipolar world order. The removal of the 'Soviet threat' created a disjuncture between world events and Turkey's traditional stance, eroding the basic tenets of Turkish foreign policy, along with the power of that section of the bureaucracy which had specialized in Cold War politics.

In conjunction with these events, the United States withdrew its support from Turkey in many different areas. The US Congress found it easier to put pressure on Turkey on the various issues that Turkey was sensitive about, such as Cyprus and the Armenian question. By 1986, US foreign aid to Turkey began to decline and continued to do so until the end of the decade *(see table 4)*. Economic assistance expected from the EEC was also halted as a result of the latter's slowing down of the Turkish application for full membership. Finally, trade with the Middle East suffered a severe setback by the mid-1980s, mainly as a result of the decline in Arab oil revenues *(see table 6)*. Rather hasty pro-Arab policies (such as Turkey's immediate recognition of Palestine and its refusal to follow US policy in isolating Libya) taken by the Turkish government in an effort to stem this decline only served further to strain its relations with its traditional Western allies, especially the United States, until the Gulf Crisis. It was then that improved relations with the Gulf states came in handy for Turkey in its attempt to redefine its strategic importance in the international order.

The policies expounded by Turkey's governments in the 1980s created the grounds for a new coalition of the state with the bourgeoisie. But this time, rather than covering a large section of the private sector as it did in the 1950s, this rather short-lived coalition was established between Özal and only a small segment of the bourgeoisie, that of the large exporting groups. Importers and small-business interests increasingly lost out and gradually withdrew their support from the Motherland Party (MP) founded by Özal. Their allegiance to the state and MP politics, as well as that of the salaried classes (especially workers and civil servants), had been secured on the basis of law-and-order issues and promises of a consumer-oriented economy. As austerity measures adopted by successive MP governments served to erode the redistributive structure of the Turkish state and the consumerism promoted by Özal, it became increasingly obvious that the premises of the new social contract also stood on shaky ground. For its part, the bureaucracy also showed signs of division. Serious disagreement had strained relations not only between the traditional elite in the Ministry of Foreign Affairs and the economic-minded government, but the latter itself became increasingly more divided in terms of economic policy. Advocates of a complete break with the West competed with more traditional secular bureaucrats and the more pragmatic compromisers in the struggle to shape the economy and polity. The same division was also echoed among the ranks of industrialists and entrepreneurs, cross-cutting the old division between the bureaucracy on one side and private entrepreneurs on the other. The crushing of socialist activism by the military, following the coup and the changed political climate, created a situation in which discontent began to be voiced through a search for new identities. Westernization no longer seemed the only alternative for Turkey, and the very tenets of modernization came to be questioned. The final link of the development-Westernization-modernization packet was also thus severed. It is in this context that a proliferation of Islamic ideologies in the late 1980s can be understood. These trends led to a situation of nonviolent internal strife that many observers have called a "crisis of legitimacy." For a short period at the end of 1989, it seemed as though the internal and external premises on which domestic social order was based had disappeared for good. The Gulf Crisis broke out as the increasingly fragile MP government began to grope for a new basis of legitimacy.

The Gulf Crisis: A Chance to Restore Internal and External Coalitions?

The Gulf Crisis seems to have offered Turkey's ruling elite solutions, at least in the short term, to the three interrelated problems delineated above: strategic position, transfer of external resources to Turkey, and internal order. The crisis helped resolve the ambivalence in Turkey's traditional approach to the Middle East by striking a balance between its attachment to the West and its new links with the Middle East. By adopting the role of broker between the West and the Middle East, remaining all the while a close ally of the former, Turkey has taken a decisive step with regard to the Middle East as well as diminishing its global isolation. In the process, Turkey's strategic role was redefined. Thus, in place of the East–West axis, Turkey began to look towards the region in shaping its new strategic role, changing drastically its post-Cyprus foreign-policy orientation of noninvolvement in intra-Arab conflicts. As recent events in the Gulf have patently demonstrated, regional conflicts in the Middle East tend quickly to become global issues, and it is at this level that Turkey decided to regain strategic importance. Although this is reminiscent of Turkey's foreign policy during the 1950s, it must be remembered that the former alignment had its rationale in anti-Sovietism, whereas today, it is the absence of the Soviet threat that made this shift possible. Furthermore, since the 1980s, Western powers were no longer unified in their assessment of the Turkish role in the international system. It is the Gulf Crisis which finally induced the Turkish leadership to recognize this division and opt for the United States rather than Europe, a tendency which had already appeared in the early 1980s.

The economic ramifications of the Gulf Crisis are yet to be determined. The economic performance of the Özal governments had begun to suffer a serious downturn after 1986. Turkey had found it increasingly difficult to secure external funds for the smooth running of the economy ever since the decline of US assistance in 1986. Turkey's external debts rose from $25.5 billion in 1985 to $49 billion in 1990.[35] Short-term loans, totaling $9.5 billion in 1990, have once more began to loom large in Turkey's foreign-debt bill (20 percent in 1990), increasing by about 65 percent between 1989 and 1990.[36] Different estimates show that the Turkish economy suffered a loss of $3 billion in 1990, as a result of the Gulf Crisis and the embargo on Iraqi trade, with greater losses expected in 1991. Many sectors of the Turkish economy, including construction, transport, and tourism, were adversely affected, as were the consumers, who had to bear the brunt of the rising oil bill. In this context the compensatory aid expected from various sources after the Gulf War acquired added urgency, leading to wild speculations in the daily press and the statements of officials. The whole episode has served to reinforce doubts regarding Turkey's relations with the West. It seemed that, once again, Western powers had disregarded the sacrifices Turkey undertook in order to align itself with the West, especially in view of the amount of material benefit that Egypt managed to obtain.[37]

Perhaps one of the most important domestic aspects of the Gulf Crisis has been the opportunity it provided for Özal to try to boost his declining prestige. To this end, he attempted to enlist the support of the United States, and especially that of President Bush, by providing a strong backing to US strategies in the region. Managing the Gulf Crisis almost single-handedly, he allowed the United States the use of the NATO bases in southern Turkey, thus providing the Western alliance crucial support, as well as meeting domestic demand for noninvolvement. For a while it seemed as though Turkey had finally obtained the international visibility and acclaim it deserved, through the efforts of its president. President Bush's visit to Turkey was yet another indicator of Turkey's (and Özal's) increasing prestige abroad, a prestige which was quickly tarnished by Turkey's handling of the Kurdish refugees from Iraq. Whether these moves allowed Özal to regain lost popularity domestically cannot be so easily ascertained. His promises were too many and too large. Not only did Turkey not obtain the economic aid it hoped for, but there have not been too many victories on the political front either, especially with regard to Turkey's accession to the European Community and the Cyprus question.

Finally, it was this solution to problems of domestic and regional order that Özal began to propound as a model to be emulated by other countries of the Middle East. According to Özal, the Turkish example demonstrates how radical Islam, which challenges Western interests, could be successfully contained while promoting Islamic values at the same time. Özal was also trying to export the model for social order which seemed successful domestically: the promotion of trade as a way of minimizing political tensions in the region. Thus the Turkish foreign ministry has tentatively begun to develop a strategy of exchanging water in return for oil. At the moment, the basic obstacle to these plans seem to be the unwillingness of Arab nations to accept Turkey as a viable broker in regional affairs. Wedding Islamic identity and aspirations to Western modernity in this fashion, Özal hoped that the Turkish example might be perceived and therefore financially supported as such by the West, lending Turkey the credibility it lacks within the region. Again, as usual in postwar Turkish history, the linchpin of this whole edifice is the inflow of economic support from Western countries to support economic growth domestically, and political and military power regionally.

Conclusion

In this essay I have tried to show that development policies in Turkey were based on a particular configuration of internal and external forces that together managed to sustain a specific understanding of development. The articulation of Turkey to the international system in terms of its geopolitical significance constituted the basis of this configuration. It was through this articulation that the funds needed to carry out development policies, whether ISI or EP, flowed into the country. The seemingly final demise of the bipolar world on which such a strategy depended makes it increasingly urgent for Turkey to find new ways of inserting itself into the world system. One of the possible alternatives, that favored by the United States, seems to direct Turkey towards a position of regional brokerage, a region which includes the Soviet–Turkish republics and the Middle East. This shift has serious implications for the nature of the social contract on which internal order was based. Above all, it requires a reconsideration of the rejection of the Ottoman identity (including its pan-Turkish and pan-Islamic variants) on the basis which the Turkish Republic was constituted.

There were, for a long time, important differences in the ways Turkey and Egypt related to the West. While the former chose to ally itself both politically and culturally with the Western tradition, Egypt assumed strategic importance with respect to its role in regional matters. The stalemate reached in the Arab–Israeli conflict in the early 1970s forced Egypt to change its foreign policy as well as its development strategy at an early date. Turkey followed suit only at the very end of the 1970s. In both countries, lack of external funds for development seems to have prompted economic changes as well as a revision in foreign policy.

Opening up to US influence has meant greater involvement in regional affairs for both countries. The new role of brokerage that both countries are being pushed into seems to engender competition rather than cooperation between Turkey and Egypt. US aid figures to both countries,[38] as well as the rumors following the Gulf War, seem to indicate that Egypt enjoys considerable advantage over Turkey. The Ottoman past, which Turkish policy-makers are trying to remember in their efforts to negotiate with Arabs, is a double-edged sword. It was, after all, against the Ottoman yoke that Arab nationalism first defined itself. For their part, Turkish foreign-policy-makers are heirs to the republican tradition which has distanced itself from the Middle East in its efforts to emulate the West. They thus find themselves incapable of defining their own identity in the changing world order, and as a result are unable to offer a specifically Turkish solution to regional problems. This dithering in turn inspires no confidence among Arab nations that continue to regard Turkey as a past imperial power acting in line with Western and US interests.

Notes

1 Nilüfer Göle, "Engineers and Technicist Ideology," in M. Heper and A. Öncü, *Changing Political and Cultural Identities* (London: I. B. Tauris, 1993).

2 For an early treatment of the subject, see Niyazi Berkes, *The Development of Secularism in Turkey* (Montreal: McGill University Press, 1964).

3 Ernest Gellner, *Thought and Change* (Cambridge: Cambridge University Press, 1964), p. 33.

4 Ibid., p. 36.

5 K. Atatürk, quoted in Bernard Lewis, *The Emergence of Modern Turkey* (Princeton: Princeton University Press, 1968), p. 480.

6 See Mehmet Gönlübol et al, *Olaylarla Türk Dış Politikası* (Ankara: SBF Yayınları, 1987).

7 See Mehmet Gönlübol and Haluk Ülman, "İkinci Dünya Savaşından Sonra Türk Dış Politikası," in Gönlübol et al.

8 For an estimate of the amount of agricultural aid received by Turkey, see Ronnie Margulies and Ergin Yıldızoğlu, "Agrarian Change: 1923–1970," in Irvin C. Schick and E. Ahmet Tonak, eds., *Turkey in Transition: New Perspectives* (Oxford: Oxford University Press, 1987), pp. 269–92.

9 Oral Sander, *Türk–Amerikan İlişkileri 1947–1964* (Ankara: SBF Yayınları, 1979), p. 74.

10 Gönlübol et al.

11 See for example Çağlar Keyder, *State and Class in Turkey* (London: Verso, 1987); and Haim Gerber, *The Social Origins of the Modern Middle East* (Boulder: Lynne Reiner, 1987).

12 See Faruk Birtek and Çağlar Keyder, "Agriculture and the State: An Inquiry into Agricultural Differences and Political Alliances, The Case of Turkey," in *Journal of Peasant Studies* , 2, no. 2, 1975, pp. 446–67.

13 Galip Yalman, "The Politics of Structural Adjustment: The Case of Turkey," paper presented to the Conference on Dynamics of States and Societies in the Middle East, Cairo, 17–19 June 1989.

14 Albert O. Hirschmann, "The Political Economy of Import Substituting Industrialisation in Latin America," in *The Quarterly Journal of Economics,* 82, no. 1, 1968, pp. 1–32.

15 See Ali Karaosmanoğlu, "Turkey and the Southern Flank: Domestic and External Contexts," in J. Chipman, ed., *NATO's Southern Allies: Internal and External Challenges* (London: Routledge, 1988), pp. 287–335.

16 See Tosun Arıcanlı, "The Political Economy of Turkey's External Debt: The Bearing of Exogenous Factors," in Tosun Arıcanlı and Dani Rodrik, eds., *The Political Economy of Turkey: Debt, Adjustment, and Sustainability* (London: MacMillan, 1990), p. 234.

17 Merih Celasun and Dani Rodrik, "Debt, Adjustment and Growth: Turkey," in Jeffrey D. Sachs and Susan M. Collins, eds., *Developing Country Debt*

and Economic Performance, Vol. 3: Country Studies, Indonesia, Korea, Philippines and Turkey (Chicago: Chicago University Press, 1989), p. 31.

18 Korkut Boratav, *Stabilization and Adjustment Policies and Programmes, Country Study: Turkey* (Helsinki: Wider, 1987), p. 2.

19 Celasun and Rodrik, p. 19.

20 Duygu Sezer, "Turkey's Security Policies," *Adelphi Paper* no. 164, IISS, London, 1981.

21 See Arıcanlı,"The Political Economy of Turkey's External Debt."

22 Ali Karaosmanoğlu, "Turkey's Security and the Middle East," in *Foreign Affairs*, 62, no. 1, Fall 1983, p. 163.

23 Atila Eralp, "Turkey and the European Community: Prospects for a New Relationship," in Atila Eralp, Muharrem Tümay, and Birol Yeşilada, eds., *Socioeconomic Transformation in Turkey Since 1980* (New York: Praeger, 1993).

24 *cf.* John Waterbury, *The Egypt of Nasser and Sadat: The Political Economy of Two Regimes* (Princeton: Princeton University Press, 1983), and John Waterbury and Alan Richards, *A Political Economy of the Middle East: State, Class, and Economic Development* (Boulder: Westview Press, 1990).

25 Duygu Sezer, "Turkey in the Western Alliance in the 1980s," in Eralp, Tünay, and Yeşilada, *Socioeconomic Transformation.*

26 Celasun and Rodrik, p.757–58 (SDR: Special Drawing Rights).

27 Ibid.

28 Ali Karaosmanoğlu, "Turkey's Security and the Middle East," p. 165.

29 Atila Eralp, "The Politics of Turkish Development Policy," in Andrew Finkel and Nükhet Sirman, eds., *Turkish State, Turkish Society* (London: Routledge, 1990), p. 251.

30 The phrase is Nilüfer Göle's. See her "Towards an Automization of Politics and Civil Society in Turkey," unpublished paper, Deutsches Orient Institut, Hamburg, 1988.

31 Ibid.

32 Nilüfer Göle, "Engineers and Technicist Ideology," p. 9.

33 Ibid.

34 Atila Eralp, "The Politics of Turkish Development Policy."

35 State Treasury, *External Debt Bulletin* (Ankara: Undersecretariat for Treasury and Foreign Trade Publication, 1990).

36 *Milliyet*, 14 April 1991.

37 The Turkish press made a big issue of the fact that Egypt's foreign debt had been halved after the Gulf War.

38 See Aly, this volume.

Interest Articulation and the Management of Discontent

10

Political and Institutional Context of Business Activity in Turkey

Ayşe Buğra

Introduction

This essay is based on some of the findings of a research project on big business activity in republican Turkey.[1] The analytical framework of the study reflects a certain dissatisfaction with the two broad theories that provide us with coherent models of business activity, namely mainstream economic theory and Marxist analysis. In spite of their many differences, these two approaches share two common characteristics. One of these characteristics is the treatment of private (or class) interest as an exogenous variable. Second, both approaches operate on the basis of a clear dichotomy between the market as the realm of private interest and the state as the realm of public policy.

Instead of adopting a research agenda based on one of these broad theories, this study draws extensively upon other theoretical contributions and currents of analysis which move beyond the two characteristics mentioned above. Karl Polanyi's work, for example, is central to the analysis of the business community as a socially created entity, as opposed to a class which acts according to exogenously given principles of behavior and influences the course of social life.[2] C. Lindblom's emphasis on the inherent tension between the business community and the state has also been a highly useful source of insight for our research.[3] As Lindblom argues, because of the crucial significance of private business decisions for overall economic performance, government leadership must often defer to business leadership.

It must nevertheless do so without compromising the interests of the wider public and endangering social stability. The way this somewhat uneasy relationship is managed appears as one of the key determinants of successful economic performance.

The significance of this task of skillful management of state–business relations has been underlined in analyses of developed, industrialized economies in "state-centered approaches"[4] as well as in "coalition models of state–business relations."[5] The implications of state–business relations for policy implementation and policy outcome are also emphasized within the neo-corporatist literature of the 1980s.[6]

Empirical studies on business activity in late-industrializing countries suggest that in the context of late industrialization, the state appears as a central actor in business life. In this context, the management of state–business relations, too, becomes both more important and more difficult than elsewhere.[7] It becomes more important because of the existence of pressing economic problems and severe social discontent which can only be dealt with by rapid economic growth. In a private-enterprise economy, rapid growth is possible only if productive private investment is forthcoming. On the other hand, the capabilities and habits of businessmen rarely match the magnitude of this task and considerable state support is required. Under these circumstances, governments can be very demanding of and impatient with businessmen. Even the threat of terminating private enterprise in a firm, industry, or the entire system is not unusual in these countries. Turkish businessmen have heard such threats quite a few times during republican history, while in Egypt they were actually put in practice.

In general, the social legitimacy of business activity in late industrializing countries does not seem to be as clearly established as in developed countries. It frequently seems to be contingent on the successful performance of businessmen in contributing to the objectives of development. At the same time, however, the kind of support they can get from the government often far exceeds what their counterparts in developed, industrialized countries can hope to get. This could not always be interpreted as a sign of corruption. As in South Korea, or even in Japan, special privileges accorded to businessmen might be regarded as a necessary condition of successful economic performance. In very general terms, it seems possible to suggest that, in many late industrializing countries, the business community finds itself in a strange position of power and weakness at the same time.

Nevertheless, it would be unjustified to classify all late-industrializing countries in one group and attempt to study the social and political context of business activity on the basis of the same criteria in all of them. Comparative studies suggest that the specificity of business life in any single country is given by a configuration of factors each of which might, in isolation or combined with a different set of factors, give us a totally different picture. This essay will not attempt to present a full discussion of all the factors which shape and mold the business life in Turkey. It will try to cover, instead, three areas which appear to be of particular significance in contrasting the characteristics of business activity in Turkey and in Egypt. What will be presented here is not an explicit comparison, but rather a discussion of the Turkish case with a view to highlighting some of the points which might be contrasted with the characteristics of the Egyptian one in analyses based on a more thorough knowledge of the latter.

One major difference between the Turkish and Egyptian business histories seems to lie in the distinctive social origins of the business class in the two countries. As the essays by Ibrahim and Keyder in this volume suggest, the insignificance of large landowners among the founders of big Turkish enterprises presents a contrast with the Egyptian case, where landed property appears as the main source of capital accumulation. In contrast with the Egyptian bourgeoisie that has emerged on the basis of a tradition of wealth and social status, the Turkish bourgeoisie appears as a largely state-created entity with no links with land ownership and, moreover, with no tradition of craftsmanship. It is a class formed of former small merchants and civil servants, largely depending on the state as the provider of financial resources and market opportunities and, more significantly, as the major source of social status. As such, it is a class which historically owes its existence and social legitimacy largely to its relations with the state.

This relationship of dependency has significantly affected Turkish business outlook and behavior, not only because of the extent of state intervention, but also because of the uncertainty-inducing nature of the policy-formation and -implementation process in the country. Throughout republican history, there have been two types of uncertainty characterizing business life in Turkey. The first type of uncertainty prevails with regard to the exact coordinates of the businessman's position in society. In an atmosphere of doubt concerning the social legitimacy of business activity, the future of the private-enterprise system could at times seem uncertain, especially in periods of rising antibusiness ideology. Nevertheless, even during the terms in office of governments contributing to the establishment of a pro-business ideology, Turkish businessmen had to operate in a highly uncertain environment because of the arbitrary policy changes which led to unexpected changes in the values of major economic indicators. In fact, under the Democratic Party governments in the 1950s and the Motherland Party governments in the 1980s, both committed to the establishment of a private-enterprise economy, the second type of uncertainty reached unprecedented dimensions due to the extent of discretionary policy changes with an enormous impact on business activity.

The environment in which Turkish business life has evolved is thus characterized by the overwhelming importance of the state as an actor which, by frequent changes of economic policy, shapes and directs private sector activities. The legitimate domain of state intervention has remained ambiguous, and this ambiguity has been a constant which business had to take into account in its decisions pertaining both to business strategy and enterprise structure.

Nevertheless, the fear of systemic change has never become a reality in Turkey, while in Egypt the failure to conform to the requirements of the social and economic objectives set by the Nasser government led to massive nationalizations and the virtual termination of private enterprise in many sectors of the Egyptian economy. As is underlined by several Egyptian scholars, these nationalizations have not led to the disappearance of old wealth, and the old elite surfaced in the 1970s ready to assume a significant economic role in the Egyptian Infitah.[8] In both the Nasser era and afterwards, there seems to have been an intermingling between the private- and public-sector representatives. The tenure of bureaucratic and political positions by private wealth-holders seems to be quite common, and some writers see in the "involvement of the State in the world of business and the intended mixture between policy and economy, wealth and power, public money and private money," an incentive to the development of parasitic elements.[9]

In contrast to the Egyptian case, in Turkey—despite the significant role the state plays in the economy—such a disappearance of the strictures on the private sector has not been observed. One notices, rather, an increasing consolidation of the position of the private sector manifested in the nature and the scope of its activities, and, especially, in the institutional structure of entrepreneurship. The structural characteristics of the big Turkish enterprises in fact constitute the second area where interesting questions pertaining to the comparative evaluation of business activity in Egypt and in Turkey can be raised.

In Turkey, the changing nature of industrial enterprise, culminating in the emergence and the development of the 'holding' form, has largely contributed to the consolidation of the place of the private sector as an irreversible social process. While the Turkish holding company appears as a social institution which reflects the vulnerability of private enterprise to the process of policy formation and implementation, it also appears as a structural component of the economic system and plays a crucial role in determining policy outcome. This is a major difference between Turkey and Egypt. In Egypt, the quantitative significance of private wealth-accumulation does not seem to be accompanied by parallel developments in organizational structuring and managerial professionalization. One could perhaps see here a rather significant characteristic of the Egyptian Infitah. One could assume that the institutionally precarious nature of private Egyptian capital is likely to have left the public sector as the main engine of transformation as far as the integration with the world economy is concerned.

Another area which appears to be important for a comparative evaluation of the place of private business in Turkish and Egyptian societies is the nature of business associations. This will constitute the third area of our discussion of the Turkish case. The diversity and vitality observed in the activity of business associations in Turkey constitutes a significant point that should be highlighted here. In Turkey, the *institutional* membership of the Union of the Chambers of Industry and Trade, and Stock Exchanges, has reached three hundred.[10] This represents an individual membership of approximately 600,000. Apart from the Chambers, the 1988–89 membership of the Turkish Industrialists' and Businessmen's Association (TÜSİAD) is 270. Sixteen regional business councils, under the umbrella of the Foreign Economic Relations Organization (DEİK), have a total membership of about five hundred. There are seventeen Employers' Unions within the Turkish Confederation of Employers' Unions (TİSK). These seventeen unions, which include three public-sector ones, have an individual enterprise membership of about 1,500. Only one of the many sectoral business associations, the Association of the Investors in Tourism, has a membership of 150. Naturally, there is some overlapping membership, but the quantitative significance of business association membership in Turkey can not be overlooked.

For the purposes of comparing Egyptian business associations with Turkish ones, two observations made in this volume by Amani Kandil are particularly interesting. Kandil writes, first, that business interest-group activity in Egypt became significant after the death of Sadat, especially after the foundation of new forms of associations in the late 1970s and the early 1980s. This coincided with a wave of political liberalization in general, and the increasing rigor of interest-group activity in particular. In Turkey, too, we observe, in the same period, that business associations, both the Chambers and other, relatively new, organizations, have gained an increasingly important social position. In Turkey, however, this constitutes a period of severe political repression, where association life and interest activity for non-business groups were largely curtailed. Union activity in general, and labor unions in particular, have been very weak since the beginning of the 1980s. Unlike the situation in Egypt, labor union demands or labor problems in general have constituted a very negligible portion of business concerns. Throughout the past decade, until very recently, industrial conflict was largely absent in the Turkish economy. With the labor movement largely silenced, the energies of business associations were channeled in other directions.

In fact, this situation presents a continuity with the past history of Turkish business, whose primary concern has traditionally been the impact of government policy on business life. In contrast with another observation made by Kandil on the totally favorable stand of the Egyptian business vis-à-vis the open-door policies, Turkish businessmen were highly critical of some of the policies implemented by the Motherland Party government. The criticism, however, was often toned down in conformity with the legacy of government–business relations in the country. While greatly appreciating the pro-business ideological stand of the government, businessmen have often preferred to take advantage of the prevailing ideological atmosphere and to use their organizational base to influence broader social and political trends with a view to consolidating their position in society.

Private Business in Turkey: Past and Present

Several historians have already drawn attention to the fact that in modern Turkey, state-building and the development of a bourgeois class were interdependent. Social and economic policies designed to create a Turkish–Muslim business class can in fact be traced back to the Union and Progress Party era between 1908 and 1918.[11] The policy of indigenization adopted in this period was probably instrumental in increasing the importance of Muslim businessmen during the final years of the empire. The information given in table 1, which shows the sectoral distribution of enterprises in Istanbul in 1924–25 according to the ethnic origin of the owner, in fact sheds some doubt on the widely held view that Muslim businessmen were practically nonexistent in the beginning of the republican era. Nevertheless, the policies of indigenization were also adopted by the republican government, and they led to the appropriation of many enterprises belonging to the emigrating minorities by aspiring Muslim entrepreneurs.

That the modern Turkish bourgeoisie largely owes its existence to the state appears, therefore, as a generally accepted fact. What is somewhat less emphasized is the nature of the social groups out of which the state has chosen to recruit the elements of the new class. The data that we have on the social background of big businessmen seem to indicate the absence of a systematic effort to channel the existing wealth, especially of the landowning segments of the population, to industrial and commercial activities. We could in fact suggest that the absence of special incentives to encourage the landlords to convert their wealth into industrial and commercial capital reflects the distrust of the builders of the new state for the alternative, nonpolitical sources of power which might have been inimical to the radical project of social transformation. The nature of the discussions of the Land Reform Bill of 1945, for example, supports this view. In some of these discussions, it is explicitly suggested that land reform is necessary because large property constitutes a threat to the state authority and conflicts with the mentality of the new republican state.[12]

Studies on Turkish business history show that, like landowners, former artisans do not figure prominently among business leaders. The fact that very few Turkish entrepreneurs were artisans or children of artisans might reflect, firstly, the significance of minorities in artisanal occupations in the late Ottoman era. Policies aimed at creating an indigenous business class naturally excluded the encouragement of Greek or Armenian artisans to use their skills in the establishment of modern industry. Moreover, the emigration of minorities is likely to have caused an important shortage of artisanal skills in

Table 1 Enterprises in Istanbul Benefiting from the Industrial Promotion Law: 1924–25

Owner	Sectors																								Total
	Food processing			Leather and leather products			Textiles			Construction materials			Carpentry			Mining and metal products			Chemicals			Paper products and misc.			
	a	b	c	a	b	c	a	b	c	a	b	c	a	b	c	a	b	c	a	b	c	a	b	c	
Muslim	8	2		1	5	2	2	6	3		3	2	2	1	2	5	3	1		4			3		55
Non-Muslim	10	9	3	1	4	1	1	1			4	2		5		3	3	3		1			4	3	58
Total TC*	18	11	3	2	9	3	3	7	3		7	4	2	6	2	8	6	4		5			7	3	113
Non-TC	1	2			1											1								1	6
Total	19	13	3	2	10	3	3	7	3		7	4	2	6	2	9	6	4		5			7	4	119

* Turkish citizens
a Employing ten or fewer workers
b Employing more than ten workers
c Information on the number of employees n.a.

The data on ethnic origins and nationality of the owners (far left column) is estimated on the basis of the table given in S. İlkin and İ. Tekeli, "1923 yılında İstanbul'un İktisadi Durumu ve İstanbul Sanayi ve Ticaret Odası İktisat Komisyonu Raporu," in *Tarih Boyunca İstanbul Semineri,* İstanbul: İstanbul Üniversitesi Edebiyat Fakültesi yayınları, 1989.

the country.[13] While the exclusion of Muslims from commercial activities in the Ottoman era is often emphasized, we find many fewer references to this absence of artisanal skills among the Muslim population. Yet, the shortage of indigenous artisans can be an important factor in defining the nature of the original sources of entrepreneurship in the country. Apart from the supply factors affecting the sources of entrepreneurship, government policies are also likely to have played a significant role in this area. The deliberate neglect of small industry and the lack of incentives designed for the modernization of small enterprises by successive governments combine to constitute another important factor limiting the opportunities of transition from small artisanal production to modern industrial activity. The political discourse, especially in the 1930s, reflected a strong distaste by government authorities for small enterprises, which were found undesirable because of their lack of conformity to the state-builders' ideal image of a modern, large-scale industry like that in developed Western nations. Along with this 'aesthetic' concern, governments' preference for large-scale enterprises might have been based on the relative ease with which such enterprises could be controlled and made subservient to government-set objectives of social and economic policy.[14]

The attitude of state authorities, therefore, provides at least a partial explanation of the insignificance of the number of landowners and artisans among the founders of big Turkish enterprises. Studies on this subject tend to indicate that the latter mostly come from the ranks of civil servants and small merchants. Especially among the businessmen who made their début in the 1950s, engineers, too, seem to have an important place.[15] Table 2 gives a summary of the former occupations of the founders of enterprises operating in the early 1970s according to the period of foundation of the enterprise. Table 3 complements the previous one by providing information on the occupation of the father of the founding entrepreneur. The available information suggests that the typical big businessman in Turkey is an individual who begins his career with a small initial capital outlay, and develops his business by relying on family support and by taking advantage of the opportunities provided by the state.

Nevertheless, these observations concerning the origins of the Turkish business class should not lead us to underestimate the social and economic role this class has come to play in Turkey. As table 4 shows, the private sector has played an increasingly significant role in the Turkish economy, in spite of the rather important periodic fluctuations in its share in total payments to employees, in total fixed investment, and in the value added.[16] While the figures in these areas suggest that the share of the public sector in the Turkish economy is also quite important, they should be interpreted by taking into account some characteristics of the Turkish experiment in mixed economic development. First, until the 1980s, 'mixed economy' remained an ambiguous term, which at times created a considerable degree of uneasiness among

Table 2 Previous Occupation of Entrepreneurs According to Date of Foundation of Enterprise

Period of establishment	Previous occupation (%)									Number of enterprises
	Merchant	Industrialist	Farmer	Professional	Civil servant	Shopkeeper	Artisan	No occupation	Total	
pre-1900	19.17	-	-	-	10.83	-	-	70	100	120
1901–10	-	-	-	-	-	-	-	-	-	
1911–20	3.85	-	-	-	3.85	-	-	92.3	100	26
1921–30	27.03	-	-	2.7	10.81	27.03	-	32.43	100	37
1931–40	3.23	1.61	-	-	74.19	-	1.61	19.36	100	62
1941–50	35.71	-	-	4.55	31.17	6.49	-	22.08	100	154
1951–60	18.92	4.3	5.16	6.45	18.93	-	1.51	44.73	100	465
1961–69	22.97	0.35	4.24	13.08	26.15	4.59	-	28.62	100	283
Total	239	21	36	75	280	33	8	455	100	1,147
%	20.83	1.83	3.14	6.54	24.41	2.88	0.7	39.67		7

Source: E. Soral, *Özel Kesimde Türk Müteşebbisleri,* Ankara: İktisadi ve Ticari İlimler Akademisi Yayınları, 1974, p. 36.

Table 3 Previous Occupation of Entrepreneurs by Occupation of Father

	Father's occupation (%)						
Previous occupation	Merchant	Industrialist	Farmer	Professional	Civil servant	Shopkeeper	Artisan
Merchant	68.2	7.11	14.64	4.6	1.27	4.18	
Industrialist	47.63	47.69			4.68		
Farmer	5.56		94.44				
Professional	21.33	32	17.33	16		13.34	
Civil servant	21.79	3.93	10	5.71	32.5	17.86	8.21
Shopkeeper			21.21	3.03		75.76	
Artisan	12.5						87.5
No occupation	38.24	20.44	19.34	5.71	4.84	8.01	3.32
% of fathers in the occupational category	37.23	14.12	19.44	5.67	10.29	9.85	3.4

Source: E. Soral, *Özel Kesimde Türk Müteşebbisleri,* Ankara: İktisadi ve Ticari İlimler Akademisi Yayınları, 1974, p. 42.

private businessmen concerning the coordinates of their social position. While this ambiguity was instrumental in shaping the business attitude prevailing in the country, the actual growth of the public sector in Turkey has never occurred in a manner which could threaten the realm of the public sector. The latter has always had sufficient investment outlets, as demonstrated by its lack of interest in the purchasing of public-sector companies during the privatization attempts of several governments, especially in the 1950s and 1980s. Second, joint ventures with public enterprises, especially with public banks, have facilitated the expansion of private firms by enabling them to realize large-scale, high-technology investments in many areas of the economy. Third, the growth of private enterprise in Turkey has taken place along with the development of the highly structured form of the Turkish holding company. Private wealth has been organized in the structure of large multiactivity firms which form the dynamic force both in the development of the Turkish economy and in its articulation with the world economy.

The Turkish Holding Company as a Social Institution

Like holding companies in general, Turkish holding companies are established to purchase the shares of other firms. However, in Turkey these companies appear more like management units maintaining an active entrepreneurial participation in their manifold activities. The first legal provisions for the

Table 4 Turkish Manufacturing Industry: 1950–1986

Year	Number of establishments (%)		Annual payments to employees (%)		Gross additions to fixed assets during the year (%)		Value added (%)	
	public	private	public	private	public	private	public	private
1950	3.93	96.07	59.37	40.63	53.98	46.02	58.33	41.67
1951	4.04	95.96	58.68	41.32	55.90	44.10	59.24	40.76
1952	3.80	96.20	55.74	44.26	46.89	53.11	61.34	38.66
1953	4.25	95.75	53.98	46.02	44.79	55.21	55.77	44.23
1954	3.79	96.21	51.38	48.62	61.55	38.45	50.55	49.45
1955	3.66	96.34	50.42	49.58	59.51	40.49	50.14	49.86
1956	3.66	96.34	50.77	49.23	61.13	38.87	47.03	52.97
1957	3.95	96.05	47.39	52.61	54.36	45.64	44.47	55.53
1958	3.81	96.19	44.28	55.72	57.09	42.91	45.09	54.91
1959	3.95	96.05	47.30	52.70	36.55	63.45	54.34	45.66
1960	3.98	96.02	49.08	50.92	48.36	51.64	59.11	40.89
1961	3.29	96.71	45.78	54.22	47.80	52.20	51.41	48.59
1962	5.71	94.29	48.24	51.76	78.21	21.79	52.64	47.36
1963	7.87	92.13	51.09	48.91	51.74	48.26	52.69	47.31
1964	8.03	91.97	49.09	50.91	59.24	40.76	51.73	48.27
1965	9.26	90.74	50.46	49.54	44.60	55.40	57.13	42.87
1966	9.35	90.65	50.76	49.24	36.56	63.44	54.67	45.33
1967	8.68	91.32	49.19	50.81	36.84	63.16	62.89	37.11
1968	8.65	91.35	48.32	51.68	35.05	64.95	61.99	38.01
1969								
1970								
1971	6.73	93.27	41.40	58.60	37.79	62.21	56.01	43.99
1972	6.72	93.28	40.46	59.54	38.47	61.53	51.81	48.19
1973	6.37	93.63	38.36	61.64	36.39	63.61	46.52	53.48
1974	6.60	93.40	38.85	61.15	34.84	65.16	50.24	49.76
1975	6.41	93.59	41.74	58.26	32.96	67.04	48.05	51.95
1976	5.65	94.35	44.05	55.95	31.69	68.31	35.54	64.46
1977	5.81	94.19	43.15	56.85	30.69	69.31	39.89	60.11
1978	5.34	94.66	42.39	57.61	38.10	61.90	33.40	66.60
1979	5.31	94.69	44.35	55.65	18.38	81.62	33.14	66.86
1980	4.68	95.32	46.49	53.51			40.41	59.59
1981	4.63	95.37	44.47	55.53	24.57	75.43	49.26	50.74
1982	4.48	95.52	40.46	59.54	29.01	70.99	46.84	53.16
1983	8.93	91.07	40.77	59.23	29.09	70.91	43.52	56.48
1984	8.37	91.63	37.53	62.47			38.47	61.53
1985	8.05	91.95	34.73	65.27			39.44	60.56
1986	7.86	92.14	33.01	66.99	32.24	67.76	40.72	59.28

Source: State Statistical Institute.

establishment of holding companies in Turkey were introduced in 1960. The changes that were made in the corporate tax system in 1961 rendered the holding form more attractive for private firms. In 1964, another legal change introduced further tax advantages for holding companies.[17] As I have argued elsewhere,[18] while these advantages stemming from the tax system have undoubtedly played a role in the increase in the number of holding companies, the possibility of the centralized management of physical and financial resources in highly diversified activities, under the umbrella of the holding company, appears to have been equally important. In fact, with the legal changes that were made in 1986, many of the tax advantages hitherto enjoyed by holding companies were eliminated. Yet many new holdings were formed after this date, indicating the significance of administrative concerns in determining this particular institutional form of business activity.

According to a list compiled by the Istanbul Chamber of Commerce, there were 210 holding companies in Istanbul in April 1990. Thirteen of these companies assumed the holding form in the 1960s, ninety-six in the 1970s, eighty-seven in the 1980s, and six during the first quarter of 1990.[19] Since 1986, thirty-five Istanbul-based companies became holdings.

Because of the absence of reliable statistical data, it was not possible for us to estimate numerically the significance of holding companies in national production and income. It is possible, however, to get a fairly accurate idea of the economic significance of these companies by looking at their position among the 500 largest companies in Turkey. According to the 1988 annual survey of the Istanbul Chamber of Commerce, there were ninety-five public and 405 private firms among the largest five hundred. Of these 405 private firms, nine belong to producers' cooperatives. Only seventy of those remaining are independent firms, with the shares of 314 of the largest 500 Turkish enterprises held either by one or more holding companies or groups. Five large holding companies (Koç, Sabancı, Yaşar, Anadolu Endüstri, and Çukurova Holding) appear as the shareholders of eighty-five companies among the largest 500. It is also significant that in the ranking of these 500 companies, none of the independent enterprises appears in the first 250. In fact, most of the independents are ranked among the last one hundred companies.[20]

Also indicating the significance of multiactivity firms in the Turkish economy is the involvement of these firms in the financial sector. As of December 1988, of the ten Turkish banks that held about 80 percent of the total assets of deposit banks, five were group-owned and four were state banks. The tenth, İş Bankası, has a rather peculiar legal structure, and itself constitutes a quasi-private group. After the post-1980 changes in banking regulation, the groups have begun to play an important role also in the newly flourishing investment banking by forming joint ventures with foreign banks.[21]

In fact, as mentioned earlier, holding companies have played a significant role in the recent increase in foreign direct investment in Turkey through the formation of joint ventures with foreign companies. In 1989, among the 500 largest Turkish companies, seventy-two had a foreign firm among the investors. Thirteen of these firms have either no Turkish partner or one with negligible shares (less than 2 percent). Of the remaining firms, five have a public company as the Turkish partner, while in forty-seven the Turkish partner is a holding company. Among these partly foreign-owned firms, only one has a Turkish partner which is not group affiliated.[22]

Tables 5–7 provide information on the scale and types of diversification in the activities of Turkish holding companies. One observes three distinct types of diversification. Yaşar Holding is typical of large conglomerates with very highly diversified activities in many unrelated fields. The activity diversification chart of Borusan shows that it is a company where the diversification is extensive, but the fields are not totally unrelated. In the case of Tamek, the activities largely remain in alcoholic beverages and food-processing, but the number of enterprises in this area is fairly large.

This diversification strategy seems to reflect the historical legacy of private enterprise and the social environment of business activity in Turkey. It involves, first, a certain weakness of industrial outlook observed in the coexistence of service- and financial-sector activities along with industrial ones, and in the lack of commitment to any particular line of activity. This conforms to the idea that Turkish industrial development has taken place without an accompanying ideology of industrialization, a point highlighted by several studies on Turkish entrepreneurial history. A. Payaslıoğlu writes, for example, that in Turkey, "industry, by virtue of its origins, its character, and the manner in which it is operated, manifests close and strong ties with commerce and does not appear as a separate field of activity."[23] Similarly, according to R.W. Kerwin, Turkish businessmen lack a long-term commitment to industrial activity, they demand abnormal returns and rapid amortization, and the tendency to sink a large portion of funds in inventory seems to indicate that objectives of a speculative nature often dominate the objective of enhanced efficiency and profitability of industrial production.[24] In the course of my interviews, too, when I asked businessmen to talk about their strategy of diversification, the answers were almost never formulated in terms of the possibility of using the acquired expertise in one area in a different, yet related, field of activity.

The reason behind the entry into a new field was almost always formulated with reference to risk-aversion or to the expectation of high profits. As the Austrian economists have argued extensively, in business life, uncertainty appears as the source of both profit and loss. The peculiarity of business life in Turkey is that the fundamental source of uncertainty that businessmen try to manage is not the market but the state. The tendency to operate in many different and often unrelated areas is in fact explained by many private-sector representatives with reference to this state-induced uncertainty. We were told that, in Turkey, the risk and profitability of industrial ventures largely stem

Table 5 Activity Diversification: Yaşar Holding

Year	Paint	Husbandry/ food processing	Alcoholic beverages	Tourism	Fertilizers/ agricultural inputs	Paper products/ data proc.	Clothing/ leather prod.	Foreign trade/trans- portation	Con- struction/ machinery
1946	imports								
1954	production								
1963	production	milk prod.							
1967			beer prod.						
1968	packaging								
1970				rest.-cafe					boilers, machinery
1971								foreign trade	
1973				holiday village	fertilizer production			trans. corp.	constr. corp.
1974	chemical products sale								
1977	chemical products			tourism agency	fertilizer & seed sales				
1978	paint raw materials								
1979	production, marketing								
1980								foreign trade	
1981	paint & deriv.	flour & meat prod.							
1982	paint & deriv					paper prod.			
1983		marketing & distrib.				data processing		trans. corp.	
1984	paint & deriv.	water & sea products			tobacco processing				
1985				aviation					
1986		regional distrib.	regional distrib.				clothing		
1987		husbandry				paper marketing			
1988		supermarket		holiday village			leather business		

Table 6 Activity Diversification: Borusan Holding

	Iron/steel	Machinery	Automotive	Construction & contracting	Marketing & transportation
1953	marketing of products				
1958	pipe production				
1960	steel production & sale				
1969		machinery production			
1970			engine production		
1975					marketing abroad
1976	iron production		galvanized iron plate		
1984			automobile representative		
1988			coordination of automotive group	housing, industrial, and touristic establishments	
year unknown			shock-absorber production		warehouse & transportation; 7 domestic trade corps.; 2 international trade corps

from economic policies, which, in the absence of a long-term industrial strategy, often change and alternately affect different sectors in highly unexpected ways.

In other words, the fluctuations in input supply and output demand, to which the companies respond by diversifying their activities, almost exclusively originate in economic policy changes, especially in three key areas: interest-rate policy, foreign-exchange policy, and the foreign-trade regime. Extremely frequent and highly unpredictable changes in these areas seem to have taught the Turkish businessmen that it is important, first, to have one foot in the banking sector to ensure access to credit, and second, to have the ability to move easily between import and export activities. More specifically, it appears important to have the flexibility to move between particular import and export sectors which periodically receive changing degrees of preferential treatment. The importance of government policy in the structure of activity

Table 7 Activity Diversification: Tamek Holding

	Non-alcoholic beverages & food processing	Advertising
1955	fruit juice & canned vegetables	
1961	distribution	
1962	fruit juice production	
1969		advertisement corp.
1974	marketing, distribution	
1977	bottling	
1981	fruit juice production/Cyprus	
1983	fruit & vegetable processing	
joint ventures	4 fruit juice enterprises; eau-de-cologne enterprise; metal cap enterprise	

diversification is manifested, for example, in the number of companies entering into the field of tourism in the 1980s, when this sector benefited from a large variety of incentives. Of the twenty-six companies for which I have activity diversification charts, ten have tourism-related activities. Seven of these ten companies entered the sector in the 1980s.

What is important to note here is that while businessmen quickly respond to opportunities stemming from economic policy changes, this does not lead them to abandon their former areas of activity. They thus maintain their activities in the formerly privileged sectors in order to have the flexibility to face any unexpected changes in the type of economic policies implemented. Since policy changes are so frequent in Turkey, this strategy appears to be a fairly rational one, even though it is highly unlikely to be conducive to the development of an industrial outlook among Turkish businessmen.

In fact, the weakness of an industrialist's mentality among the businessmen is enhanced by another characteristic of the historical legacy of Turkish business. As highlighted by previous research in the area, the support of the family of the entrepreneur has played a very significant role in the accumulation of capital and in the subsequent development of the enterprise. In the course of my interviews, businessmen invariably referred to the government as the major source of their difficulties. Nevertheless, most of them shared the opinion that these difficulties would not lead to the actual collapse of the enterprise as long as the family remains as a closely knit unit. Hence the significance attached to the intergenerational continuity of family control over business operations, which does not seem to be seriously challenged by the younger generation. We thus observe highly conscious efforts to combine a viable organizational structure with continuing family control. Moreover, by making sure that the heirs get a first-class training in business administration, big-business families attempt to overcome the potential contradiction between family control and professional management of the enterprise.

My study indicates that Turkish holding companies present a highly centralized structure, where the board of directors of the mother company, dominated by the members of the owning family, very closely control the operations of the subsidiary firms. The general managers of individual companies who, by virtue of their function, are more closely involved in the production process, have little autonomy in their decisions. Moreover, the nature of the relations between owners and professional managers is such that the degree of commitment of the latter to the enterprise is often quite low. Under these circumstances, matters pertaining specifically to production tend to be dominated by financial concerns. The family-dominated structure of the holding company thus enhances the weakness of the industrial outlook in the country.

The continuity of family control over the manifold activities of Turkish holding companies is made possible, at least partially, by the nature of these companies' relations with the state. By virtue of their size and the scope of their activities, holding companies enjoy special advantages in their relations with the government, especially in as far as the access to subsidized credit resources is concerned. The fact that large companies often have their own banks does not reduce their financial dependence on the state. It might even enhance it, because having one's own bank does not reduce the use of subsidized credit but facilitates its use by eliminating the discretion of commercial banks in the allocation of such credits.[25] In fact, it is documented that large Turkish companies have very high debt/equity ratios which tend to increase with company size.[26]

The possibility of easy access to credit is one of the reasons behind the unsatisfactory development of Turkish capital markets, in spite of the efforts made in this direction in the 1980s. Given this possibility, Turkish companies could indulge in their desire to remain as family concerns and avoid the loss of control over their business which the issuing of shares in the stock market might imply. It has also given them the opportunity to act according to their traders' mentality instead of concentrating on the profitability of industrial operations. Although it would be difficult to document it, government authorities have repeatedly referred to the significance of enterprise funds used to purchase government bonds rather than to redress the company's fragile financial position. Real estate speculation, too, seems to be quite important.[27]

It is possible to predict that the increasingly acute fiscal crisis of the Turkish state would eventually lead the holding companies to reconsider their financial strategies and to reduce their dependence on the state. One could predict, for example, that Turkish companies would eventually give up their reluctance to raise funds by issuing shares in the stock market. While it is possible to observe certain trends in this direction, the alternative preferred by Turkish big-businessmen seems to be the formation of partnerships with foreign capital as a way of dealing with financial bottlenecks. The foreign firm investing in Turkey thus appears as a new actor which might alleviate the relations of dependency between the state and the Turkish business, but, at least in the near future, it is not at all certain that the joint ventures with foreign companies would necessarily end the family domination of the Turkish holding company.

At present, the Turkish holding company appears as a family-run giant with very close relations with the state. One area where the close ties between holding companies and the state have significant implications is the business association activity in the country.

Business Organizations in Turkey

The size and the multisectoral character of holding companies enable them to enjoy important advantages in their relations with government authorities. These companies have, in particular, highly significant channels of presenting and negotiating for their demands from the government. In this regard, they seem to render redundant, in many ways, the organized channels of interest representation. In this section, this idea will be pursued by concentrating on four types of business organizations: Chambers of Commerce and Industry, sectoral associations, the Turkish Industrialists' and Businessmen's Association (TÜSİAD), and organizations like the Foreign Economic Relations Organization (DEİK) and the Economic Development Foundation (İKV), which play a quasi-governmental role in international economic relations.

The relations between the government and the Chambers is extensively explored in studies by Öncü and Sayıbaşılı.[28] Both writers emphasize the close government control exercised over the activities of the Chambers, and document the extent of political patronage involved in the allocation of foreign-currency quotas, which remained a prerogative of the Chambers until 1971. After the 1971 military coup, the powers of the Chambers were significantly curtailed by the centralization of the allocation of foreign-currency quotas under the responsibility of the Ministry of Commerce. The Chambers continued to fulfill certain bureaucratic functions, like the registration and control of the prices of imported goods, but these functions, too, have largely lost their significance with the changes that have taken place in the foreign-trade regime in the 1980s.

Some of my interviewees thought that with the declining importance of their bureaucratic functions, the Chambers could probably be more successful as interest organizations in the future. Most of them noted, however, that the heterogeneity of the membership, the cleavages between big- and small-business interests in particular, would hamper the role of the Chambers as interest organizations. Big businessmen in general did not seem to think of the Chambers as a significant forum for the articulation and promotion of their interests, although some of them argued that the Professional Committees of the Chambers of Industry were quite effective in promoting the interests of small-businessmen. The presidents of the two sectoral associations that we interviewed said, however, that there was no way these committees could be effective, given the heterogeneity of the enterprises brought together under the same professional grouping. They believed, therefore, that sectoral associations had a very important role to fulfill, in spite of the reluctance of the Chambers to admit the significance of their role.

In fact, during the 1980s, these associations gradually became an important component of the state–industry relations in Turkey. However, there are certain problems preventing them from being fully effective. Firstly, they have financial difficulties because of the refusal of the government to accord them the status of 'socially useful association', which would enable them to benefit from tax-deductible contributions. Secondly, as one of the interviewees bitterly complained, the lack of interest and commitment of businessmen prevents sectoral associations from becoming really influential. "The big think that they do not need the association," he said, "and the smaller ones feel that the association is there anyway and would try to solve their problems without their contribution." He also thought that the government did not try to curb the particularist tendencies, and continued to receive individual pleas which should be channeled through the association.

The president of another association seemed to be happier with the attitude of the membership, and also with the association's relations with the state. According to him, the solidarity of the members of his association was an exceptional one, largely owing to the strong guild tradition which is still dominant in the trade. As to their good relations with the state, he explained it with reference to their compliant attitude and their care in limiting their demands to strictly technical issues, and in avoiding any discussion of broader policy matters. Since their sector was very closely affected by the foreign-exchange policy, then in implementation, I asked him whether it was not too difficult to avoid expressing their views on this particular policy issue. As an answer, he complained about the seriousness of the harm inflicted on their sector by the current government policy in that area, but concluded that it was not their business to deal with it. "Let the Chambers do it," he said. "Let TÜSİAD do it . . . "

This was the attitude of a quite typical member of a class whose social position is not fully consolidated. In this regard, TÜSİAD, the increasingly influential representative of big business that has an important presence on the public scene, has an entirely different image. In fact, in a period when association activity was severely curtailed, when the workers, civil servants and intellectuals were faced with serious obstacles in presenting their pleas and voicing their criticisms against government policy, TÜSİAD could play a very important public-opinion-forming role by advocating the merits of the private-enterprise system. As an interest association, however, its role is limited by the widely shared view of the membership that TÜSİAD should take care to avoid getting involved in pressure-group politics and concentrate on questions pertaining to national objectives. As most of the interviewees indicated, the big businesses in TÜSİAD are too big to need the association to take their problems to the government. They do not seem to have any difficulty in meeting government authorities to present their cases. In fact, the big-business community in general believes that the government prefers this individual contact to association-mediated relations. Two of the interviewees explicitly said that this is especially true for right-wing, pro-business governments which tend to have a pragmatic approach and believe that the intermediation of organizations complicates things. "They view this type of indirect contact as being too bureaucratic," one businessman said. He thought that other types of governments, on the other hand, are reluctant to discuss policy matters with the representatives of business organizations, because they fear appearing to be guided by business interests. This observation, whether well-founded or not, is interesting, since it reflects the views of businessmen on the limited effectiveness of organized channels of contact with the government.

While the business community seems to be discouraged from acting as a class in the pursuit of its interests (the word 'class', like the words 'interest' and 'lobby', was avoided like an obscenity by the private-sector representatives I interviewed), in recent years they were given a quasi-governmental role in specific areas of public policy, especially in the realm of foreign economic relations. The fourth type of business organization that we mentioned is important in this context. Among these, İKV was established in the 1960s to deal with economic relations between Turkey and the EEC. It was founded by the Istanbul Chambers of Industry and Trade, and its membership includes several business organizations like TİSK (Turkish Confederation of Employers' Unions) and TÜSİAD. DEİK, on the other hand, was founded through the initiative of the Union of Chambers as an organization bringing together several regional business councils (such as the Turkish–American Business Council) and major business organizations. While it is active in the area of foreign economic relations, one of its major objectives is the establishment of a healthy dialogue between different private-sector organizations and the coordination of their activities.[29]

In spite of their wide organizational membership, both İKV and DEİK appear as organizations whose effective role in public policy is largely determined by the personalities of a few individuals who maintain good relations with the government. As such, their nature is in conformity with the particularism which traditionally pervades state–business relations in Turkey. Yet they also reflect some new trends in this area, in that the increasing economic significance of the big-business community is accompanied by the special position it has acquired in policy formation and implementation.

It is doubtful that this represents a development whereby the state-created bourgeoisie of Turkey would finally become a 'class for itself'. It seems to define, rather, a novel form of corporatism where labor is conspicuously absent. As such, it might not be too different from the South Korean model, where an unequal partnership between the strong and highly autonomous state and the state-dependent big conglomerates determines the course of economic life to the exclusion of third parties. This particular model has in fact been a major source of inspiration for Turkish policy-makers throughout the last decade.

There are, of course, significant differences between the Turkish and South Korean business environments, reflecting the differences in many societal variables. Nevertheless, with regard to the three areas covered in this essay, the difference between the political and institutional context of business activity in Egypt and in Turkey might even be greater.

Notes

1 The data are mainly derived from an analysis of company reports, autobiographies, and biographies of businessmen, and a series of personal interviews conducted with private-sector representatives. Reports prepared by different business organizations, official documents, and an extensive survey of newspapers and magazines are also used to study the evolution of the business environment in the country.

2 K. Polanyi, *The Great Transformation* (Boston: Beacon Press, 1957).

3 C. Lindblom, *Politics and Markets* (New York: Basic Books, 1977).

4 See, for example, P. B. Evans, D. Rueschemeyer, and T. Skocpol, eds., *Bringing the State Back In* (Cambridge: Cambridge University Press, 1985).

5 See, in particular, P. Katzenstein, "Domestic and International Structures and Strategies of Foreign Economic Policy" in *International Organization*, vol. 31, no. 4, 1977, pp. 587–606, 879–919; see also C. J. Martin, "Business Influence and State Power: The Case of US Corporate Tax Policy," in *Politics and Society*, vol. 17, 1989.

6 See, among others, W. Grant, ed., *Introduction to the Political Economy of Corporatism* (London: MacMillan, 1985); W. Streeck and P.C. Schimitter, "Community, Market, State- and Associations? The Prospective Contribution of Interest Governance to Social Order," in W. Streeck and P. C. Schimitter, *Private Interest Government* (London: Sage Series in New Corporatism, 1985); W. Streeck, "Between Pluralism and

Corporatism: German Business Associations and the State," in *Journal of Public Policy*, vol. 3, August 1983.

7 We adopt here the definition of late industrialization given by A. H. Amsden, "Third World Industrialization: 'Global Fordism' or a New Model?" in *New Left Review*, no. 182, July–August 1990. Amsden defines late industrializing countries as those whose industrializing process takes place without an indigenous technology-producing capacity. Hence, not only countries like South Korea and Turkey, but also Japan can be placed in this category.

8 See, for example, M. Shumizu et al., *Introductory Notes for the Study of Pressure Groups in Egypt* (Cairo: Middle East Studies Series, 1988).

9 See Samia Said Imam, "Three Tributaries of Egyptian Capitalism in the Open Door Policy" in Shumizu et al., p. 197.

10 There are 152 Chambers of Industry and Trade, sixty Chambers of Trade, eleven Chambers of Industry, one Maritime Chamber of Trade, and seventy-six local stock exchanges among the members of the Union.

11 See, especially, Z. Toprak, *Türkiye'de Milli İktisat* (Ankara: Yurt Yayınları, 1982); F. Ahmad, *İttihat ve Terakki: 1908–1914* (Istanbul: Sander Yayınları, 1971).

12 See, for example, F. Ahmad's reference to Necmettin Sadak's views on this subject in F. Ahmad, *The Turkish Experiment with Democracy* (London: C. Hurst and Co., 1977).

13 One study conducted in 1960 documents that a significant percentage of the Greek industrialists whose previous occupation was craftsmanship were either immigrants from Anatolia or sons of artisans from Anatolia: A.P. Alexander, "Greek Industrialists," discussed in E. Soral, *Özel Kesimde Türk Müteşebbisleri* (Ankara: İktisadi ve Ticari İlimler Akademisi, 1974).

14 In one of his articles, Ş. Mardin refers to the traditional suspicion of intermediate classes, which continued in the early years of the republican era in a new form. He writes that, "The top of the capitalistic entrepreneurial iceberg, the few industrialists and businessmen of Turkey, is allowed to figure in the system because they are just easily controllable as the moneylenders were in the traditional system." In A. Ulusan and E. Özbudun, eds., *The Political Economy of Income Distribution in Turkey* (New York: Holmes and Meier, 1980).

15 R. W. Kerwin, "Private Enterprise in Turkish Economic Development," in *Middle East Journal*, vol. 5, no. 1, winter 1951; A.P. Alexander, "Industrial Entrepreneurship in Turkey: Origins and Growth," in *Economic Development and Cultural Change*, vol. 8, July 1960; A. Payaslıoğlu, *Türkiye'de Özel Sanayi Alanında Müteşebbisler ve Teşebbüsler* (Ankara: Siyasal Bilgiler Fakültesi, 1961); G.G. Alpander, "Big Business and Big Business Leaders in Turkey," unpublished Ph.D. thesis, Department of Management, Michigan State University, 1966; D. La Vere Bates, "The Origins and Career Path Development of the Modern Turkish Business Elite," unpublished Ph.D.

thesis, Department of Business Administration, University of Arkansas, 1973; E. Soral, *op. cit.*; for a nonacademic study also containing valuable information on enterprise history for holding companies, see M. Sönmez, *Kırk Haramiler* (Istanbul: Gözlem Yayıncılık, 1987).

16 The decline in the share of the private sector in total number of establishments indicates the increasing size of private firms.

17 See M. S. Tekbaş, "Türkiye'de Holding Uygulaması Üzerine Bir Çalışma," unpublished Ph.D. thesis, Istanbul, 1972.

18 A. Buğra, "Turkish Holding Company as a Social Institution," in *Journal of Economics and Administrative Studies*, vol. 4, no. 1, winter 1990.

19 It is indicated that eight of these 210 holdings were established before the 1960s, which obviously reflects an error, since the holding company as a legal entity was established only after 1960. The dates given in these cases probably pertain to the establishment of these enterprises which have later assumed the holding form. The error does not seem to have been repeated for the enterprises assuming the holding form after 1960.

20 We have compiled this information from the *Journal of the Istanbul Chamber of Industry*, vol. 24, no. 282, 15 August 1989, and by consulting the president of the chamber on the shareholding structures of the enterprises. It was not possible to have information on the shareholding structure of twelve enterprises.

21 See A. Öncü and D. Gökçe, "Macro-Politics of De-Regulation and Micro-Politics of Banks," in M. Heper, ed., *Strong State and Economic Interest Groups: The Post-1980 Experience* (New York: Walter de Gruyter, 1992).

22 Data compiled on the basis of the information given by the *Journal of the Istanbul Chamber of Industry*, vol. 25, no. 294, 22 August 1990. We could not obtain information on the ownership structure of nine private Turkish firms in joint ventures with foreign enterprises.

23 Payaslıoğlu, pp. 64–65.

24 Kerwin, "Private Enterprise in Turkish Economic Development."

25 This was a point made by several of my interviewees.

26 See B. Yaşer, *A Comparative Analysis of Selected Financial Ratios of Private Manufacturing Firms in USA and in Turkey, 1983–1984* (Istanbul: Istanbul Chamber of Industry Publication, 1988).

27 Indirectly indicating the significance of real-estate speculation is the evidence on the ample use of the transfer of real-estate property between the portfolios of companies in the same group to enable the desired capital increases. See *Cumhuriyet*, 24 December 1988.

28 A. Öncü, "Chambers of Industry in Turkey: An Inquiry into State–Industry Relations as a Distributive Domain," in A. Ulusan and E. Özbudun, eds., *op. cit.*; and K. Saybaşılı, "Chambers of Commerce and Industry, Political Parties and Governments: An Analysis of the British and Turkish Cases," in *METU Studies in Development*, 11, spring 1976.

29 See the interview with Feyyaz Berker, the president of DEİK, in *Dış Ticarette Durum*, November–December 1988.

11

Socioeconomic Policies and Interest Groups in Egypt

Amani Kandil

Introduction

The aim of this essay is to study the interaction between socioeconomic policies and interest groups in Egypt from 1952 to 1990. The essay assumes that the change from one policy to another has been closely linked to the changing roles of interest groups and the nature of the issues of concern to these groups.

First, this essay is *not* concerned with interest groups per se, nor with the state's socioeconomic policies as such. What it is concerned with is the impact of interest groups on such policies. The essay also shows that such policies affect the legal and organizational structure of interest groups, and have great impact on the issues they raise and the tactics they use. Moreover, it also presumes that such policies, however different they may be, create new forces which work for their own interests, either from within existing groups or through new groups. In addition to the fact that socioeconomic policies affect interest groups, the latter may also affect such policies by taking supportive, neutral, or opposing positions towards such policies, or even by being an instrument in implementing them. In this context, this essay is concerned with the role played by interest groups, as civil society institutions, in the process of making policies.

Second, in studying interest groups' interaction with socioeconomic policies, we will focus particularly on three groups: professional syndicates, labor unions, and business associations. The first represents the middle class, the second represents workers, and the third represents those higher strata which possess wealth, influence, and power and are interested in open-door policies. By following the development of these different social formations, it is possible to trace their different and changing interests, and their effects on, as well as their reaction to, different and changing policies.

The essay is divided into two main parts: a) a historical framework of the structural development of socioeconomic policies and of interest groups over the last forty years (1952–90); and b) a review of the main issues raised as a result of the interaction between interest groups and socioeconomic policies. These include specific issues of economic policy, education, unemployment, as well as general issues of democracy and civil liberties both in the socialist period and in the later and relatively liberal period of the Open-Door Policy.

The Historical Framework of the Development of Socioeconomic Policies and Interest Groups

It is important to describe first the prerevolutionary phase, specifically the so-called Liberal Age, in order to understand the development of interest groups in the postrevolution period. Before 1952 there were nine professional syndicates,[1] all of which were established in the 1940s, except for the lawyers' syndicate which was established in 1912. Labor unions, on the other hand, had begun to emerge in the early twentieth century, and in 1931 there were estimated to be about thirty-eight of them. They were not legally recognized, however, until 10 September 1942, when Law 85 of 1942 was issued.

This delay in attaining legal recognition may explain successive governments' denials of the right to establish unions. Even after the issuance of the 1942 law, the laborers' right to organize unions was highly restricted both in relation to the categories of laborers permitted to join, and due to the fact that they were controlled by the Ministry of Social Affairs.

Like business associations, industrial unions had a special relationship with landlords and merchants and thereby managed to retain many privileges, especially during and immediately following World War II.

There were also several teachers' associations, whose differences were rooted in the sort of training teachers had received, but which, as a group, could not be included among any of the above three categories. The three most important of these teachers' associations were the League of Compulsory Education (1942), the League of al-Azhar Graduate Teachers (1941), and the Association of University Graduate Teachers (1942).[2]

The prerevolutionary period witnessed the growth and establishment of a limited number of syndicates and professional associations, and some restrictions on the organization of labor unions. Of particular interest is the fact that the laws governing professional associations and labor unions included clauses which totally prohibited involvement in political and religious actions. Furthermore, the government disbanded the councils of a number of syndicates, such as that of lawyers. This has led some scholars to conclude that the Nasserist period did not impose new restrictions on the formation of professional associations, but merely extended the state corporatist pattern that prevailed in the pre-1952 period.[3]

After the 1952 Revolution and during the two-year transitional period that followed it, the number of professional syndicates remained stable (nine) and the same was true for the labor unions and the Egyptian Industries Union, which included both businessmen and industrialists. The revolution was initially welcomed by almost all groups, and it was only the March 1954 crisis that created political opposition to the new regime and its policies. For example, the engineers' syndicate officially sanctioned the maintenance of the Revolution Command Council and the nonresumption of party politics in a statement issued on 29 March 1954, and the transportation unions had recognized and accepted the Revolution Command Council fully enough to go on strike to force it to comply with their demands. Other labor unions, with the exception of a very few (mostly in Alexandria), also took the same stand in favor of, or at least recognizing, the Revolution Command Council.

On the other hand, the syndicates of journalists and lawyers opposed the Revolution Command Council. The general assembly of the lawyers' syndicate called for the resumption of parliamentary life, the repeal of martial law, and the release of all detainees, and the journalists' syndicate issued a statement advocating the holding of new elections and the end of martial law.

The supportive positions were, in fact, a result of the advantages gained by laborers during the first few months after the revolution. By the same logic, the position taken by the engineers' syndicate's leaders was due to the fact that they belonged to the same new elite to which the revolution's officers belonged. On the other hand, opposition stances conformed to the liberal trends followed by the leaders of both the lawyers' and journalists' syndicates. They also matched the previous role played by the lawyers' syndicate in protecting civil liberties.

It was in relation to these fundamental positions that policies dealing with interest groups were framed. During the transitional period, the government of the revolution agreed, in principle, to the establishment of the General Labor Union, and granted the right to form unions to farm laborers and other categories of labor. Restrictions on professional syndicates' involvement in political and religious affairs were maintained,[4] and the councils of the journalists' and lawyers' syndicates were dissolved on 15 April 1954 and 23 December 1954 respectively.

What most deserves attention is the fact that the Revolution Command Council was keen to placate and please both labor unions and professional syndicates. The Council called for opening communication channels with such bodies, through the presence of a delegate from each at the Liberation Organization, and through the appointment of representatives from them to attend the technical committees of the Organization. Furthermore, the RCC allowed representatives of syndicates to participate in the ad hoc committee formed to frame new legislation regulating the work of professional syndicates.[5]

The significance of the transitional period (1952–54) is that it gave interest groups the opportunity to demonstrate their aims, principles, and working methods; it showed such groups the strength of the relations between their interests and the incumbent regime, and, conversely, showed the ruling elite the value of such groups. Unions and the syndicates that supported the Command Council were the forces that shifted the balance of popularity in favor of Nasser and against his opponents, consequently paving the way to the formulation of the regime's new policies towards such groups. Thus, the relationship between interest groups and the state developed in such a way that guaranteed the loyalty of such groups to the regime, or at least their neutrality. Thereafter, the importance of the labor unions was recognized and their opinions taken into consideration.

Moving to the next period which, retrospectively, can be said to have begun in the mid-1950s and ended at the end of Nasser's period in power (1970), a question should be raised concerning the repercussions of the socioeconomic policies on interest groups, and the political role played by the latter with regard to such policies.

First, it should be noted that the number of syndicates increased overall, as five more were established,[6] and only one, the *sharia* lawyers' syndicate, was disbanded, upon the cancellation of the sharia courts. Secondly, it may be observed that the regime tended to broaden the base of membership by giving new categories the right to join such syndicates. The best example of this was the extension of the lawyers' syndicate membership to include lawyers of the public sector and general institutions, a step which led to the involvement of thousands of members who served later as the pro-regime tool inside that syndicate. Moreover, military engineers were accepted in the engineers' syndicate, and they too later represented the same pro-regime bloc. Labor unions also witnessed an extension in membership conditions to include new categories of labor employed by the government. On the other hand there was a tendency towards the centralization and unification of the various unions by reducing their numbers and establishing the General Labor Union, while preserving the optional right to join unions (in accordance with Law 91 of 1959).[7] Thirdly, professional syndicates' laws on the election of chairs were amended so that re-election several times over was permitted, and the period of each term of office was lengthened (lawyers' and journalists' syndicates).

These, then, were the general features which characterized the development of unions and syndicates during Nasser's period in power, and within which the study of the interaction between the state and interest groups during that period must be placed. Not surprisingly, the socialist policies had produced important gains for laborers, so labor unions supported state policies. Additionally, most of the professional syndicates were supportive, or at least neutral, the only exception being the lawyers' syndicate, which represented the political opposition to the incumbent regime, especially on the issues of civil liberties and democracy. We will discuss this later in this essay.

During the socialist stage, political leadership was fully aware of the effective role played by interest groups. For example, this awareness was indicated in the leadership's eagerness to represent syndicates and unions in the National Conference of Popular Forces in 1962. Moreover, the broadening of the membership to include new categories (mainly those who worked in governmental bodies) was a good indication of the regime's eagerness to encourage and secure the support of such groups. Furthermore, amendments to union and syndicate laws repealed the articles which prohibited involvement in politics and thereby showed the government's willingness to mobilize such unions to serve the 'socialist transformation', a term which was used in almost all these laws. More importantly, it was stipulated that top posts in such groups be confined to members of the political organization (the National Union in the 1950s and the Arab National Socialist Union in the 1960s).[8]

In this period of 'socialist transformation', President Nasser initiated and encouraged discussion on themes like, 'Whose interests are represented by syndicates?' and 'Unions to protect workers or owners?' This development reflects the impact of the socioeconomic[9] policies on the political leadership's perception of the interests of such groups and the tendency to be in favor of the interests of laborers.

In this context it is worth mentioning that there were several unsuccessful attempts made by the state to found a general association of professional syndicates. The only exception was the Professionals' Association Council, which lasted from 1964 to 1965. Strangely enough, the idea of establishing a general association for professional syndicates was revived in 1989–90, in a completely different context and for different purposes; in spite of the relatively free atmosphere and the existence of political plurality and an open-door policy, the resurrection of such an idea was in fact due to the state's attempt to suppress those professional syndicates which opposed the regime—especially on the subject of democracy.

The third distinct period which witnessed a measurable change in state policies was 1970–81. This period, especially since the mid-1970s, was characterized by the shift to an open-door policy and the gradual economic liberation of market forces, and by the resumption of a restricted multiparty political system. In this atmosphere, five new professional syndicates were founded, laws on syndicates were amended, and restrictions on their freedom were variously lessened.

On one hand, the requirement of membership in the socialist union as a condition for nomination to syndicates' top offices was lifted. On the other hand, all syndicates were represented in the Future of Political Endeavor Committee in 1976. In a conciliation between the political leadership and the syndicates and unions, chairmen of such syndicates and unions were appointed advisers to the president of the republic. New laws were issued, allowing unions to participate more fully in projects of social and economic development; for example, the labor unions' Law 35 of 1976 and the law concerning the engineers' syndicate (Law 66 of 1974). Finally, the state agreed to the demands of some groups, notably the engineers' syndicate, a consideration which partially explains the political support of the syndicate for the regime during the second half of the 1970s. In this period, the syndicate's leaders were considered a part of the political ruling elite, in spite of the fact that during the first half of the 1970s the same syndicate had opposed the regime, especially concerning the issues of democracy and civil liberties.

While it might have been expected that labor unions would oppose the Open-Door Policy, an occurrence which would certainly have dissipated the socialist advantages, the fact is to the contrary: the General Labor Union continued to support the new policies, while only a few labor unions opposed specific economic policies that were concerned with the public sector.

Nonetheless, the most important result of the socioeconomic policies in this period was the emergence of new sorts of interest groups.[10] The relative freedom and the Open-Door Policy encouraged the founding of new groups, such as the Egyptian Businessmen's Association (1977), The American–Egyptian Businessmen's Council (1975), and the American Chamber of Commerce (1981). These groups represented new socioeconomic forces interested in the new economic policies, and some of them, notably the American–Egyptian Council and the American Chamber of Commerce, had relations with American investors and began defending their interests.

The period 1981–90 was an extension of the previous one, though it has some specific features of its own. On the political level, it was characterized by a more democratic atmosphere, which allowed a higher degree of freedom of expression and representation of interests, while on the economic level it witnessed a closer linking to the world economic system, due to the aggravating economic crisis and the debt burden, all of which led to the recent wave of privatization.

The socioeconomic policies introduced in this period had a significant impact on interest groups if one considers the fact that they became highly vocal in the expression of their views and opinions on those policies—whether supportive or opposing. Also, issues of concern to those groups multiplied and varied widely to include economic, political, and social issues (education and social justice). This period also witnessed the businessmen's associations taking a more active role, pressing the government to make decisions to meet their demands or to cancel already-made economic decisions that were against their interests. The activities of the American Chamber of Commerce were, and still are, clearly based on their view of their role as mediator between American businesses and the Egyptian government. Moreover, USAID relations with businessmen's associations intensified.

The 1981–90 period was characterized by the politicization of the unions' and syndicates' activities, due to the fact that political parties (the National Democratic Party and the Wafd Party) and other political forces (Islamic groups and the left) entered the elections of some syndicates and unions. It was also affected by the aggravation of the democratic crisis.

In conclusion, the evolution of the Egyptian political system and the adopted socioeconomic policies have positively and/or negatively affected both groups which supported the regime and others which opposed it. Leading the latter was the lawyers' syndicate, especially on issues of democracy, whether in the state-socialism period or the open-door era, followed closely by the syndicates of engineers in the first half of the 1970s and the second half of the 1980s, and the physicians' syndicate in the mid-1980s. Some labor unions also opposed the state policies of privatization.

All of this indicates that the change in the positions held by interest groups towards state policies is in some measure due to the transfer of leadership in such groups and sometimes due to the range of freedom permitted such groups by the state.

Interest Groups' Positions on Socioeconomic Policies: Some Major Issues

The positions of interest groups on different state policies have focused on three main issues: the first is related to economic policies (in both public and private sectors), the second is related to social justice (especially education policies), and the third is the issue of democracy and civil liberties.

The Issue of Public and/or Private Control

The issue of public and/or private control has been ranked high among the top priorities concerning the development of socioeconomic policies throughout the last four decades. With the 1952 Revolution, laborers attained some advantages which were further intensified by the adoption of nationalization. However, when the state shifted to open-door policies, such advantages were gradually reduced. Therefore, it is important to study the relationship between interest groups and the state, in the light of the evolution of public and private sector policies.

Labor Unions. The interests of labor unions matched state policies, a coincidence which made them main supporters of the socialism-oriented regime. However, since the mid-1970s and the beginning of the Open-Door Policy and the raising of the notion of 'developing the public sector', interests have partially diverged.

It is important to make clear that labor unions do not represent all laborers (more than 13 million), only 25 percent of them. Also, individual labor unions, and the unions in different sectors of the economy, have different interests and there is little unity of policy or activity.[11] For example, laborers in joint ventures have quite different interests and aims from laborers in the national public sector. Emigration of labor to Arab countries helped change the makeup of labor unions. Restrictive laws regulating labor unions' political activities have never been rescinded, not even during the relatively democratic mood of the 1980s. So labor unions and their leaders have always been tied to the state. From the early 1960s and up to 1987, it was the minister of labor who occupied the office of chair of the General Labor Union. In the last three years, the minister of labor has become one of the top figures of the ruling elite and the deputy speaker of the *Shura* council (consultative council).

In October 1976, the chair of the General Labor Union drafted the so-called 'Moral code of ethics,' in which he expressed his support for the Open-Door Policy, "on condition that it does not conflict with socialism."[12] On another occasion he demanded that it should be a "productive open-door policy that might provide new job opportunities" to laborers.[13] On a previous occasion in 1975, when a law extending the right of private capital to invest in joint ventures was issued (Law 11 of 1975), the General Labor Union sent a memo to the political leadership stating that "public sector companies are not for sale and are not open for private sector participation."[14] These statements clearly demonstrate that union leaders wished to reassure the government of their support of the economic policies, while simultaneously opposing any encroachment into the public sector, a trend which prevailed throughout the 1970s and 1980s.

In 1980, when the Ministry of Industry initiated a project for developing the public sector, labor unions countered with demands that were to freeze the project; they stipulated that laborers should participate on boards of directors and in profits, that state control should continue, and that company profits should not be repatriated.

In the early 1980s, the state adopted, for the first time, the policy of selling shares of the public sector. There was fierce opposition to this from some unions, such as the Public Union for Chemicals, though it was greeted with complete silence by other unions, and the General Labor Union tried to make a compromise. However, there were some distinct and individual opposing positions taken by some labor unions in the 1980s, particularly opposing the alternatives offered by the economic policy to solve the public sector's problems. One of the most obvious was the stance taken by the General Union of Engineering Industries against the General Motors project. The opposition staged by this union and its ability to mobilize other unions in support of its opposition forced the government to shelve the project.

State policies in the textile sector were considered to be the root cause of the crisis in public-sector production companies, and serious opposition entailing a program of strikes and sit-ins was carried out by the Spinning and Weaving Union in 1986. It was also in 1986 that railway workers asked for a dialogue with the government to discuss the question of developing that sector. When the government refused, they went on strike. In this case, however, neither the Railway Union nor the General Labor Union supported the workers. It was only the Railway Laborers' Association that effectively held workers together.[15]

By the end of the 1980s, when the government openly raised the issue of privatization, the official stance of the General Labor Union was represented in the signing of the Joint Manifesto of Laborers and Businessmen.[16] This manifesto was considered to be a formal conciliation which included an acceptance of the importance and value of the public sector, the need for its development and liberation from bureaucracy, and the separation of its administration from ownership. At the same time, it included an acceptance of the value and importance of the private sector and the inevitability of its liberation from bureaucracy.[17] It did not include, however, a single mention of the subject of privatization. In other words, the Joint Manifesto represented a conciliation between laborers and businessmen and an agreement on the outline of the economic reform, but did not consider the details of the means of this reform, thus ignoring the controversial issues. Nevertheless, individual unions declared their rejection of privatization, and considered the Manifesto a betrayal of the interests of laborers.

From the preceding overview, it is obvious that the official stance of the General Labor Union was mostly in favor of state policies and sometimes neutral, while certain individual unions expressed opposing views. The violent forms of rejection (such as strikes and demonstrations) were carried out within some labor sectors and not by the official organizations representing general labor. This mix, undoubtedly, demonstrates the hegemony of the state over the General Labor Union and the failure of labor solidarity because of an absence of homogeneity of interest.

Businessmen's Associations. The businessmen's associations have shown a higher degree of effectiveness and homogeneity on the issue of public and private sector. Several demands have been made calling for the liquidation of the losing public-sector companies, and suggesting tax and customs facilities for the private sector, with a view to liberating it from state bureaucracy. However, the strongest action taken by the businessmen's groups in the last two years has been that concerned with the implementation of privatization. Three businessmen's groups (the Egyptian Businessmen's Association, the American Chamber of Commerce, and the Economic Committee of Alexandria Businessmen)—besides the investors' societies in the new cities—have jointly devised an outline for their participation in the privatization program. It advances various ways of achieving goals and representing interests, the most immediate of which include communicating with top officials, organizing meetings and joint committees, convening conferences and symposiums, publicizing views through the mass media, and arranging for continuous meetings with the top political leadership.

Such groups perceived that the initial conciliation with the chambers of commerce and industry (after a ten-year struggle)[18] was a turning point on the way to privatization. However, what deserves attention in this context is that businessmen's groups sought to intensify relations with US businesses and the United States Agency for International Development (USAID) in Cairo. Special departments within such groups were entitled to contact USAID officials and submit proposals and requests for direct aid for supporting private-sector projects. The American Chamber of Commerce in Cairo has played a major role in establishing cooperation between the two parties and arranging meetings between Egyptian and American businessmen.[19]

A study of the role of businessmen's groups in foreign policy,[20] has shown that the Egyptian Foreign Ministry has depended greatly on such groups to persuade the United States to increase its aid to Egypt. Moreover, it has shown the United States' dependence on such groups to encourage further privatization and move towards the liquidation of the public sector.

Professional Syndicates. The professional syndicates' attitudes to privatization, which remained staunchly pro-socialist during the 1960s, underwent some cautious alterations in the 1970s, notably the engineers' syndicate's initially reserved acceptance of the Open-Door Policy.

In the first half of the 1970s, the engineers' syndicate firmly opposed the Oil Pipeline Project (SUMED) and the Aluminum Project of Nag Hammady. The head of the syndicate drafted a new law giving the syndicate the right to participate in making economic policy and studying development plans. Later, however, the syndicate was completely converted to full support of the new socioeconomic policies. By the 1980s, the syndicate was actually participating in supporting the private sector at the expense of the public sector.

The syndicates of lawyers and physicians took declared positions in the 1980s against privatization. The physicians' syndicate's concern with national issues is a new phenomenon which began only in the mid-1980s. In its general conference in June 1990, the syndicate declared its opposition to reform and development. Moreover, the conference voiced several reservations on the subject of transferring certain public sector units to foreign investors. Specific conditions and guarantees were demanded to protect national labor rights.

In conclusion, the attention given by some interest groups to the issue of private and public sectors has coincided with the Open-Door Policy. The new state economic policy has been weakly opposed by labor unions. Violent forms of rejection have been practiced by a limited number of unions, and more often by unofficial groups of laborers and not by the unions representing them. In the meantime, businessmen's groups have been highly successful in supporting open-door policies and pushing towards privatization.

Issues of Social Justice and Equity of Opportunities: The Case of Education

Educational policy is considered one of the most important areas of concern to interest groups. Education is one of the main targets of general development and has a specific importance in Egypt, because it was a major instrument upon which the 1952 Revolution depended to attract support and achieve political mobilization. Free school and university education has been one of the most important advantages attained by the masses since 1952, both for themselves and as a means of social mobility. Egyptian political discourse throughout the 1950s and 1960s addressed the topic of free education as being the essence of social justice.

By the 1970s, however, educational policy had become a political and controversial issue for several reasons. First, the demand for education increased to such an extent that it surpassed the government's capability to provide it. For example, free education for students in the preuniversity stages soared from five million students in 1975–76 to more than nine million students in 1985–86. Over the same period the ratio of educational spending to the national income decreased from 4.9 percent in the 1970s to 3.5 percent in the 1980s. Economic difficulties are now so serious that it is not possible to accept all applicants to primary education; 90 percent, at best, is the highest percentage of admission.[21] Second, school buildings have deteriorated so far in quality, as well as having reached a point now where there are not nearly enough of them, that only 59 percent of the available buildings are usable. Third, the quality of the educational process, in all stages, has deteriorated considerably. The development of educational processes needs substantial resources—which Egypt simply does not have. Fourth, USAID participation in financing education continued to grow throughout the 1980s, ultimately reaching about $300 million, the largest part of which was used to build new schools.[22] Fifth, the crisis of graduate unemployment worsened steadily. Without a close relationship between education and development plans, unemployment levels among university graduates reached 38 percent in 1985 estimates; in addition, there is an average five-year wait for a job after graduation. Technical education graduates have experienced unemployment levels that reached about 43 percent of total graduates in 1985.[23]

Therefore, education is no longer the means of social mobility that it was in the early 1970s. Nor is it a means of political mobilization and attraction of mass support. Instead, it is an insolvable national crisis. In this context, socioeconomic policies offer various alternatives, the most serious of which is the suggestion that free education and admission to universities be restricted, and that a great number of students be transferred from universities to technical education. There have also been several calls for private education and private universities.

As the issue became a national one in the 1980s, interest groups displayed considerable and varied concerns and reactions. Businessmen's associations called for the elimination of free education and the restriction of admission to universities. They also made offers to the state to build private universities. They have recommended that technical education be extended and that the state's guarantee to employ new graduates be abolished.[24] More significantly, the businessmen's associations have presented such demands within the general economic reforms they call for. In their analysis educational policies were considered to have caused many of the economic policy problems.

It is worth noting that the Joint Manifesto of Laborers and Businessmen discussed above was silent on the issue of free education, as laborers naturally rejected any suggestion of curtailing the free-education-for-all policy. The communiqué therefore called only for general educational reforms and the creation of better relations between education and job opportunities.[25]

Workers' organizations, on the other hand, insisted on the right to free education. The General Labor Union perceived any restriction of this right to be to the detriment of labor interests. Their perception, and description, of the problem was stated in terms of *how to employ people positively and effectively*, rather than as "an unemployment problem."[26]

To face the deteriorating standard of graduates' qualifications caused by oversubscription to faculties, syndicates of physicians, engineers, and lawyers called for restricting admission to universities. The physicians' syndicate has managed to persuade the Ministry of Health and the Supreme Council for Universities to decrease the number of medical students admitted annually and to continue to reduce the admission rate gradually, by 10 percent annually.[27]

Since 1985 the syndicate of engineers has declared its opposition to the establishment of engineering departments in regional universities. It has asked, instead, for an improvement in the educational process. This position has initiated a fierce struggle between the syndicate and the Ministry of Education. The syndicate convened a conference to debate the subject of the unemployment of engineering graduates, estimated at twenty thousand people. First on the list of alternatives proposed to tackle the problem was the recommendation that the syndicate, in collaboration with the Supreme Council for Universities, should determine the number of students to be admitted annually. The conference called first for an improvement in the standards of engineering teaching, by establishing permanent in-service training programs for engineers, with an ultimate view to putting an end to the role of foreign engineers in Egyptian projects, and second for a ratification of the syndicate's rule which states that "non-engineers may not be allowed to work in engineering fields."[28]

Ironically, the half-million-strong teachers' syndicate played no positive role in influencing educational policies, at a time when other professional syndicates escalated their pressure in this field. It merely supported the policies declared by the Ministry of Education. This was an unexpected reaction, which gives rise to questions about why some interest groups are impelled to play a political role, while others remain neutral.

The 1980s, imbued as they were with the crisis of developing and financing education, and with the retreat from socialist advantages, caused certain interest groups to become politically concerned with taking part in making policies by making suggestions and proposing alternative agenda.

Democracy and Issues of Civil Liberty

Initially, in the 1950s and 1960s, the lawyers' syndicate constituted virtually the only opposition group. It held well-established opinions on the issues of civil liberties, notably in its demand in 1908 for the foundation of a Supreme Constitutional Court, its call for a free press, and for guarantees of civil liberties. The lawyers' syndicate also reacted positively to students' demonstrations in 1968, and called for legislation to "protect socialism from its executors."[29]

In the early 1970s, engineers' and journalists' syndicates joined the lawyers in calling for a civil liberties program and in supporting student movements (in 1972). However, the support soon faded away when the syndicates' leaders allied with the ruling elite. In 1977, the engineers' syndicate denounced the mass riots of January 18th, leaving the lawyers' syndicate as the only professional syndicate defending civil liberties throughout the 1970s. Other professional syndicates (such as the teachers' and agriculturalists' syndicates) had never opposed the regime; rather, they were supportive, even at the expense of democracy and civil liberties.

What was even more surprising, perhaps, was the official position of the labor unions in favor of the regime. They declared no position when the student demonstrations took place in the early 1970s, nor did they support the masses in the 1977 riots. In fact, they grossly underestimated the gravity of the situation and actually helped the government in containing the riots.[30]

In the 1980s, however, syndicates actively supported civil liberties programs and the move towards democracy. The physicians' syndicate actively continued to condemn torture and violations of human rights, and called for the abolition of martial law and all liberty-restricting laws. By the end of the 1980s, the engineers' syndicate mobilized its members against the nondemocratic practices of the security forces, at a time when the journalists' syndicate positively advocated freedom of expression and opinion and called for the release of political detainees (1989).

In spite of the fact that it experienced disagreement within its own membership during the second half of the 1980s, the lawyers' syndicate kept defending democracy and civil liberties. It played a vital role in the 1987

Table 1 The Turnout of the Elections of the Physicians' Syndicate

Year	Turnout	Votes gained by Islamists
1986	11,800	40%
1988	19,100	60%
1990	21,500	65%

Source: Amani Kandil, "Islamic Movement in Some Civil Society Institutions: The Case of Professional Syndicates," in *Modernisation et nouvelles formes de mobilisation sociale: Egypte, Turquie,* (Edege), Cairo, 1990.

People's Assembly elections, figured prominently in support of the railway laborers in 1988, and was involved in frequent skirmishes with security forces over the question of human-rights violations. It declared its support of the artists' and journalists' syndicates' arguments in favor of democracy, and has continuously called for the abolition of martial law.

Conclusions

From the previous discussion, it is clear that there are certain circumstances that determine the political role of interest groups. Some aspects have been outlined above, and could be considered obvious anyway; the nature of the political regime matters, in that it is true that an atmosphere of relative freedom for groups to operate in leads to higher degrees of participation, and further representations of interests. Still, there are anomalies. For instance:

a) The lawyers' syndicate played an opposition role during Gamal Abd al-Nasser's period in power.

b) Throughout the last four decades, the syndicates of agriculturalists and teachers played no political role.

c) The physicians' syndicate began to take on a considerable political role only in the mid-1980s.

d) The engineers' syndicate opposed the state's position only in the early 1970s and the late 1980s.

e) The artists' syndicate played its political role through the medium of strikes and sit-ins as an expression of its opposition to nondemocratic practices.

f) Labor unions have continued to declare pro-regime allegiances even in the atmosphere of political pluralism.

g) Businessmen's groups have never held opposing views on the issues of civil liberties and democracy.

There are, however, factors, which, in certain combinations, may go some way towards explaining these seemingly inconsistent and incongruous aspects. Some of these factors are related to the political regime and the others are related to the interest groups.

The Political Regime . Certainly, the nature and attitudes of the political regime in power initially determine the range of activities permitted to groups. In general, the atmosphere of political pluralism and Open-Door Policy has been accompanied by a higher level of action by interest groups. It has allowed new socioeconomic forces to be represented institutionally as never before. While this is true concerning the laws regulating the relationship between civil society institutions, i.e. professional syndicates, and the state, the equivalent laws concerning labor unions have remained continuously restrictive and have allowed the state the right to maintain full hegemony over them.

Moreover, the regime, which shifted in the mid-1970s to political plurality, continued nonetheless to deprive certain political bodies of legitimate representation. In particular, such forces as the Islamic trend (mainly the brotherhood group *Ikhwan),* Nasserists, and Marxists failed to attain legitimacy or to found independent parties. Such forces realized that the only way they would be able to take any form of political action or mobilize support was through professional syndicates. However, in spite of the fact that the door was open to all such forces, only Islamists—because of their historical position—have managed to enter and even dominate the councils of the most important syndicates, mainly physicians, engineers, and commerce syndicates, and lately, the pharmacists' syndicate, of which Christians constitute 60 percent of the members.

The study of the development of political participation in the physicians' syndicate, for example, demonstrates the success of the Islamic trend in mobilizing ardent supporters on the one hand, and inciting the left and the state on the other.[31]

The politicization of syndicate action has not resulted only from the participation of the Islamic trend, but also from the competition and struggle among political parties. For example, the National Democratic Party has always been keen to preserve its chairs of syndicates at the expense of the Wafd Party, which it views as having been responsible for the lawyers' syndicate's inner conflicts. Undoubtedly, the parties' lack of a consensus of opinion has led to some of the parties' functions being transferred to interest groups.

Interest Groups. The long history of the lawyers' syndicate, which began in 1912, has naturally given it the opportunity to develop a political role, which equally naturally coincides with its defense of civil liberties and democracy. In other words, the nature of the profession has been a critical factor in determining the action of a group. Similarly, in a study of the teachers' syndicate, it has been demonstrated that the history of the syndicate, the different methods of training teachers, their economic and social status,

Table 2 Islamic Trend in Syndicates' Councils

Syndicate	Number of seats	Date of elections
Engineers	41 (out of 43)	1989
Pharmacists	10 (out of 12)	1990
Physicians	11 (out of 12)	1990

Source: Amani Kandil, "Islamic Movement in Some Civil Society Institutions: The Case of Professional Syndicates," in *Modernisation et nouvelles formes de mobilisation sociale: Egypte, Turquie,* (Edege), Cairo, 1990.

and the nature of the profession itself have contributed to the fact that this syndicate does *not* play a political role as an opposition group. Moreover, the goals of a group significantly influence the independence of its decisions; the teachers' syndicate is still, and has been since its foundation, concerned primarily with achieving some improvement in the profession's conditions and pay, issues that indisputably depend on the will of the incumbent authorities. Although it is the biggest syndicate group in Egypt (750,000 members) it is very weak and dominated by government types with low socioeconomic status. Hence, teachers support the regime.

Another important factor is the influence of syndicates' leaderships on decision-making. In some periods, syndicates of engineers and journalists played crucial roles, and in others, were quite self-effacing. Furthermore, the leadership of certain syndicates (such as those of teachers or agriculturalists) is sometimes assumed by a member of the ruling elite or even by the relevant minister himself (as in the case of the teachers' syndicate, when the minister of education was the head of the syndicate), thus restricting the body's role and negatively affecting political action.

All these considerations constitute a complicated fabric that constitutes and explains the action and role of a group. It is, therefore, unwise to see only one factor as explaining the interaction between interest groups and socioeconomic policies in Egypt.

Notes

1 The nine syndicates are: lawyers (*shari'a* and civil), journalists, engineers, physicians, dentists, pharmacists, veterinarians, and agriculturalists.

2 Amani Kandil, "Interest Groups and Political Power in Egypt," paper submitted to the Annual Political Science Conference, Center for Political Studies, Cairo University, 1987.

3 Ahmad Fares Abdel Moneim, "Interest Groups," in Aly Din Helal, ed., *Egyptian Political System* (Cairo: Cairo University Press, 1986), p. 304.

4 Article no. 109 of Law 98 of 1944 on the legal profession, Law 10 of 1941 on journalists' syndicate and Law 98 of 1946 on the engineers' syndicate, prohibiting involvement in political and religous affairs.

5 Fares Abdel Moneim, p. 271.

6 The syndicates are: actors, show business (movie industry), musicians, scientists, and accountants.

7 Egyptian labor amounts to 13 million, but union members do not exceed three million (about 25 percent), distributed among twenty-one unions.

8 Presidential decree no. 8 of 1958. It was noticed that a professional syndicate (the agriculturalists' syndicate) had gone thus far when in 1966 it stipulated that the membership of the Socialist Union was obligatory in order to attend the Syndicates' National Assembly. For more details see Law 31 of 1966 on the agriculturalists' syndicate.

9 Fares Abdel Moneim, p. 283.

10 Amani Kandil, "Interest Groups and the Development of the Egyptian Political System," paper presented to the Symposium on Political System, Faculty of Economics and Commercial Syndicate, 1986.

11 Amani Kandil, "Labour and Business Interest Representation in Egypt," paper delivered at the Conference on Dynamics of State and Society in the Middle East, Cairo, 1989, pp. 9–10.

12 *Al-Ahram* daily newspaper, 18 October 1976.

13 *Al-Ahram* daily newspaper, 21 October 1980.

14 *Al-Ahram al-Iqtisadi*, no. 481, 1 September 1975.

15 A league is a voluntary society of workers within the same job and is registered at the Ministry of Social Affairs. See "The Arab Strategic Report," (Cairo: al-Ahram, 1987), p. 386.

16 Joint Manifesto, 29 May 1989.

17 Ibid., pp. 5–6.

18 Chambers of Commerce and Industry carried on a fierce struggle with businessmen's groups throughout the 1980s. The chambers accused the said groups of being illegal as they did not represent the wider base of businessmen.

19 See papers and monthly reports of the Egyptian Businessmen's Association. See also *Business Monthly*, the magazine of the American Chamber of Commerce, especially 1989 and 1990 editions.

20 Amani Kandil, "Interest Groups and Foreign Policy," paper delivered at the Second Political Science Conference, Cairo, 1988.

21 Amani Kandil, "Educational Policy in Egypt and the Nile Valley," Arab Thought Forum, 1989, pp. 85–86.

22 *Status Report*, United States Economic Assistance to Egypt, Cairo, 1988

23 Amani Kandil, "Education and the Challenge of the 1990s," paper delivered at the Third Political Science Annual Conference, Faculty of Economics and Political Science, Cairo, 1989.

24 The Annual Meeting of Businessman Association, Alexandria, 1987.

25 Joint Manifesto, p. 3.

26 Speech by the Head of the General Association of Labor Unions, reproduced in *al-Ahram*, 26 March 1989.

27 Meeting of the General Assembly of the Physicians' Syndicate, Cairo, 1987

28 "The Arab Strategic Report," p. 353.

29 Article no. 7 of Law 66 of 1974.

30 Fares Abdel Moneim, pp. 274–75.

31 *Al-'Ummal*, Labor magazine, 24 January 1977, 31 January 1977.

12

Street Politics

Ayşe Öncü

> A group of police mutinied in protest against the death of their colleagues. They marched to the palace. At the same time groups of people in Cairo began to go on the rampage. This was the beginning of Black Saturday, 26 January 1952. At the end of the day over 750 establishments had been burned, at least thirty people were dead including eleven British and other foreigners, and hundreds injured. ... The main thrust of the attacks was on British property—Shepherds Hotel, BOAC, Barclays Bank, Cook's, British car showrooms—but the mob went beyond these. Other symbols of the Western presence and decadence, were also attacked—cafes, cinemas, bars, luxury shops. Organized or not, encouraged or not, Black Saturday was an outburst of frustrated fury, vented on symbols of that frustration. ... Black Saturday was the death spasm of the monarchical regime.

> The government announced in 1977 the ending of several subsidies—including those on flour, rice, and cooking oil—together with the cancellation of bonuses and pay increases. . . . The result was immediate and shocking. On 18 and 19 January there was heavy rioting, ... variously described as the biggest upheaval since the rising against the British in 1919. . . . There was apparently little animosity towards foreigners: targets were institutions such as ASU offices and police stations and signs of wealth and corruption such as large cars and nightclubs. It was the uprising of the ruled against the rulers. . . . In Cairo alone, seventy-seven people were killed. The price rises were immediately rescinded, the bonuses and pay increases retained. The rioters had won.[1]

These passages frame the problem I wish to identify and address in this essay—a difference in 'repertoires' of political protest and activism at the grassroots level among workers in Egypt and Turkey. From the burning of Cairo in 1919 to the food riots of 1977, we witness the crises of Egyptian politics spilling over into the streets of Cairo and Alexandria. The propensity of various segments of Egyptian workers to unite in spontaneous mass action, taking their grievances into the streets to fashion the course of political events, has few parallels in Turkish history. How can we explain the difference?

The Name of the Phenomenon: Street Politics

'Street politics' refers to a phenomenon that is difficult to pinpoint and capture in the current language and discourse of various social disciplines. It brings together a diversity of social groupings—students, elements of the 'bazaar', segments of unionized labor, employees from the lower rungs of municipal and state bureaucracy, as well as vast numbers of workers engaged in the myriad of floating occupational pursuits associated with the Third World city ('marginals', 'proto- or sub-proletariat', or 'informal workers', etc.). It manifests itself as a bonding of emotions, fury, euphoria, or jubilation, translating itself, literally, into waves of motion and movement on the streets. It signals and articulates a prevailing mood of impatience with established authority and defiance of conventional practice, triggering a chain of official political action and reaction. It is thus a political phenomenon that lacks a name in the vocabulary of political science, in the absence of institutional underpinnings, ideological coherence, hierarchy, or leadership.

In its ephemeral and episodic manifestations, it reminds us of the sociologists' fascination with mobs, riots, crowds, panics, crazes, wildcat strikes—grouped together with fads and fashions under the category of 'collective phenomena' in the literature. Ever since Le Bon and Gabriel Tarde, 'collectivities' have captured the imagination of sociologists because they fall outside the institutional realm. In numerous contemporary case studies, the words 'crowd', 'mob', and 'craze' remain imbued with connotations of irrationality, simultaneously intriguing and fearsome, symbolizing a defiance not only of authority and officialdom but of common sense, sanity, and logic. They continue to remain encapsulated in the historical accounts of Victorian cities or Paris barricades, aberrations of a distant past in Western society, only to reappear, in all its diabolical destructiveness, in the teeming cities of the contemporary Third World.

In suggesting the name 'street politics', I wish to emphasize the political nature of the phenomenon, extending its connotations beyond episodic incidents to encompass street action in all the variety of its manifestations, often clustered in time, and cumulative in its reverberations, to propose that it is a paradigmatic form of articulating discontent. In defining the 'street' as an arena of politics, I wish to draw attention to its increasing importance as a mode of political action against established authority in contemporary politics.

Street Politics as a Focus of Comparison

For a Turkish student of contemporary Egyptian history, the way momentous political events are bound up with street action in all the variety of its manifestations is striking. This is not only because it lends Egyptian history a drama against which the milestones of Turkish politics remain insipid. The kind of street politics in Egypt that the Turkish comparison beckons us to explain is of broader significance.

As a specific mode of articulating discontent, street politics transcend diverse lines of cleavage, structural and ideological, to mobilize and unite a variety of social groupings in joint action against established authority. What lends analytical interest to the Egypt–Turkey contrast in this context is that each social formation is one of a family sharing common traits associated with peripheral capitalism. The fault lines dividing and fragmenting the urban workforce are more or less the same in the two countries.

Table 1 Structure of the Labor Force: Egypt–Turkey

	Egypt (1984)		**Turkey** (1985)	
	No. of persons (millions)	Share of total (%)	No. of persons (millions)	Share of total (%)
Economic sector				
Agriculture	4.8	36	9.4	51
Private non-agricultural	3.2	23	4.3	22
Public enterprises	1.3	10	0.7	4
Government	2.5	19	1.6	10
Migrant workers	0.7	5	-	-
Unemployment	0.8	6	2.3	13
Total labor force	13.2	99	18.3	100

Note: As a percentage of the total labor force, agricultural employment appears to be much more significant in Turkey (51 percent) than it does in Egypt. But absolute numbers tell a different story. In both countries, the non-agricultural labor force is about 8–9 million. The total population of each country is about 50 million. But the total labor force in Turkey is about 18 million as opposed to 13 million in Egypt. The inevitable conclusion is that the Turkish census tends to count women as part of the agricultural labor force, while the Egyptian census does not.

Sources:
Egypt: Ragui Assaad, "The Unemployment Crisis in Egypt: Trends and Issues," unpublished paper, Cairo, 1989, p. 14.
Turkey: State Planning Organization; TUSIAD, *1980 Sonrası Ekonomide Kamu-Özel Sektör Dengesi,* 1988.

The highly segmented nature of labor markets in both Egypt and Turkey is self-evident from table 1. We observe that in both countries, a large proportion of the labor force remains in agriculture.[2] In both, the category of the private nonagricultural sector subsumes vast numbers of small, family-owned enterprises together with a floating population of self-employed, next to (and in stark contrast with) capital-intensive, large-scale enterprises. Hence, a thriving 'informal economy' is a characteristic feature of large cities in both countries. The most important single difference between the two cases is in state-sector employment. Both in absolute numbers and also as a proportion of the total nonagricultural labor force, the Egyptian state is a much more significant employer.

The parallelism in the labor-force profiles outlined above points toward similar structural cleavages—between unionized labor in large scale enterprises and casual workers in small-scale production, between public- and private-sector employees; between the quasi-employed in petty services and trades and formal wageworkers. Hence to try to ascertain how closely Turkish and/or Egyptian workers approximate the paradigmatic case[3] of 'genuine' working class development would be a debilitating exercise both analytically and empirically.[4]

The contrast between the Egyptian and Turkish cases leads away from accounts based on such criteria as wage levels, regularity of work, trade union membership, etc. It forewarns against the assumption that patterns of political mobilization and activism reflect or mirror underlying social structural cleavages. Instead, it raises the question of why some lines of social cleavage are politicized rather than others, why some potential group identities are activated and reinforced, but not others. Hence we must turn to history and its variations to try to understand the distinctive political experiences of workers which have served to accentuate divergent modes of articulation of discontent. But what history and what variations?

An Outline of the Argument

This essay focuses upon variations in the *timing* and *sequence* of three transformative processes which have shaped the historical trajectories of Egypt and Turkey in the first half of the twentieth century. In both countries, popular wars of liberation against a foreign power were followed by the establishment of postcolonial, independent state structures. In both countries, traditional agrarian export economies were substantially transformed under the impact of the Great Depression and initial industrialization attempts. Finally, both countries experienced massive dislocation of agrarian populations and rural exodus, transforming the shape of urban space.

The thrust of my argument is that owing to differences in *sequence* and *timing,* these same historical processes have combined to produce distinctive sociopolitical configurations in the two cases. In Turkey, the earlier success of the nationalist movement meant that interwar industrialization efforts took place under the aegis of a centrist-bureaucratic state, before substantial dislocation from agriculture. In Egypt, important political and economic breaks with colonial powers were postponed until the end of World War II, after major rural exodus had occurred and a sizable industrial sector was already in existence.

These variations are critical for identifying the broader matrix of social forces that have shaped the distinctive content, definition, and 'repertoires' of political action among urban workers in the two contexts. The specificity of the Egyptian experience (in contrast to Turkey), resides in the articulation of the forces of anticolonialism, nationalism, and Islamic fundamentalism, mutually reinforcing one another in an interactive pattern and uniting various segments of the urban workforce in recurrent upsurges of militant street action. In the case of Turkey, the earlier consolidation of a nationalist-secularist state in the 1920s yielded a different political matrix. It served to reproduce and reinforce small-scale peasant ownership in agriculture. It gave birth to a state-owned industrial sector composed of large manufacturing enterprises deliberately located away from Istanbul, and hence yielded an isolated, dispersed workforce. Thus peasant exodus from the rural countryside and urban industrial agglomeration were postponed until the 1950s in Turkey and coincided with the postwar boom. In Egypt by contrast, major agrarian dislocation began much earlier, during the interwar period of stagnation in world trade for cotton. The subsequent residential ordering of space in large cities of Cairo and Alexandria differed dramatically from Istanbul, Ankara, or Izmir, whose growth gained momentum in the post-1950 period.

To elaborate and link these arguments to street politics, I have organized the substantive sections of this essay in two major parts. In the first part, I focus on the contrast between the two cases in terms of the sequence and timing of independent state formation in relation to industrialization. How did they lead to major differences in the kinds of political struggles which shaped the first popular mobilization experiences of workers in the two contexts? Drawing on sources of labor historiography in Egypt and Turkey, I discuss different patterns of opposition and confrontation which initially served to mobilize workers, uniting and/or dividing them, depending upon the nature of other dominant social forces in the political arena. In the second part, I am concerned with how repertoires of political action acquired in the past are produced and reproduced in the present. Hence I turn to contemporary differences in the social organization of residential space in large cities, and discuss variations in the timing and patterns of the dislocation of labor from agriculture which gave birth to them. Here, I draw on sources of historical and contemporary Cairo and Istanbul. My emphasis is on the ways contemporary organization of urban social space conditions potential social cleavages and group identities, and serves to reconstruct past experiences in the present.

1. Industrial Transitions and Independent State Formation

A parallel reading of Turkish and Egyptian labor historiography reveals a remarkably similar story, up to World War I. In both cases, the beginnings of labor unrest and agitation can be traced back to the emergence of a new group of urban wageworkers towards the end of the nineteenth century. While based on agricultural exports, integration into world markets spurred similar kinds of investments in transport (tramways and railways), public services (light, gas, etc.), enterprises processing agricultural products, as well as in the manufacturing of limited kinds of goods for the Europeanized segments of the urban population. Despite their small numbers, wageworkers employed in these enterprises came to constitute an active core of organized and politicized workers who, along with some of the artisans, began to engage in collective action in the period leading up to World War I.[5]

Two features of this early period of labor activism become significant in light of subsequent developments. First and foremost was the cleavage between domestic workers and foreign management. Not only were virtually all the large private companies owned by foreigners or Levantines, but in state-owned enterprises, public-service companies, etc., the supervisory personnel and technical staff who oversaw the workforce were also usually foreigners. Hence in both countries, the members of the active core of laborers were united by the fact of their employment in relatively large-scale enterprises under foreign and/or Levantine management. The fact that Egypt was directly colonized lent foreign investment in Egypt a more prominent role. But in both cases, the center of gravity of labor activism resided in foreign-owned and/or -operated enterprises.

A second important feature of this early period of labor activism concerns the ethnic heterogeneity of indigenous workers themselves. The skilled, relatively high-wage workers such as electricians, machinists, plumbers, etc. were predominantly of Armenian, Syrian, or Greek origin in both cases. Workers of Egyptian and Turkish ethnic origin were mainly concentrated at the bottom, in the unskilled and low-paid, often temporary jobs. Thus ethnic cleavages among indigenous workers overlapped with variations in job security and benefits as well as skill levels. And, it was from among workers of non-Turkish/non-Egyptian ethnic origin that labor militancy and radicalism initially germinated and later spread.

Thus the 'first wave' of labor activism unfolded in broadly parallel lines in the two countries during the prewar decades. The common matrix which served to define this parallelism was dramatically altered, in the Turkish case, by the early success of the nationalist movement. Had the Turkish War of Independence been postponed until the end of World War II, the Turkish labor movement would perhaps have evolved along the same lines as the Egyptian. Egypt's continued domination by British colonialism during the interwar years forged an inextricable link between the nationalist movement and the workers' movement during the interwar decades. In Turkey by contrast, the devastating War of Independence, which followed immediately upon the ravages of World War I, constituted a dramatic rupture—economic and political. The subsequent industrialization efforts during the interwar decades brought peasants from the countryside into state-owned manufacturing plants, and fashioned an industrial workforce but not a labor movement.

A. Interwar Decades: The Political Nexus of Early Industrialization Efforts In Egypt and Turkey

The broader sociopolitical matrix of the interwar decades in Egypt, in contrast to the Turkish case, may be rendered in summary terms as follows:

EGYPT	TURKEY
(Official Independence from Britain in 1922)	(Establishment of Republic in 1923)
A quasi-colonial state with the Wafd as the ruling party	Military-civilian bureaucrats in control of the state apparatus
A powerful commercial bourgeoisie with organic links with international capital	Muslim merchants seeking to replace departed minorities
An entrenched landed oligarchy (dominating the Wafd)	Provincial landed notables and small peasantry
Foreign capital and investment	Absence of foreign capital and investment
Emergence of an increasingly politicized labor movement	Growth of an industrial workforce under state tutelage

This crude summary chart pinpoints the divergence in the matrix of social forces within which interwar industrialization efforts began in the two countries. In the case of Egypt, the gathering momentum of a nationalist movement meant that workers were rapidly mobilized in the struggles against the ancien regime, against colonial presence, and against foreign capital. In the Turkish case, by contrast, interwar industrialization efforts took place within the nexus of a nationalist state and gave birth to an apolitical workforce. Below I will highlight these differences.

Turkey: Creation of a New Industrial Workforce under State Sponsorship

The Turkish War of Liberation was essentially a peasant war. It entailed four years of devastating struggle, following upon the heels of serious Ottoman defeats in the Balkan Wars of 1911–13 and later World War I, entered and lost. Between 1912 to 1922, the population of Anatolia fell by about 30 percent: approximately 20 percent died and 10 percent emigrated.[6] After the military victory of the nationalist movement, what remained of the dismembered Ottoman empire consisted of Anatolia and Thrace, with a population of less than 15 million, ravaged by wars, massacres, and migrations.

The nationalist struggle had been waged as much against the great Western powers as against other ethnic groups of the empire which had hoped to benefit from the partitioning of the Ottoman empire in order to realize their own nationalist aims. Hence the military struggle simultaneously entailed the expulsion and emigration of Christian minorities which had hitherto constituted the metropolitan commercial bourgeoisie of the empire, with organic links to international capital. The vast majority of the non-Muslim merchants and industrialists disappeared from the scene, together with a large segment of the skilled labor force and artisans.[7] The devastation in agriculture was equally dramatic, with significant declines in land under cultivation and production, due partly to the loss of rural population and partly to the loss of export trade in foodstuffs. In short, the economy was in shambles, burdened with the Ottoman debt as well as the Capitulations which continued until 1929.

It is against this background of social and economic devastation that the transformational 'success' of the Kemalists in their nationalist, secularist, and modernist project must be couched. The theory and practice of the Kemalist 'transformation' was stamped by the ideology and peculiar gestalt of its military–civilian bureaucratic cadres. It combined corporatist legislation and institutions with state-capitalistic economic policies. But it was the weakness of a resistance matrix of opposing social forces which enabled the centralist–bureaucratic consolidation of the state apparatus to proceed in a fairly autonomous fashion, insulated from the 'pulls' of compromise. Among the groups aligned behind the nationalist struggle, both the provincial landed notables (never a landed oligarchy to begin with) and also Anatolian merchant-commercialists, stood to benefit from centrist consolidation, initially to expropriate and replace Levantine and minority interests, and later to increase their accumulation through political connections with the center. The only real threat lay in Islam, in whose name the War of Liberation was fought. The cooperation of the Kemalists with the local clerics and religious authorities, a key element in the successful mobilization of peasantry during the war, was short-lived. The success of the Kemalist cadres in eliminating the institutional underpinnings of Islam (administrative, legal, educational, and economic) in a series of radical, militant steps indicates that the religious establishment was strong enough, on its own, to be threatening, yet at the same time lacking powerful allies to forge concession and compromise towards some sort of accommodation. The militant secularism of Kemalist cadres, in succeeding in reducing Islam to its 'folk' variety and purging the center of its institutional vestiges, ensured ideological consolidation around ethnic nationalism.

The emergent configuration of the interwar decades entailed a single-party system, incorporating major segments of the most strategic social forces—military, bureaucracy, local notability—into a ruling coalition, astride an overwhelmingly rural society of peasant cultivators. The party itself formed the organizational link between the military–civilian bureaucratic cadres and the local notables, who represented its core support and its link to the peasantry. Istanbul- and Izmir-based economic interest groups, now composed of ethnic Turks moving into the vacuum left by the departed commercial and industrial bourgeoisie of the Ottoman empire, were soon stifled by the onset of the Great Depression. The Ankara regime consolidated its power, cut off from political networks based in the previous Ottoman establishment, and increasingly isolated from international markets. The political powers and social status of the bureaucracy reigned supreme, pristine in its ethnic nationalism and militant secularism, for nearly three decades.

The balance sheet of etatist industrialization efforts during the interwar decades added up to an impressive figure of more than a hundred state-run enterprises by the end of the 1940s.[8] By 1950, when etatism theoretically ended, these public enterprises employed 76,000 workers, or 45.9 percent of the manufacturing labor force, in enterprises employing more than ten workers. The remaining 54.1 percent of the workers were distributed among 2,515 private manufacturing establishments *(see table 2).*

In terms of both the numbers of large-scale plants as well as the size of the labor force employed, the accomplishments of the etatist decades were impressive. But given the ban on any form of labor organization—unions, voluntary organizations, etc.—among workers from 1928 to 1946, this was a labor force with no experience in any form of mobilization. Since the new plants were almost exclusively located in Anatolia, the workforce was composed of peasants recruited from nearby villages who were allowed to go back during harvest to help out on the family farms. The geographical dispersion of large-scale mechanized production away from Istanbul, as a deliberate state policy, isolated the labor force from the urban wageworkers

Table 2 Emergence of an Industrial Workforce: Interwar Decades

	Egypt (1946)	Turkey (1950)		
		public	private	total
Number of enterprises (employing 10+)	3,381	103	2,515	2,618
Number of workers	271,000	76,033	86,826	162,859

Sources:
Egypt: J. Beinin and Z. Lochman, *Workers on the Nile,* Princeton University Press, Princeton, 1987, p. 265.
Turkey: SSI, *Türkiye'de Toplumsal Gelişmenin 50.* Ankara: Yılı,1973, p. 206.

of the metropolis. The politically repressive mono-party decades allowed little scope for diverse ideological currents which may have, in a more liberal environment, drawn the workers into the arena of political contestation. In sum, interwar industrialization efforts in Turkey yielded a geographically dispersed, semi-peasant labor force but not a workers' movement. It is the absence of labor as a historical actor until well into the 1950s that marks the specificity of the Turkish case.

Egypt: Politicization of Workers Through Nationalist Struggles

By contrast, Egyptian workers evolved into a highly visible and politically significant force during the interwar decades, the continuation of colonial presence serving to lend it coherence and a common front.

Though Britain was unilaterally forced to declare Egypt an independent state in 1922, following the popular uprisings of 1919, its active presence continued until the 1952 Revolution. The political configuration of the interwar decades, as represented by the ruling Wafd Party, entailed a narrowly based alliance between large landowners, who controlled the peasantry in the countryside, and a foreign-resident bourgeoisie that managed Egypt's links to external markets through ownership and control of banking, insurance, transport, and communication facilities. This narrow alliance, which was exclusively centered upon the cultivation and export of a single cash crop—cotton—dated back to the mid-nineteenth century, and continued to prevail after Egypt's official independence in 1922.

The impetus for initial industrialization efforts was broadly parallel to the Turkish case. The onset of the World Depression towards the end of the 1920s was accompanied, in the case of Egypt, by a dramatic decline in export markets for cotton and a fall in cotton prices. The sharp reduction in trans-Mediterranean trade stimulated local manufacturing, allowing scope for indigenous investments and an enhanced role for Egypt's nascent local bourgeoisie. The enactment of a series of protective tariffs for manufactured goods in the early 1930s was followed in 1937 by the abolishment of the Capitulations, which reduced the advantages of foreign investors vis-à-vis local capital. Thus, increasing numbers of Egypt's indigenous capitalists joined the ranks of Cairo's 'haute bourgeoisie'[9] throughout the interwar decades, during what is often referred to as Egypt's Liberal Age. In the early 1920s there was only one Egyptian-run joint-stock company, Bank Misr, which had been established on nationalist principles. By the conclusion of World War II, among purely national companies, Egyptian firms outnumbered other firms. But despite the impressive growth of native Egyptian industrial capital, foreign and Levantine capital continued to play a major role. Foreign participation in industrial development (while a minor share of total foreign investment) remained considerable. Some of the major monopolies or semi-monopolies in key sectors of the economy remained under foreign control.

Similarly to the Turkish case, interwar industrialization efforts in Egypt took the form of early industries of import substitution—primarily in textiles, cement, and processed food. The presence of Allied armies in Egypt during World War II served as an additional stimulus, by temporarily expanding the internal market for Egyptian manufactures, as well as creating additional employment. Thus by the end of World War II, the numbers of Egyptian wageworkers employed in relatively large-scale manufacturing establishments were appreciably higher than in Turkey *(see table 2).*

Given the recent origin of this industrial workforce, it is not difficult to surmise that the peasant ethos remained strong—as in the Turkish case. What proved to be a much more crucial difference was the geographical concentration of wageworkers in Egypt, which served to increase their importance and visibility for various ideological appeals, and enhanced possibilities for political mobilization. Among textile workers, for instance, who became the strength and center of gravity of the emergent labor movement, it was the medium-sized, poorly capitalized spinning and weaving mills around Shubra al-Khayma, where labor militancy was strongest. Shubra's proximity to Cairo, and the prevalence of foreign and Levantine capital, enhanced its importance for nationalist politicians as well as labor activists.[10] By contrast, at the giant mills of the Misr Company located in the Delta, the combination of distance from large urban centers, a largely illiterate peasant labor force, and the 'national' character of ownership meant that labor activism was much slower to develop and did not gain real momentum until into the 1940s.

It would undoubtedly be misleading to read undue cohesiveness, organizational unity, and consciousness into the labor activism of the interwar decades in Egypt. What served to mobilize Egyptian workers was the growing momentum of the nationalist struggle. The continuing dominance of foreign capital in Egypt meant that nationalist sentiment came to play a major role as a justifying framework and ideology for political activism and militancy. The demands of Egyptian wageworkers merged with the political movement for national independence in a mutually reinforcing pattern. Trade unions existed, regardless of how corporatist, paternalistic, or passive they were. And most important, wageworkers gradually became the focus of contestation to competing ideological appeals. While the liberal nationalism of the Wafd Party continued to be the hegemonic ideological and organizational force, both communists and Muslim Brothers emerged as rival, new, political forces. Thus workers became the testing ground for diverse political currents, and participated in recurrent upsurges of militant street action. They were an important component of the social and political upheaval that undermined the monarchy and ended the era of British colonialism in Egypt. Together with the emergent new middle classes of the interwar decades and the peasantry in the countryside, they formed part of the broad constituency upon which the Nasser regime consolidated its power.

B. The Post–World War II Era: Developmentalist Strategies and Populist Dilemmas

For states at the periphery of the international system and the global economy, the post–World War II decades offered new possibilities. The new cycle of expansion in world markets opened the way for industrialization of the import-substituting variety. Bolstered by a faith in the efficacy of bureaucratic technoplanning, the thrust of the developmentalist strategies of the 1950s and 1960s hinged upon the expansion of internal consumer markets simultaneously with massive industrial investments. The benchmark of this new era of developmentalism was the political and economic inclusion of various segments of the working classes through increasing state expenditures and redistributive measures. The dilemmas and stalemates of the model itself resided in the clash between investment demands of rapid industrialization and the consumption demands of 'populism'. Hence its sustainability was contingent on substantial infusions of foreign aid in the favorable international conjuncture of the 1950s and 1960s.

The distinctive political configurations within which the quintessential dilemmas of a 'populist' economy unfolded in the two countries led to progressively divergent political outcomes. Egypt evolved towards an avowedly socialist path and a mono-party regime. Turkey by contrast professed to embrace capitalism, and developed a crisis-prone multiparty system. The emergent patterns of political incorporation of labor differed.

Egypt's Populist Interlude: Charisma and Co-optation

It is tempting to start by referring to parallels between Nasserism in Egypt and Kemalism in Turkey. In both, radical officers of petit-bourgeois origin were at the forefront of the nationalist movement, initially spearheading popular wars of liberation to throw off Western political power, and later furnishing the political cadres of military-bureaucratic, single-party structures. The ideological and intentional content of both revolutions was typical of the petit-bourgeois style of politics as embodied in the catchword 'third way'—between capitalism and socialism. The defining essence of their initial vision was a capitalist society without a liberal rationale, a bourgeois society without bourgeois politics and economics.[11]

These similarities in the vision and/or ideologies of their political cadres notwithstanding, the two revolutions were products of very different historical moments, both in terms of the matrix of the domestic social forces they were located in as well as the international context. The series of choices that charted the path of Nasserism in Egypt entailed juggling a much more complex set of political forces and alliances. Nasser had to deal with much stronger opponents—the old landed aristocracy and the metropolitan bourgeoisie—because of Egypt's interwar legacy. He was also able to develop and mobilize a much wider constituency, owing in no small part to the new opportunities of economic growth in the post–World War II era. Until around the mid-1950s, Egypt was riding comfortably on the cushion of sterling balances which were accumulated during World War II, and later, beginning with the first Soviet loan for industrialization in 1958, it received substantial amounts of aid from all sources, East and West. Between 1960 to 1974, foreign aid financed perhaps "one-fifth to one-third of Egypt's investment and growth."[12]

Much has been written on the "alliance of popular working forces," (to use the well-known slogan espoused by Nasser), which took shape in the political struggles against the dominant forces of the interwar era. It included the trade unions and organized labor; the middle peasantry which emerged through the land reform of 1952, or what Leonard Binder calls the "second stratum"[13] and the "new middle class" of professionals and bureaucrats who were a key group among the original supporters and, later, beneficiaries of the regime. For the purposes of the present analysis, a number of specific features of Nasser's mobilizational formula vis-à-vis the labor force are worth reiterating briefly.

One of the key elements in the equation was Nasser's awesome charisma and his remarkable success in forging a psychological bond with the masses. Nasser's stature as a leader extended far beyond those around and below him. He was a popular hero with a mass following. His direct personal identification with the common people, capable of inspiring faith and trust as well as rallying mass support, was a "tremendous fund of political capital."[14] It served simultaneously to mobilize and channel the activism of the working classes in support of the regime.

A second important dimension of the regime's relationship with the labor movement was a combination of repression and co-optation which served to create a cadre of loyal trade-union leadership. In the years 1952–56, bracketed by the collapse of the monarchy, the Suez Crisis, and the 1956 War, when the winds of revolution were blowing in various directions, the RCC government moved to harness labor militancy by purging the 'extremist' elements from the trade unions to replace them with cadres loyal to the RCC.[15] Simultaneously, a series of long-standing demands of the trade-union movement were legislated to improve the status of labor. This pattern of co-optation of the trade-union leadership aligned the labor movement behind Nasser in the struggles among the various wings of the RCC. The nationalist, anti-imperialist fervor of the Suez Crisis and the 1956 War solidified the relationship. Later, when the corporatist instruments of government control were in place, syndicate elections could be counted upon to produce 'co-operative' leadership.

The last, but most important, component of workers' support of the regime was the real, tangible benefits it extended. The ten years which marked the height of Nasser's social experiment, beginning with the Egyptianization of foreign interests between 1956–57, and continuing with the implementation of the comprehensive national plan of 1960–65, constituted a period of genuine redistribution. The redistributive impact of the radical social reforms of this period—nationalizations, educational expansion, and consumption subsidies—have been well documented.[16]

The nationalizations in both industry and services brought organized labor into the fold of the public sector, new industrial investments serving to expand the organized labor market. Public-sector employment grew from about 10 percent of the entire workforce in 1960 to nearly one third by 1976.[17] Job security, provisions for pensions, and health and accident insurance, coupled with politically determined high wage rates, meant real and substantial gains for organized labor.

Egypt's populist interlude thus robbed the formal union movement of much of its raison d'être, with the Egyptian Trade Union Federation strictly supporting of Nasser's economic policies. It was only after an interplay of internal and external forces emasculated the thrust of Nasser's social experiment, and began to threaten the gains workers had made in the 1960s, that union organizations acquired a fresh breath of life.[18]

Turkey's Populist Interlude: the Politicization of a Labor Movement

By contrast, the three decades following World War II gave birth to an increasingly politicized trade union movement in Turkey. Its timing proved crucial in two important respects.

First, it meant that the genesis and subsequent evolution of Turkey's trade-union movement were defined within the parameters of a 'mixed economy' with a large state manufacturing sector. Emphasizing Turkey's economic liberalism in contrast to Egypt's socialist course serves well as a heuristic device making the divergence between the two cases more transparent. But it can also be misleading. Critics of Egypt's social experiment never fail to remark on its shortcomings in achieving a genuine socialist economy. Nor did Turkey's choice of 'capitalism' in the conjuncture of the 1950s diminish the importance of state investments.[19] Rather, it implied the nurturing of a private sector behind protective state barriers.

Second, the emergence and politicization of Turkey's trade-union movement coincided with decades of expansionist growth in the Turkish economy. In its broad contours, the 1950–75 was the period when the exuberance of the import-substituting drive, coupled with substantial infusions of foreign aid and credit, made redistribution through public expenditure affordable. The descriptive account below will try to elucidate exactly how these broader features of the post-1950 conjuncture shaped the unfolding of Turkey's trade-union movement.

Trade unionism was legislated into existence in the early 1950s, introduced under US auspices. Its initiation was more of an attempt to preempt potential labor mobilization in state enterprises than to curb existing ferment. The establishment in 1952 of Turk-Is as the first union confederation, with its leaders trained in the United States, was little more than a political move to put on a democratic face in the new era of liberalism in Turkey. It was only in the 1960s, and coinciding with capital concentration in private enterprise and the consolidation of Turkish family-owned holdings, that a labor movement in the political sense of the term, began to gain momentum.

Turk-Is, the original giant of Turkish unionism, never transcended the state sponsorship which marked its birth. Drawing its membership overwhelmingly from among the ranks of workers in state economic enterprises, it rapidly developed a highly oligarchical leadership structure and acquired a conservative ideological cast from the very beginning. Its functions remained confined to negotiating 'pace-setting' agreements in key state enterprises. Thus Turk-Is evolved as an appendage to state labor-management policies. Inflationary state fiscal policies meant that wage levels in the state sector were invariably higher than in private enterprise, throughout the 1950–80 period. The practice of using state enterprises as sources of employment patronage in electoral politics served to further consolidate the clientelistic powers of the Turk-Is oligarchy, its survival becoming more dependent on governmental grants of patronage than its own activism.

The beginnings of opposition and ferment at the grassroots level, which surfaced immediately after the 1961 Constitution granted unions the right to strike, initially took the form of extreme organizational fragmentation. An estimated two million registered union members were divided among some eight hundred rival local unions by the end of the 1960s.[20] The rank-and-file members, unable to consolidate broader opposition against the entrenched union oligarchy, tended to switch from one local union to another to register dissatisfaction. Hence, to maintain membership commitment, local unions were forced to demonstrate strong action vis-à-vis employers, rapidly moving into and organizing workers in large-scale private enterprises.

It was from among these affiliated local unions of Turk-Is that a second labor confederation, DİSK, was born in 1967, much more radically oriented in ideology, and prominently based in private enterprise. This was followed, in the 1970s, with the establishment of Hak-Is (affiliated with the religious right National Salvation Party) and MISK (affiliated with the nationalist right). Thus the ideological spectrum of trade-union confederations began to approximate the four major ideological divisions in the political party system of the 1970s.

The 'ideological flowering' of the Turkish trade-union movement in the 1960s and 1970s coincided with increasing capital concentration in private enterprise, next to, and interlocked with, a vast state sector. Joint ventures with the state, rather than international capital, provided the motor of growth and accumulation. The extensive interlocking of private and state-owned banks with corporations, which resulted in a series of family-dominated, oligopolistic, public-private conglomerates—the Turkish family holdings—is beyond the scope of discussion here. What is significant in this analysis is that, while capital concentration in Turkish private enterprise was heavily reliant upon foreign loans and credit, it did not entail direct foreign investment. Organic links with the state, rather than with international capital, was its salient characteristic.

In the absence of foreign capital, nationalist sentiment never assumed importance as a major justifying framework and ideology for labor activism in Turkey. The labor movement was mobilized against domestic capital from the beginning. Its ideological 'radicalism' was shaped and dominated by the secular left. The Islamist appeal of Hak-Is was emasculated not so much by direct repression (which was equally valid for the militant left) as by the absence of the 'infidel.'

When Turkish labor did become organized against large-scale domestic capital, 'big business' proved essentially a 'soft' opponent. Under conditions of high inflation, coupled with rapid expansion of the domestic consumer market, large-scale manufacturing enterprises of the import-substituting variety tended to opt for short-term benefits of continued production rather than risk lengthy strikes. Employers' associations which were organized in the early 1970s consistently failed to come up with industry-wide collective-bargaining agreements, because the larger enterprises among their ranks refused to dig in the ditches for an extended fight or risk intransigent counter-action.[21] The ease with which large enterprises could absorb wage hikes, and thereby set the pace for increasing wage concessions, depended upon the cycles of the import-substituting economy. Tense confrontations surfaced towards the end of the 1960s, concomitantly with a major foreign-currency crisis, but were suspended in the early 1970s when remittances of Turkish workers abroad provided temporary relief, to be reactivated much more dramatically in the latter half of the 1970s.

Hence it was only when the import-substituting economy was squeezed from the mid-1970s onwards, with all its usual manifestations—rampant inflation, dramatic reductions in consumer demand, actual negative rates of growth, and the IMF at the doorstep—that organized labor encountered its first real test of confrontation. And it seemed equal to the challenge of contestation; a real force, mobilized and organized. The number of strikes was phenomenal, workers occupied factories, their footsteps echoed on the streets—years of 'sound and fury' which were later described by the engineers of the Turkish Infitah as the reign of anarchy and terror.

Yet in the 1980s conjuncture, it became apparent that at the grassroots level the labor movement had acquired little capacity of its own to withstand and combat repression. The apparent radicalization and militancy of the masses of workers proved to be a myth. With the hindsight of the 1990s, what seems remarkable is the ease with which the labor movement was totally leveled and reduced to quiescence. True, the labor movement was the primary target of attack by the military, its leaders imprisoned, its organizational base dismantled, and corporatist controls imposed. But it seems as if the labor movement itself was legislated out of existence. Once the workers who provided leadership in trade unions, pressure groups, and political-party machines disappeared from the arena, the Turkish working classes appear to have succumbed into apathy. In the progressively widening political arena of the postmilitary period (1983–90), labor has been noteworthy for its absence more than anything else. And this is so despite the dramatic and continuing real reductions in wage levels and worsening income distribution which has accompanied the Turkish Infitah.[22]

Why the total lack of intransigence, wildcat strikes, mob action, riots, etc., on the part of Turkish workers? Why the absence of street politics? This question brings me back to the original puzzle set forward in the introduction of this essay. Differences in the first popular mobilization experiences of workers in Egypt and Turkey, and the kinds of political struggles which shaped them, constitute only one component of the explanation, and provide a partial answer at best. Unless we resort to a kind of historical and cultural essentialism which assumes that events and configurations of the past determine or limit future possibilities, the question of how earlier experiences are reconstructed in the present remains to be answered. Hence, the second substantive part of this essay will focus on differences in the social organization of urban residential space in the two contexts and argue that it has been a important factor in reinforcing divergent potential group identities.

2. Patterns of Agrarian Dislocation and the Organization of Urban Residential Space

The major concern here will be the ways in which the contemporary social order of residential space in large metropolitan agglomerations, notably of Cairo and Alexandria in contrast to Istanbul and Ankara, serves to reinforce diverse social cleavages and potential group identities, and lends itself to alternative modes of articulation of discontent in moments of crisis. My assumption is that the initial political mobilization experiences of workers, and the kinds of political struggles which shaped them, condition—but do not determine—contemporary patterns of political activism. The significance of urban social space resides in facilitating the reproduction of past experiences in the present.

I have already provided a lengthy descriptive account (albeit all too brief and oversimplified for the informed reader) of variations in patterns of industrial growth in the two contexts. To start from the beginning, describing concomitant changes in agriculture is neither my intention nor is it necessary for this analysis. It is clear that the two processes are inextricably interlinked parts of what constitutes, in each case, a unique drama of change. But at the expense of breaking up the temporal unity of the account at this point, I would like to highlight two historical dimensions of agrarian dislocation, which led to differences in the residential order of space in large cities and thereby served to reinforce different cleavages among workers in the two cases.

Differences in the Timing and Patterns of Agrarian Dislocation

In Egypt, population pressure on land began much earlier than it did in Turkey. Egypt had reached the limits of cultivable land by 1900, so that in 1950, when Egypt's total population was still 20 million, Cairo had already reached the 2.5 million mark. By contrast, Turkey was able to extend cultivable land up until the late 1950s. In 1950, Istanbul's population had yet to reach one million, and Ankara was about half a million—although the population of the two countries was identical, i.e., 20 million *(see table 3).*

Currently, with its population of more than 10 million, Cairo accounts for one fifth of Egypt's population. But much more significant for our purposes is that roughly 70 percent of this population was born *in* Cairo. Of Istanbul's current population of approximately 6.5 million, 70 percent were born *outside* Istanbul according to recent estimates. Thus Cairo's current expansion is predominantly a product of its own population growth. Istanbul remains a city of immigrants.

Equally significant has been the pattern of dislocation of labor from land. In Egypt, the rural exodus of interwar decades was predominantly composed of landless, destitute *fellahin,* given the dominance of the traditional landed elite in the countryside and the prevailing pattern of large ownership. Never having been landowners to begin with, their ties to the countryside were totally severed. They constituted a bloated lumpen segment, much exceeding

Table 3 Patterns of Population Growth

	Total population		Metropolitan Cairo		Istanbul province	
Censuses	Egypt	Turkey	Percent of Egypt	Size (1,000)	Percent of Turkey	Size (1,000)
1927	14,178	13,648	11.1	1,572	5.8	794
1947; 1945	18,967	18,790	14.7	2,779	5.7	1,078
1960	25,984	27,755	17.5	4,530	6.8	1,802
1986; 1985	48,205	50,412	20.2	9,754	11.5	5,843
1990*	52,061	56,473	20.5	10,679	12.9	7,309
1995*	57,396	61,643	20.7	11,887	14.3	8,815

* Projected for Egypt; census for Turkey for 1990 and projected for 1995.

Sources:
Egypt: F. Shorter, "Cairo's Leap Forward," *Cairo Papers in Social Science,* volume 12, monograph 1, Spring 1989; Eduard Bos, My T. Uu, Ann Levin, and Rudolfo A. Bulatao, *World Population Projections: 1992–93 Edition,* Johns Hopkins University Press for the World Bank, Baltimore 1992.
Turkey: Turkish Population Censuses, 1927–1990. Projections by the State Institute of Statistics.

the absorptive capacity of the interwar economy where the mass standard of living fell continuously, per capita income dropping almost 50 percent in the first half of the century.

This is in contrast to the Turkish case, where rural exodus began in the early 1950s, its major thrust coinciding with the inflationary-expansionist decades of the 1950s and 1960s when the Turkish economy grew at the rate of 6–9 percent per annum. Rural exodus in the Turkish case was predominantly an outgrowth of the process of fragmentation of landownership among small peasantry. Thus in each generation some members of the household left while others stayed on to manage the family holding, the continuity of ties becoming a part of the strategy for survival and maximization at both ends. Differences in the timing and pattern of agricultural dislocation thus generated different social configurations in the urban arena.

Transformations of Urban Space [23]

The divergence in the residential ordering of space in large cities becomes more transparent in the contrast between Cairo and Istanbul—cities which dominate the economic and demographic landscapes of their respective countries.

The influx of landless *fellahin* into Cairo during the interwar decades paved the way for unprecedented congestion and density in inner-city slums. Cairo had already developed into what is often considered the paradigmatic case of a dual colonial city by 1900s. The 'traditional' core of Cairo, in and around the medieval center of the city, had deteriorated sharply by the turn of the century, as the movement of the original upper-income groups was followed by the middle classes in the 1920s, thus leaving the old quarters to the urban poor. The interwar flux of immigrants led to further concentration of population in inner-city slums, flowing over to semi-vacant areas surrounding the medieval core, once the subdivided structures in the traditional quarters could no longer accommodate the soaring densities. The notorious slums of interwar Cairo were an outgrowth of a combination of factors which prohibited low-density peripheral sprawl. In what was essentially a pedestrian city, proximity to the railway terminals leading up the newly emergent manufacturing zones remained crucial. But also land on the fringes of the built-up city was either desert or, if arable, was under the control of powerful landlords who could police encroachment.[24]

The resultant residential configuration of interwar Cairo, with all its concomitant social cleavages, was an important catalyst in giving the initial spark to the 1952 Revolution. It was from the inner slums of Cairo that the mass revolt and rampage of Black Saturday in January of 1952 began and culminated in the burning of Cairo's modern business district. The massive social housing projects of the subsequent Nasser decades, which were mainly oriented towards industrial workers to begin with, (together with the 'new middle class' which constituted its base) did not begin to alleviate the congestion in Cairo's inner-city slums. Paradoxically, it was Nasser's 'land reform' in the early 1950s, which created a stratum of middle peasantry, that paved the way to the much-lamented peripheral sprawl towards arable land during the Infitah decades. Peasants benefiting from the 1952 land distribution found that income obtainable from using land for building was much higher than that obtained from its use for agriculture, and began to sell on a large scale in the 1970s and 1980s.[25] Hence some of the groups long-trapped in the inner slums of Cairo began to move towards the periphery.

In contrast to Cairo, whose sociohistorical legacy intertwined with its distinctive physical ecology to produce a city of working-class slums, Istanbul exploded in the postwar decades to become a city of peasants.

Istanbul's population explosion coincided with its ascendance as the major growth pole of the economy in the post–World War II decades. The swift progress of large-scale plants in the outer zones of the metropolis during the 1960s and 1970s was accompanied by the growth of a flourishing 'informal economy'—a proliferation of vast numbers of labor-intensive, small-scale manufacturing, and petty commercial activities which formed a refuge sector for the bulk of the urban poor.

It was in the residential patterns of the urban poor that Istanbul's growth differed markedly from Cairo. The expansion of immigrant neighborhoods took the form of peripheral sprawl from the beginning, given the possibilities of motorized transport in the decades of microbuses and the availability of agricultural land on the fringes of the city. The initial 'squatments' on vacant state land in the 1950s were succeeded in the 1960s by subdivisions of privately owned agricultural land, older neighborhoods progressively becoming rapidly absorbed into the expanding fabric of the city. There were two implications of this residential patterning from the point of view of working-class politics. First, the majority of incoming rural immigrants (who retained their social and often economic ties with their villages of origin through 'family holdings', however small) became landowners in the city, security of tenure virtually guaranteed by successive party governments. Delivery of basic services—roads, electricity, and water—as well as legalization of property rights, formed the basis of urban populism of the postwar decades.[26] A second important dimension of this pattern was the replication, in the residential order of the large city, of the various ethnic, religious, and regional differences. A first-generation 'immigrant' population, engaged in a variety of pursuits ranging from factory work to the marginal pursuits of the large metropolis, remained embedded in village-based communal networks. With continuing roots in small peasant agriculture, and security of land tenure in the city, they remained essentially peasants, seeking and accepting state intervention in periods of crisis, and returning back into the fold of regional, ethnic, and sectarian neighborhoods.

Concluding Remarks

I have attempted in this essay to weave together various factors which have shaped the distinctive political content and repertoires of action among workers in Egypt and Turkey, emphasizing street politics as a specific mode of articulation of discontent. The significance of street politics resides in transcending diverse lines of cleavage, structural and ideological, to mobilize and unite workers in joint action against established authority. The propensity of Egyptian workers (including segments of unionized labor, petty-service employees, elements of the bazaar, as well as a vast substratum of semi-employed or unemployed) to unite in joint action on the streets of Cairo and Alexandria, has rendered them a visible political force on the arena of Egyptian history, a critical social actor—however volatile and unpredictable—in shaping the course of events. By contrast, moments of crisis in republican history have tended to accentuate the fault lines dividing Turkish workers; instead of mobilizing into sweeping waves of motion, emotion, and movement on the streets of Istanbul and Ankara, to demand voice through direct action and confrontation, Turkish workers have tended to retreat from the arena of politics, quiescent and marginalized in the course of momentous historical events.

In attempting to develop explanations, I have tried to avoid the pitfalls of the proletarianization problematique, i.e., trying to compare the two cases in terms of a theoretically constructed proletariat to assess which is 'weaker' or 'stronger'. In both Egypt and Turkey, workers have been and continue to be segmented into disparate labor markets, fragmented along diverse ideological appeals, and divided among competing allegiances of class and community. Hence I focused upon the distinctive political experiences of workers in the two contexts, experiences which have served to produce and reproduce alternative modes of articulation of discontent and political action.

The initial popular mobilization experience of workers in the two contexts and the nature of the political struggles which shaped them was my major concern in the first substantive section of the essay. In Egypt, the newly emergent industrial workforce of the interwar decades was rapidly politicized in the context of competing ideological currents. It was mobilized in struggles against colonial presence, against foreign capital, against an ancien regime of monarchy and landed aristocracy. In the gathering momentum of the nationalist movement, wageworkers and the unemployed, elements of the bazaar, and unionized labor were united in repeated upsurges of militant street action. In Turkey by contrast, the initial political mobilization of workers occurred in the post-1950 period, coinciding with a cycle of inflationist expansion and exuberant growth in the broader economy. The prior existence of a vast state-enterprise sector (where cost-cutting and profitability were never the primary concern), coupled with the vigorous expansion of private industry oriented towards a growing domestic consumer market, meant that the demands of unionized workers could be met relatively easily and rapidly. Hence political mobilization paved the way for increasing ideological fragmentation, accentuating structural cleavages—between unionized workers in large enterprises and nonunionized labor in small-scale production; between public- and private-sector employees; between the floating quasi-employed of the informal economy and the formal job market.

Crucial and formative as they are, these differences in the kinds of political struggles which shaped the initial political mobilization experience of workers do not account for contemporary differences. Unless we assume that earlier, and ultimately earliest, events determine what comes later, the question of how past experiences are reconstructed in the present remains. 'Traditions' are not simply traces of a distant past, surviving in the recesses of a collective memory; they are produced and reproduced in the present. Hence in the second substantive part of this essay, I turned to contemporary differences in the social organization of space, contrasting Cairo and Istanbul as the two major metropolitan agglomerations. I tried to elucidate how variations in the timing, sequence, and patterns of agrarian dislocation in the two contexts have been solidified in the social organization of urban space, accentuating and politicizing, in the Turkish context, ethno-communal cleavages.

At the more analytical level, the substantive themes I have elaborated in different subsections of this essay are interlinked components of a broader comparative scheme. The logic of the comparative analysis I have pursued throughout has been based upon variations in the sequence and timing of three general, transformative processes which have shaped the historical trajectories of Egypt and Turkey in the twentieth century. In both countries, popular wars of liberation against colonial powers paved the way for the establishment of independent, nationalist state structures. Both countries have undergone substantial industrialization. Both have experienced massive rural exodus and urban migration. The analytical centerpiece of my argument is that owing to variations of timing and sequence, the same processes have unfolded to generate and shape different political forces, actions, and solidarities in the two contexts. Hence, instead of emphasizing the special affinity of certain classes to particular ideological positions, or attributing permanent political significance to communal loyalties on a basis of religion, ethnicity, or tribal origin, I have sought to understand how the interaction of various social groupings within particular historical conjunctures have served to produce and reproduce divergent political cleavages and repertoires of political action. The puzzle of street politics is, from a methodological point of view, a heuristic device enabling me to select and juxtapose case materials on Egypt and Turkey, to build and follow through a comparative scheme which I believe to be of broader relevance in understanding the divergent political trajectories of the two countries.

At the expense of a tidy substantive conclusion, I will end with a methodological caveat. A proclivity for what Skocpol and Somers call 'genetic determinism' inevitably creeps in when contrasting two historical cases which are distinctive wholes, each a unique configuration in itself.[27] The tendency is to look for earlier happenings and configurations, and ultimately the earliest, to explain contemporary differences. I have sought to avoid the pitfalls of such historical essentialism, by breaking up the chronological unity of what constitutes a unique drama of change in Egypt and Turkey, and introducing analytical distinctions between general social processes which are inextricably interrelated. In centering my analysis on variations of timing and sequence in the unfolding of historical events and their distinctive combinations, I have emphasized the specificity of particular historical conjunctures in redefining paths of change. My own intellectual aversion to historical inevitabilities aside, the cases of Egypt and Turkey underscore the importance of timing and conjuncture in redefining the parameters of political choice and action. If past continuities condition but do not determine future alternatives, then the divergent political experiences of workers in Egypt and Turkey do not foreclose, in either case, future possibilities in the arena of street politics.

Notes

1 Quoted from Derek Hopwood, *Egypt: Politics and Society 1945–1981* (London: George Allen and Unwin, 1982), pp. 31–32, 109.

2 As a percentage of the total labor force, agricultural employment appears to be much more significant in Turkey (51 percent) as opposed to Egypt (36 percent). But absolute numbers tell a different story. In both countries, the nonagricultural labor force is around 8–9 million. The total population of both countries is around 50 million. But the total labor force in Turkey is around 18 million as opposed to 13 million in Egypt. The inevitable conclusion is that the Turkish census tends to enumerate women among the agricultural labor force, whereas the Egyptian census does not.

3 In discussions of labor, the paradigmatic case is almost always based upon British working-class history. In analysis of the emergence and development of a 'bourgeoisie', by contrast, the paradigmatic case is invariably built upon the French experience.

4 We would first have to identify the 'real' proletariat. The minimalist definition favoured by labor legislation and by planners or international agencies is often 'those working in full-time wage employment in establishments employing over ten persons.' This would immediately lead to the question of how state employees are to be classified, and the whole labor aristocracy debate. Given that in both countries state employees constitute a privileged group, do they act as a conservative force against the underlying radicalism of masses of workers; or do they constitute the radical element vis-à-vis the apathetic majority? What about the rest of the workers—semi-, sub-, lumpen- or proto-proletariat?, etc.

5 My main sources on labor activism before and during the interwar period in Egypt is Joel Beinin and Zachary Lockman, *Workers on the Nile* (Princeton: Princeton University Press, 1987); and Ellis Goldberg, *Tinker, Tailor and Textile Worker: Class and Politics in Egypt* (Berkeley: University of California Press, 1986). On pre–World War I labor activism in the Ottoman empire, a very useful summary and extensive bibliography is available in "Işçi Hareketleri," in *Tanzimat'tan Cumhuriyet'e Türkiye Ansiklopedisi*, vol. 3, pp. 791–830.

6 See Justin McCarthy, "Foundations of the Turkish Republic: Social and Economic Change," in *Middle Eastern Studies*, vol. 19, no. 2, April 1983, pp. 139–51.

7 The ethnic composition of such major manufacturing and commercial cities as Istanbul, Izmir, and Bursa was dramatically altered. Izmir, for instance, with an estimated 60 percent non-Muslim population in 1912, had become 86 percent Muslim according to the 1927 census. Ibid. pp. 142–43.

8 Notably among these were a stock of twelve spinning and textile mills completed by 1940, five sugar factories under the jurisdiction of Turkish Sugar Factories Co. (Türkiye Şeker Fabrikaları A.O.), eight mining industry groups managed by Etibank, seven industry groups with a steel complex, and twenty-two factories under the jurisdiction of Sümerbank. For a succinct account, in English, of the mono-party decades, with an extensive bibliography, see Stephane Yerasimos, "The Monoparty Period," in Irvin Schick and Ahmet Tonak, eds., *Turkey in Transition* (New York: Oxford University Press, 1987).

9 I borrow the term from Robert Tignor, "The Economic Activities of Foreigners in Egypt, 1920–1950: From Millet to Haute Bourgeoisie," in *Comparative Studies in Society and History*, vol. 22, July 1980, pp. 416–49.

10 Beinen and Lockman, pp. 273–75.

11 Various interpretations of Nasser's social experiment would require an inventory of their own. I have found Fouad Ajami's work most inspiring, probably because it fits nicely with my own understanding of Kemalism. See Fouad Ajami, "The Open-Door Economy: Its Roots and Welfare Consequences," in Gouda Abdel Khalek and Robert Tignor, eds., *The Political Economy of Income Distribution in Egypt* (New York: Holmes and Meier, 1982).

12 Gouda Abdel Khalek, "Foreign Economic Aid and Income Distribution in Egypt, 1952–1977," in Abdel Khalek and Tignor, pp. 435–68.

13 Leonard Binder, *In a Moment of Enthusiasm: Political Power and the Second Stratum in Egypt* (Chicago: University of Chicago Press, 1978).

14 Quoted from Raymond Hinnebusch, *Egyptian Politics Under Sadat* (New York: Lynne Rienner Publishers, Inc., 1988) (updated edition), p. 14. According to Hinnebusch, Nasser's "finger over the pulse of public opinion" was in part responsible for the failure of the regime to develop institutionalized channels of participation. It also enabled Nasser to

intervene periodically in struggles among various wings of the ASU in the name of 'public interest'. Television enhanced Nasser's appeal by projecting him as a leader of world stature. The 'people-ism' of the Kemalist decades in Turkey seem emasculated by contrast.

15 For an extended account, see Joel Beinin, "Labor, Capital and the State in Nasserist Egypt, 1952–1961," in *International Journal of Middle East Studies* vol. 12, no. 1, February 1989, pp. 71–90.

16 See articles by Ali Hillal Dessouki, "The Politics of Income Distribution in Egypt," and Saad Eddin Ibrahim, "Social Mobility and Income Distribution in Egypt: 1952–1977," in Abdel Khalek and Tignor, pp. 55–87 and 375–434.

17 See Samir Radwan and Bent Hansen, *Employment Opportunities and Equity in Egypt: A Labor Market Approach* (Geneva: International Labor Office, 1982), p. 62. Ragui Assaad provides evidence that public-sector employment rose equally rapidly during the Infitah decades. See Ragui Assaad, "Labor Underutilization and Segmented Labor Markets: The Case of Egypt," paper presented at the Cairo University Conference on Unemployment, January 1989.

18 For more details, see Marsha Rosusney, "Workers Against the State: Wage Protest in Egypt, 1952–1988," paper presented at MESA Annual Meeting, Los Angeles, 1988, and "Labor as as Obstacle to Privatization: The Case of Egypt," paper presented at the MESA Annual Meeting, Toronto, 1989.

19 Between 1951 and 1960, the government's share in total investment increased from about 38 percent to 56 percent.

20 See Maksut Mumcuoğlu, "Political Activites of Trade Unions and Income Distribution," in Ergun Özbudun and Aydın Ulusan, *The Political Economy of Income Distribution in Turkey* (New York: Holmes and Meier, 1980); and Alpaslan Işıklı, "Wage Labor and Unionization," in Schick and Tonak, pp. 309–32.

What makes estimates of aggregate union membership in the pre-1980 period so unreliable is the possibility of multiple registration, with workers belonging to several unions simultaneously. Competition among the major confederations inclined them to exaggerate their membership; their combined claims adding up to some five million unionized workers. When the military regime legislatively enforced a centralized registration system in the aftermath of the 1980 coup, membership figures dropped down dramatically. But once again, it is difficult to assess how many former union members simply failed to register, with DİSK permanently closed down. For a detailed account of post-1980 changes in labor legislation and its implications, see Taha Parla and Ayşe Öncü, "Militarism and Corporatism in Turkish Politics," paper presented at the Conference on "History and Society in Turkey," Berlin Institute for Comparative Social Research, Berlin, December 1981.

21 Ataman Aksoy, on the basis of a comparative analysis of wage levels in unionized versus nonunionized workers in private manufacturing, has argued that without unionization, labor would have lost tremendously against other groups in the post-1963 period. But in assessing the potency of unionization during this period, the broader economic conjuncture which made large business a particularly 'soft' opponent must also be kept in mind. See Ataman Aksoy, "Wages, Relative Shares, and Unionization in Turkish Manufacturing," in Özbudun and Ulusan, pp. 409–54, 630.

22 See Merih Celasun, "Income Distribution and Employment Aspects of Turkey's Post-1980 Adjustment," in *ME TU Studies in Development*, vol. 16, no. 3–4, 1980, pp. 1–30.

23 My point on the significance of residential ordering of space is inspired by Katznelson's comparison of American and British working-class politics. See Ira Katznelson, *City Trenches* (New York: Pantheon, 1981), and his extension of the argument in "Working Class Formation and the State: Nineteenth-Century England in American Perspective," in Peter B. Evans *et. al.*, eds., *Bringing the State Back In* (Cambridge: Cambridge University Press, 1985), pp. 257–84.

24 On the historical evolution of Cairo's social ecology, see Abu Lughod, *Cairo: 1000 Years of the City of the Victorious* (Princeton: Princeton University Press, 1971); and also Saad Eddin Ibrahim, "Cairo: A Sociological Profile," in *The Expanding Metropolis: Coping with the Growth of Cairo*, Proceedings of the Aga Khan Seminar, held in Cairo, 1984. The volume contains a series of other useful articles on the ecology of contemporary Cairo.

25 See Galila el Kadi, "Market Mechanisms and Spontaneous Urbanization in Egypt: The Cairo Case," in *International Journal of Urban and Regional Research*, vol. 12, no. 1, March 1988, pp. 22–37.

26 For a discussion of informal land and housing markets in Istanbul from a planner's perspective, see Ayşe Yönder, "Informal Land and Housing Markets: The Case of Istanbul," in *American Planning Journal*, Spring 1987; on its political implications, see Ayşe Öncü, "The Politics of the Urban Land Market in Turkey: 1950–1980," in *International Journal of Urban and Regional Research*, vol. 12, no. 1, March 1988, pp. 65–86.

27 Theda Skocpol and Margaret Somers, "The Uses of Comparative History in Macrosocial Inquiry," *Comparative Studies in Society and History*, vol. 25, no. 2, April 1980, pp. 174–97.

Notes on Contributors

ABDEL MONEM SAID ALY is the Deputy Director for Research and Publications at the al-Ahram Center for Political and Strategic Studies in Cairo. He has been a fellow at the Brookings Institution, Washington, D.C., and has participated in research projects with similar institutions in Egypt and the Arab world and in the United States (Maryland University, Harvard University, Georgetown University) and France (EFRI). He has published in both Arabic and English on the topics of world systems, Middle East regional security, and Egypt's political system and national security.

GALAL A. AMIN is professor of economics at the American University in Cairo. He is the author of several books and numerous articles on economic theory, economic development, and the economic and cultural problems of the Arab world. His works include *The Modernization of Poverty* (Brill: 1974, 1980) and *The Arab East and the West* (in Arabic).

KORKUT BORATAV is professor of economics at the University of Ankara. He is the author of numerous books and collected volumes on the Turkish economy, including *Etatism in Turkey* (1974 and 1982, in Turkish); *Income Distribution* (1969, 1972, and 1980, in Turkish); *Agrarian Structures and Capitalism* (1980 and 1982, in Turkish). His recent publications in English have focused on the post–1980 structural adjustment policies in Turkey, such as *Stabilization and Adjustment Policies and Programs, Country Study 5: Turkey* (Helsinki, 1987) and numerous contributions to such collected volumes as *The Political Economy of Turkey: Debt, Adjustment, and Sustainability* (MacMillan, 1990) and *Problems of Developing Countries in the 1990s, Volume 2: Country Studies* (World Bank, 1990).

AYŞE BUĞRA is associate professor of economics at Boğaziçi University, Istanbul. She is the author of *Economics and People* (1989, in Turkish). Her works in English and French include articles on development theory and policy, the methodology of economics, and the history of economic thought in *Current Anthropology, Technological Forecasting and Social Change* , *Review of Radical Political Economics, Labor, Capital and Society, Interventions economiques*, *Mauss,* and other journals. Her current research is on the political context of business activity in Turkey.

ALI E. HILLAL DESSOUKI is professor of political science and director of the Center for Political Research and Studies at Cairo University. He has been a visiting professor at the University of California at Los Angeles and Princeton. His publications include *Islam and Power* (1981), *Islamic Resurgence in the Arab World* (1982), *Egypt and the Great Powers* (1983), *Egypt's Economic Policies* (1984), *The Foreign Policies of the States* (1984 and 1991), and *The Future of the Arab Nation* (1991).

ATILA ERALP is associate professor of international relations at the Middle East Technical University in Ankara. His current research interests include North–South relations in the changing international system and the role of foreign relations in constituting Turkish national identity. He has contributed articles on Turkey's political economy in such edited volumes as *Turkish State, Turkish Society* (Routledge, 1990) as well as various scholarly journals in both English and Turkish. He is the co-editor of *Socioeconomic Transformation of Turkey in the 1980s* (Praeger, 1993).

NADIA RAMSIS FARAH is a professor of economics and is currently director of the Arab Women's Center for Training and Research. She is the author of numerous publications concerning the problems of development in Egypt and the Arab world, the most recent of which are: *Religion in Egypt: Crisis and Ideological Conflict in the Seventies* (Gordon and Breech, 1986); *Women's Life and Helath in Egypt* (1991); *Population Profile in Egypt* (co-authored, 1991), and *Patterns of Arab Women Employment* (in press). Her articles on development have appeared in journals and collected volumes in both English and Arabic.

SAAD EDDIN IBRAHIM (co-editor) is professor of political sociology at the American University in Cairo, board member of the al-Ahram Center of Political and Strategic Studies, and Chairman of the Board of the Ibn Khaldun Center for Developmental Studies. Dr. Ibrahim has published extensively in both English and Arabic. His books include *The New Arab Social Order* (Westview, 1982); *Society and the State in The Arab World* (Beirut, 1988, in Arabic); *Minorities and Political Integration in the Arab World* (Beirut, 1988, in Arabic). He is the co-editor of *Arab Society in Transition* (AUC Press, 1977) and editor of *Egypt in a Quarter of a Century (1952-1977)* (Beirut, 1981, in Arabic).

AMANI KANDIL is senior research fellow at the Egyptian National Center for Sociological Research. Her fields of interest are that of public policies and interest groups and political parties in Egypt. Dr. Kandil's recent publications in Arabic include *Educational Policy in Egypt* (1990); *Privatization in Egypt* (ed., 1991); *Professional Associations and the Gulf War* (1992); *Public Opinion Polls on Political Parties* (1992). She has also contributed to various collected volumes in English.

ÇAĞLAR KEYDER (co-editor) was at the Department of Economics of the Middle East Technical University in Ankara and is currently associate professor of sociology at the State University of New York, Binghamton. He has published extensively in both English and Turkish in economic history, agrarian transformations, and political economy. His books include *Definition of a Peripheral Economy: Turkey 1923–29* (Cambridge, 1981); and *State and Class in Turkey: A Study in Capitalist Development* (Verso, 1987). Most recently, he has edited *Land and Commercial Agriculture in the Middle East* (1992).

AYŞE ÖNCÜ (co-editor) is professor of sociology at Boğaziçi University, Istanbul. She has been a visiting scholar at the G. E. von Grunebaum Center for Near Eastern Studies at the University of California. Her research interests include urban studies, economy–society relations, and interest organizations. Her articles have appeared in *International Social Science Journal, Current Sociology, International Journal of Urban and Regional Studies*, as well as various collected volumes. Most recently, she is the co-editor of *Turkey and the West: Changing Political and Cultural Identities* (Tauris, 1993).

İLKAY SUNAR is professor of political science at Boğaziçi University, Istanbul. He was an international fellow at the Hoover Institution, Stanford University, and visiting professor of political science at the University of California, Berkeley. His published works on state–society relations in Turkey and Turkish politics have appeared in *Annales E.S.C., Government and Opposition, Il Politico,* and also such collected volumes as *Transitions from Authoritarian Rule: Southern Europe* (Johns Hopkins University Press, 1986). Most recently, he is the co-author of *Policy Networks and Industrialization* (1992, in Turkish). He is currently interested in the problems of democratization and economic change in the Middle East.

Bibliography

al-Abd, Atif Adli, *The History of Egyptian Broadcasting*, UAE Broadcasting Institution, 1970.

———, *Egyptian Information: Past, Present and Future*, Ministry of Information, Cairo, 1988.

Abdel Khalek, Gouda, "Foreign Economic Aid and Income Distribution in Egypt, 1952–1977," in Gouda Abdel Khalek and Robert Tignor, eds., *The Political Economy of Income Distribution in Egypt*, Holmes and Meier, New York, 1982.

———, ed., *The Open Door Policy (Infitah)*, forthcoming.

——— and Robert Tignor, eds., *The Political Economy of Income Distribution in Egypt*, Holmes and Meier, New York, 1982.

Abdel Malek, Anouar, Anthologie de la Litérature Arabe Contemporaine, Editions de Seuil, Paris, 1965.

Abdel Rahman, Ibrahim Helmy and Mohammed Sultan Abu Ali, "Role of the Public and Private Sectors with Special Reference to Privatization: The Case of Egypt," in Said al-Naggar, ed., *Privatization and Structural Adjustment in the Arab Countries*, International Monetary Fund, Washington, D.C., 1989.

Abu Lughod, Janet, *Cairo: One Thousand and One Years of the City Victorious*, Princeton University Press, Princeton, 1971.

Abu Talib, Sufi, *Democratic Socialism* (in Arabic) Cairo, 1978.

Ahmad, Feroz, *İttihat ve Terakki: 1908–1914*, Sander Yayınları, Istanbul, 1971.

———, *The Turkish Experiment with Democracy*, C. Hurst and Co., London, 1977.

———, "Vanguard of a Nascent Bourgeoisie: The Social and Economic Policy of the Young Turks, 1908–1918," in Osman Okyar and Halil İnalcık, eds., *Social and Economic Policy of Turkey, 1081–1971*, Ankara, 1980.

Ahmed, Husni Khalil, "The Development of Capital Market in Egypt," paper presented at the Conference on Saving in Egypt, al-Mansura University, al-Mansura, April 1989.

Ajami, Fouad, "The Open-Door Economy: Its Roots and Welfare Consequences," in Gouda Abdel Khalek and Robert Tignor, eds., *The Political Economy of Income Distribution in Egypt*, Holmes and Meier, New York, 1982.

Akgüç, Öztin, *Türkiye'de Bankacılık*, Gerçek Yayınevi, Istanbul, 1987.
Aksoy, Ataman, "Wages, Relative Shares, and Unionization in Turkish Manufacturing," in Aydın Ulusan and Ergun Özbudun, eds., *The Political Economy of Income Distribution in Turkey*, Holmes and Meier, New York, 1980.
Alexander, Alec P., "Greek Industrialists," discussed in Erdoğan Soral, *Özel Kesimde Türk Müteşebbisleri*, AİTİA, Ankara, 1974.
———, "Industrial Entrepreneurship in Turkey: Origins and Growth," in *Economic Development and Cultural Change*, vol. 8, July 1960.
Alexandris, Alexis, *The Greek Minority of Istanbul and Greek–Turkish Relations, 1918–1974*, Center for Asia Minor Studies, Athens, 1983.
Alpander, Güvenç G., "Big Business and Big Business Leaders in Turkey," unpublished Ph.D. thesis, Michigan State University, 1966.
Aly, Abdel Monem Said, "The Superpowers and Regional Security in the Middle East: The Threat is Real," in Mohammed Ayoob, ed., *Regional Security in the Third World*, Croom Helm, London, 1986.
———, "The External Factors in the Security of the Middle East," in *Europe and the Security of the Middle East*, Arab Thought Forum, Amman, 1986.
———, "Democratization in Egypt," in *American–Arab Affairs*, Fall 1987.
———, "Egypt: A Decade After Camp David," in William B. Quandt, ed., *The Middle East: Ten Years After Camp David*, The Brookings Institution, Washington, D.C., 1988.
———, "Back to the Fold? Egypt and the Arab World," *Occasional Papers Series*, Center for Contemporary Arab Studies, Georgetown University, September 1988.
———, "Quality versus Ouantity: The Arab Perspective of the Arms Race in the Middle East," paper presented at the Conference on Arms Control and the Proliferation of High Technology Weapons in the Near East and South Asia, Bellagio, October 1989.
———, "The Myth and The Reality: The Four Faces of the Islamic Investment Companies," in Louis J. Cantori, ed., *Democratization of Egypt*, forthcoming.
———, "Privatization in Egypt: The Regional Dimensions," in Iliya Harik and Dennis Sullivan, eds., *Privatization and Liberalization in the Middle East*, Indiana University Press, Bloomington, 1992.
Amin, Galal A., *The Arab East and the West* (in Arabic), Center for Arab Unity Studies, Beirut, 1979.
———, "External Factors in the Reorientation of Egypt's Economic Policy," in Malcolm H. Kerr and Sayed el Yassin, eds., *Rich and Poor States in the Arab World*, Westview Press, Boulder, 1982.
———, "Adjustment and Development: The Case of Egypt," in Said el Nassar, ed., *Adjustment and Development Strategies in the Arab World*, International Monetary Fund, Washington, D.C., 1987.

———, *The Story of Egypt's External Debt* (in Arabic) Ali-Mukhtar, Cairo, 1987.

———, "The External Factors Leading to the Infitah (Open-Door)," in Gouda Abdel Khalek, ed., *The Open Door Policy (Infitah)*, forthcoming.

——— and E. Awny, *International Migration of Egyptian Labor*, International Development Research Center, Ottawa, 1985.

Amsden, Alice H., "Third World Industrialization: 'Global Fordism' or a New Model?" in *New Left Review*, no. 182, July/August 1990.

Anderson, Benedict, *Imagined Communities*, Verso, London, 1983.

Anderson, Lisa, "The State in the Middle East and North Africa," in *Comparative Politics*, vol. 20, no. 1, 1987.

Ansari, Hamied, *Egypt: The Stalled Society*, SUNY Press, Albany, 1986.

Arıcanlı, Tosun, "The Political Economy of Turkey's External Debt, the Bearing of Exogenous Factors," in Tosun Arıcanlı and Dani Rodrik, eds., *The Political Economy of Turkey: Debt, Adjustment and Sustainability*, MacMillan, London, 1990.

Arrighi, Giovanni, ed., *Semiperipheral Development: The Politics of Southern Europe in the Twentieth Century*, Sage, Beverly Hills, 1985.

Ashford, Douglas E., "The Challenge of Diversity to the Single Party States," paper presented at the 1963 Meeting of the American Political Science Association.

Assaad, Ragui, "Labor Underutilization and Segmented Labor Markets: The Case of Egypt," paper presented at the Cairo University Conference on Unemployment, January 1989.

Aston, Trevor Henry and C. H. E. Philpin, eds., *The Brenner Debate*, Cambridge University Press, Cambridge, 1985.

Awad, Lewis, "The Dialogue of Generations," in *al-Ahram*, 13 May 1989.

Ayoob, Mohammed, ed., *Regional Security in the Third World*, Croom Helm, London, 1986.

Ayubi, Nazih, *Bureaucracy and Politics in Contemporary Egypt*, Ithaca Press, London, 1980.

Babi, Don, "The World Bank and the IMF: Rolling Back the State or Backing Its Role," in Raymond Vernon, ed., *The Promise of Privatization*, Council on Foreign Relations, New York, 1988.

Baer, Gabriel, "Social Change in Egypt: 1821–1962," in Peter Malcolm Holt, ed., *Political and Social Change in Egypt, Historical Studies from the Ottoman Conquest to the United Arab Republic*, Oxford University Press, London, 1968.

Baker, Raymond William, *Egypt's Uncertain Revolution Under Nasser and Sadat*, Harvard University Press, Cambridge, 1978.

Bates, D. La Vere, "The Origins and Career Path Development of the Modern Turkish Business Elite," unpublished Ph.D. thesis, University of Arkansas, 1973.

Batou, Jean, ed., *Between Development and Underdevelopment: the Precocious Attempts at Industrialization of the Periphery, 1800–1870*, Droz, Geneva, 1991.
Bayar, Turgut, *La Türkiye İş Bankası*, Montreux, 1938.
Beinin, Joel, "Labor, Capital and the State in Nasserist Egypt, 1952–1961," in *International Journal of Middle East Studies* vol. 12, no. 1, 1989.
——— and Zachary Lockman, *Workers on the Nile*, Princeton University Press, Princeton, 1987.
Bell, Coral, *The Diplomacy of Detente, The Kissinger Era*, Martin Robertson, London, 1977.
Berkes, Niyazi, *The Development of Secularism in Turkey*, McGill University Press, Montreal, 1964.
Bianchi, Robert, *Interest Groups and Political Development in Turkey*, Princeton University Press, Princeton, 1983.
Binder, Leonard, *In a Moment of Enthusiasm: Political Power and the Second Stratum in Egypt*, University of Chicago Press, Chicago, 1978.
Birtek, Faruk, "The Rise and Fall of Etatism in Turkey, 1932–1950," in *Review*, vol. 8, no. 3, 1985.
——— and Çağlar Keyder, "Agriculture and the State: An Inquiry into Agricultural Differences and Political Alliances, The Case of Turkey," in *Journal of Peasant Studies*, vol. 2, no. 2, 1975.
al-Bishry, Tarek, *Democracy and Nasserism*, (in Arabic) al-Thaqafa al-Gadida, Cairo, 1975.
Blaisdell, D. C., *European Financial Control in the Ottoman Empire*, New York, 1929.
Blechman, Barry M. and Stephen S. Kaplan, *Force Without War: US Armed Forces as a Political Instrument*, The Brookings Institution, Washington, D.C., 1978.
Boratav, Korkut, "Kemalist Economic Policies and Etatism" in Ali Kazancıgil and Ergun Özbudun, eds., *Atatürk, Founder of a Modern State*, Archon Books, Hamden, 1981.
———, *Stabilization and Adjustment Policies and Programs, Country Study 5: Turkey*, Wider, Helsinki, 1987.
———, "Birikim Biçimleri ve Tarım," in Şevket Pamuk and Zafer Toprak, eds., *Türkiye'de Tarımsal Yapılar: 1923–2000*, Yurt Yayınları, Ankara, 1988.
———, "The Turkish Bourgeoisie and the State During a Major Reorientation of Economic Policies," paper presented at the Conference on Dynamics of State and Societies in the Middle East, Center for Political Research and Studies, Cairo University, June 1989.
———, "Intra-class and Inter-class Relations of Distribution under 'Structural Adjustment': Turkey during the 1980s," in Tosun Arıcanlı and Dani Rodrik, eds., *The Political Economy of Turkey: Debt, Adjustment and Sustainability*, Macmillan, London, 1990.

———, "The Medium-Term Prospects for the Turkish Economy," in F. Desmond McCarthy, ed., *Problems of Developing Countries in the 1990s, Volume 2: Country Studies*, The World Bank, Washington, D.C., 1990.

———, *1980'li Yıllarda Türkiye'de Sosyal Sınıflar ve Bölüşüm*, Gerçek Yayınevi, Istanbul, 1991.

——— and Galip Yalman, "A Study on the Political Economy of Structural Adjustment: Workers and Peasants during a Major Reorientation of Economic Policies: Turkey, 1980–1987," research paper prepared for IDRC, Canada, mimeo, 1989.

Borthwick, Bruce M., "Religion and Politics in Israel and Egypt," in *The Middle East Journal*, vol. 33, no. 2, 1979.

Bos, Eduard, My T. Uu, Ann Levin, and Rudolfo A. Bulatao, *World Population Projections: 1992–93,* Johns Hopkins University Press for the World Bank, 1992.

Boyd, Douglas A., *Broadcasting in the Arab World,* Temple University Press, Philadelphia, 1982.

Brecher, Michael, "The Middle East Subordinate System and Its Impact on Israel's Foreign Policy," in *International Studies Quarterly*, vol. 13, June 1969.

Buğra, Ayşe, "Turkish Holding Company as a Social Institution," in *Journal of Economics and Administrative Studies*, vol. 4, no. 1, 1990.

———, *State and Business in Modern Turkey: A Comparative Study,* State University of New York Press, Albany, 1994.

Burton, John W., *World Society*, Cambridge University Press, Cambridge, 1981.

Buss, Robin, "Wary Partners, The Soviet Union and Arab Socialism," *Adelphi Papers,* no. 73, International Institute for Strategic Studies, London, 1970.

Cantori, Louis J., ed., *Democratization of Egypt*, forthcoming.

——— and Iliya Harik, eds., *Local Politics and Development in the Middle East*, Westview Press, Boulder, 1984.

Cardoso, Fernando H. and Enzo Faletto, *Dependency and Development in Latin America*, University of California Press, Berkeley, 1979.

Celasun, Merih, "Income Distribution and Employment Aspects of Turkey's Post-1980 Adjustment," in *METU Studies in Development*, vol. 16, no. 3–4, 1989.

——— and Dani Rodrik, "Debt, Adjustment and Growth: Turkey," in Jeffrey D. Sachs and Susan M. Collins, eds., *Developing Country Debt and Economic Performance, Vol. 3: Country Studies, Indonesia, Korea, Philippines and Turkey*, University of Chicago Press, Chicago, 1989.

Central Agency for Public Mobilization and Statistics, *Statistical Indicators 1952–1973*, Cairo, 1974.

———, *Arab Republic of Egypt: Statistical Yearbook 1988*, Cairo, 1988.

Center for Political and Strategic Studies, "Interest Groups," in *The Arab Strategic Report 1986 and 1987, al-Ahram*, Cairo, 1987 and 1988.

Chelkowski, Peter and Robert J. Pranger, eds., *Ideology and Power in the Middle East,* Duke University Press, Durham, 1988.
Childs, W. J., "Armenia," in *Encyclopedia Britannica*, twelfth edition, vol. 30, 1922 (supplementary volume to the eleventh edition published in 1909).
Chipman, John, ed., *NATO's Southern Allies: Internal and External Challenges*, Routledge, London, 1988.
Chucri, Nazli, "Dimensions of National Security: The Case of Egypt," unpublished paper for the World Resource Institute, March 1987.
Clark, Edward C., "The Turkish Varlık Vergisi Reconsidered," in *Middle Eastern Studies*, vol. 8, no. 2, 1972.
Clarke, Michael, "Transnationalism," in Steve Smith, ed., *International Relations: British and American Prospectives*, Basil Blackwell, New York, 1985.
Cooper, Mark N., *The Transformation of Egypt*, Croome Helm, London, 1982.
Crecelius, Daniel, "Al-Azhar in the Revolution," in *The Middle East Journal*, vol. 20, no. 1, 1966.
———, "The Course of Secularisation in Modern Egypt," unpublished paper.
Crouchley, Arthur Edwin, *The Economic Development of Modern Egypt*, Longman Green Ltd., London, 1938.
Cuno, Kenneth, "The Origins of Private Ownership of Land in Egypt: A Reappraisal," in *International Journal of Middle East Studies*, vol. 12, no. 3, 1980.
Çetin, B., *Soygun: Hayali İhracatın Boyutları*, Bilgi, Ankara, 1988.
Davison, Roderic H., "Nationalism as an Ottoman Problem and the Ottoman Response," in William W. Haddad and William Ochsenwald, eds., *Nationalism in a Non-National State: The Dissolution of the Ottoman Empire*, Ohio State University Press, Columbus, 1977.
Denoueux, Guilain, "State and Society in Egypt," in *Comparative Politics*, vol. 20, no. 3, 1988.
Dessouki, Ali E. Hillal, "Arab Intellectuals and al-Nakba: The Search of Fundamentalism," in *Middle Eastern Studies*, vol. 9, no. 2, 1973.
———, *Big Land-Owners and Their Role in Egyptian Society* (in Arabic), al-Thaqafa al-Gadida, Cairo, 1975.
———, *Politics and Government in Egypt* (in Arabic) al-Sharq, Cairo, 1977.
———, ed., "Democracy in Egypt: Problems and Prospects," *Cairo Papers in Social Sciences*, vol. I, monograph no. 2, The American University in Cairo Press, Cairo, 1978.
———, "The Politics of Income Distribution in Egypt," in Gouda Abdel Khalek and Robert Tignor, eds., *The Political Economy of Income Distribution in Egypt*, Holmes and Meier, New York, 1982.
———, ed., *The Democratic Evolution in Egypt: Issues and Discussions* (in Arabic) Maktabat Nahdat al-Sharq, Cairo, 1986.

Deyo, Frederic, *The Political Economy of New Asian Industrialism*, Cornell University Press, Ithaca, 1987.

Di Tella, Torcuata, "Populism and Reform in Latin America" in Claudio Veliz, ed., *Obstacles to Change in Latin America*, Oxford University Press, London, 1970.

Dodwell, Henry Herbert, *The Founder of Modern Egypt: A Study of Mohamed Ali*, Cambridge University Press, Cambridge, 1931.

Dumont, Paul, "A propos de la classe ouvrière Ottomane à la veille de la révolution Jeune Turque," in *Turcica*, vol. 9, no. 1, 1977.

Egyptian National Center for Sociological and Criminological Research, *The Comprehensive Survey of the Egyptian Society, 1952–1980*, Cairo, 1985.

Egyptian Economic Society, *Proceedings of the 50th Anniversary*, Cairo, 1960.

Egyptian National Bank, *Economic Bulletin*, no. 3 and 4, 1987, Arabic version.

Eisenstadt, Shmuel Noah, *Modernization Protest and Change*, Prentice Hall, Inc., Englewood Cliffs, 1966.

Eldem, Vedat, *Osmanlı İmparatorluğunun İktisadi Şartları Hakkında bir Tetkik*, Türkiye İş Bankası Kültür Yayınları, Istanbul, 1970.

Eralp, Atila, "The Politics of Turkish Development Policy," in Andrew Finkel and Nükhet Sirman, eds., *Turkish State, Turkish Society*, Routledge, London, 1990.

———, "Turkey and the European Community: Prospects for a New Relationship," in Atila Eralp, Muharrem Tümay and Birol Yeşilada, eds., *Socioeconomic Transformation in Turkey Since 1980*, Praeger, New York, 1993.

Evans, Peter B., *Dependent Development: The Alliance of Multinationals, State and Local Capital in Brazil*, Princeton University Press, Princeton, 1979.

———, "Predatory, Developmental and Other Apparatuses: A Comparative Analysis of the Third World State," in *Sociological Forum*, no. 4, 1989.

——— and John D. Stephens, "Studying Development Since the Sixties: The Emergence of a New Comparative Political Economy," in *Theory and Society*, vol. 17, no. 6, 1988.

———, Deitrich Rueschemeyer and Theda Skocpol, eds., *Bringing the State Back In*, Cambridge University Press, Cambridge, 1985.

Fadil, M. Adel, *Development, Income Distribution and Social Change in Rural Egypt: 1952–1970*, Cambridge University Press, Cambridge, 1975.

Farah, Nadia Ramsis, "Science, Ideology and Authoritarianism in Middle East Economics," in Earl L. Sullivan and Jacqueline S. Ismael, eds., *The Contemporary Study of the Arab World*, University of Alberta Press, Edmonton, Alberta, 1991.

———, *Religious Strife in Egypt: Crisis and Ideological Conflict in the Seventies*, Gordon and Breach, New York and London, 1986.

Finkel, Andrew and Nükhet Sirman, eds., *Turkish State, Turkish Society*, Routledge, London, 1990.
Fergany, Nader, *Going After Salary: A Field Research on the Egyptian Migration to Work in Arab Countries* (in Arabic) Center for Arab Unity Studies, Beirut, 1988.
Gaddis, John L., *The United States and the Origins of the Cold War 1941–1947*, Columbus Press, New York, 1972.
Gameson, William A. and Andre Modigliani, *Untangling the Cold War*, Little, Brown, Boston, 1971.
Geddes, Barbara, "Building 'State' Autonomy in Brazil, 1930–1964," in *Comparative Politics*, vol. 22, no. 2, 1990.
Gellner, Ernest, *Thought and Change*, Cambridge University Press, Cambridge, 1964.
———, *Nations and Nationalism*, Cornell University Press, Ithaca, 1983.
Gerber, Haim, *The Social Origins of the Modern Middle East*, Lynne Reiner, Boulder, 1987.
Ghanem, Muhammed Hafez, "The Arab Socialist Union: A Comparative Study," (in Arabic) in *Egyptian Journal of Political Sciences*, no. 24, March 1963.
Goldberg, Ellis, *Tinker, Tailor, and Textile Worker: Class and Politics in Egypt*, University of California Press, Berkeley, 1986.
Gould, Andrew G., "Lords or Bandits? The Derebeys of Cilicia," in *International Journal of Middle East Studies*, vol. 7, no. 4, 1976.
Göle, Nilüfer, "Towards an Automization of Politics and Civil Society in Turkey," unpublished paper, Deutsches Orient Institut, Hamburg, 1988.
———, "Engineers and Technicist Ideology," in Metin Heper and Ayşe Öncü, eds., *Turkey and the West: Changing Political and Cultural Identities*, I. B. Tauris, London, 1993.
Gönlübol, Mehmet and Haluk Ulman, "İkinci Dünya Savaşından Sonra Türk Dış Politikası," in Mehmet Gönlübol et. al., *Olaylarla Türk Dış Politikası*, SBF, Ankara, 1987.
Gövsa, İbrahim Alaettin, *Sabatay Sevi, İzmir'li Meşhur Sahte Mesih Hakkında Tarihi ve İçtimai Tetkik Tecrübesi*, Semih Lütfi Kitabevi, Istanbul, 1940.
Grant, Wyn, ed., *Introduction to the Political Economy of Corporatism*, MacMillan, London, 1985.
Haddad, William W. and William Ochsenwald, eds., *Nationalism in a Non-National State: The Dissolution of the Ottoman Empire*, Ohio State University Press, Columbus, 1977.
Hafez, Afify, *On The Periphery of Egyptian Politics* (in Arabic) al-Kutub al-Misriya, Cairo, 1938.
Hale, William, *Political and Economic Development of Modern Turkey*, Croom Helm, London, 1981.
Halliday, Fred, *The Making of the Second Cold War*, Verso, London, 1984.

Halpern, Manfred, *Politics of Social Change in the Middle East and North Africa*, Princeton University Press, Princeton, 1963.

Handoussa, Heba, "Egypt's Investment Strategy, Policies and Performance since the *Infitah*," paper presented at the Seminar on Investment Policies in Arab Countries, Kuwait, 1989.

———, Mieko Nishimizu and John M. Page, "Productivity Change in Egyptian Public Sector Industries After 'The Opening', 1973–1979," in *Journal of Development Economics*, vol. 20, no. 1, 1986.

Hanke, Steve H., ed., *Prospects for Privatization*, The Academy of Political Science, New York, 1987.

Hanna, Sami and George Gardner, eds., *Arab Socialism*, E. J. Brill, Leiden, 1969.

Hansen, Bent, "Planning and Economic Growth in the UAR 1960–1963," in Panayiotis J. Vatikiotis, ed., *Egypt Since the Revolution*, Allen and Unwin, London, 1968.

Harb, Osama al-Gazali, "The Civil Society in Egypt', in *al-Ahram*, 8 April 1988.

Harik, Iliya, "Continuity and Change in Local Development Policies in Egypt: From Nasser to Sadat," in Louis J. Cantori and Iliya Harik, eds., *Local Politics and Development in the Middle East*, Westview Press, Boulder, 1984.

——— and Dennis Sullivan, eds., *Privatization and Liberalization in the Middle East*, Indiana University Press, Bloomington, 1992.

Heaphy, James, "The Organisation of Egypt," in *World Politics*, vol. 15, no. 3, 1966.

Heikal, Muhammad, *Sphinx and Commissar: The Rise and Fall of Soviet Influence in the Arab World*, Butler and Tanner, London, 1978.

———, *Years of Turmoil* (in Arabic), al-Ahram Center for Translation and Publications, Cairo, 1988, in Arabic.

Helal, Aly Din, ed., *Egyptian Political System*, Cairo University, 1986.

Heper, Metin, ed., *Strong State and Economic Interest Groups: The Post-1980 Experience*, Walter de Gruyter, New York, 1992.

——— and Ayşe Öncü, eds., *Turkey and the West: Changing Political and Cultural Identities*, I. B. Tauris, London, 1993.

Herschlag, Zvi Yehuda, *Introduction to the Modern Economic History of the Middle East*, E. J. Brill, Leiden, 1964

Hill, Enid, "Legislating Development in Egypt: 1971–1986," paper presented at the Conference on Dynamics of States and Societies in the Middle East, Center for Political Research and Studies, Cairo, June 1989.

Herz, John H., "The Rise and Demise of the Territorial State," in *World Politics*, vol. 13, no. 3, 1961.

———, *The Nation State and the Crisis in World Politics*, McKay, New York, 1976.

Hila, Rida, *The Making of Dependency* (in Arabic) Dar al-Mustaqbal al-'Arabi, Cairo, 1987.
Hilal, Ali E., "Mubarak and the Completion of the Democratic March," in *al-Ahram al-Iqtisadi*, 20 April 1987.
Hinnebusch, Raymond, "Egypt Under Sadat: Elites, Power Structure, and Political Change in a Post-Populist State," in *Social Problems*, vol. 28, no. 4, 1981.
———, *Egyptian Politics Under Sadat*, Lynne Rienner Publishers, Inc., New York, 1988 (updated edition).
Hirschmann, Albert O., "The Political Economy of Import Substituting Industrialisation in Latin America," in *The Quarterly Journal of Economics*, vol. 82, no. 1, 1968.
Holt, Peter Malcolm, ed., *Political and Social Change in Egypt, Historical Studies from the Ottoman Conquest to the United Arab Republic*, Oxford University Press, London, 1968.
Hoopwood, Derek, *Egypt: Politics and Society: 1945–1984*, Allen and Unwin, London, 1985.
Hussein, Adel, *Egyptian Economy From Independence to Dependency: 1974–1979* (in Arabic) (2 vols.), Dar al-Mustaqbal al-'Arabi, Cairo, 1982.
Hussein, Mahmoud, *Class Conflict in Egypt: 1945–1970*, Monthly Review Press, New York, 1973.
Ibrahim, I. I., "The Egyptian Intellectuals Between Tradition and Modernity: A Study in Some Important Trends in Egyptian Thought: 1922–1952," unpublished Ph.D. thesis, Oxford University, 1967.
Ibrahim, Saad Eddin, "The Social Project," in Saad Eddin Ibrahim, ed., *Egypt in a Quarter of a Century*, Arab Institute of Development Studies, Beirut, 1980.
———, "The Social Project of the July Revolution," in Saad Eddin Ibrahim, ed., *Egypt, Arabism and the July Revolution* (in Arabic) Center for Arab Unity Studies, Beirut, 1982.
———, "Social Mobility and Income Distribution in Egypt: 1952–1977," in Gouda Abdel Khalek and Robert Tignor, eds., *The Political Economy of Income Distribution in Egypt*, Holmes and Meier, New York, 1982.
———, *The New Arab Social Order*, Westview Press, Boulder, 1982.
———, "Cairo: A Sociological Profile," in *The Expanding Metropolis: Coping with the Growth of Cairo*, The Aga Khan Award, Geneva, 1985.
International Labor Organization, *Employment Opportunities and Equity in Egypt*, Geneva, 1982.
Imam, Samia, *Who Owns Egypt? An Analytical Study of the Social Origins of the Infitah Elite: 1974–1980* (in Arabic) Dar al-Mustaqbal al-'Arabi, Cairo, 1986.
———, *Analyzing the Social Roots of the Open-Door Policy in Egypt* (in Arabic) Dar al-Mustaqbal al-'Arabi, Cairo, 1986.

———, "Three Tributaries of Egyptian Capitalism in the Open Door Policy" in Shumizu et. al., *Introductory Notes for the Study of Pressure Groups in Egypt*, Middle East Studies Series, Cairo, 1988.

İnalcık, Halil, "Centralization and Decentralization in Ottoman Administration," in Thomas Naff and Roger Owen, eds., *Studies in Eighteenth Century Islamic History*, University of Southern Illinois Press, Carbondale, 1977.

İnan, Afet, *Devletçilik İlkesi ve Türkiye Cumhuriyetinin Birinci Sanayi Planı*, Türk Tarih Kurumu, Ankara, 1975.

Issawi, Charles, *Egypt at Mid-Century: An Economic Survey*, Oxford University Press, London, 1954.

———, *Egypt in Revolution: An Economic Analysis*, Oxford University Press, London, 1963.

———, ed., *The Economic History of the Middle East*, University of Chicago Press, Chicago, 1966.

Issawi, Ibrahim, "The Internal Factors Leading to the Infitah (Open-Door)," in Abdel Khalek, ed., *The Open Door Policy (Infitah)*, forthcoming.

Işıklı, Alpaslan, "Wage Labor and Unionization," in Irvin C. Schick and Ahmet Tonak, eds., *Turkey in Transition: New Pespectives*, Oxford University Press, New York, 1987.

Japanese Embassy, Cairo, *Japan Information Bulletin*, 15 April 1989.

Jargy, Simon, "La Syrie à la veille d'une nouvelle expérience," in *Orient*, no. 10, 1958.

El Kadi, Galila, "Market Mechanisms and Spontaneous Urbanization in Egypt: The Cairo Case," in *International Journal of Urban and Regional Research*, vol. 12, no. 1, 1988.

Kandil, Amani, "Public Policy-Making in Egypt: A Case Study of Economic Policy: 1974–1981," unpublished Ph.D. thesis, Cairo University, 1985.

———, "Political Evolution in Egypt and the Making of Public Policies," in Ali E. Hillal Dessouki, ed., *The Democratic Evolution in Egypt: Issues and Discussions* (in Arabic) Maktabat Nahdat al-Sharq, Cairo, 1986.

———, "Interest Groups and Foreign Policy," paper presented at the Annual Conference of Political Research, Cairo University, December 1988.

———, "Labor and Business Interest Representation in Egypt," paper presented at the Conference on Dynamics of State and Society in the Middle East, Cairo, 1989.

———, ed., *The Transfer Towards the Private Sector*, Center for Political Research and Studies, Cairo, 1989.

———, "Educational Policy in Egypt and the Nile Valley," Arab Thought Forum, 1989.

Kandil, Hamdi, "Mass Communication and Integration in the Arab World," in *al-Mustaqbal al-'Arabi*, no. 107, January 1988.

———, "The Future of the Arab Television," in *al-Ahram*, 11 June 1990.

Kaplan, Stephen S., *Diplomacy of Power: Soviet Armed Forces as a Political Instrument*, The Brookings Institution, Washington, D.C., 1981.

Karaosmanoğlu, Ali, "Turkey's Security and the Middle East," in *Foreign Affairs*, vol. 62, no. 1, 1983.
———, "Turkey and the Southern Flank: Domestic and External Contexts," in John Chipman, ed., *NATO's Southern Allies: Internal and External Challenges*, Routledge, London, 1988.
Karpat, Kemal H., *Ottoman Population 1830–1914, Demographic and Social Characteristics*, University of Wisconsin Press, Madison, 1985.
Kasaba, Reşat, *The Ottoman Empire and the World Economy*, SUNY Press, Albany, 1988.
———, "Was There a Comprador Bourgeoisie in Mid-Nineteenth Century Western Anatolia?" in Çağlar Keyder, ed., *Ottoman Empire: Nineteenth-Century Transformations*, special issue of *Review*, vol. 11, no. 2, 1988.
Kass, Iiana, *Soviet Involvement in the Middle East: Policy Formulation, 1966–1973*, Westview Press, Boulder, 1978.
Katzenstein, Peter, "Domestic and International Structures and Strategies of Foreign Economic Policy" in *International Organization*, vol. 31, no. 4, 1977.
Katznelson, Ira, *City Trenches*, Pantheon, New York, 1981.
———, "Working Class Formation and the State: Nineteenth-Century England in American Perspective," in Peter B. Evans, Dietrich Rueschemeyer and Theda Skocpol, eds., *Bringing the State Back In*, Cambridge University Press, Cambridge, 1985.
Kazancıgil, Ali and Ergun Özbudun, eds., *Atatürk, Founder of a Modern State*, Archon Books, Hamden, 1981.
Keohane, Robert O., "Transnational Relations and World Politics," in *International Organization*, vol. 25, no. 3, 1971.
——— and Joseph S. Nye, *Power and Interdependence*, Little, Brown, Boston, 1977.
Kerr, Malcolm H., *The Arab Cold War: Gamal Abdel Nassir and His Rivals 1958–1970*, Oxford University Press, New York, 1971.
——— and Sayed el Yassin, eds., *Rich and Poor States in the Arab World*, Westview Press, Boulder, 1982.
Kerwin, R.W., "Private Enterprise in Turkish Economic Development," in *Middle East Journal*, vol. 5, no. 1, 1951.
Keyder, Çağlar, *The Definition of a Peripheral Economy: Turkey 1923–1929*, Cambridge University Press and Maison des Sciences de l'Homme, Cambridge, 1981.
———, "The Genesis and Structure of Small Peasant Ownership in Agriculture," in *Review*, vol. 7, no. 1, 1983.
———, "The American Recovery of Europe: Aid and Hegemony," in Giovanni Arrighi, ed., *Semiperipheral Development: The Politics of Southern Europe in the Twentieth Century*, Sage, Beverly Hills, 1985.
———, *State and Class in Turkey. A Study in Capitalist Development*, Verso, London, 1987.

———, ed., *Ottoman Empire: Nineteenth-Century Transformations*, special issue of *Review*, vol. 11, no. 2, 1988.
———, "Creation and Destruction of Forms of Manufacturing: the Ottoman Example," in Jean Batou, ed., *Between Development and Underdevelopment: the Precocious Attempts at Industrialization of the Periphery, 1800–1870*, Droz, Geneva, 1991.
——— and Faruk Tabak, eds., *Landholding and Commercial Agriculture in the Middle East*, SUNY Press, Albany, 1991.
——— and Donald Quataert, eds., "The Impact of 1838 on Anatolia and Egypt," special issue of *New Perspectives on Turkey*, no. 7, Spring 1992.
——— and Donald Quataert, eds., *Port-Cities in the Eastern Mediterranean*, special issue of *Review*, forthcoming.
al-Khafif, Mohamed, "Tahaluf quwwat al-sha'b" (The Alliance of people's forces), paper written for the Higher Institute for Socialist Studies, formerly the Arab Socialist Union Cadre School, mimeo.
Khalil, Mohamed, *The Arab States and the Arab League* (in Arabic) vol. I, Khayat, Beirut, 1962.
al-Khatib, M. Fathalla, "Egypt's New Constitution: An Appraisal in the Light of Past Experiences," in *Review of Economics, Political and Business Studies*, Faculty of Commerce, Cairo University, vol. 4, no. 3–4, 1956.
Khedr, Hassan and Amin Hassouna, *Egypt's Republic in its First Year*, the Department of Public Relations of the Egyptian Armed Forces, Cairo, 1957.
Kissinger, Henry, *White House Years*, Little, Brown, Boston, 1979.
———, *Years of Upheaval*, Little, Brown, Boston, 1982.
Kitab al-Ahram al-Iqtisadi, *Islamic Investment Companies: The Rise, The Collapse, and the Future*, Cairo, June 1988.
Koç, Vehbi, *Hayat Hikayem*, Istanbul, 1973.
Korany, Baghat, "The Crisis of Arab Society: A Research on the Premises and Consequences of the Contemporary Arab Political Economy," in *al-Mustaqbal al-Arabi*, no. 60, February 1984.
Kurmuş, Orhan, *Emperyalizmin Türkiye'ye Girişi*, Bilim, Istanbul, 1974.
Laclau, Ernesto, *Politics and Ideology in Marxist Theory*, New Left Review Books, London, 1977.
Lacouture, Jean and Simone, *Egypt in Transition*, Criterion Books, New York, 1959.
Landes, David S., *Bankers and Pashas: International Finance and Economic Imperialism in Egypt*, Harvard University Press, Cambridge, 1958.
Lapidus, Ira, *A History of Islamic Societies*, Cambridge University Press, Cambridge, 1988.
Laroui, Abdullah, *The Crisis of Arab Intellectuals*, University of California Press, Berkeley, 1976.
Lerner, Daniel, *The Passing of Traditional Society*, The Free Press of Glencoe, New York, 1964.

Lewis, Bernard, *The Emergence of Modern Turkey*, Princeton University Press, Princeton, 1968.

Lindblom, Charles Edward, *Politics and Markets*, Basic Books, New York, 1977.

Lipset, Seymour M., *Political Man*, Doubleday, New York, 1963.

Mabro, Robert, *The Egyptian Economy: 1952–1972*, Clarendon Press, Oxford, 1974.

——— and Samir Radwan, *The Industrialisation of Egypt 1939–1973*, Clarendon Press, Oxford, 1976.

Mannheim, Karl, *Ideology and Utopia*, Routledge and Kegan Paul, London, 1952.

———, *Essays on Sociology and Social Psychology*, MacMillan, London, 1953.

Marguiles, Ronnie and Ergin Yıldızoğlu, "Agrarian Change: 1923–1970," in Irvin C. Schick and E. Ahmet Tonak, eds., *Turkey in Transition: New Perspectives*, Oxford University Press, Oxford, 1987.

Martin, Cathie Jo, "Business Influence and State Power: The Case of US Corporate Tax Policy," in *Politics and Society*, vol. 17, no. 2, 1989.

Maxfield, S. and J. H. Nolt, "Protectionism and the Internationalization of Capital: US Sponsorship of Import Substitution Industrialization in the Philippines, Turkey, and Argentina," in *International Studies Quarterly*, vol. 34, no. 1, 1990.

McCarthy, Desmond, ed., *Problems of Developing Countries in the 1990s, Volume 2: Country Studies*, The World Bank, Washington, D.C., 1990.

McCarthy, Justin, "Foundations of the Turkish Republic: Social and Economic Change," in *Middle Eastern Studies*, vol. 19, no. 2, 1983.

Meyer, Gunter, "Employment in Small-Scale Manufacturing in Cairo: A Socio-Economic Survey," in *British Society for Middle Eastern Studies Bulletin*, vol. 14, no. 2, 1988.

Migdal, Joel S., *Strong Societies and Weak States: State–Society Relations and State Capabilities in the Third World*, Princeton University Press, Princeton, 1988.

Mohyeddin, A. and Saad Eddin Ibrahim "State Socialism and Economic Development," in Saad Eddin Ibrahim, ed., *Egypt in a Quarter of a Century*, Arab Institute of Development Studies, Beirut, 1980.

Mokhtar, Ibrahim, *Egypt's Banks* (in Arabic) Kitab al-Ahram al-Iqtisadi, Cairo, 1988.

Moneim, Ahmad Fares Abdel, "Interest Groups," in Aly Din Helal, ed., *Egyptian Political System*, Cairo University, 1986.

Morsy, F., *This Open Door Economic Policy* (in Arabic) al-Wihda, Beirut, 1981.

Mourad, M., *Who Ruled Egypt?* (in Arabic) Madbuli, Cairo, 1975.

Mouzelis, Nicos, *Politics in the Semi-Periphery*, Macmillan, London, 1986.

Mumcuoğlu, Maksut, "Political Activites of Trade Unions and Income Distribution," in Aydın Ulusan and Ergun Özbudun, eds., *The Political Economy of Income Distribution in Turkey*, Holmes and Meier, New York, 1980.

Naff, Thomas and Roger Owen, eds., *Studies in Eighteenth Century Islamic History*, University of Southern Illinois Press, Carbondale, 1977.
al-Naggar, Ahmad, "Temporary Migration From Egypt," unpublished research, Arab Research Center, Cairo, 1990.
al-Naggar, Said, "On The New Investment Law," in *al-Ahram*, 31 May 1989.
———, ed., *Privatization and Structural Adjustment in the Arab Countries*, International Monetary Fund, Washington, D.C., 1989.
Naguib, Mohamed, *Egypt's Destiny*, Doubleday, New York, 1955.
El Nassar, Said, ed., *Adjustment and Development Strategies in the Arab World*, International Monetary Fund, Washington, D.C., 1987.
Nasser, Gamal Abdel, *Egypt's Liberation, The Philosophy of the Revolution*, translated by Dorothy Thompson, Washington, D.C., 1953.
———, "The Egyptian Revolution," in *Foreign Affairs*, vol. 33, no. 1, 1965.
National Center for Sociological and Criminological Research, *The Comprehensive Survey of the Egyptian Society, 1952–1980* (in Arabic) Cairo, 1985.
———, *On Stratification* (in Arabic) Cairo, 1985.
Nye, Joseph S., "The Transformation of American Power," in *Aspen Institute Quarterly*, no. 2, Winter 1990.
O'Donnel, Guillermo, Philippe C. Schmitter, and Laurence Whitehead, eds., *Transitions From Authoritarian Rule: Experiences in Southern Europe and Latin America*, Johns Hopkins University Press, Baltimore, 1986.
Okyar, Osman and Halil İnalcık, eds., *Social and Economic Policy of Turkey, 1071–1920*, Ankara, 1980.
OECD, *1988 Report: Development Cooperation*, December 1988.
Osgood, Robert E., "Introduction: Reappraisal of American Policy," in Robert E. Osgood et. al., *America and the World: From the Truman Doctrine to Vietnam*, Johns Hopkins University Press, Baltimore, 1970.
——— et. al., *Retreat from Empire: The First Nixon Administration*, Johns Hopkins University Press, Baltimore, 1973.
Owen, Roger, *Cotton and the Egyptian Economy 1820–1914*, Oxford University Press, Oxford, 1969.
———, *The Middle East in the World Economy, 1800–1914*, Methuen, London, 1981.
Ökçün, Gündüz, ed., *Osmanlı Sanayii: 1913, 1915 Yılları Sanayi İstatistiki*, SBF, Ankara, 1970.
———, *1920–1930 Yılları Arasında Kurulan Türk Anonim Şirketlerinde Yabancı Sermaye Sorunu*, SBF, Ankara, 1971.
Ökte, Faik, *Varlık Vergisi Faciası*, Istanbul, 1951.
Öncü, Ayşe, "Chambers of Industry in Turkey: An Inquiry into State–Industry Relations as a Distributive Domain," in Aydın Ulusan and Ergun Özbudun, eds., *The Political Economy of Income Distribution in Turkey*, Holmes and Meier, New York, 1980.
———, "Militarism and Corporatism in Turkish Politics," paper presented at the Conference on History and Society in Turkey, Berlin Institute for Comparative Social Research, Berlin, December 1981.

———, "The Politics of the Urban Land Market in Turkey: 1950–1980," in *International Journal of Urban and Regional Research*, vol. 12, no. 1, 1988.
——— and Deniz Gökçe, "Macro-Politics of De-Regulation and Micro-Politics of Banks," in Metin Heper, ed., *Strong State and Economic Interest Groups: The Post-1980 Experience*, Walter de Gruyter, New York, 1992.
Pamuk, Şevket, *The Ottoman Empire and European Capitalism, 1820–1913*, Cambridge University Press, Cambridge, 1987.
———, "War, State Economic Policies and Resistance by Agricultural Producers in Turkey, 1939–1945," in *New Perspectives on Turkey*, vol. 2, no. 1, 1988.
———, "The Ottoman Empire in Comparative Perspective," in Çağlar Keyder, ed., *Ottoman Empire: Nineteenth-Century Transformations*, special issue of *Review*, vol. 11, no. 2, 1988.
——— and Zafer Toprak, eds., *Türkiye'de Tarımsal Yapılar: 1923–2000*, Yurt Yayınları, Ankara, 1988.
Payaslıoğlu, Arif, *Türkiye'de Özel Sanayi Alanında Müteşebbisler ve Teşebbüsler*, SBF, Ankara, 1961.
Pentzopoulos, Dimitri, *The Balkan Exchange of Minorities and its Impact upon Greece*, Mouton, Paris, 1962.
Peretz, Don, "Democracy and the Revolution in Egypt', in *Middle East Journal*, vol. 13, no. 1, 1959.
Polanyi, Karl, *The Great Transformation*, Beacon Press, Boston, 1957.
Puryear, Vernon John, *International Economics and Diplomacy in the Near East, 1834–1853*, Stanford University Press, Palo Alto, 1935.
Quandt, William B., ed., *The Middle East: Ten Years After Camp David*, The Brookings Institution, Washington, D.C., 1988.
Radwan, Samir and Bent Hansen, *Employment Opportunities and Equity in Egypt: A Labor Market Approach*, International Labor Office, Geneva, 1982.
Ramadan, A., *Class Conflict in Egypt: 1937–1952* (in Arabic) al-Mu'assasa al-'Arabiya li-l-Dirasat wa-l-Nashr, Cairo, 1978.
Richards, Alan R., "Primitive Accumulation in Egypt, 1798–1882," in *Review*, vol. 1, no. 2, 1977.
Rivlin, Helen, *The Agricultural Policy of Muhammad Ali in Egypt*, Harvard University Press, Cambridge, 1969.
Rodinson, Maxime, "The Political System," in Panayiotis J. Vatikiotis, ed., *Egypt Since the Revolution*, Allen and Unwin, London, 1968.
Rostow, Eugene V., "America, Europe and the Middle East," in *Commentary*, February 1974.
Rosusney, Marsha, "Workers Against the State: Wage Protest in Egypt, 1952–1988," paper presented at MESA Annual Meeting, Los Angeles, 1988.
———, "Labor as an Obstacle to Privatization: The Case of Egypt," paper presented at the MESA Annual Meeting, Toronto, 1989.
Runciman, Walter Garrison, *Social Science and Political Theory*, Cambridge University Press, London, 1965.

Sabancı, Sakıp, *İşte Hayatım*, Istanbul, 1985.
Sachs, Jeffrey D. and Susan M. Collins, eds., *Developing Country Debt and Economic Performance, Vol. 3: Country Studies, Indonesia, Korea, Philippines and Turkey*, University of Chicago Press, Chicago, 1989.
Sadowski, Yahya, "Is There a Civil Society in Egypt?," paper presented at the New York Social Science Research Council Conference, 1989.
Said, Mohamed al-Sayed, "The Political Economy of Migration in Egypt 1974–1989," paper presented at the Seminar on International Worker Migration: Political, Economic and Social Change in Turkey and Egypt, Istanbul, June 1989.
Salame, Ghassan, "Introduction," in Ghassan Salame, ed., *The Foundation of the Arab State*, Croom Helm, London, 1987.
Sander, Oral, *Türk-Amerikan İlişkileri 1947–1964*, SBF, Ankara, 1979.
Sayegh, Fayez, "The Theoretical Structure of Nasser's Socialism," in Sami Hanna and George Gardner, eds., *Arab Socialism*, E. J. Brill, Leiden, 1969.
Saybaşılı, Kemali, "Chambers of Commerce and Industry, Political Parties and Governments: An Analysis of the British and Turkish Cases," in *METU Studies in Development*, no. 11, Spring 1976.
Schölch, Alexander, *Egypt for the Egyptians*, Ithaca Press, London, 1981.
Segal, Ronald, *Political Africa*, Praeger, New York, 1961.
Sezer, Duygu, "Turkey's Security Policies," *Adelphi Papers*, no. 164, International Institute for Strategic Studies, London, 1981.
———, "Turkey in the Western Alliance in the 1980s," in Atila Eralp, Muharrem Tünay, and Birol Yeşilada, eds., *Socioeconomic Transformation in Turkey Since 1980*, Praeger, New York, forthcoming.
Shefter, Martin, "Party and Patronage: Germany, England, and Italy," in *Politics and Society*, vol. 7, no. 4, 1977.
Schick, Irvin C. and E. Ahmet Tonak, eds., *Turkey in Transition: New Perspectives*, Oxford University Press, Oxford, 1987.
Shihata, Ibrahim, *The World Bank and The Arab World*, al-Hilal, Cairo, 1990.
Shorter, Frederic C., "The Population of Turkey after the War of Independence," in *International Journal of Middle East Studies*, vol. 17, no. 4, 1985.
———, "Cairo's Leap Forward," *Cairo Papers in Social Science*, volume 12, monograph 1, Spring 1989.
Shumizu, M. et. al., *Introductory Notes for the Study of Pressure Groups in Egypt*, Middle East Studies Series, Cairo, 1988.
Singer, Morris, *The Economic Advance of Turkey, 1938–1960*, Ankara, 1977.
Skocpol, Theda and Margaret Somers, "The Uses of Comparative History in Macrosocial Inquiry," in *Comparative Studies in Society and History*, vol. 25, no. 2, 1980.
Smith, Steve, ed., *International Relations: British and American Prospectives*, Basil Blackwell, New York, 1985.
Soos, Regina, "The Alexandria Tire Company: An Experiment in Privatization," in *Business Monthly*, February 1989.

Soral, Erdoğan, *Özel Kesimde Türk Müteşebbisleri*, AİTİA, Ankara, 1974.
Sousa, Nasim, *The Capitulatory Regime of Turkey*, Johns Hopkins University Press, Baltimore, 1934.
Sönmez, Mustafa, *Kırk Haramiler*, Gözlem Yayıncılık, Istanbul, 1987.
Spiro, Herbert J., "The Primacy of Political Development," in Herbert J. Spiro, ed., *Africa: The Primacy of Politics*, Random House, New York, 1966.
Springborg, Robert, *Family, Power and Politics in Egypt,* University of Pennsylvania Press, Philadelphia, 1982.
———, "Approaches to the Understanding of Egypt" in Peter Chelkowski and Robert J. Pranger, eds., *Ideology and Power in the Middle East*, Duke University Press, Durham, 1988.
———, *Mubarak's Egypt: Fragmentation of the Political Order*, Westview Press, Boulder, 1989.
Streeck, Wolfgang and Philippe C. Schimitter, "Community, Market, State- and Associations? The Prospective Contribution of Interest Governance to Social Order" in Wolfgang Streeck and Philippe C. Schimitter, *Private Interest Government*, Sage, Series in New Corporatism, London, 1985.
———, "Between Pluralism and Corporatism: German Business Associations and the State," in *Journal of Public Policy*, vol. 3, August 1983.
Stuermer, Harry, *Deux ans de guerre à Constantinople*, Paris, 1914.
Sullivan, Earl L. and Jacqueline S. Ismael, eds., *The Contemporary Study of the Arab World*, University of Alberta Press, Edmonton, 1991.
Sunar, İlkay, "Populism and Patronage: The Demokrat Party and its Legacy," in *Il Politico*, October-December 1990.
——— and Sabri Sayarı, "Democracy in Turkey: Problems and Prospects," in Guillermo O'Donnell, Philippe C. Schmitter and Laurence Whitehead, eds., *Transitions From Authoritarian Rule: Experiences in Southern Europe and Latin America,* Johns Hopkins University Press, Baltimore, 1986.
Sussnitzki, A. J., "Ethnic Division of Labor," in Charles Issawi, ed., *The Economic History of the Middle East*, University of Chicago Press, Chicago, 1966.
Tahsin, Hamit and Remzi Saka, *Sermaye Hareketi*, Amedi Matbaası, Istanbul, 1930.
——— and Remzi Saka, *Sermayenin Şirketlerdeki Hareketi*, Hüsnütabiat Matbaası, Istanbul, 1929.
Tanju, Sadun, *Hacı Ömer*, Apa Ofset, Istanbul, 1983.
Tekbaş, M.S., "Türkiye'de Holding Uygulaması Üzerine Bir Çalışma," unpublished Ph.D. thesis, Istanbul, 1972.
Tekeli, İlhan and Selim İlkin, *1929 Dünya Buhranında Türkiye'nin İktisadi Politika Arayışları*, ODTÜ, Ankara, 1977.
——— and Selim İlkin, *Para ve Kredi Sisteminin Oluşumunda bir Aşama: T.C. Merkez Bankası*, Ankara, 1981.

——— and Selim İlkin, *Uygulamaya Geçerken Türkiye'de Devletçiliğin Oluşumu,* Ankara, 1982.
——— and Selim İlkin, "Savaşmayan Ülkenin Savaş Ekonomisi: Üretimden Tüketime Pamuklu Dokuma," paper presented at Türk Tarih Kongresi, Ankara, September 1986.
Thornburg, Max, *Turkey, An Economic Appraisal,* New York, 1949.
Tignor, Robert, "The Economic Activities of Foreigners in Egypt, 1920–1950: From Millet to Haute Bourgeoisie," in *Comparative Studies in Society and History,* vol. 22, no. 3, 1980.
———, *State, Private Enterprise, and Economic Change in Egypt. 1918–1952,* Princeton University Press, Princeton, 1984.
Toprak, Zafer, *Türkiye'de Milli İktisat,* Yurt Yayınları, Ankara, 1982.
Tsuji, Kiyotake, *Forecast: OPEC's 1989 Oil Revenues and Current Account,* The Japanese Institute of Middle East Economies, Tokyo, 1989.
Türel, Oktar, ed., *Two Decades of Planned Development in Turkey,* special issue of *METU Sudies in Development,* 1981.
Ulugay, Osman, *Kim Kazandı, Kim Kaybetti?,* Bilgi, Ankara, 1987.
Ulusan, Aydın and Ergun Özbudun, eds., *The Political Economy of Income Distribution in Turkey,* Holmes and Meier, New York, 1980.
USAID, *US Overseas Loans and Grants: Military Assistance and Foreign Military Sales,* Cairo, 1973.
———, *Privatization in Egypt,* Cairo, 1988.
———, *Status Report: United States' Economic Assistance to Egypt,* Cairo, 1989.
———, *Status Report 1990,* Cairo, 1990.
US Department of State, *Communist States and Developing Countries: Aid and Trade in 1972,* RECS-10, 1973.
US Embassy, Cairo, *Economic Trends Report,* 1986.
———, *Egyptian Economic Trends,* 1989.
———, *Economic Report of Egypt,* 1990.
Uygur, E., *Policy, Productivity, Growth and Employment in Turkey, 1960–1989 and Prospects for the 1990s,* mimeo, 1990.
Vacalopoulos, Apostolos E., *A History of Thessaloniki,* Institute of Balkan Studies, Salonica, 1963.
Vatikiotis, Panayiotis J., *The Egyptian Army in Politics,* Indiana University Press, Bloomington, 1961.
——— ed., *Egypt Since the Revolution,* Allen and Unwin, London, 1968.
Veliz, Claudio, ed., *Obstacles to Change in Latin America,* Oxford University Press, London, 1970.
Vernon, Raymond, "Introduction: The Promise and the Challenge," in Raymond Vernon, ed., *The Promise of Privatization,* Council on Foreign Relations, New York, 1988.
Vitalis, Robert, "On the Theory and Practice of Compradors. The Role of Abbud Pasha in Egypt's Political Economy," in *International Journal of Middle East Studies,* vol. 22, no. 3, 1990.

Von Grunebaum, Gustave E., *Modern Islam*, University of California Press, Berkeley, 1962.

Vuylsteke, Charles, *Techniques of Privatization of State-Owned Enterprises*, The World Bank, Washington, D.C., 1988.

Walker, Michael A., ed., *Privatization Tactics and Techniques*, The Fraser Institute, Vancouver, 1988.

Waterbury, John, *Egypt: Burdens of the Past / Options for the Future*, Indiana University Press, Bloomington, 1978.

———, *The Egypt of Nasser and Sadat: The Political Economy of Two Regimes*, Princeton University Press, Princeton, 1983.

——— and Alan Richards, *A Political Economy of the Middle East: State Class and Economic Development*, Westview Press, Boulder, 1990.

Whealock, Keith, *Nasser's New Egypt*, Praeger, New York, 1960.

The World Bank, *World Debt Tables 1989–90: External Debts of Developing Countries*, Washington, D.C., 1989.

———, *Development Report 1990*, Washington, D.C., 1990.

Worsley, Peter, *The Third World*, Weidenfeld and Nicolson, London, 1964.

Yalman, Ahmet Emin, *Turkey in the World War*, Yale University Press, New Haven, 1930.

Yalman, Galip, "The Politics of Structural Adjustment: The Case of Turkey," paper presented at the Conference on Dynamics of States and Societies in the Middle East, Cairo, June 1989.

Yaşer, Betty Slade, *A Comparative Analysis of Selected Financial Ratios of Private Manufacturing Firms in USA and in Turkey, 1983–1984*, Istanbul Chamber of Industry, Istanbul, 1988.

Yavuz, Erdal, "1908 Boykotu," special issue of *METU Studies in Development*, 1978.

Yerasimos, Stephane, "The Monoparty Period," in Irvin C. Schick and Ahmet Tonak, eds., *Turkey in Transition: New Pespectives*, Oxford University Press, New York, 1987.

Yönder, Ayşe, "Informal Land and Housing Markets: The Case of Istanbul," in *American Planning Association Journal*, Spring 1987.

Zaalouk, Mata, "Commercial Agents in Egypt: A Case Study in Development," Ph.D. thesis, University of Hull, 1982.

Zeitlin, Maurice, *The Civil Wars in Chile or the Bourgeois Revolutions that Never Were*, Princeton University Press, Princeton, 1984.

Index